REX MUNDI
Book Five

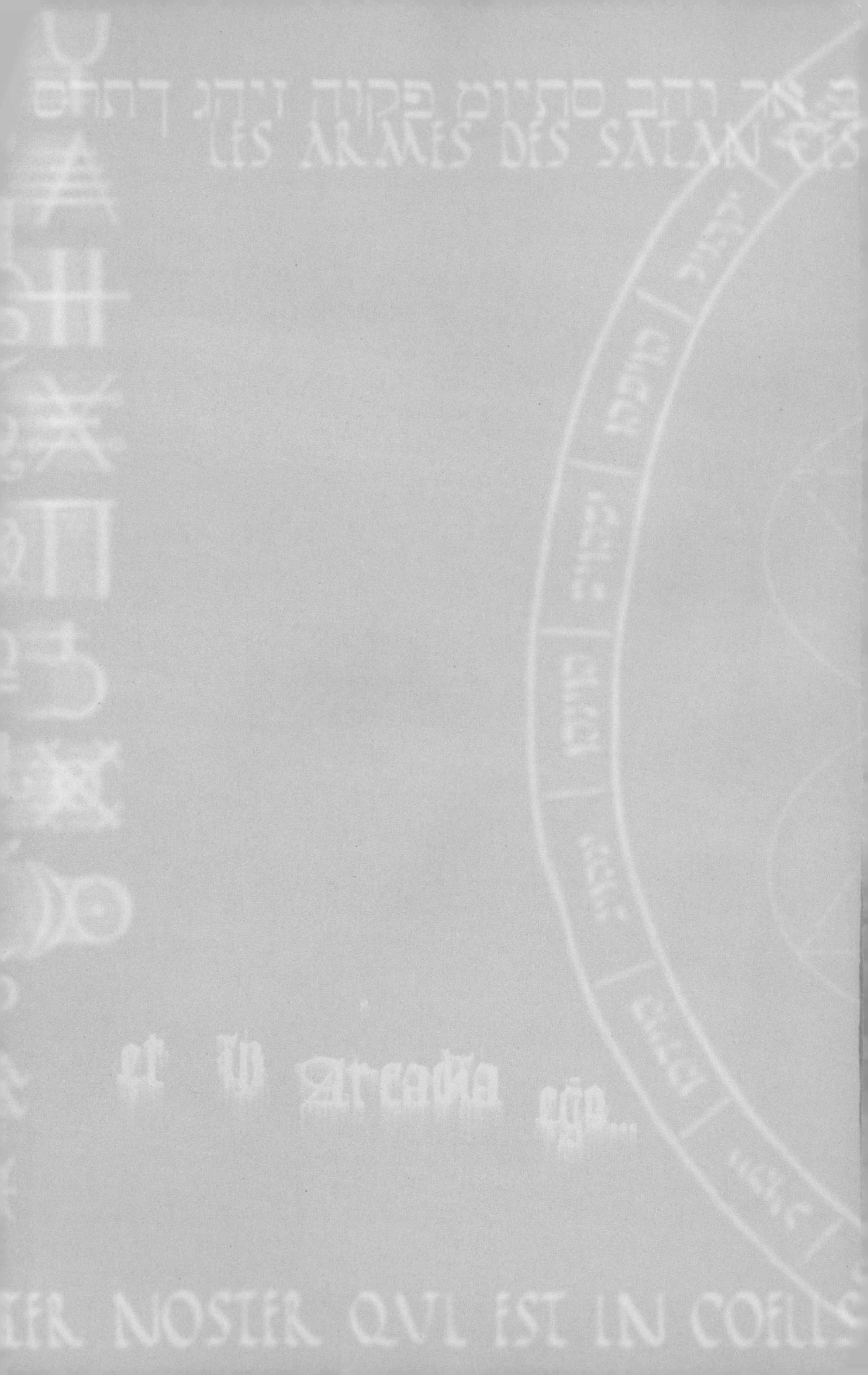
LES ARMES DES SALAMANDRES
et in Arcadia ego...
TER NOSTER QVI EST IN COELIS

REX MUNDI™

• BOOK FIVE •

The Valley at the End of the World

writer ARVID NELSON
artist JUAN FERREYRA
prologue artist JIM DI BARTOLO

Rex Mundi created by ARVID NELSON and ERIC J

DARK HORSE BOOKS®

publisher
MIKE RICHARDSON

editor
SCOTT ALLIE

assistant editor
RYAN JORGENSEN

letterer and newspaper designer
ARVID NELSON

book designer
AMY ARENDTS

art director
LIA RIBACCHI

Special thanks to Jason Hvam, Jason Rickerd, and Sam Humphries at MySpace.
Archival photographs: Eugène Atget.

character profiles • summaries of past issues • much more: www.rexmundi.net

REX MUNDI BOOK FIVE: THE VALLEY AT THE END OF THE WORLD

This volume collects issues six through twelve of the comic-book series *Rex Mundi*, published by Dark Horse Comics. Also, the story "Frailty" which appeared in *MySpace Dark Horse Presents* published online by Dark Horse Comics and MySpace.

Published by
Dark Horse Books
A division of Dark Horse Comics, Inc.
10956 SE Main Street
Milwaukie, OR 97222

darkhorse.com

To find a comics shop in your area, call the Comic Shop Locator
Service toll-free at 1-888-266-4226

First edition:
November 2008
ISBN 978-1-59582-192-8

10 9 8 7 6 5 4 3 2 1

Printed in China

THE WEIRD IS NEAR YOU

by Jim Uhls

That is, the "Wyrd" is near you. That could mean something strange and tangible is very close to you, or that you are on the verge of a strange revelation. But "Wyrd" is not limited to meaning "strange." It's an Old English noun, which originally meant "[the] becoming." What you are about to become next is near you—your becoming—your transformation to the person you will be next. It's an event that will change your chemistry, your mental landscape, and your worldview.

All of these meanings apply in *Rex Mundi*. The Wyrd, a European phenomenon, is a living entity, a personification of strangeness and fate. It walks through the pages of this story inexorably; to cross its path many times is inevitable.

The "fate" implied in the word is not one of predestination. It is plastic, malleable. When faced with it, one can choose among several ways to deal with it. Once the choice is made, the "becoming" starts.

Julien Saunière relentlessly pursues the truth buried in dark obscurity. As he discovers, so he changes. We can barely keep pace with him, for the world, which he takes for granted, is staggering and awe inspiring to us: an alternate reality, in which the great events of history happened differently. The Wyrd has met us at the starting gate. With our footing less than secure, we go on, keeping pace with Julien.

Rex Mundi is a mystical, archaeological, religious, sociological mystery—brushed by whistling gusts of terror. The terror is of a distinct and rare kind—a profound fear of finding out what we don't want to know —that what we thought was sacred is actually profane; what was blasphemy is, in fact, a paradigm-shattering truth. Unlike the thrills and chills of standard horror, this experience seems to throw open our inner doors of spiritual protection, allowing any manner of evil to reach us, allowing us no respite in the arms of faith. Most assuredly, Julien feels it—and its growing intensity—as he presses ever onward, past junctures at which we might have balked.

The alternate world is more than a backdrop. The genius of it is that it demonstrates the malleability of fate through a history in which

Man chose different paths, while at the same time it proves the alternate meaning of fate: predestination. We begin to see that the events unfolding are parallel to those that happened in our real world—the rise of a dictator aspiring to global domination, and the march toward world war.

Here, in the fifth volume of *Rex Mundi,* we find Julien making choices at every turn, attempting to solve a mystery and keep himself alive. He faces the Wyrd and changes directions—some which are good, some are grimly dead-ended. Still, there might be a predestined aspect to his fate: perhaps he was uniquely meant to go into the heart of darkness and fight the unimaginable evil.

Jim Uhls made his screenwriting debut with *Fight Club* (1999). Most recently, he collaborated with David S. Goyer on *Jumper* (2008). He's currently working on a *Rex Mundi* screenplay for Dark Horse Entertainment and Johnny Depp's production company, Infinitum Nihil.

PROLOGUE
THE TWILIGHT WOLF

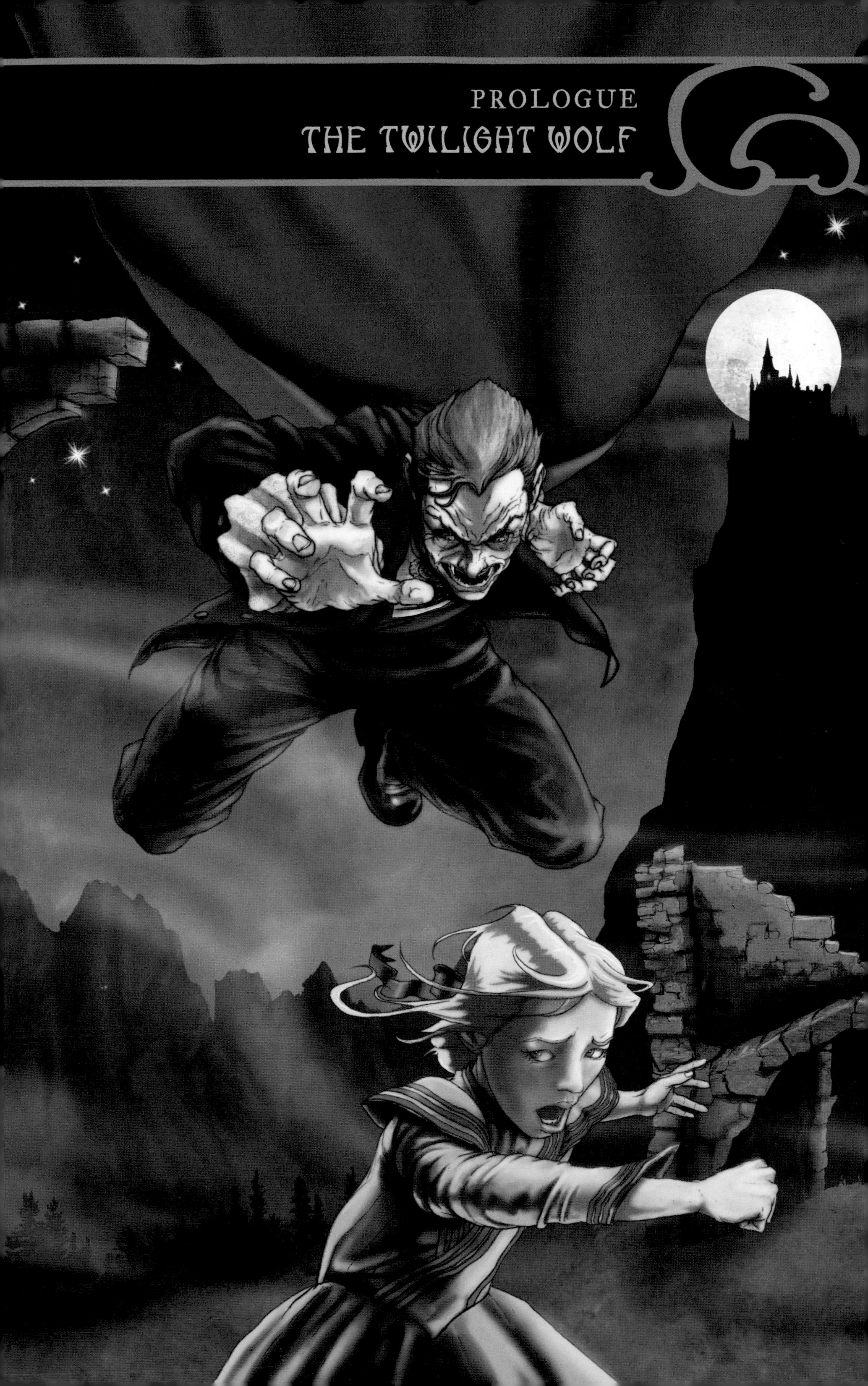

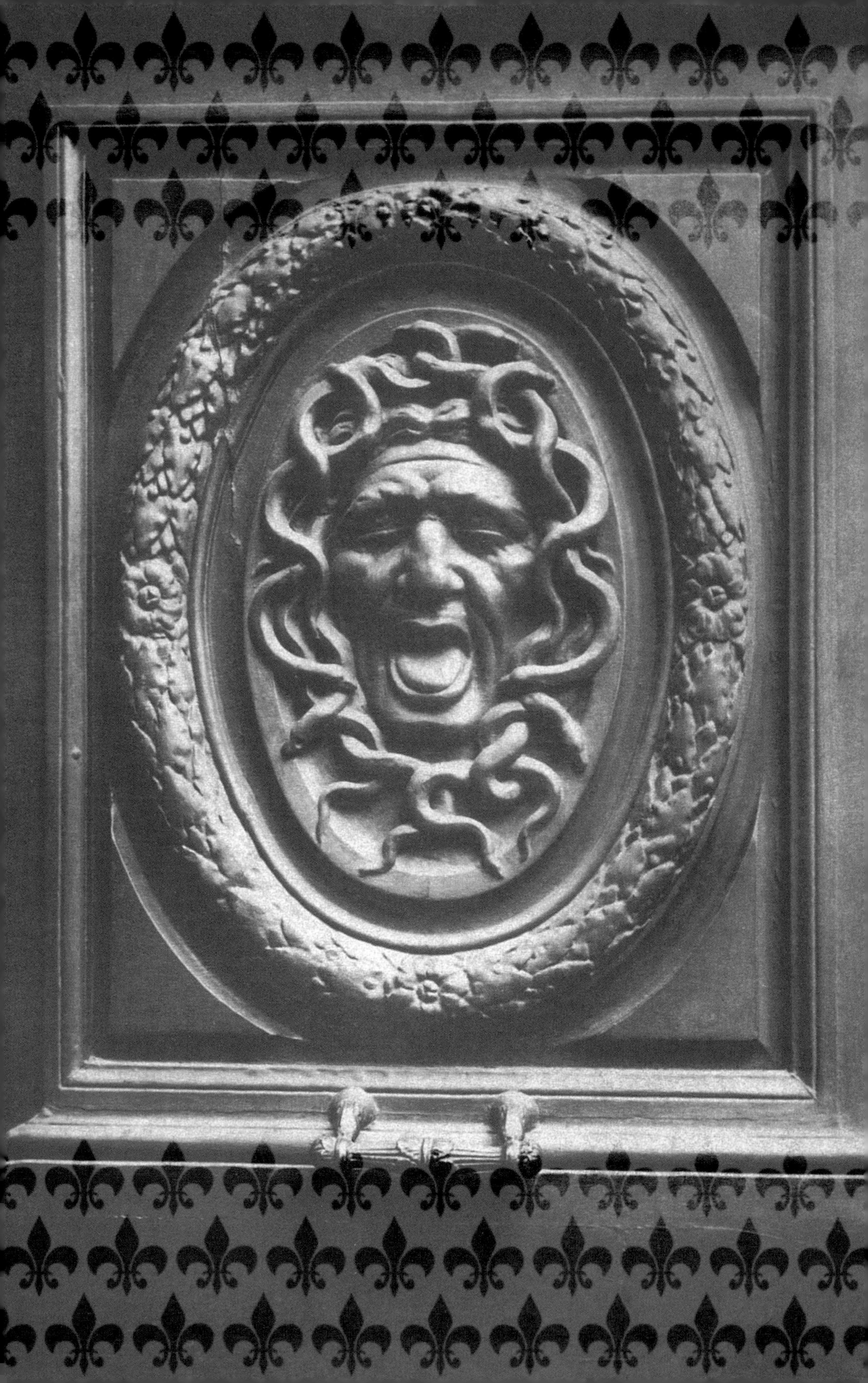

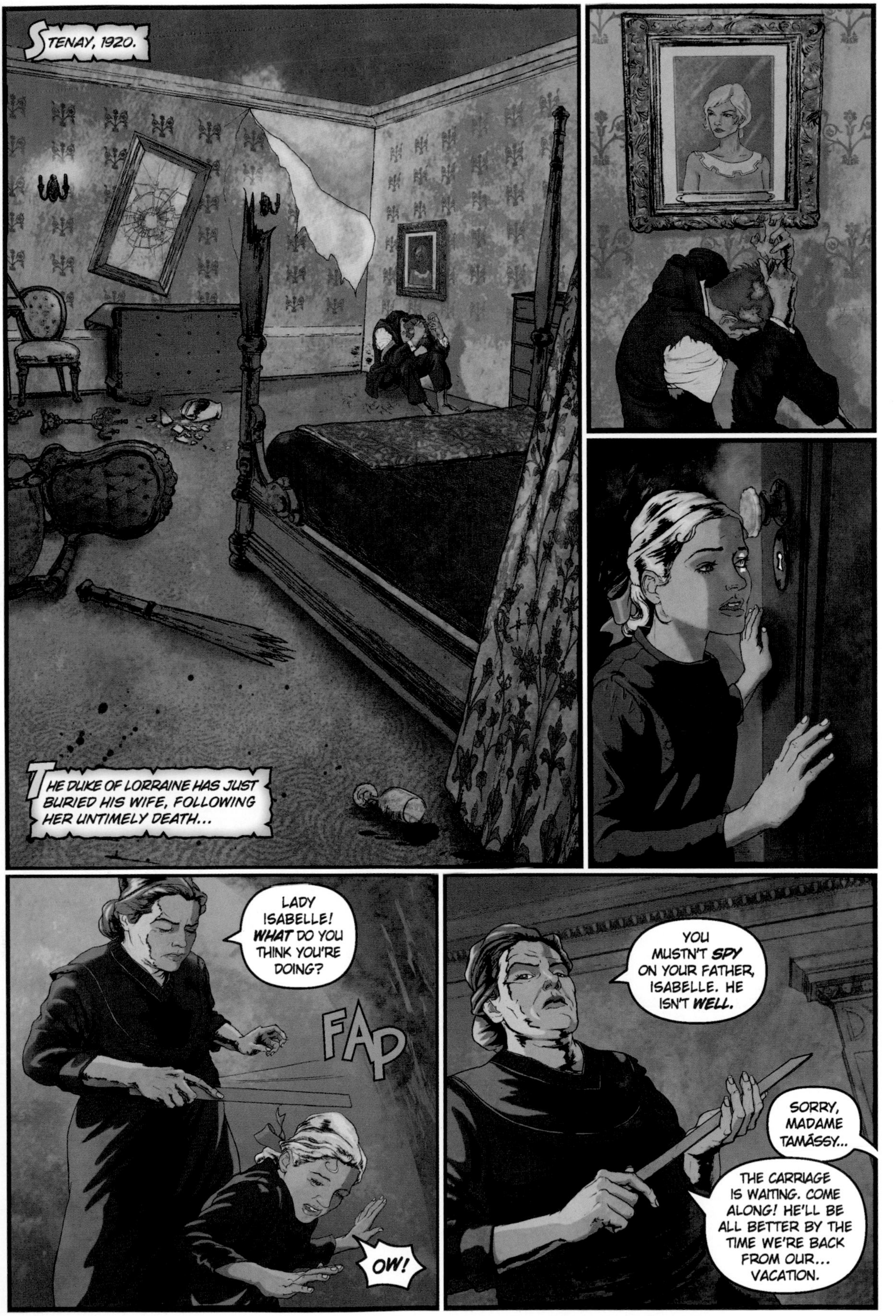
STENAY, 1920.
THE DUKE OF LORRAINE HAS JUST BURIED HIS WIFE, FOLLOWING HER UNTIMELY DEATH...
LADY ISABELLE! WHAT DO YOU THINK YOU'RE DOING?
FAP
OW!
YOU MUSTN'T SPY ON YOUR FATHER, ISABELLE. HE ISN'T WELL.
SORRY, MADAME TAMÁSSY...
THE CARRIAGE IS WAITING. COME ALONG! HE'LL BE ALL BETTER BY THE TIME WE'RE BACK FROM OUR... VACATION.

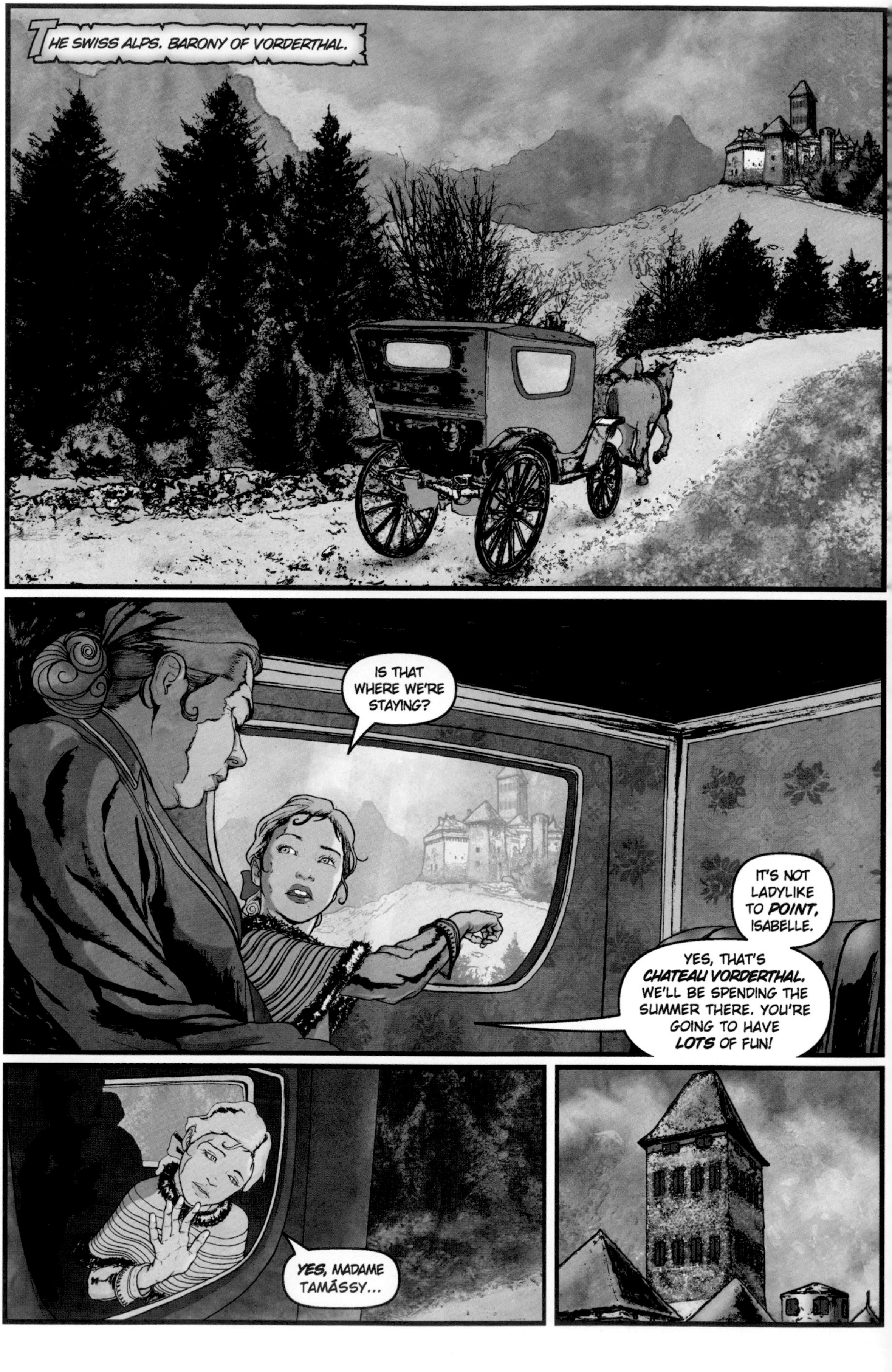
THE SWISS ALPS. BARONY OF VORDERTHAL.
IS THAT WHERE WE'RE STAYING?
IT'S NOT LADYLIKE TO POINT, ISABELLE.
YES, THAT'S CHATEAU VORDERTHAL. WE'LL BE SPENDING THE SUMMER THERE. YOU'RE GOING TO HAVE LOTS OF FUN!
YES, MADAME TAMÁSSY...

YEEW! IT SMELLS BAD...

DON'T MAKE *FACES*, ISABELLE. WE ARE GUESTS HERE, AND PROPER LADIES DON'T COMPLAIN.

ALL THE SAME--

WELCOME, BOTH OF YOU!

I AM CLAIRE ST. JEAN, THE HEAD OF BARON VORDERTHAL'S STAFF.

I APOLOGIZE FOR THE ODOR. IT SEEMS AN ANIMAL HAS DIED SOMEWHERE. WE GIRLS ARE *DESPERATELY* TRYING TO FIND IT!

I AM MADAME FLŐRA TAMÁSSY, LADY ISABELLE'S GOVERNESS.

DOES THE BARON HAVE ANY... *MALE* SERVANTS, MADEMOISELLE ST. JEAN?

AH. LORD VORDERTHAL EMPLOYS DESTITUTE LOCAL GIRLS SO THEY CAN... BETTER THEMSELVES.

WE'RE ALL *VERY* GRATEFUL FOR HIS CHARITY.

WHERE *IS* THE BARON, EXACTLY?

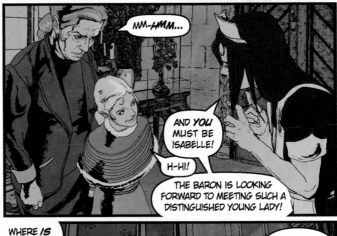

MM-HMM...

AND *YOU* MUST BE ISABELLE!

H-HI!

THE BARON IS LOOKING FORWARD TO MEETING SUCH A DISTINGUISHED YOUNG LADY!

MY LORD CONVEYS HIS APOLOGIES. HE IS ILL, AND WON'T BE ABLE TO GREET YOU UNTIL YOUR EVENING MEAL.

IN THE MEANTIME, WHY NOT GET SETTLED? COME, I'LL SHOW YOU TO YOUR QUARTERS.

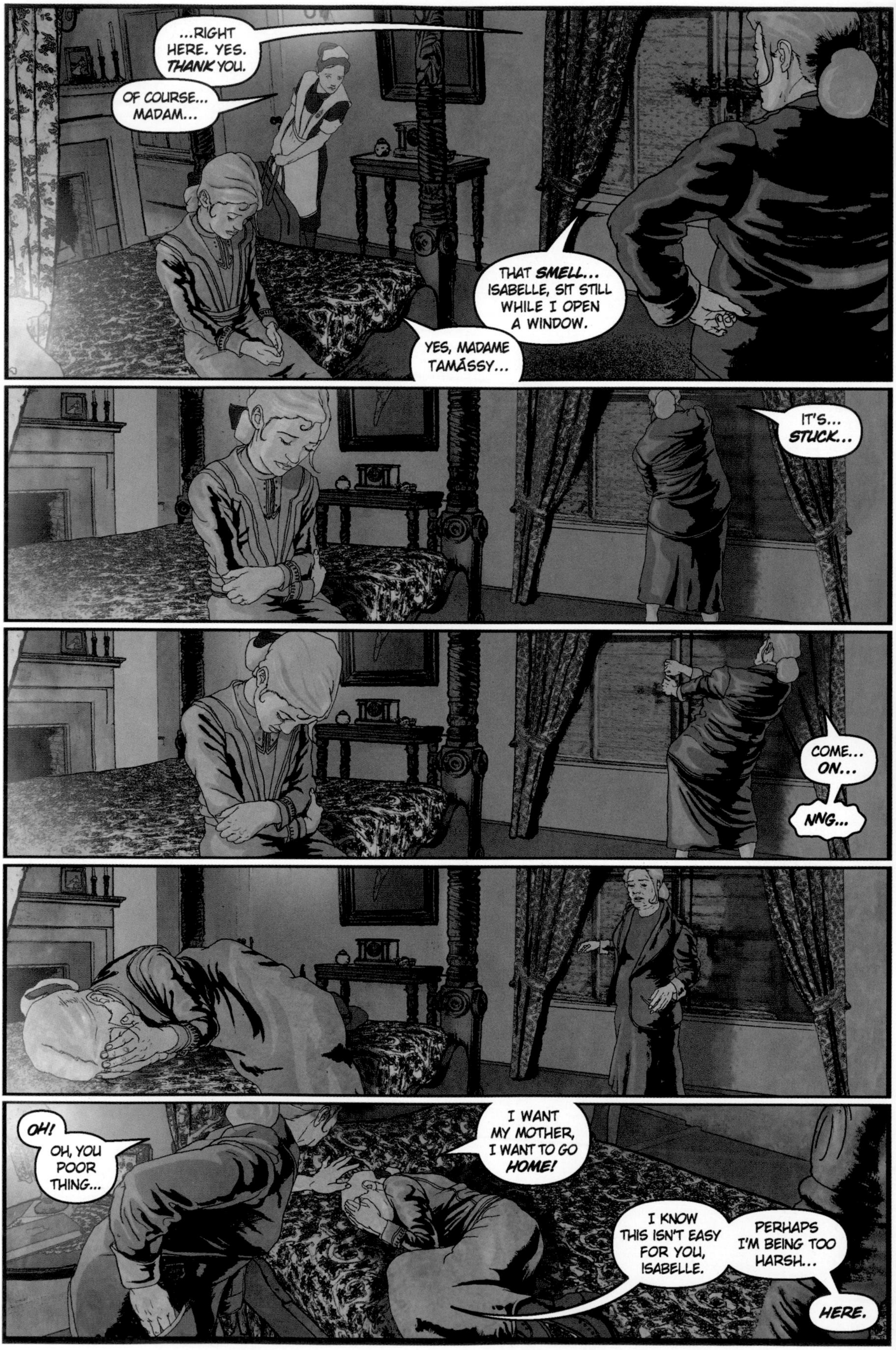
...RIGHT HERE. YES. THANK YOU.
OF COURSE... MADAM...
THAT SMELL... ISABELLE, SIT STILL WHILE I OPEN A WINDOW.
YES, MADAME TAMÁSSY...
IT'S... STUCK...
COME... ON...
NNG...
OH!
OH, YOU POOR THING...
I WANT MY MOTHER, I WANT TO GO HOME!
I KNOW THIS ISN'T EASY FOR YOU, ISABELLE.
PERHAPS I'M BEING TOO HARSH...
HERE.

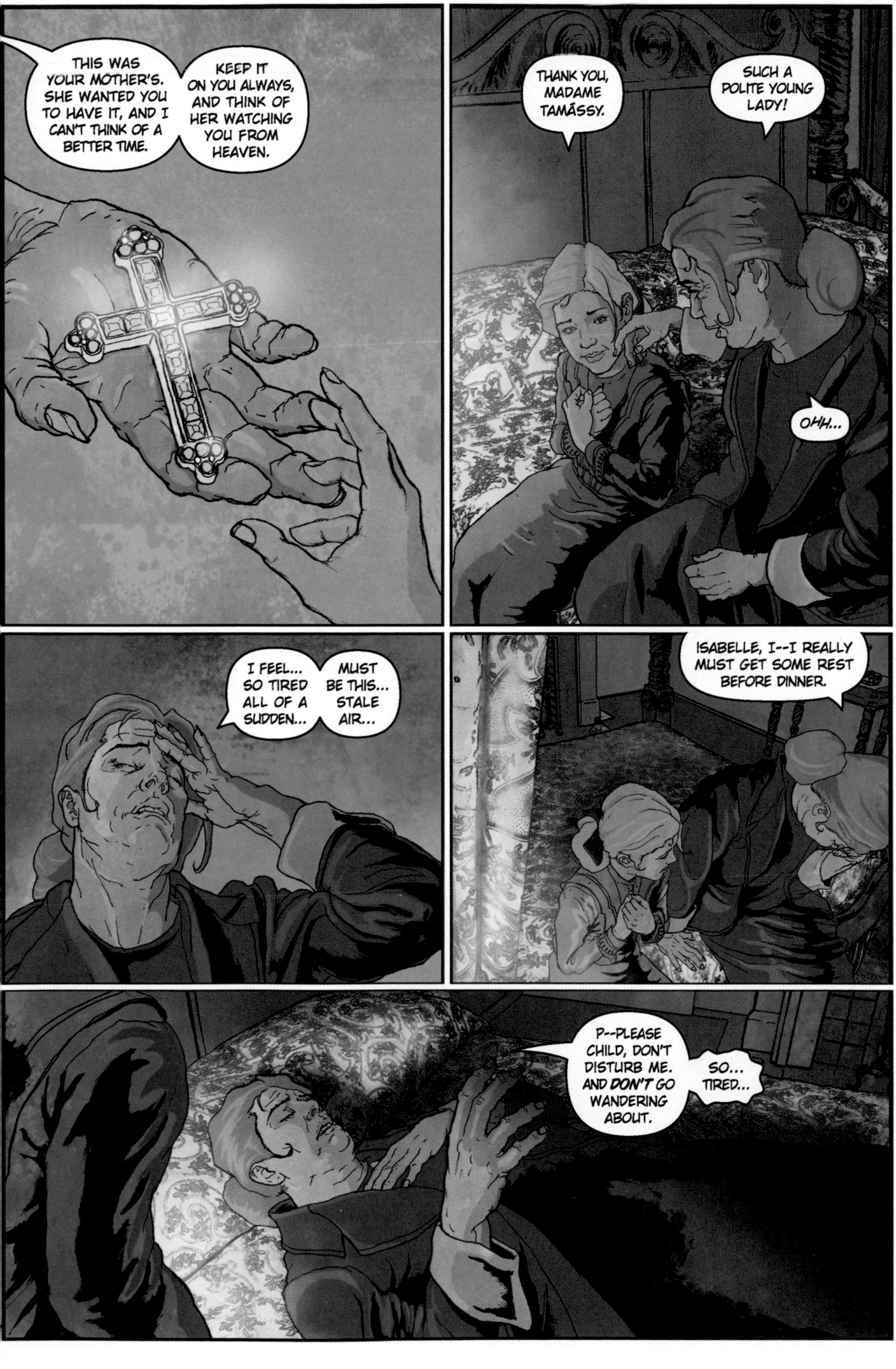
THIS WAS YOUR MOTHER'S. SHE WANTED YOU TO HAVE IT, AND I CAN'T THINK OF A BETTER TIME.
KEEP IT ON YOU ALWAYS, AND THINK OF HER WATCHING YOU FROM HEAVEN.
THANK YOU, MADAME TAMÁSSY.
SUCH A POLITE YOUNG LADY!
OHH...
I FEEL... SO TIRED ALL OF A SUDDEN...
MUST BE THIS... STALE AIR...
ISABELLE, I--I REALLY MUST GET SOME REST BEFORE DINNER.
P--PLEASE CHILD, DON'T DISTURB ME. AND *DON'T* GO WANDERING ABOUT.
SO... TIRED...

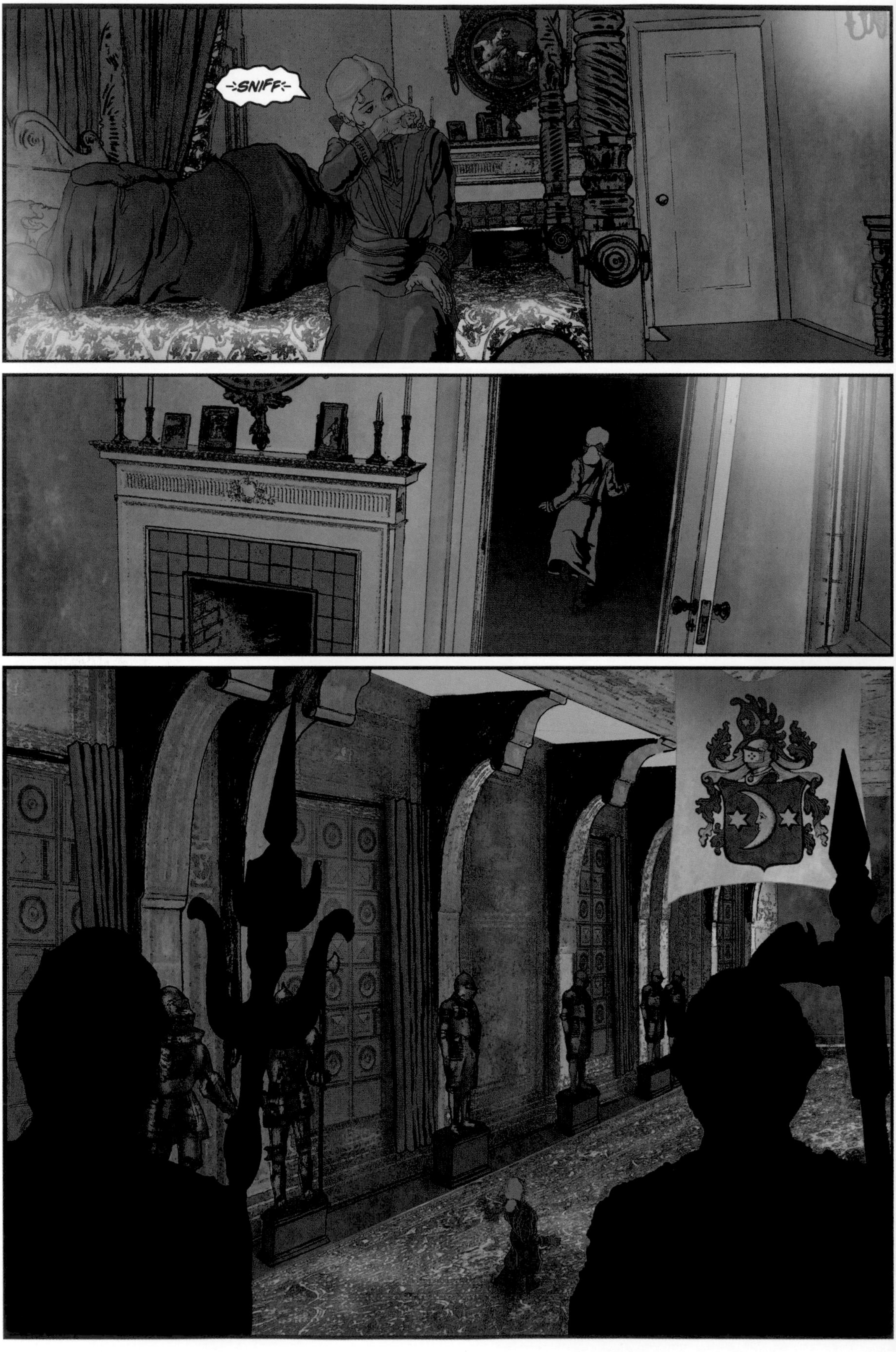
SNIFF

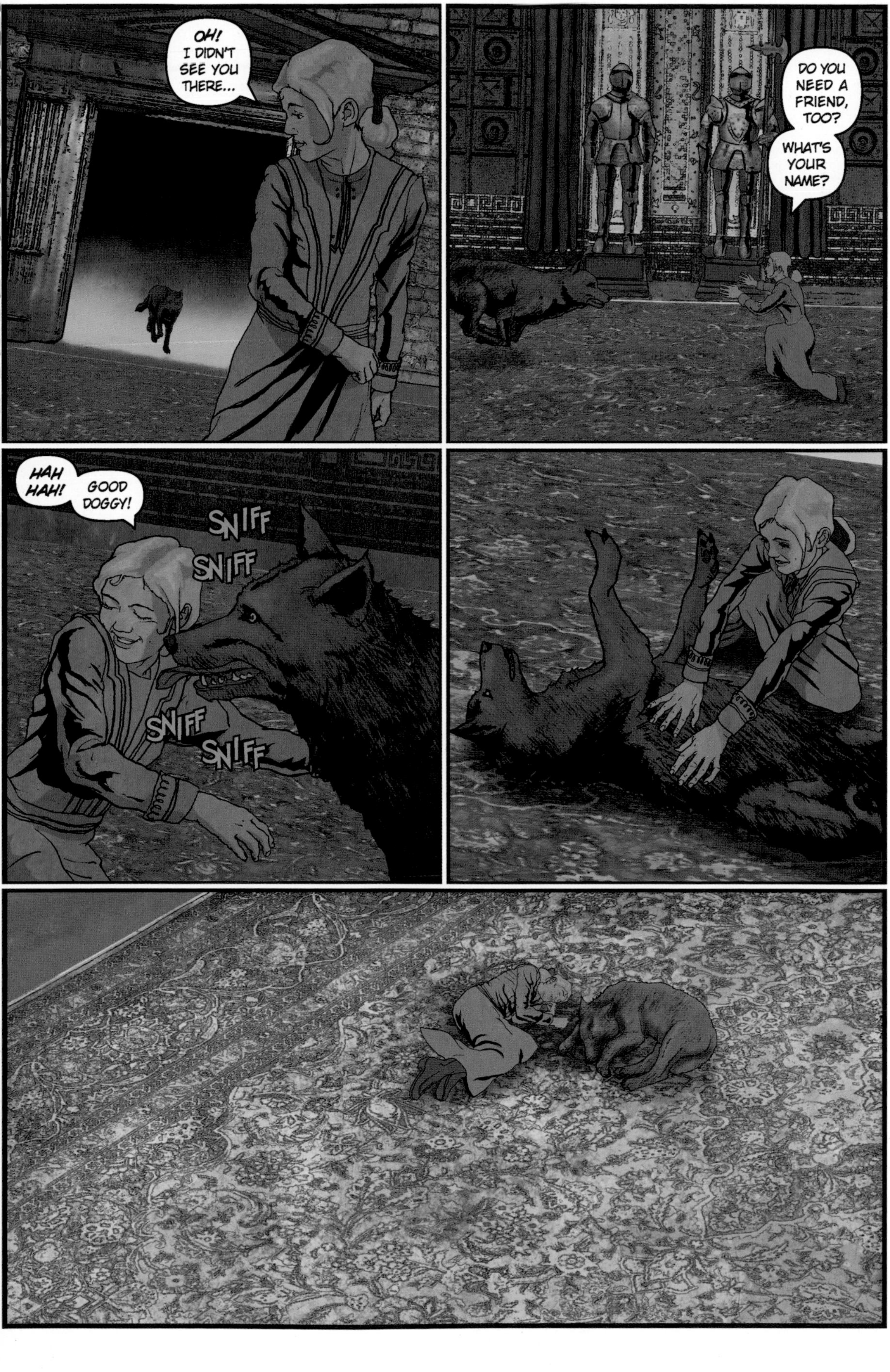
OH! I DIDN'T SEE YOU THERE...
DO YOU NEED A FRIEND, TOO?
WHAT'S YOUR NAME?
HAH HAH!
GOOD DOGGY!
SNIFF
SNIFF
SNIFF
SNIFF

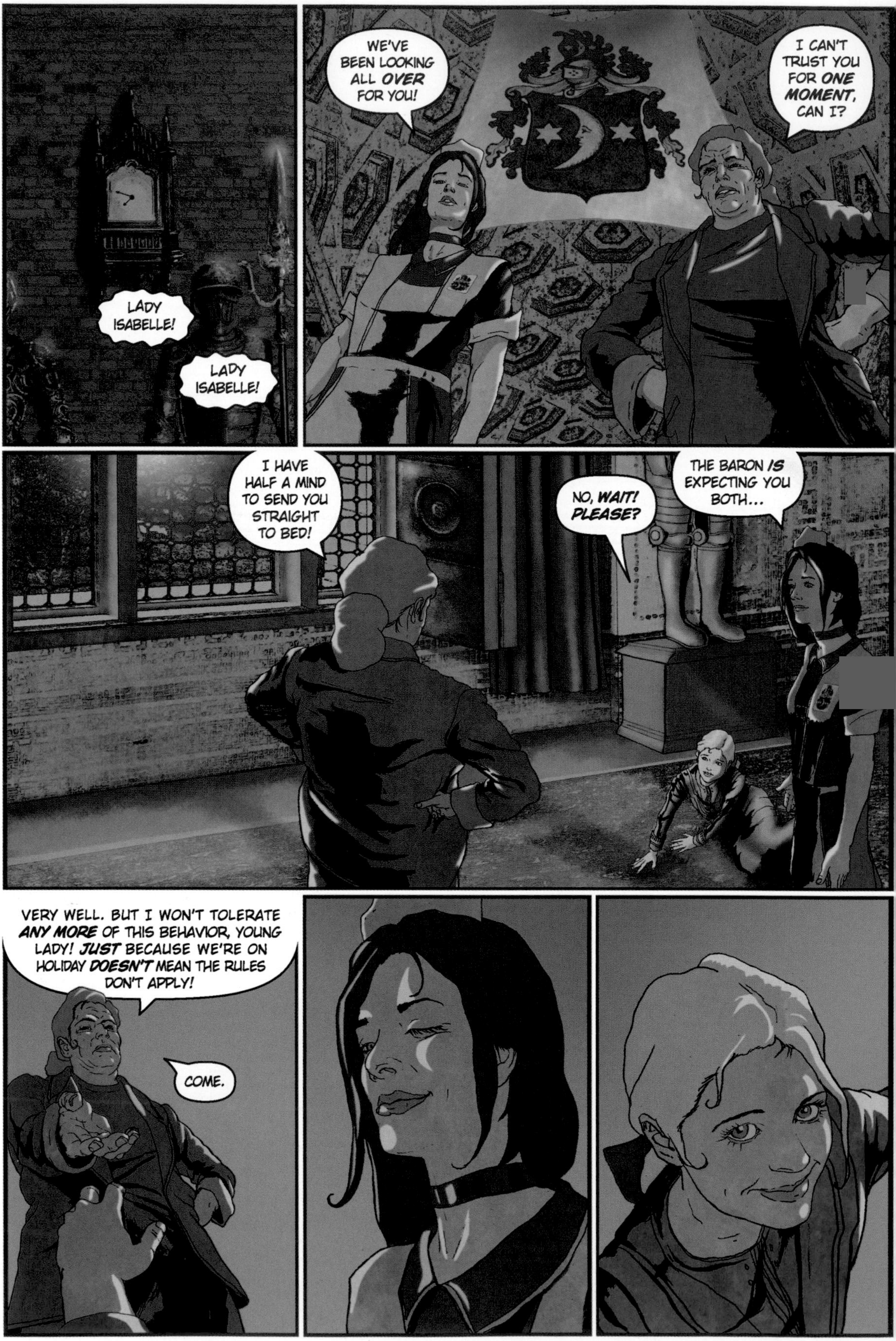
LADY ISABELLE!
LADY ISABELLE!
WE'VE BEEN LOOKING ALL *OVER* FOR YOU!
I CAN'T TRUST YOU FOR *ONE MOMENT*, CAN I?
I HAVE HALF A MIND TO SEND YOU STRAIGHT TO BED!
NO, *WAIT! PLEASE?*
THE BARON *IS* EXPECTING YOU BOTH...
VERY WELL. BUT I WON'T TOLERATE *ANY MORE* OF THIS BEHAVIOR, YOUNG LADY! *JUST* BECAUSE WE'RE ON HOLIDAY *DOESN'T* MEAN THE RULES DON'T APPLY!
COME.

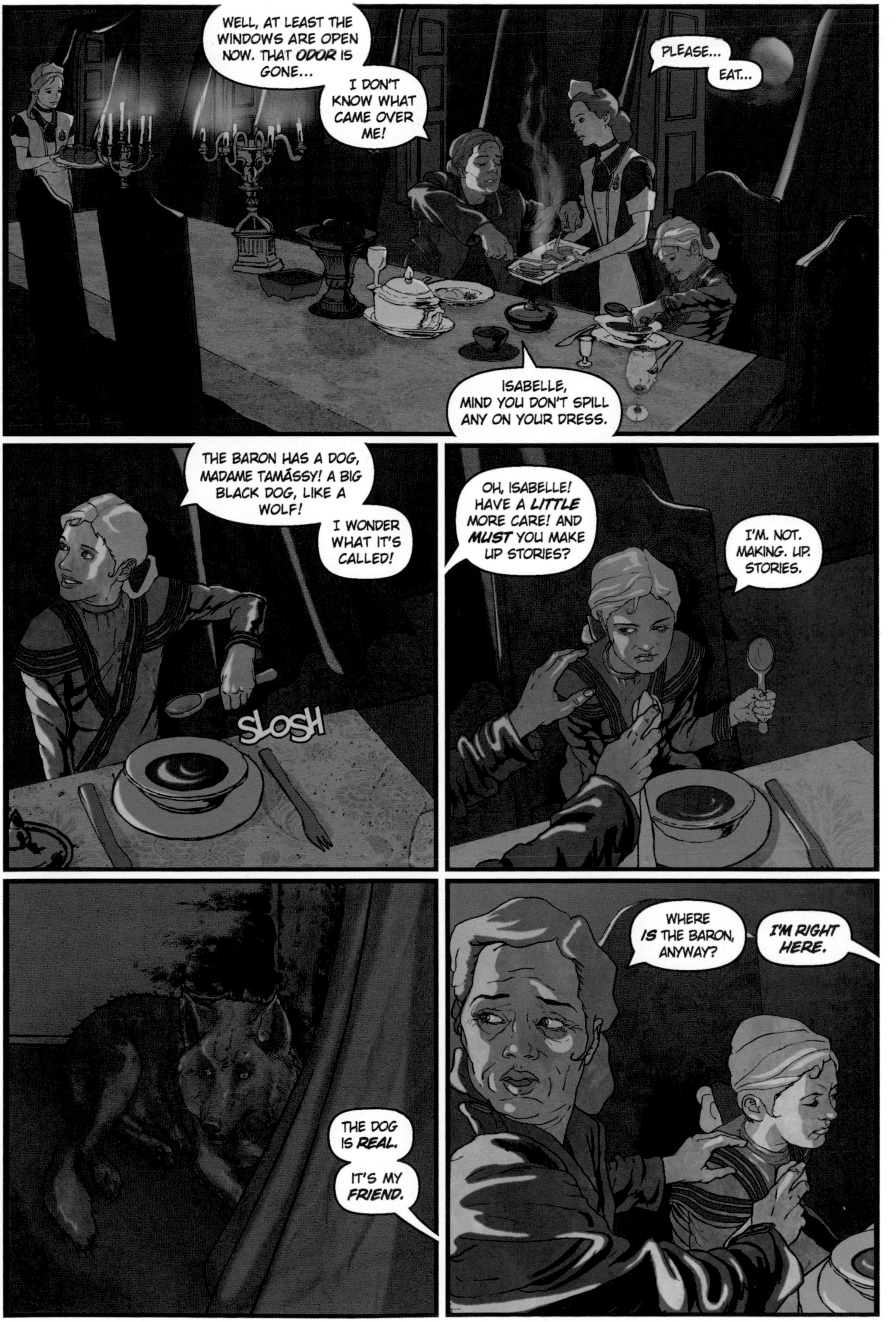
WELL, AT LEAST THE WINDOWS ARE OPEN NOW. THAT ODOR IS GONE...
I DON'T KNOW WHAT CAME OVER ME!
PLEASE...
EAT...
ISABELLE, MIND YOU DON'T SPILL ANY ON YOUR DRESS.
THE BARON HAS A DOG, MADAME TAMÁSSY! A BIG BLACK DOG, LIKE A WOLF!
I WONDER WHAT IT'S CALLED!
SLOSH
OH, ISABELLE! HAVE A LITTLE MORE CARE! AND MUST YOU MAKE UP STORIES?
I'M. NOT. MAKING. UP. STORIES.
THE DOG IS REAL.
IT'S MY FRIEND.
WHERE IS THE BARON, ANYWAY?
I'M RIGHT HERE.

WELCOME, WELCOME TO MY HOME.

I *APOLOGIZE* FOR NOT INTRODUCING MYSELF EARLIER, BUT I HAVE A CONDITION THAT INCAPACITATES ME FROM TIME TO TIME.

I--HONORED TO MEET YOU, MY LORD. I AM--

SIT, PLEASE. SIT.

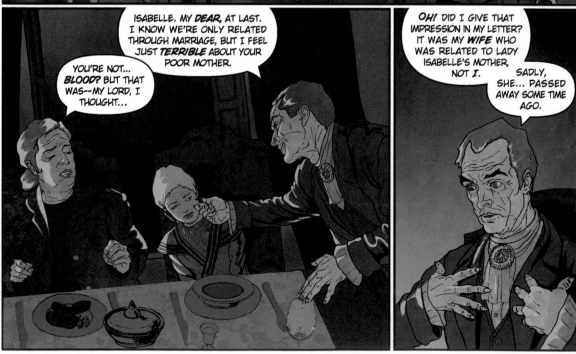

ISABELLE. MY *DEAR,* AT LAST. I KNOW WE'RE ONLY RELATED THROUGH MARRIAGE, BUT I FEEL JUST *TERRIBLE* ABOUT YOUR POOR MOTHER.

YOU'RE NOT... *BLOOD?* BUT THAT WAS--MY LORD, I THOUGHT...

OH! DID I GIVE THAT IMPRESSION IN MY LETTER? IT WAS MY *WIFE* WHO WAS RELATED TO LADY ISABELLE'S MOTHER, NOT *I.*

SADLY, SHE... PASSED AWAY SOME TIME AGO.

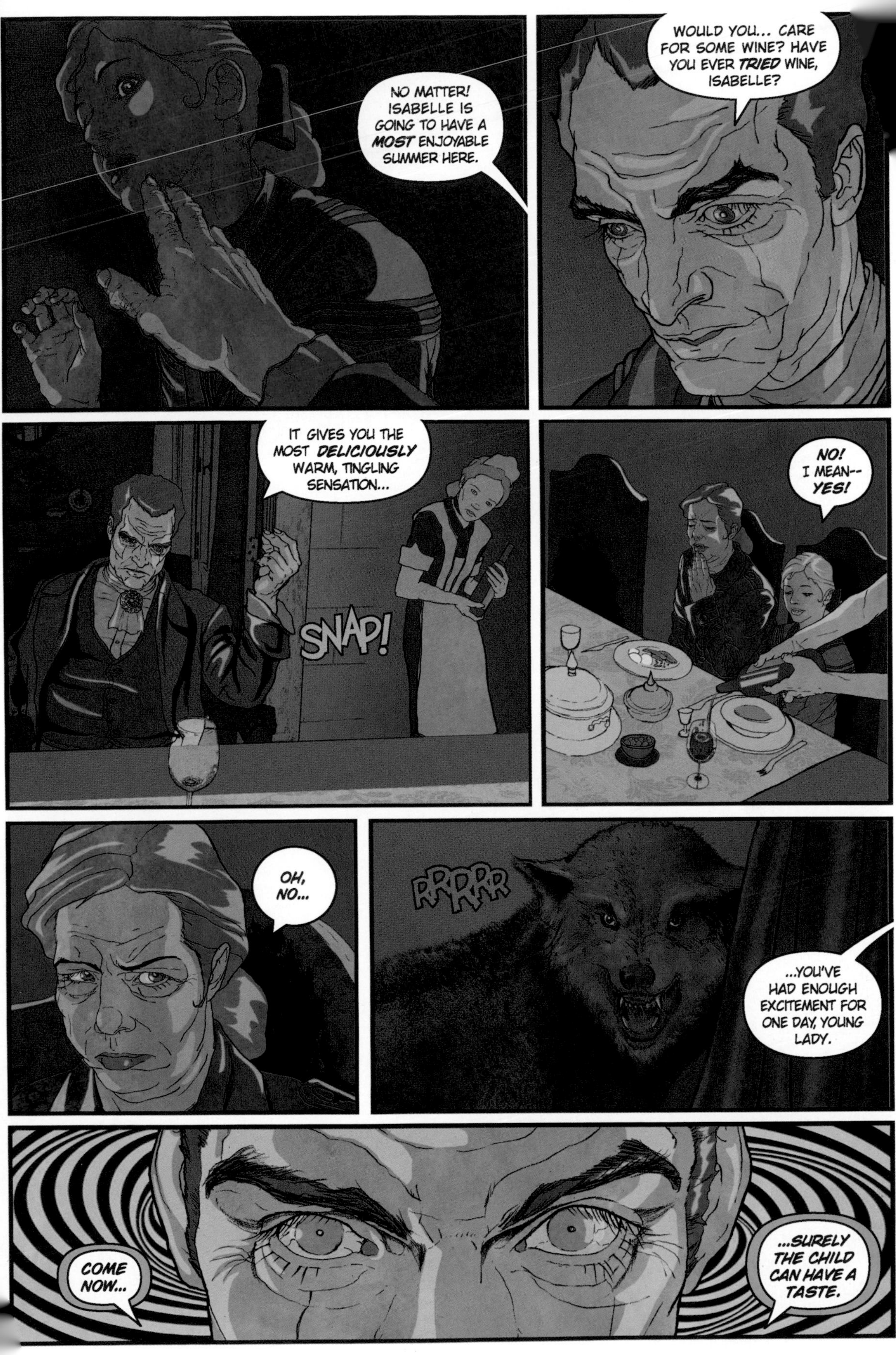
NO MATTER! ISABELLE IS GOING TO HAVE A *MOST* ENJOYABLE SUMMER HERE.
WOULD YOU... CARE FOR SOME WINE? HAVE YOU EVER *TRIED* WINE, ISABELLE?
IT GIVES YOU THE MOST *DELICIOUSLY* WARM, TINGLING SENSATION...
SNAP!
NO! I MEAN-- *YES!*
OH, NO...
RRRRR
...YOU'VE HAD ENOUGH EXCITEMENT FOR ONE DAY, YOUNG LADY.
COME NOW...
...SURELY THE CHILD CAN HAVE A TASTE.

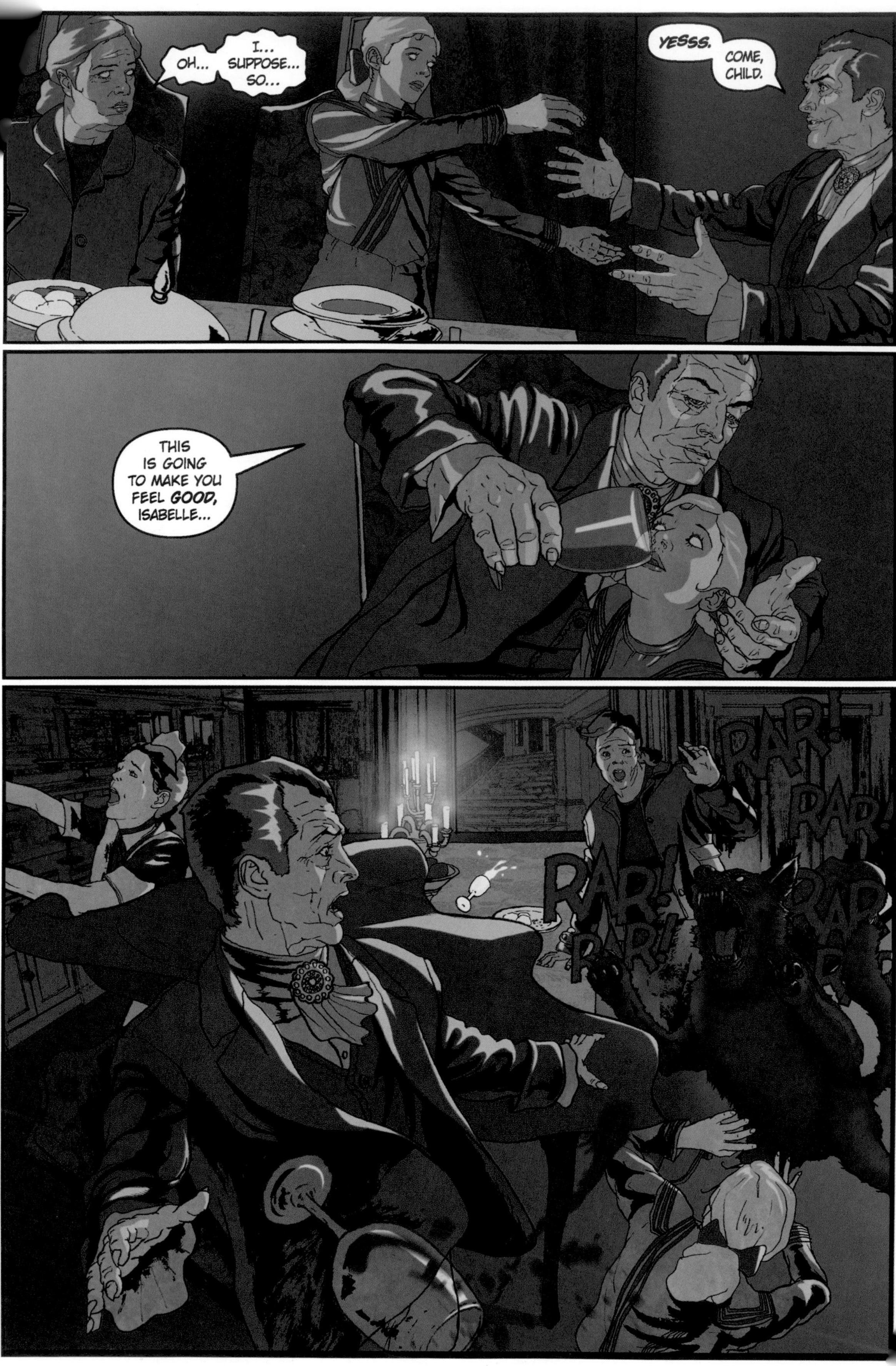
OH...
I... SUPPOSE... SO...
YESSS.
COME, CHILD.
THIS IS GOING TO MAKE YOU FEEL GOOD, ISABELLE...
RAR!
RAR!
RAR!
RAR!
RAR!

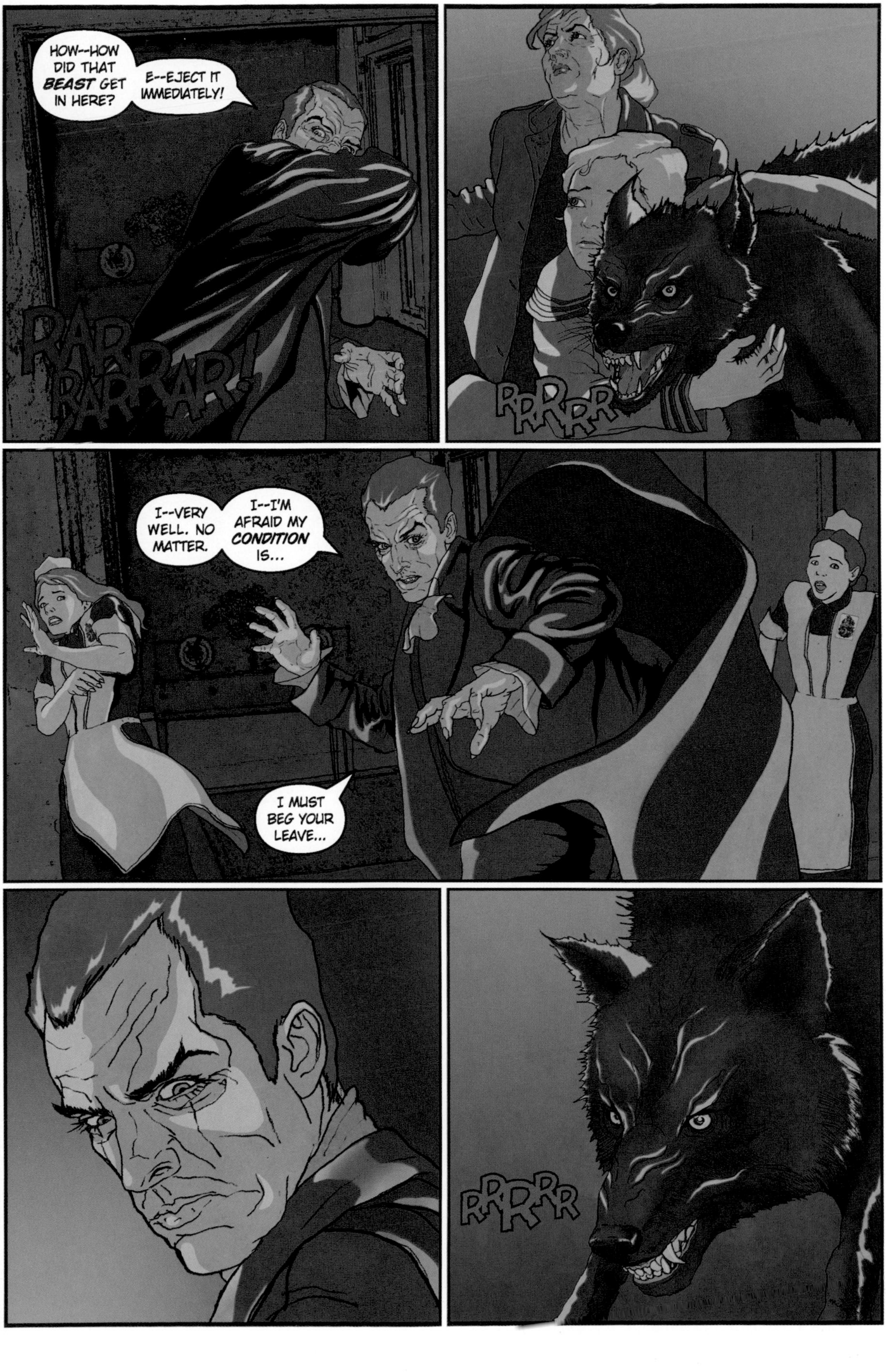
HOW--HOW DID THAT BEAST GET IN HERE?
E--EJECT IT IMMEDIATELY!
RAR RAR RAR RAR!
RRRRR
I--VERY WELL. NO MATTER.
I--I'M AFRAID MY CONDITION IS...
I MUST BEG YOUR LEAVE...
RRRRR

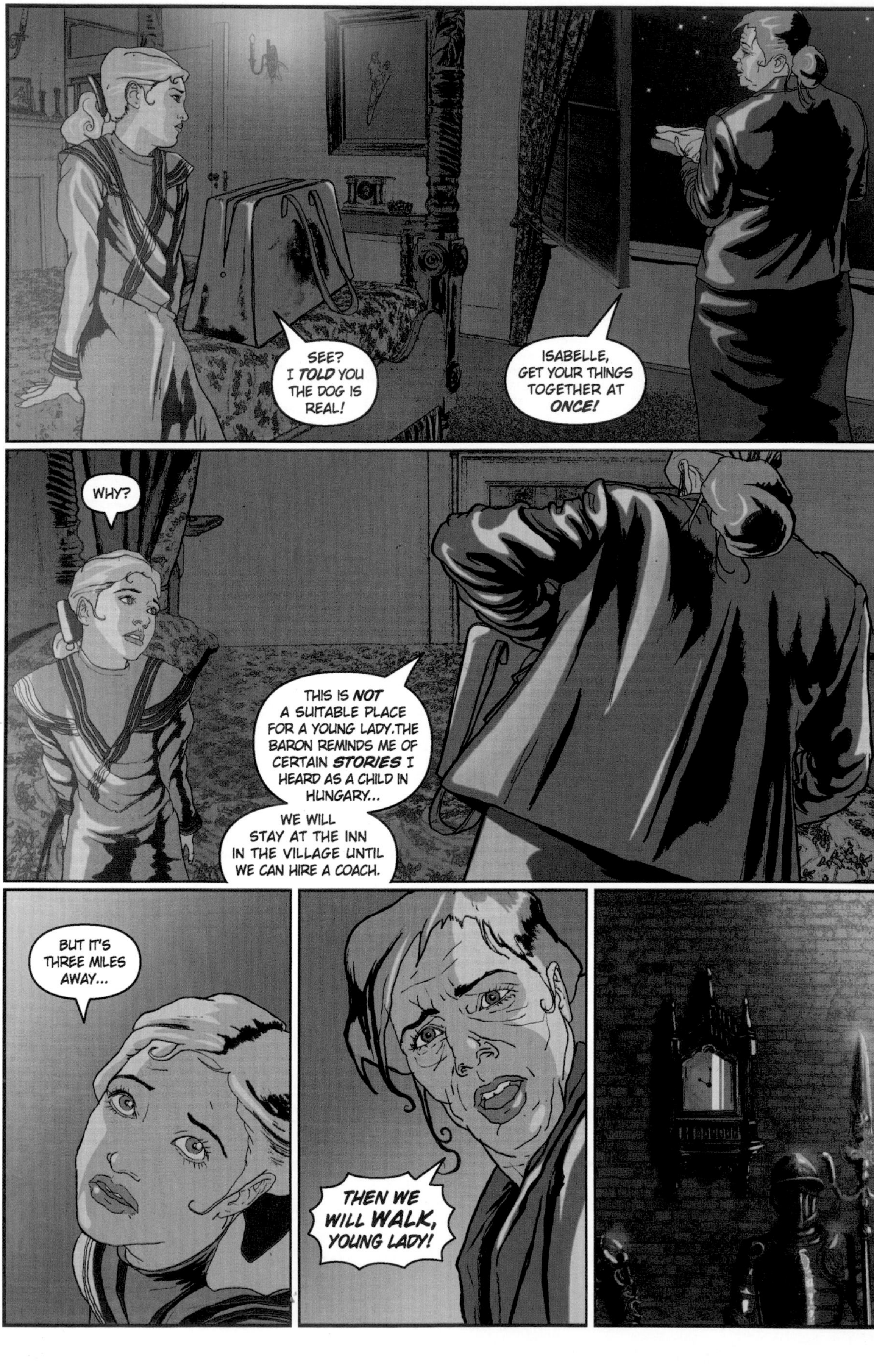
SEE? I TOLD YOU THE DOG IS REAL!
ISABELLE, GET YOUR THINGS TOGETHER AT ONCE!
WHY?
THIS IS NOT A SUITABLE PLACE FOR A YOUNG LADY.THE BARON REMINDS ME OF CERTAIN STORIES I HEARD AS A CHILD IN HUNGARY...
WE WILL STAY AT THE INN IN THE VILLAGE UNTIL WE CAN HIRE A COACH.
BUT IT'S THREE MILES AWAY...
THEN WE WILL WALK, YOUNG LADY!

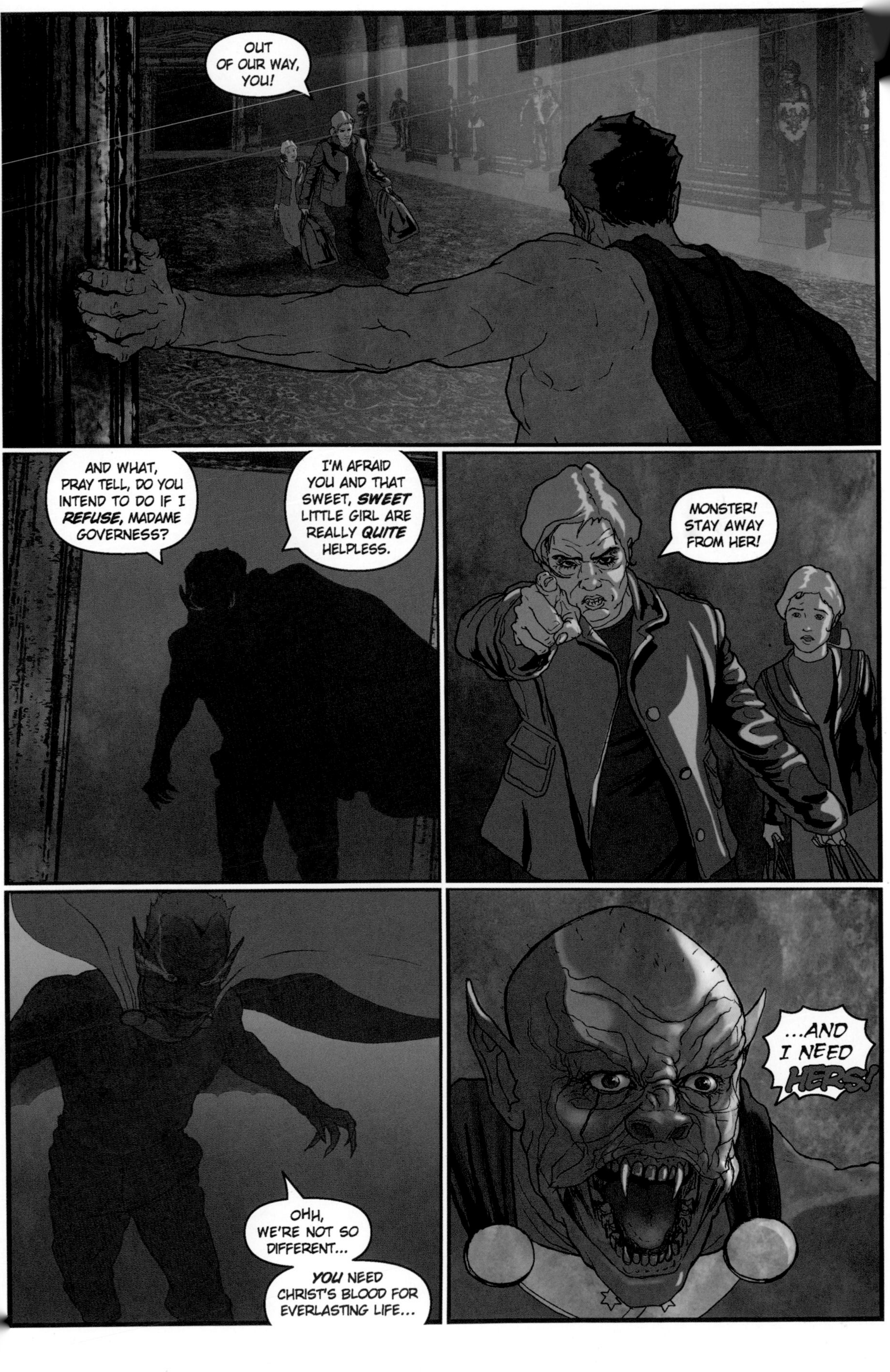
OUT OF OUR WAY, YOU!
AND WHAT, PRAY TELL, DO YOU INTEND TO DO IF I REFUSE, MADAME GOVERNESS?
I'M AFRAID YOU AND THAT SWEET, SWEET LITTLE GIRL ARE REALLY QUITE HELPLESS.
MONSTER! STAY AWAY FROM HER!
OHH, WE'RE NOT SO DIFFERENT...
YOU NEED CHRIST'S BLOOD FOR EVERLASTING LIFE...
...AND I NEED HERS!

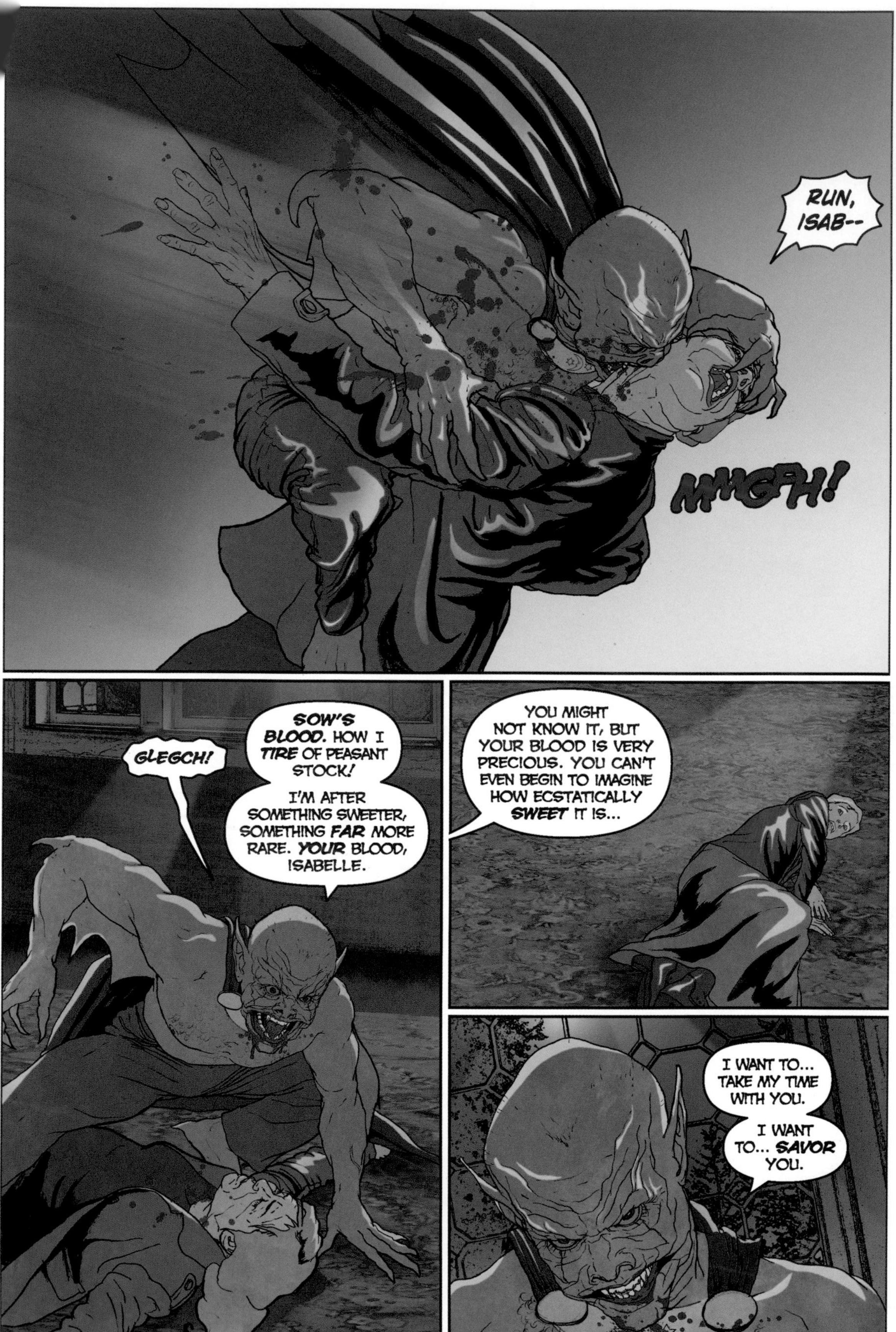
RUN, ISAB--
MMGFH!
GLEGCH!
SOW'S BLOOD. HOW I TIRE OF PEASANT STOCK!
I'M AFTER SOMETHING SWEETER, SOMETHING FAR MORE RARE. YOUR BLOOD, ISABELLE.
YOU MIGHT NOT KNOW IT, BUT YOUR BLOOD IS VERY PRECIOUS. YOU CAN'T EVEN BEGIN TO IMAGINE HOW ECSTATICALLY SWEET IT IS...
I WANT TO... TAKE MY TIME WITH YOU.
I WANT TO... SAVOR YOU.

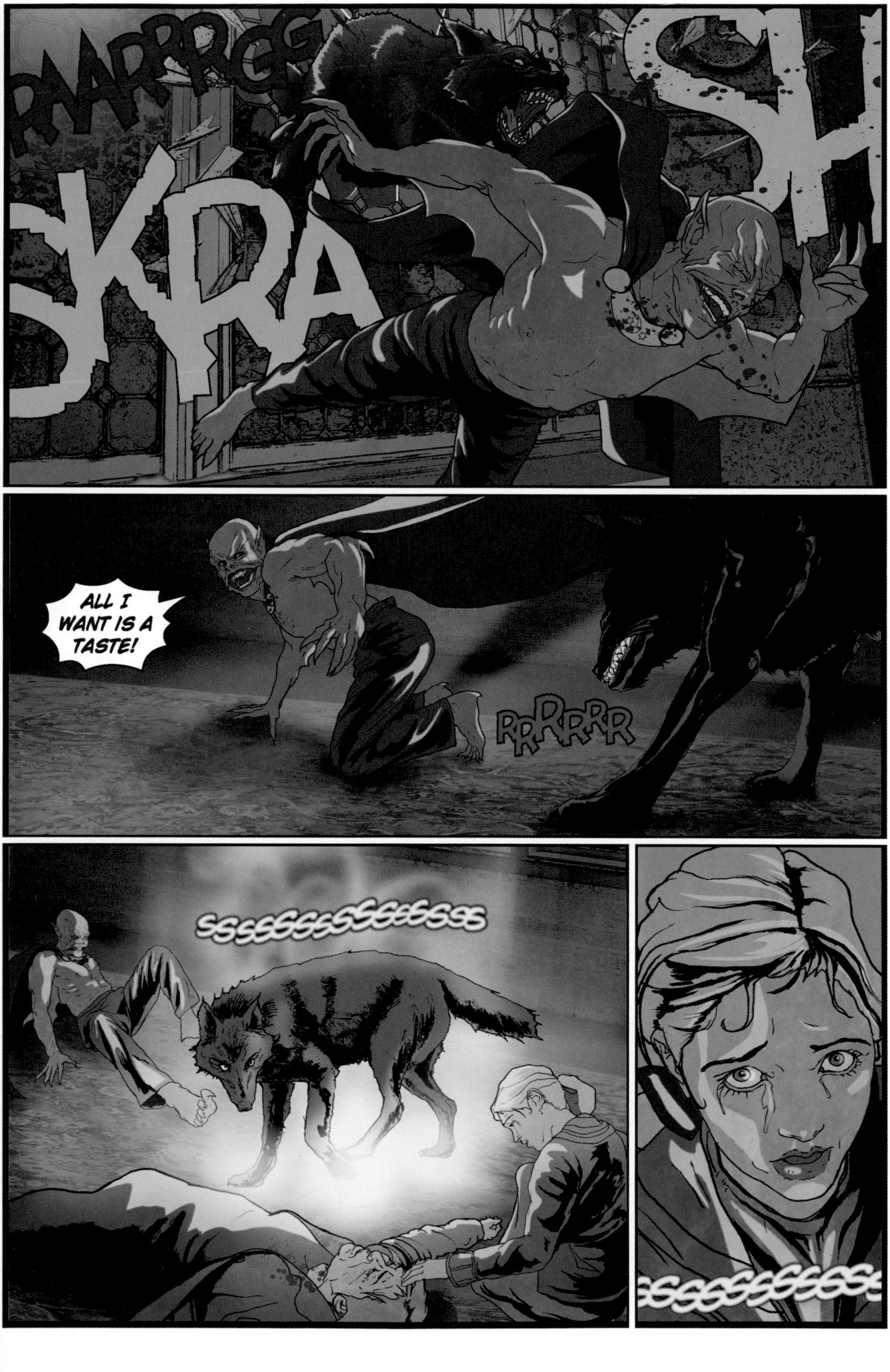
RAARRRGG
SKRA
SH
ALL I WANT IS A TASTE!
RRRRRR
SSSSSSSSSSSSSSS
SSSSSSSSSSSS

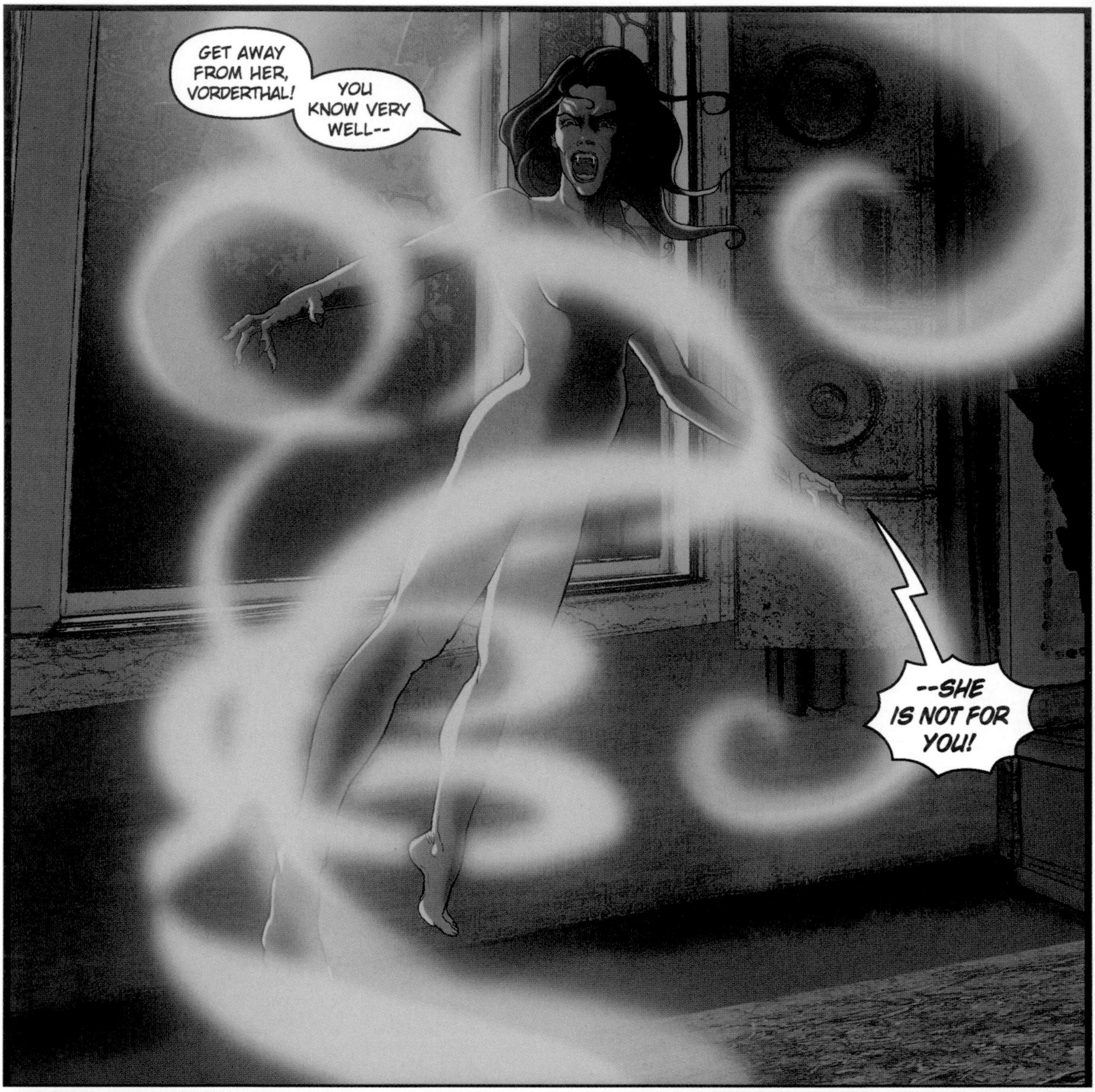
GET AWAY FROM HER, VORDERTHAL!
YOU KNOW VERY WELL--
--SHE IS NOT FOR YOU!

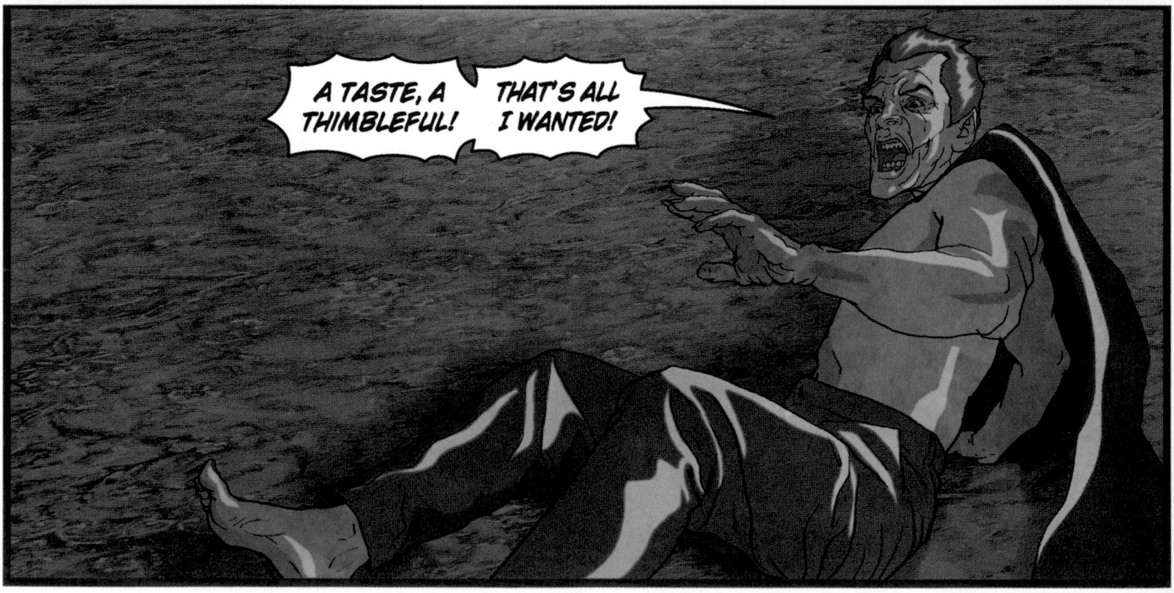
A TASTE, A THIMBLEFUL!
THAT'S ALL I WANTED!

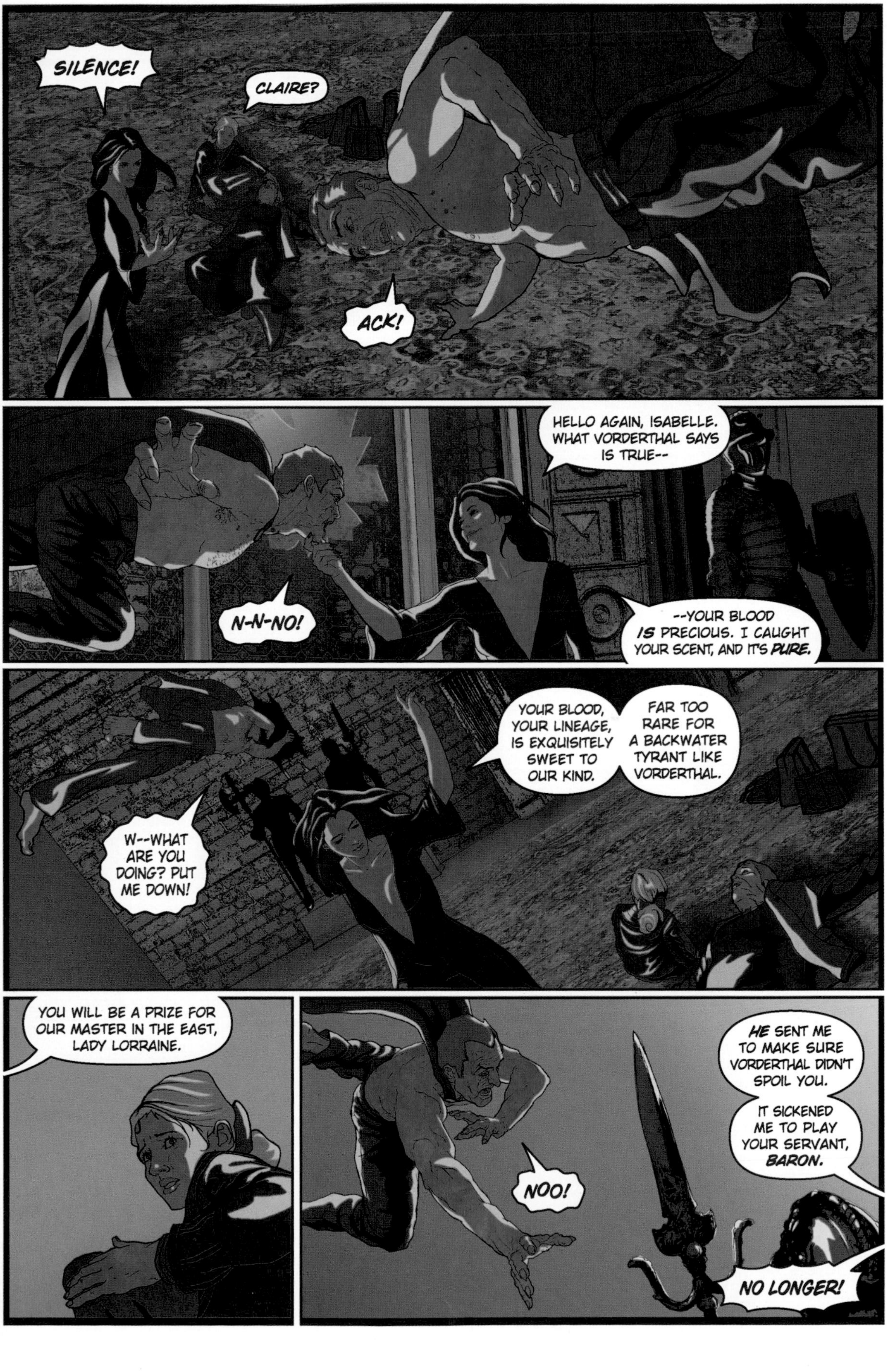
SILENCE!
CLAIRE?
ACK!
HELLO AGAIN, ISABELLE. WHAT VORDERTHAL SAYS IS TRUE--
N-N-NO!
--YOUR BLOOD IS PRECIOUS. I CAUGHT YOUR SCENT, AND IT'S PURE.
YOUR BLOOD, YOUR LINEAGE, IS EXQUISITELY SWEET TO OUR KIND.
FAR TOO RARE FOR A BACKWATER TYRANT LIKE VORDERTHAL.
W--WHAT ARE YOU DOING? PUT ME DOWN!
YOU WILL BE A PRIZE FOR OUR MASTER IN THE EAST, LADY LORRAINE.
HE SENT ME TO MAKE SURE VORDERTHAL DIDN'T SPOIL YOU.
IT SICKENED ME TO PLAY YOUR SERVANT, BARON.
NOO!
NO LONGER!

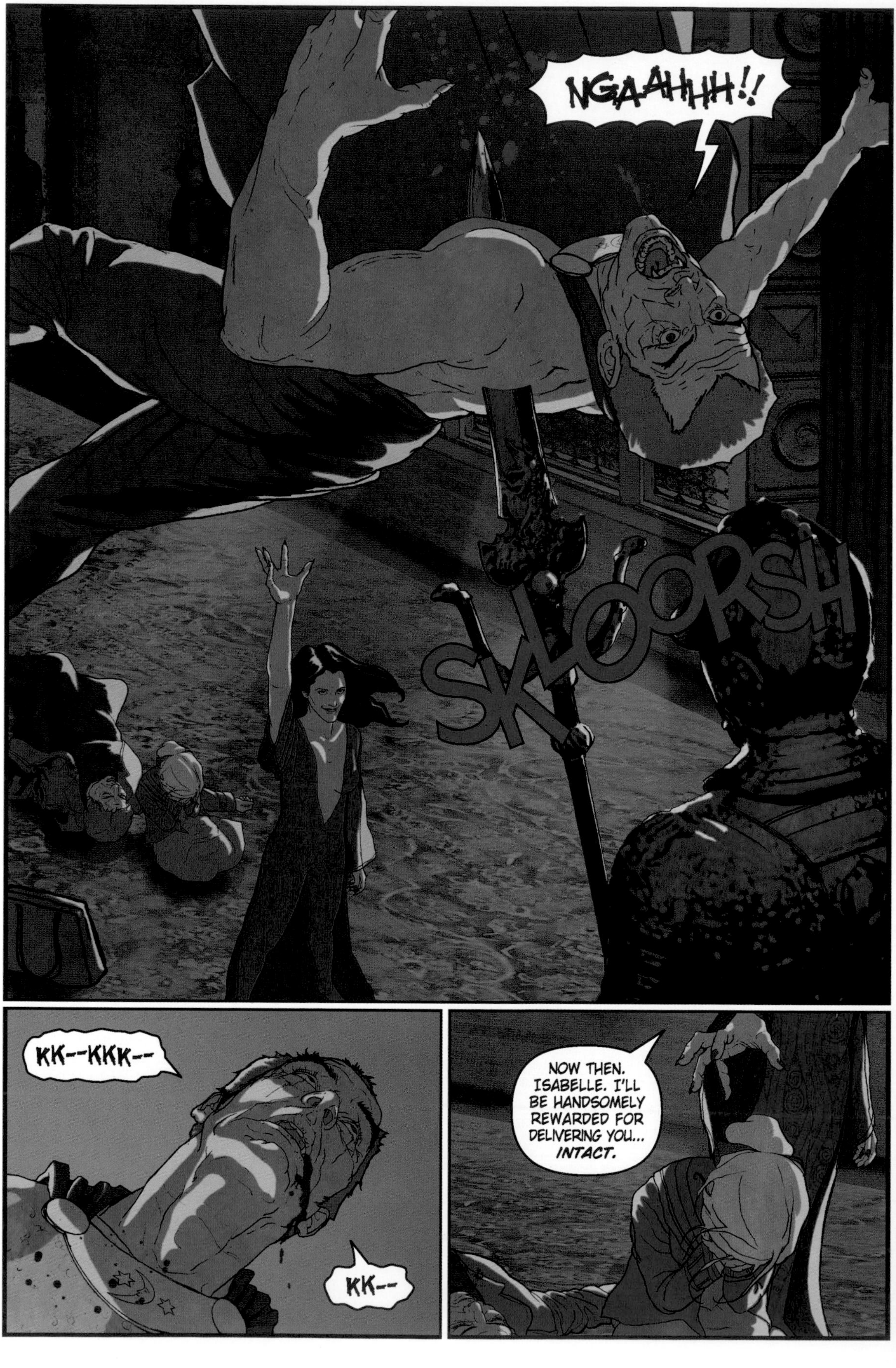
NGAAHHH!!
SKLOORSH
KK--KKK--
KK--
NOW THEN. ISABELLE. I'LL BE HANDSOMELY REWARDED FOR DELIVERING YOU... *INTACT.*

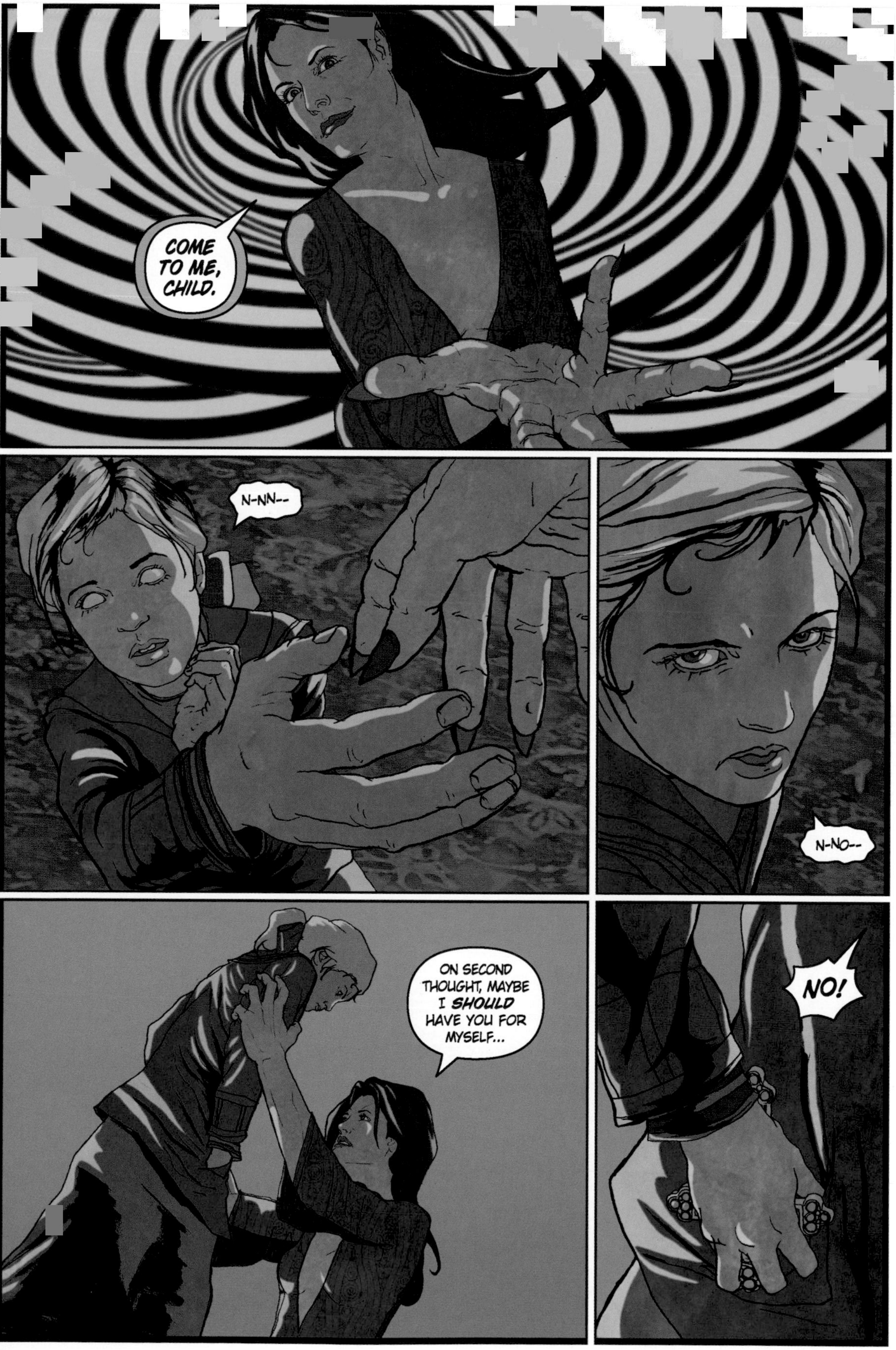
COME TO ME, CHILD.
N-NN--
N-NO--
ON SECOND THOUGHT, MAYBE I SHOULD HAVE YOU FOR MYSELF...
NO!

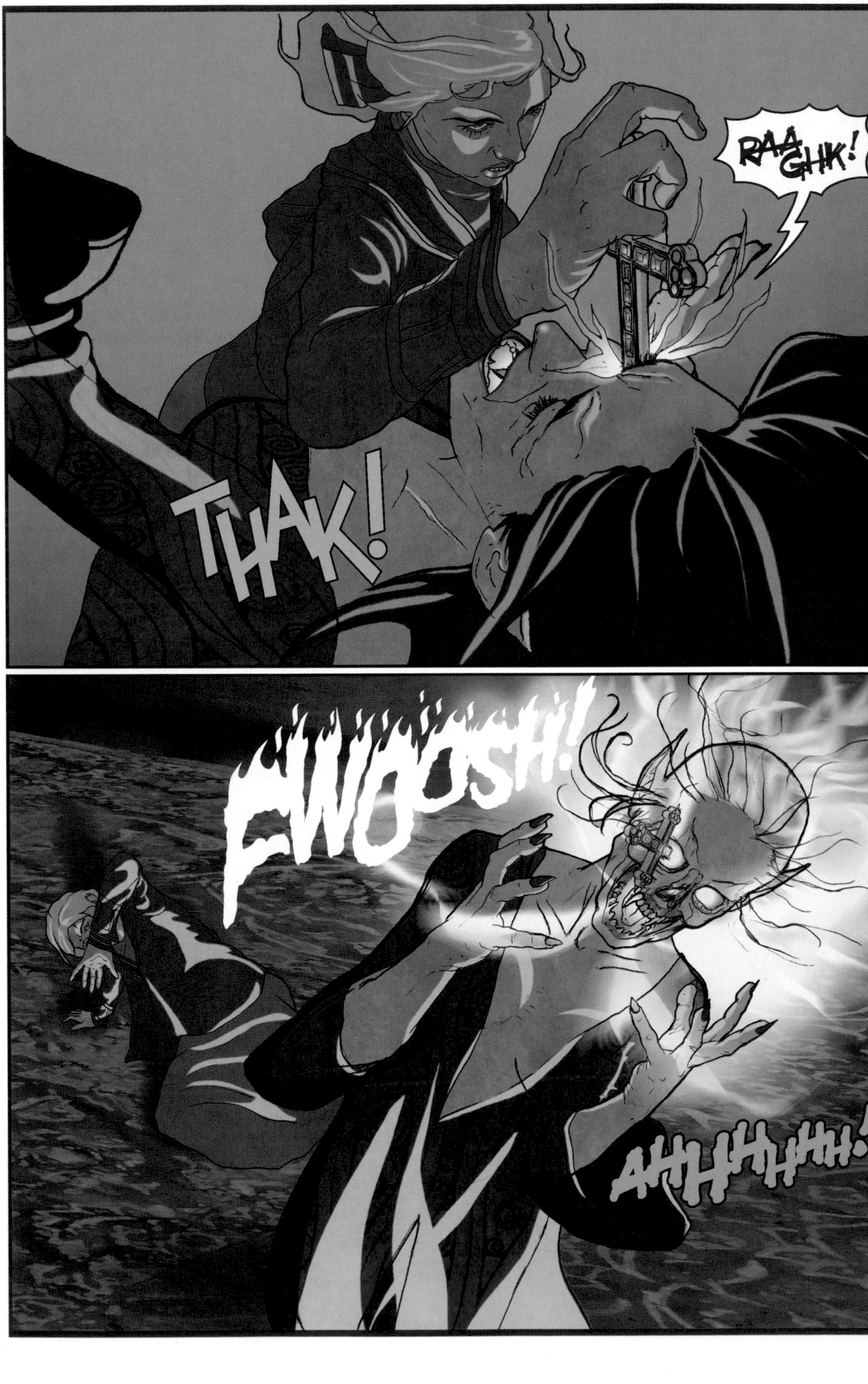
RAAGHK!
THAK!
FWOOSH!
AHHHHHH!

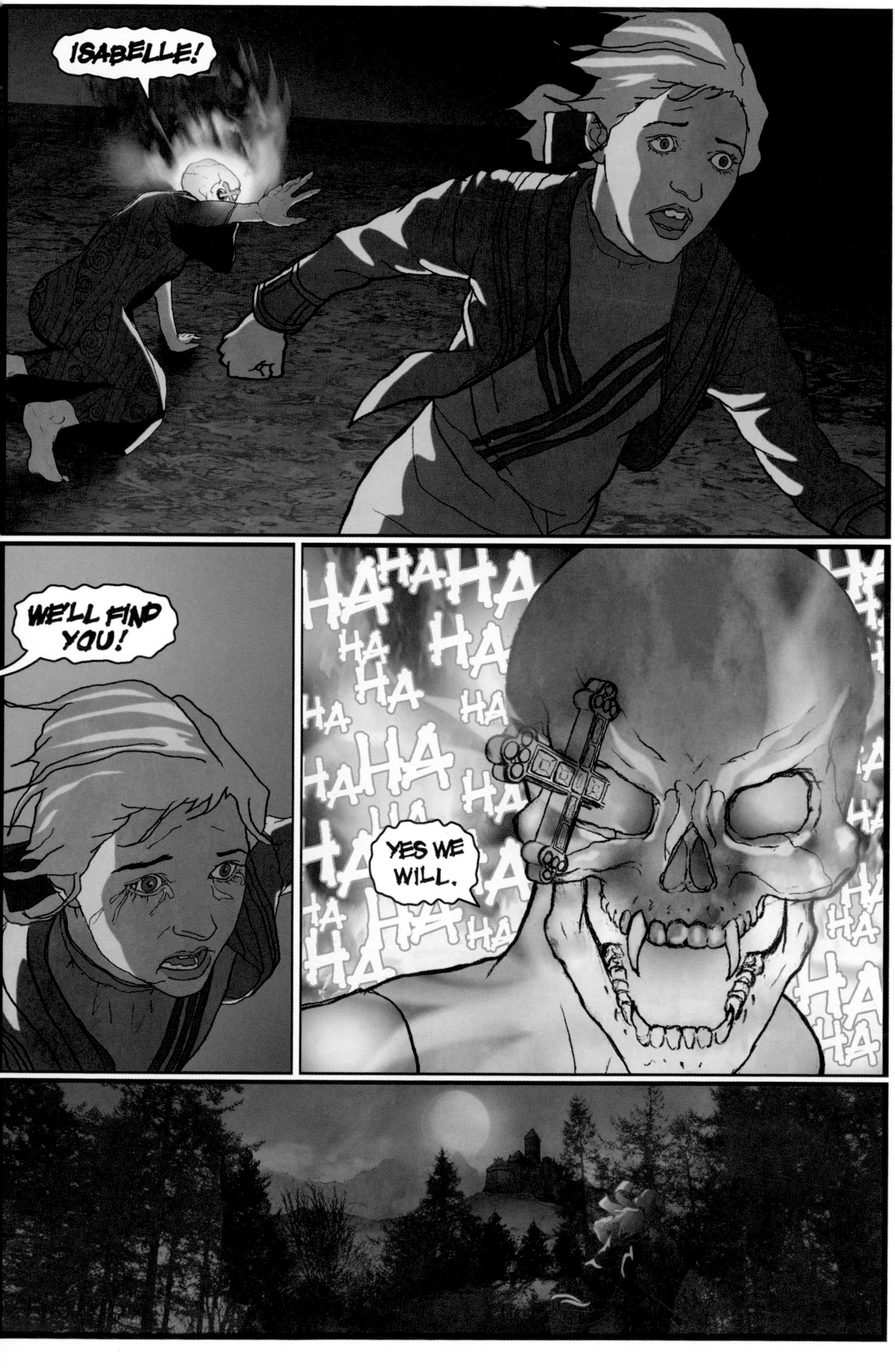
ISABELLE!
WE'LL FIND YOU!
YES WE WILL.
HAHAHA HA HA HA HA HA HAHA HA HA HA HA HA HA HA HA

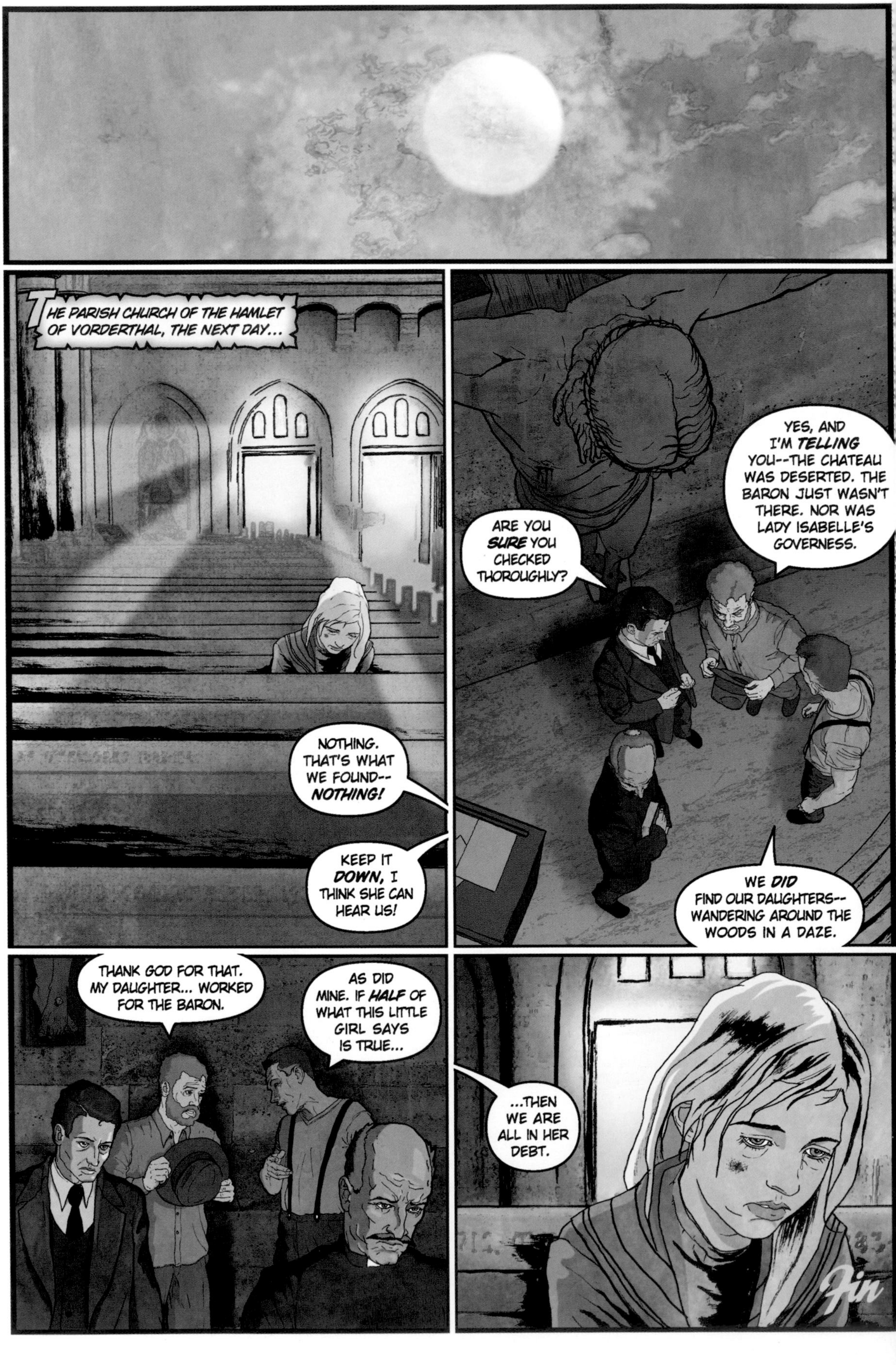
THE PARISH CHURCH OF THE HAMLET OF VORDERTHAL, THE NEXT DAY...
ARE YOU SURE YOU CHECKED THOROUGHLY?
YES, AND I'M TELLING YOU--THE CHATEAU WAS DESERTED. THE BARON JUST WASN'T THERE. NOR WAS LADY ISABELLE'S GOVERNESS.
NOTHING. THAT'S WHAT WE FOUND-- NOTHING!
KEEP IT DOWN, I THINK SHE CAN HEAR US!
WE DID FIND OUR DAUGHTERS-- WANDERING AROUND THE WOODS IN A DAZE.
THANK GOD FOR THAT. MY DAUGHTER... WORKED FOR THE BARON.
AS DID MINE. IF HALF OF WHAT THIS LITTLE GIRL SAYS IS TRUE...
...THEN WE ARE ALL IN HER DEBT.
Fin

Le Journal de la Liberté

Papal seal

of Approval

Paris's leading anglophone newspaper • vol. 192, no. 150 • Jun. 7, MCMXX

Editors in Chief: M. Tait Bergstrom, M. Matthew Pasteris. **Story Editor:** M. Arvid Nelson. **Art Editor:** M. Juan Ferreyra. **Photography Editor:** M. Alexander Waldman. **Layout Supervisor:** M. William Kartalopoulos. **Editors Emeritus:** M. Jules Verne, M. H.G. Wells, Mme. Mary Shelly. Redacted by the Holy Inquisition under the direction of His Excellency Archbishop Emile-Jean Ireneaux. *Le Journal de la Liberté* is printed under the benign auspices of his most puissant majesty KING LOUIS XXI of FRANCE. ⚜ GOD SAVE THE KING.

ALGERIAN REBELS SLAY FRENCH CITIZENS

Loyal Algerian natives assist in the recovery of the ransacked locomotive with French colonial troops.

Rebel horsemen on the move in the arid Algerian interior.

Rebels Seize Passenger Train Outside El Menia; Five French Citizens Killed

Algiers — French *spahi* cavalry on patrol in the region surrounding El Menia spotted a column of smoke in the distance early yesterday morning. They rode out to investigate and discovered a scene of carnage.

Mohammedan rebels had descended upon a French passenger train on its way to Algiers and left it a smoking ruin. Several dozen charred corpses were strewn on the ground nearby, including those of five French citizens. Women and children were among the French dead.

King Louis XXI expressed his outrage at the attack.

"We shall respond to this egregious assault on French civilization with the harshest possible measures," He said.

The perpetrators have not been apprehended and are suspected to be hiding among the populace of the nearby town. Henri Eugène Philippe Louis d'Orléans, Duke of Aumale and Governor-General of Algeria, vowed to hunt them down.

"Those who did this are little more than bandits, and the populace hiding them are no better," he said.

The duke said he would "aggressively interrogate" inhabitants of El Menia until the perpetrators were found. He also said reprisals against the town's inhabitants were forthcoming. "For every French citizen killed, we shall kill ten of them," he said.

Raids such as this are becoming more and more frequent in Algeria, as nationalists and Islamic fundamentalists gain support from the local populace.

The duke denied French policy is contributing to the unrest.

continued on next page

FANCIFUL TALES OF NIGHTTIME TERROR SEND YOUNG LADY LORRAINE BACK TO FRANCE

Vorderthal, Switzerland — Isabelle Plantard de St. Clair, daughter of the Duke of Lorraine, arrived in the remote hamlet of Vorderthal in the small hours of the morning. She was alone, shivering, and clad in a tattered dress. It was less than 24 hours after she came to the chateau of her distant relative, the baron of Vorderthal.

"The poor little thing was deathly cold. She had a dazed look on her face, but as soon as I got her into the church, she broke down," Father Olivier Chattot, priest of the parish of Vorderthal, said.

The young Lady Lorraine told Fr. Chattot she had been attacked by the baron and his head servant, one Claire St. Jean. Young Isabelle was not injured, but she said the baron had killed her governess.

There were also lurid, nightmarish details to her story, of the baron turning into a fanged monster, and of St. Jean turning into a wolf.

By the time the local constables arrived at the remote mountain chateau, it was deserted. There was no evidence of a vio-[...] attack. Lord Vorderthal, his [...] St. Jean and Lady Lorraine's governess were nowhere to be found. Their current whereabouts are unknown.

The baron's servants, all girls taken from the village, were found wandering the countryside later on that day. None of them had clear recollections of the events of the previous night. No one in the village had heard of Claire St. Jean, the woman Lady Lorraine described as the baron's head servant.

Now the inhabitants of the hamlet of Vorderthal are left to wonder what became of their lord, a reclusive baron who was rarely seen in the village and "never during the day," according to residents.

The Holy Inquisition was quick to arrive on the scene. They immediately closed off the baron's estate and dismissed Lady Lorraine's fantastic story.

"Obviously, it's just the workings of a poor young girl's distraught mind," Inquisitor Moricant, heading up the Church investigation, said. He did not speculate on what actually occurred in the chateau.

Lady Lorraine is unharmed, and is expected to return to France soon.

Ostracized Viscount Dies in Fire

Paris — A fire on the ancestral estates of the house of de Boeldieu took the life of the family's only surviving heir late last night, permanently ending the lineage.

Viscount de Boeldieu never married. He secluded himself in his estates after being evicted from the Guild of Physicians and continued his medical experiments on his own.

Two of the viscount's friends visited him the night he died. They speculate de Boeldieu's research led to the fire that claimed his life.

"When we left him he told us he was going to continue an experiment. He had a lot of volatile chemical compounds around," friend and Journeyman Physician Genevieve Tournon said.

"De Boeldieu was very troubled. All he wanted was to be a doctor, and he never got over his rejection from the Guild," Journeyman Physician Julie Saunière, also with de Boeldieu the night he died, said.

"He was brilliant. I d[...] think anyone in the Guild [...] ized how much he had to o[...] he added.

Viscount Antoine-Dav[...] Boeldieu was 27 years o[...] Guild of Physicians had r[...] ment on his death.

REX MUNDI BOOK FIVE:
The Valley at the End of the World

PARIS, 1933. THE PROTESTANT REFORMATION HAS FAILED. Europe is in the grip of feudalism, and sorcerers stalk the streets at night. It is the world of *Rex Mundi*.

The Duke of Lorraine, grand master of a secret society born in the shadows of the First Crusade, has manipulated rising political tensions to seize power in France and ignite a world war.

His reasons for doing so are connected to the secret of the Holy Grail itself.

Master Physician Julien Saunière devoted himself to uncovering that secret when an encrypted medieval scroll connected to the Grail was stolen from longtime friend Father Gérard Marin. A mysterious assassin in a white suit murdered Marin soon after, leaving Saunière no choice but to investigate.

With the help of his old flame and fellow doctor Genevieve Tournon, Julien has discovered the Grail is not, in fact, a cup—it is the royal bloodline of King David and Jesus Christ, and none other than Lorraine is a direct descendant!

Julien's prying has aroused the ire of the powerful Archbishop of Sens, head of the Holy Inquisition in Paris.

Julien has escaped from the archbishop with Genevieve's help, and the two have run to the southern hamlet of Rennes-le-Chateau, said to conceal the tomb of an ancient king of France . . . and the location of the legendary Grail Castle itself.

What Julien did not know, until recently, is that Genevieve has been having an affair with Lorraine, spying on Julien while trying to protect him at the same time. What's more, she bears a striking resemblance to the duke's dead wife, awakening long-dormant feelings in Lorraine.

Genevieve is pregnant, but she does not know if the child is Lorraine's or Julien's. When the Man in White attacks in Rennes-le-Chateau, she is finally exposed. Julien banishes her.

Things aren't faring much better for Lorraine. Thanks to an indiscretion on the part of his only daughter, Isabelle, Lorraine suffers a crushing defeat at the gates of Paris. He has fled south, abandoning the city to the Prussians . . .

"Blessed art thou among women, and blessed is the fruit of thy womb. And whence is this to me, that the mother of my Lord should come to me?"

— Luke 1:42–43

Et in Arcadia ego...

TER NOSTER QVI EST IN COELIS

CHAPTER ONE
UNEXPECTED VISITORS II

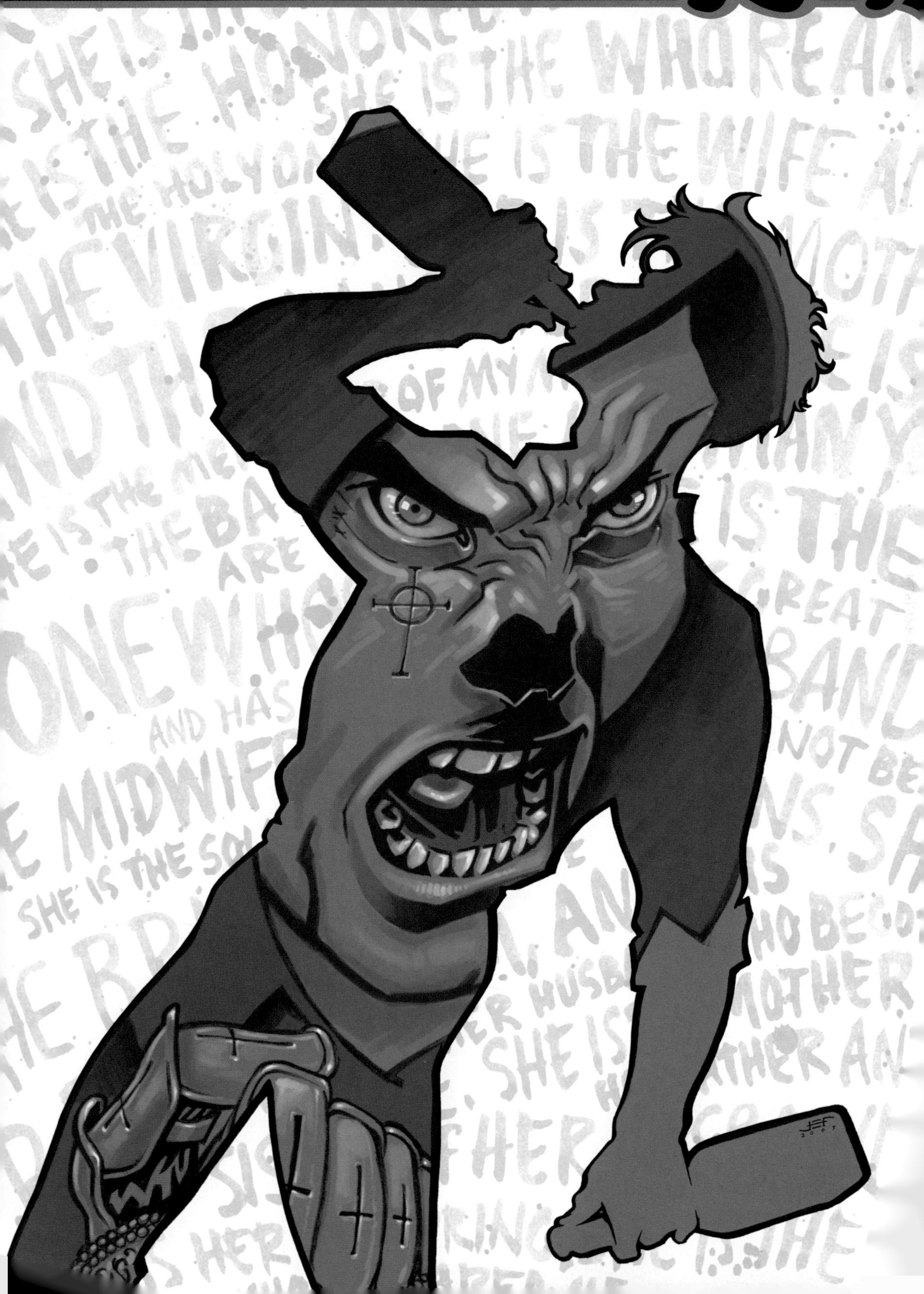

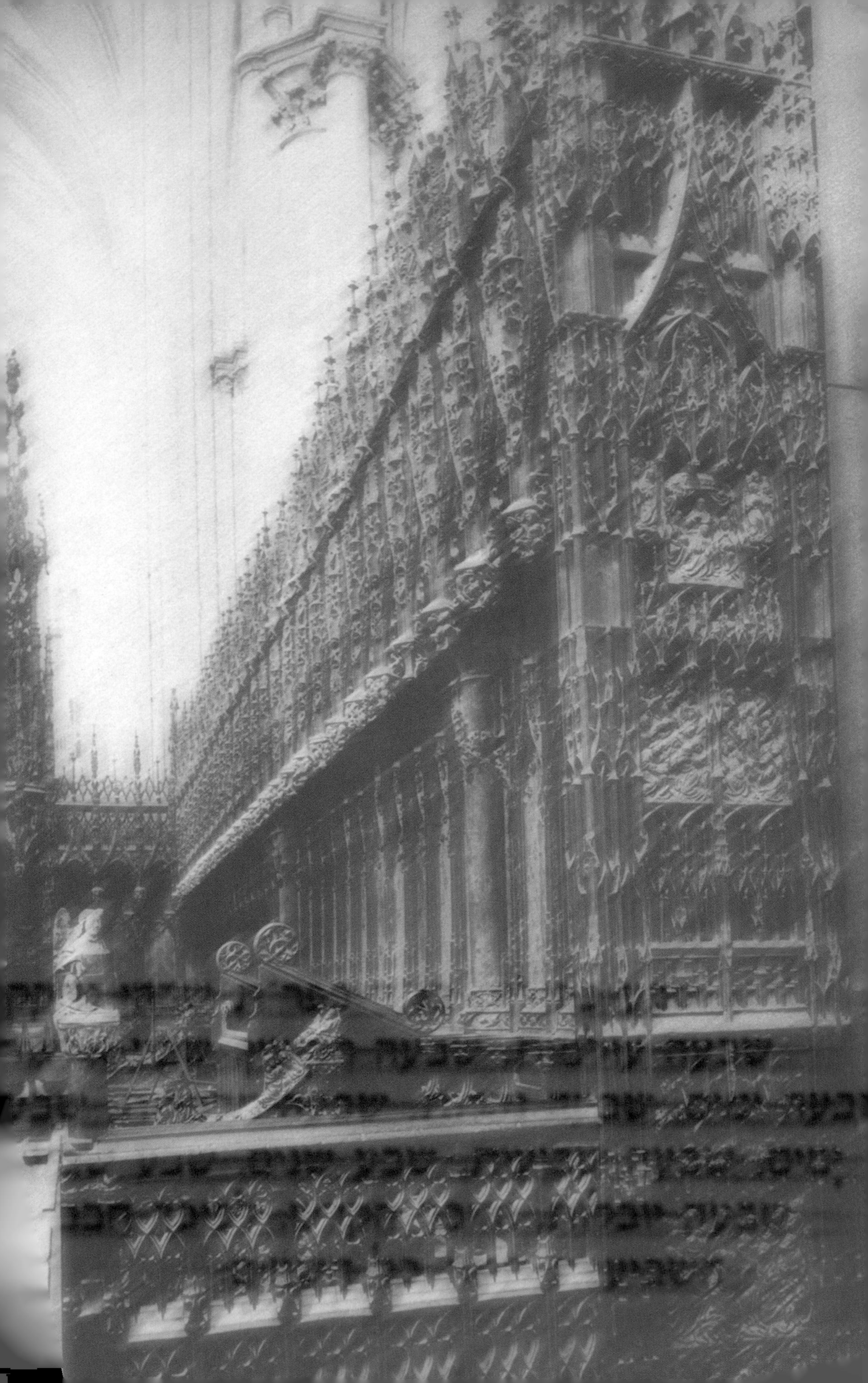

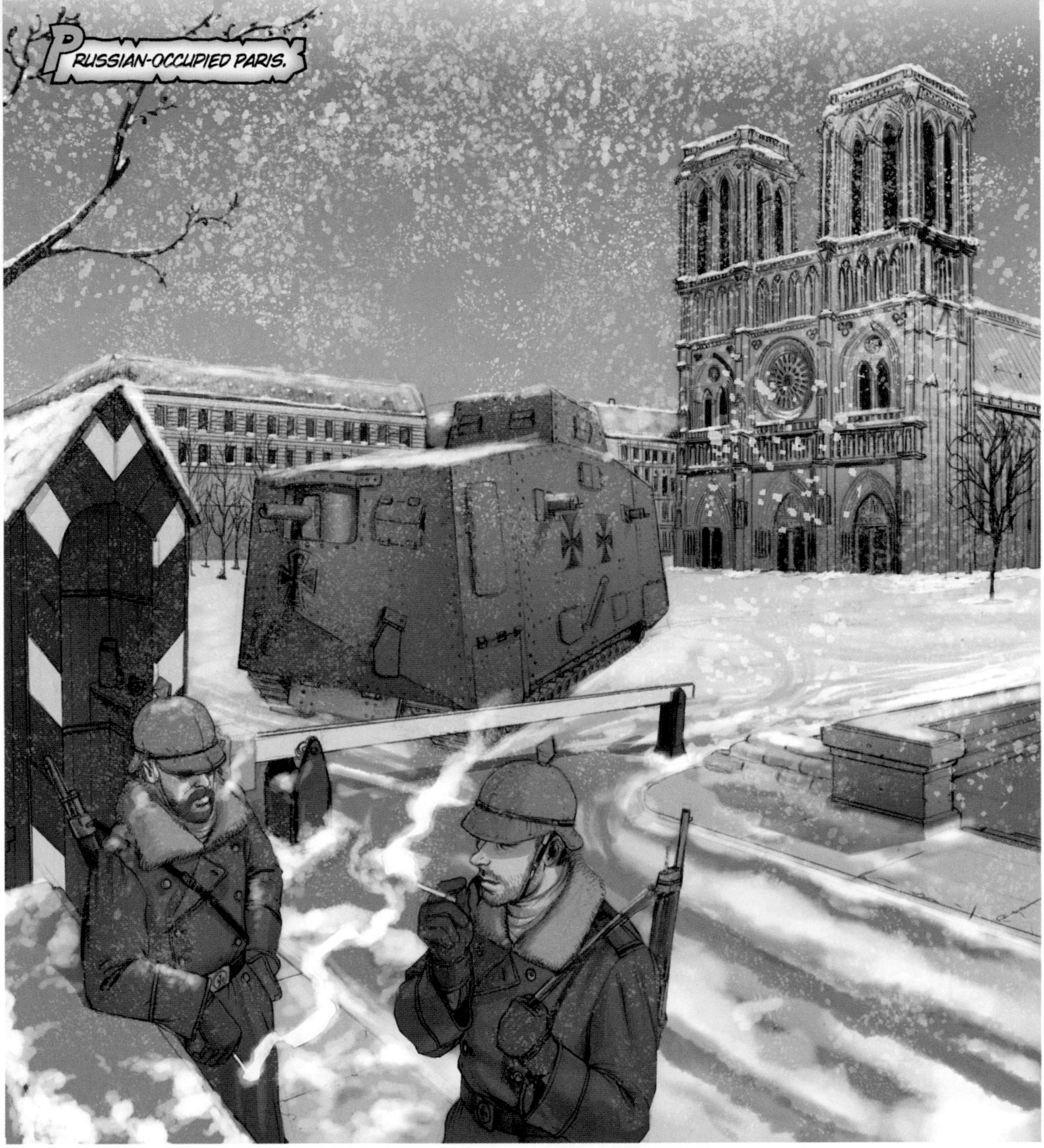
PRUSSIAN-OCCUPIED PARIS.

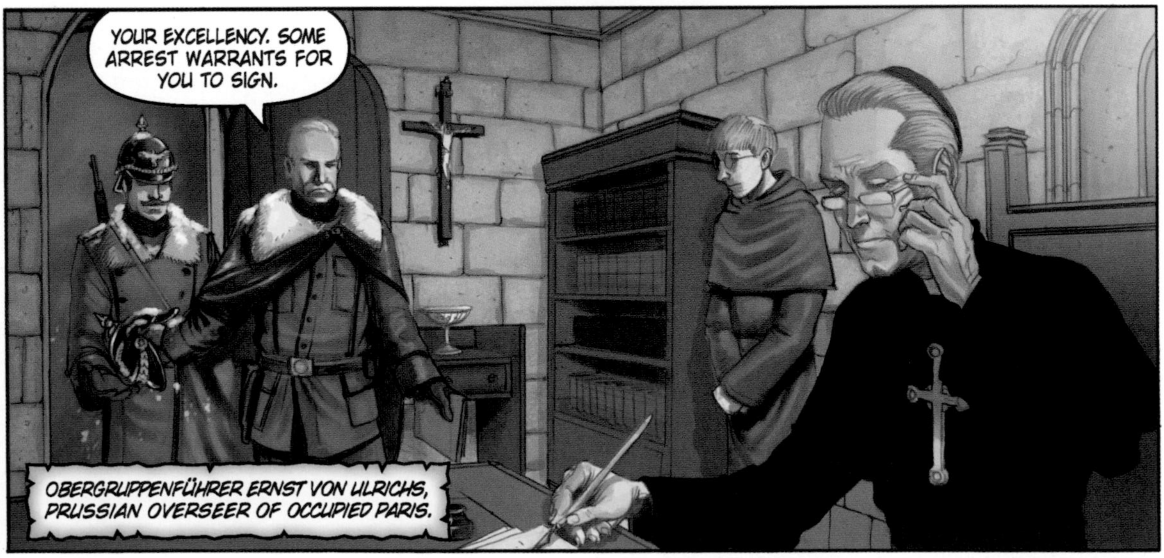
YOUR EXCELLENCY. SOME ARREST WARRANTS FOR YOU TO SIGN.
OBERGRUPPENFÜHRER ERNST VON ULRICHS, PRUSSIAN OVERSEER OF OCCUPIED PARIS.

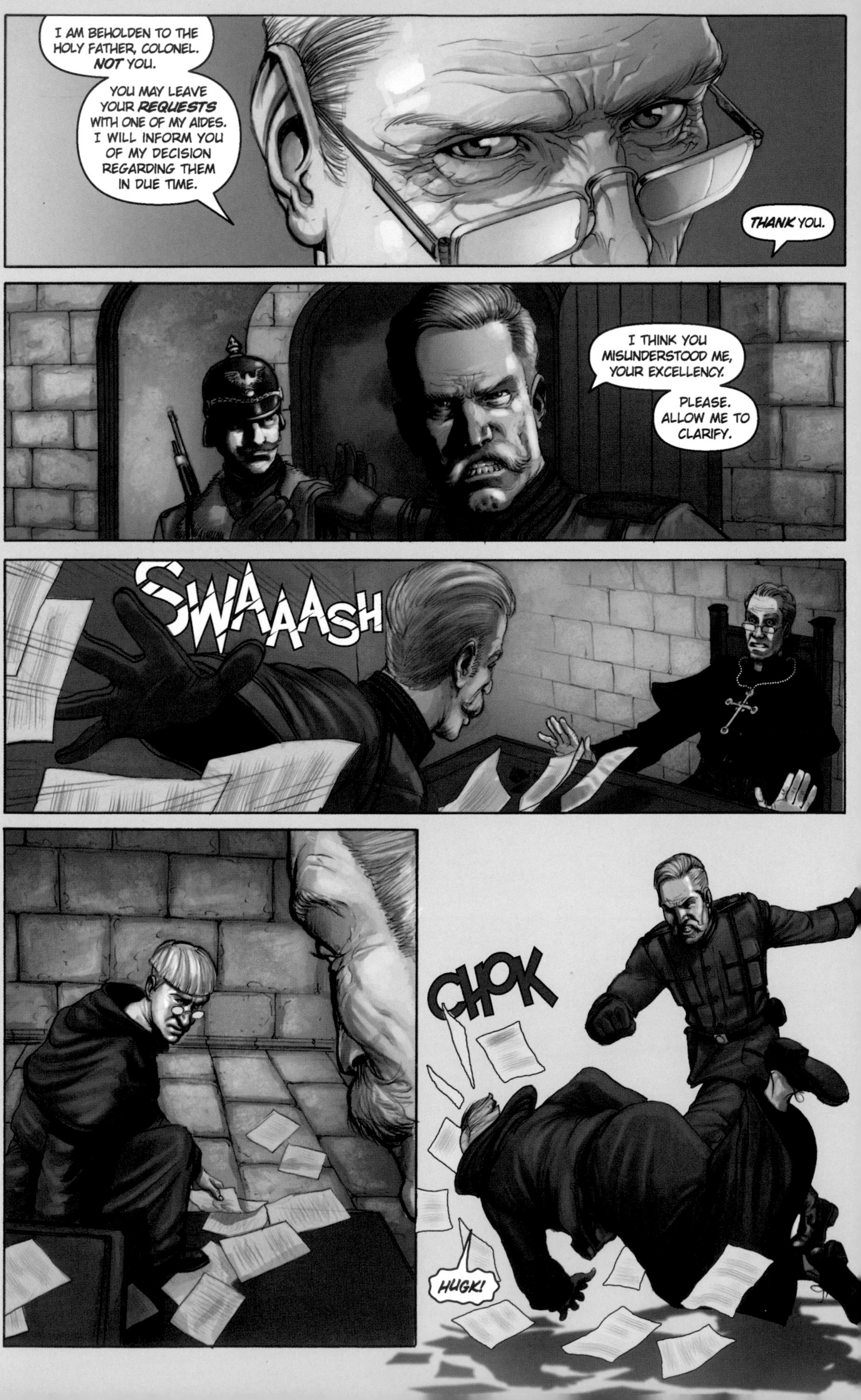
I AM BEHOLDEN TO THE HOLY FATHER, COLONEL. **NOT** YOU.
YOU MAY LEAVE YOUR **REQUESTS** WITH ONE OF MY AIDES. I WILL INFORM YOU OF MY DECISION REGARDING THEM IN DUE TIME.
THANK YOU.
I THINK YOU MISUNDERSTOOD ME, YOUR EXCELLENCY.
PLEASE. ALLOW ME TO CLARIFY.
SWAAASH
CHOK
HUGK!

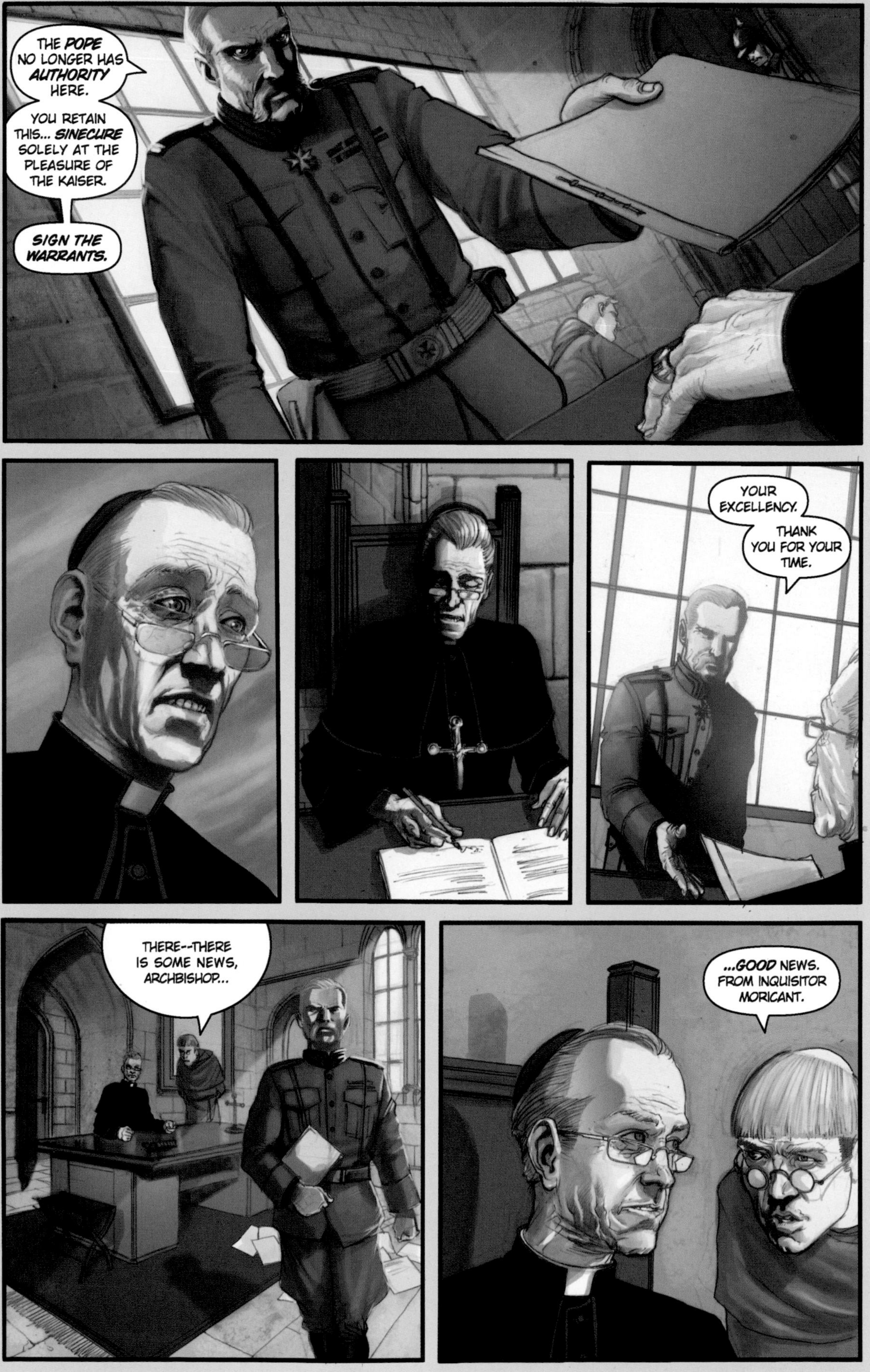
THE POPE NO LONGER HAS AUTHORITY HERE.
YOU RETAIN THIS... SINECURE SOLELY AT THE PLEASURE OF THE KAISER.
SIGN THE WARRANTS.
YOUR EXCELLENCY.
THANK YOU FOR YOUR TIME.
THERE--THERE IS SOME NEWS, ARCHBISHOP...
...GOOD NEWS. FROM INQUISITOR MORICANT.

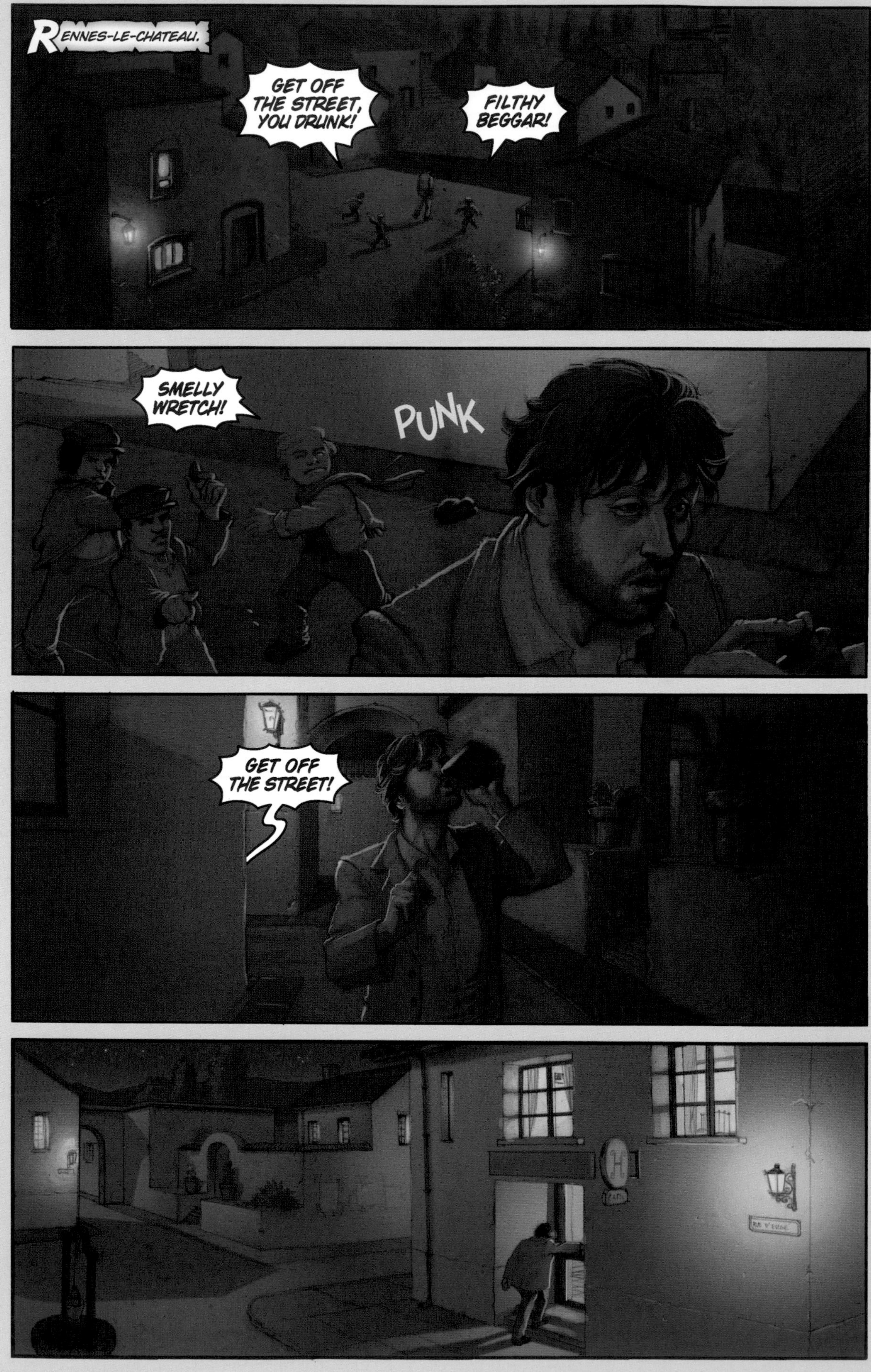
RENNES-LE-CHATEAU.
GET OFF THE STREET, YOU DRUNK!
FILTHY BEGGAR!
SMELLY WRETCH!
PUNK
GET OFF THE STREET!

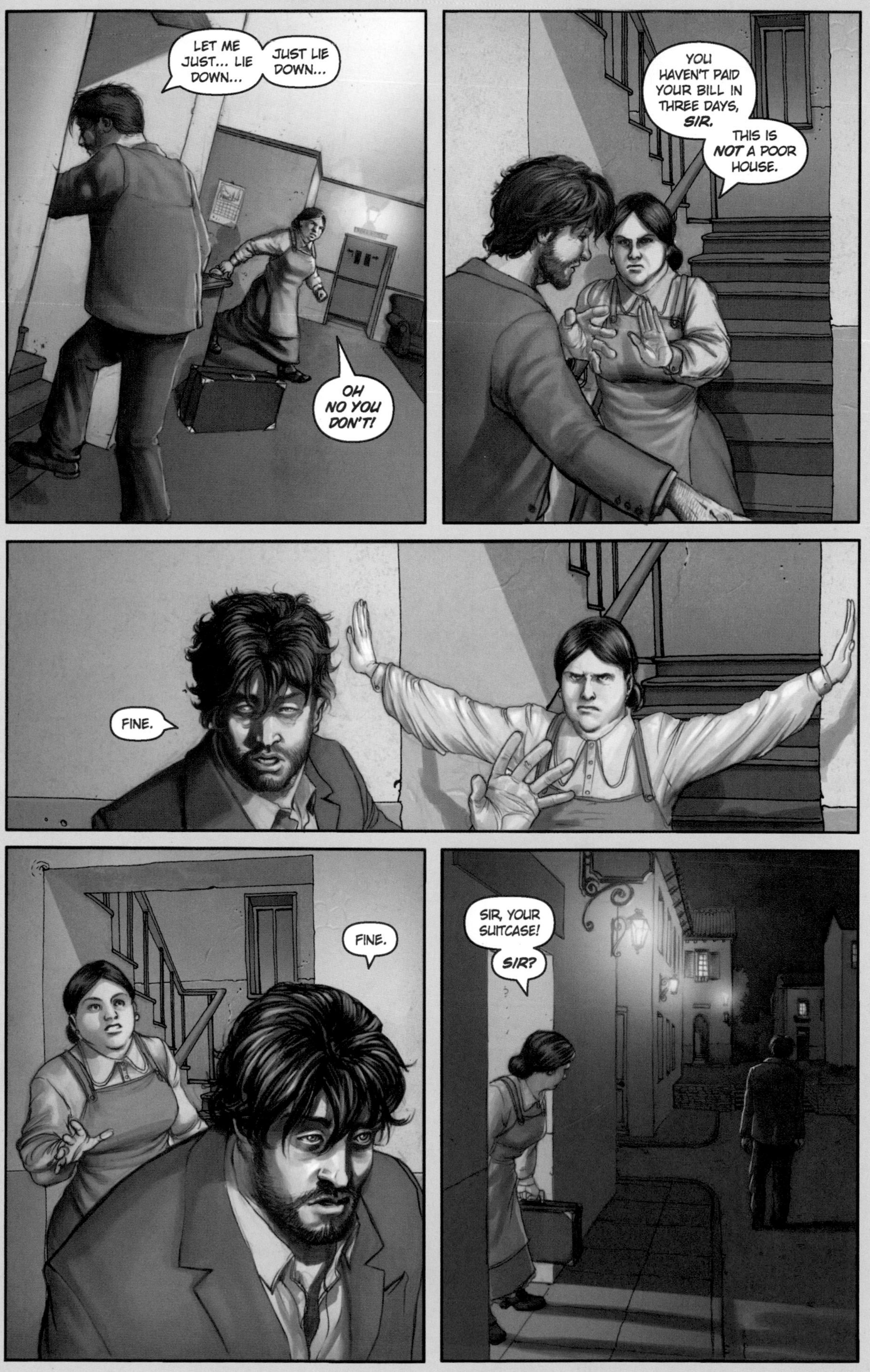
LET ME JUST... LIE DOWN...
JUST LIE DOWN...
OH NO YOU DON'T!
YOU HAVEN'T PAID YOUR BILL IN THREE DAYS, SIR.
THIS IS NOT A POOR HOUSE.
FINE.
FINE.
SIR, YOUR SUITCASE!
SIR?
?

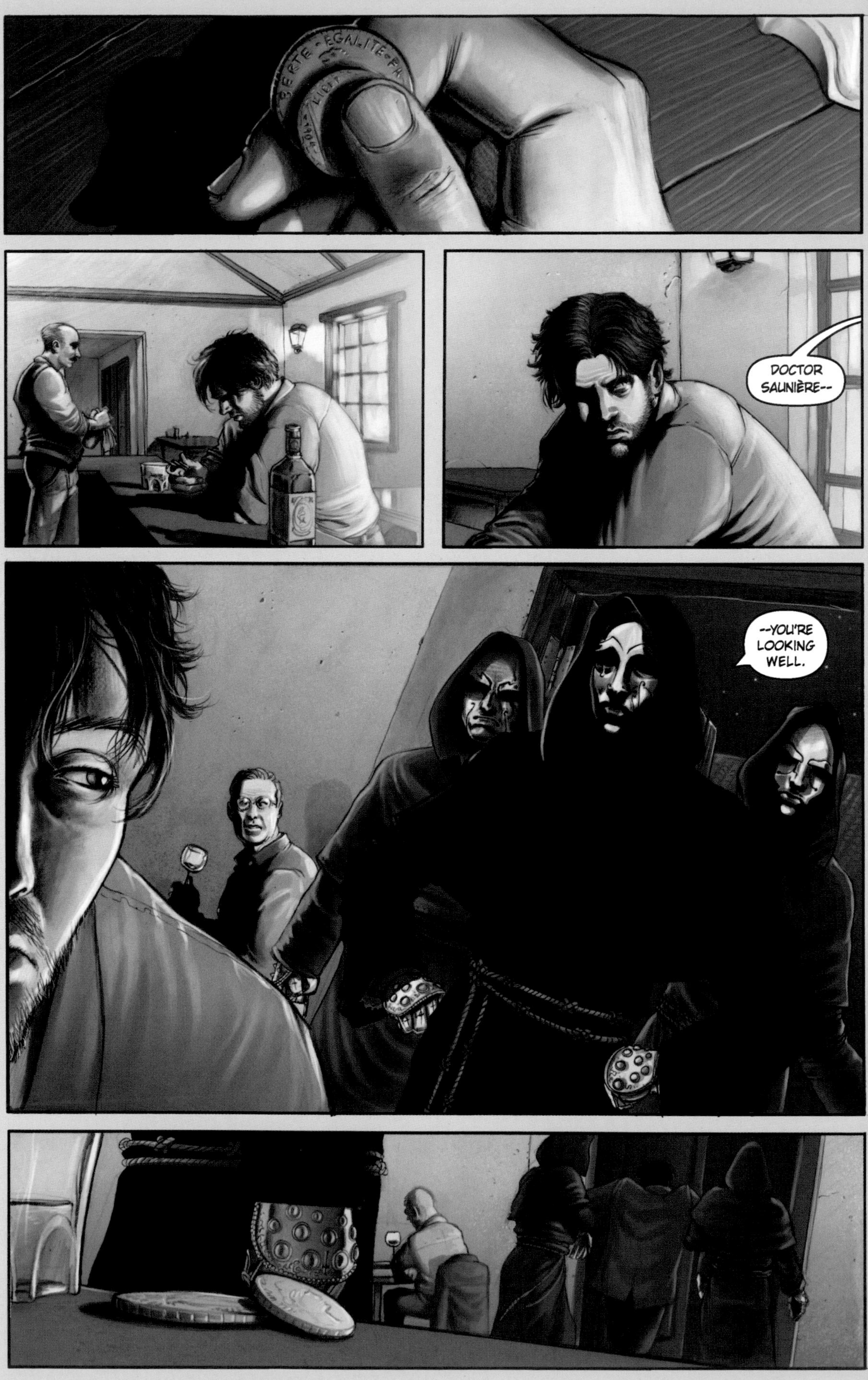
DOCTOR SAUNIÈRE--
--YOU'RE LOOKING WELL.

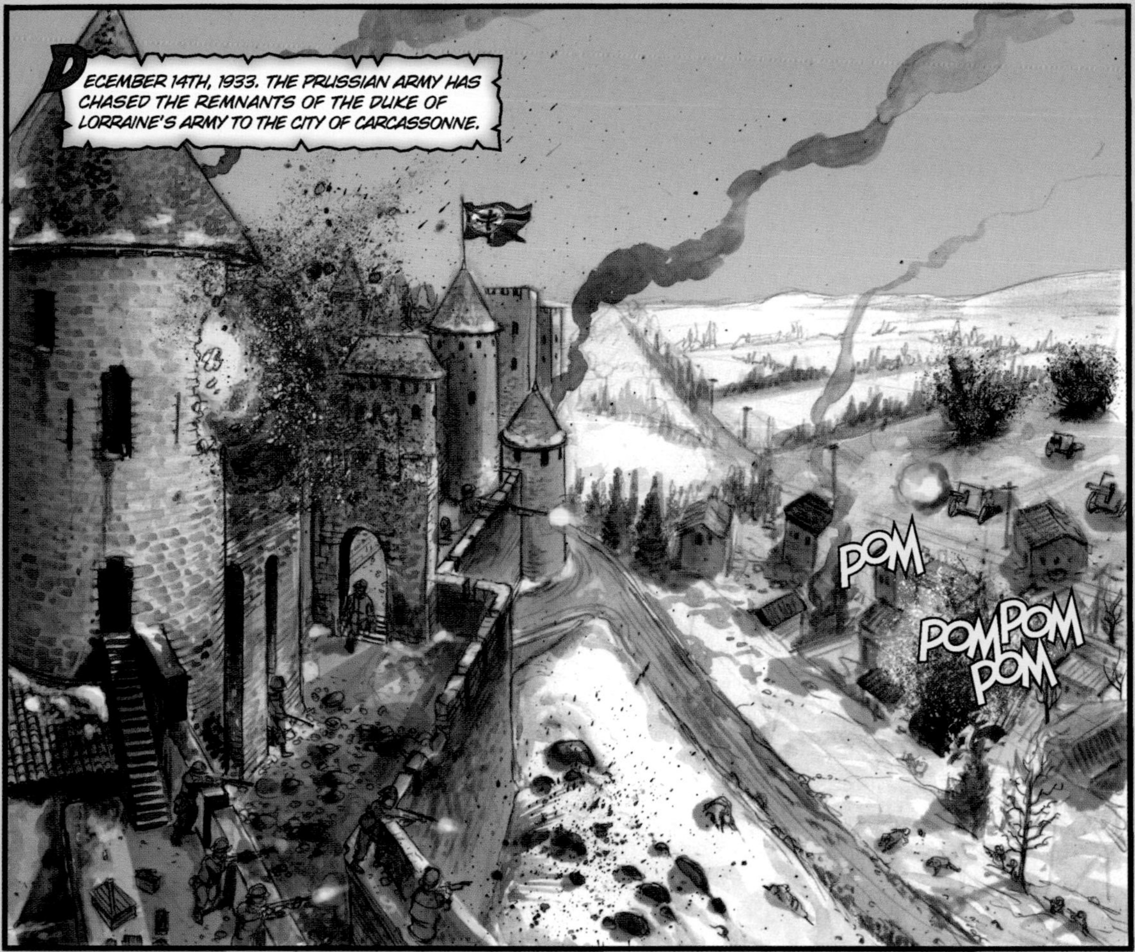
DECEMBER 14TH, 1933. THE PRUSSIAN ARMY HAS CHASED THE REMNANTS OF THE DUKE OF LORRAINE'S ARMY TO THE CITY OF CARCASSONNE.
POM
POMPOM
POM

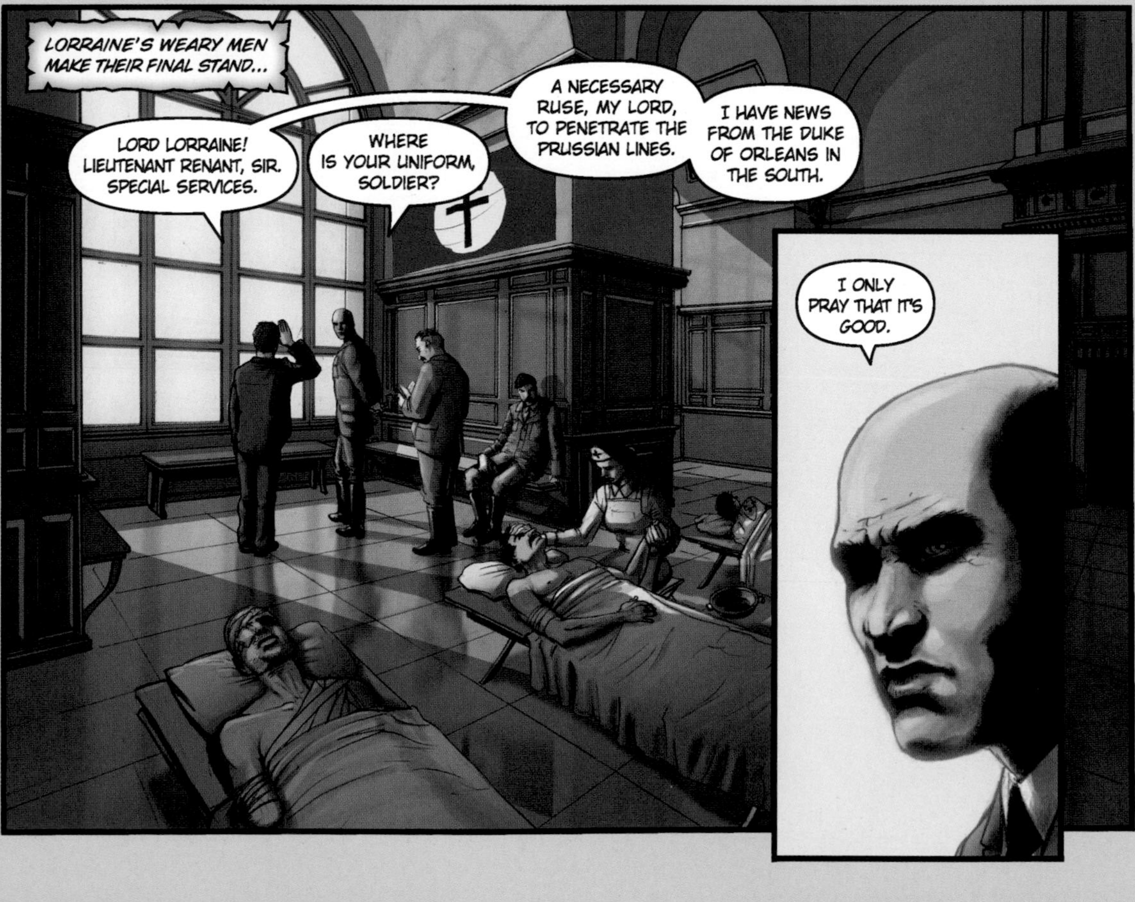
LORRAINE'S WEARY MEN MAKE THEIR FINAL STAND...
LORD LORRAINE! LIEUTENANT RENANT, SIR. SPECIAL SERVICES.
WHERE IS YOUR UNIFORM, SOLDIER?
A NECESSARY RUSE, MY LORD, TO PENETRATE THE PRUSSIAN LINES.
I HAVE NEWS FROM THE DUKE OF ORLEANS IN THE SOUTH.
I ONLY PRAY THAT IT'S GOOD.

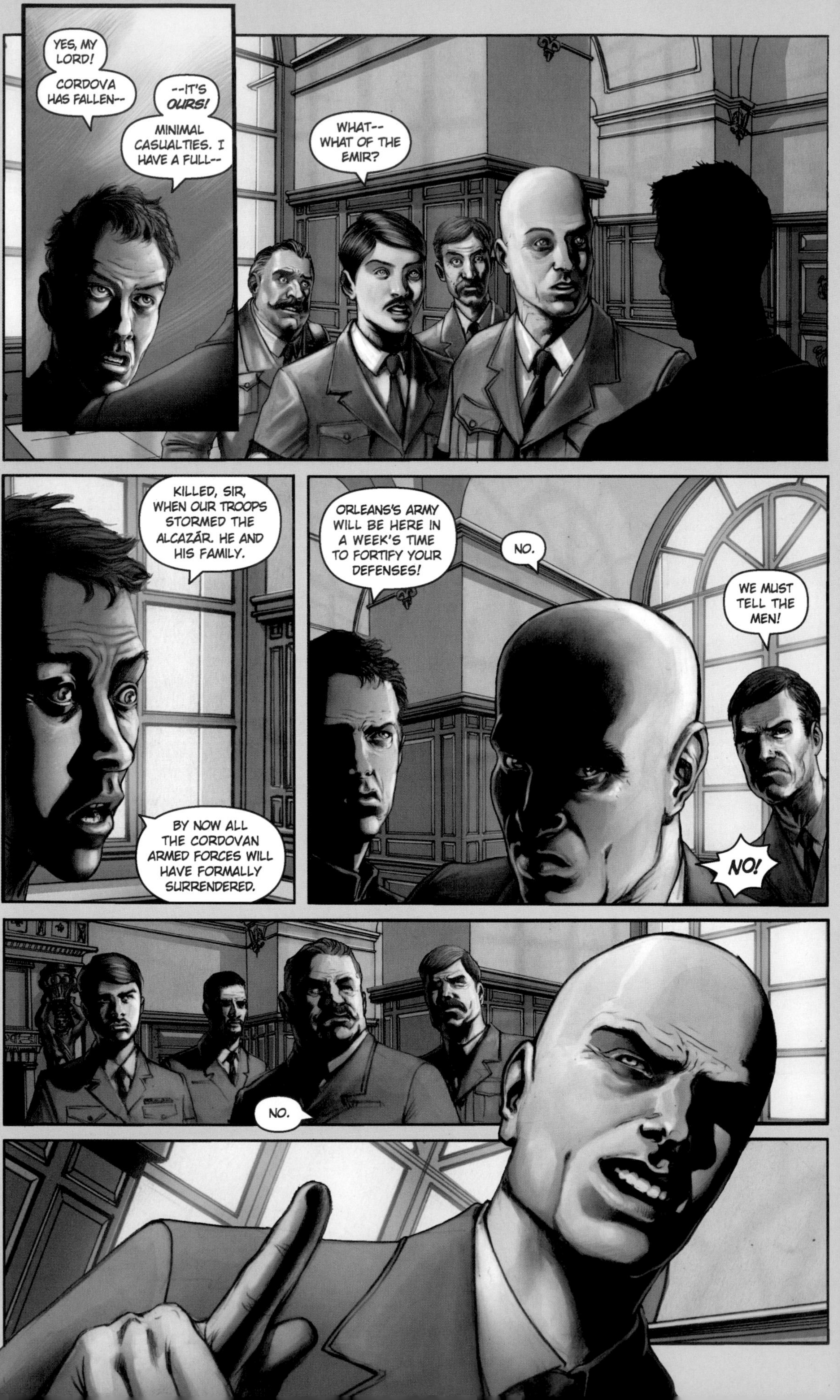
YES, MY LORD!
CORDOVA HAS FALLEN--
--IT'S OURS!
MINIMAL CASUALTIES. I HAVE A FULL--
WHAT--WHAT OF THE EMIR?
KILLED, SIR, WHEN OUR TROOPS STORMED THE ALCAZÁR. HE AND HIS FAMILY.
BY NOW ALL THE CORDOVAN ARMED FORCES WILL HAVE FORMALLY SURRENDERED.
ORLEANS'S ARMY WILL BE HERE IN A WEEK'S TIME TO FORTIFY YOUR DEFENSES!
NO.
WE MUST TELL THE MEN!
NO!
NO.

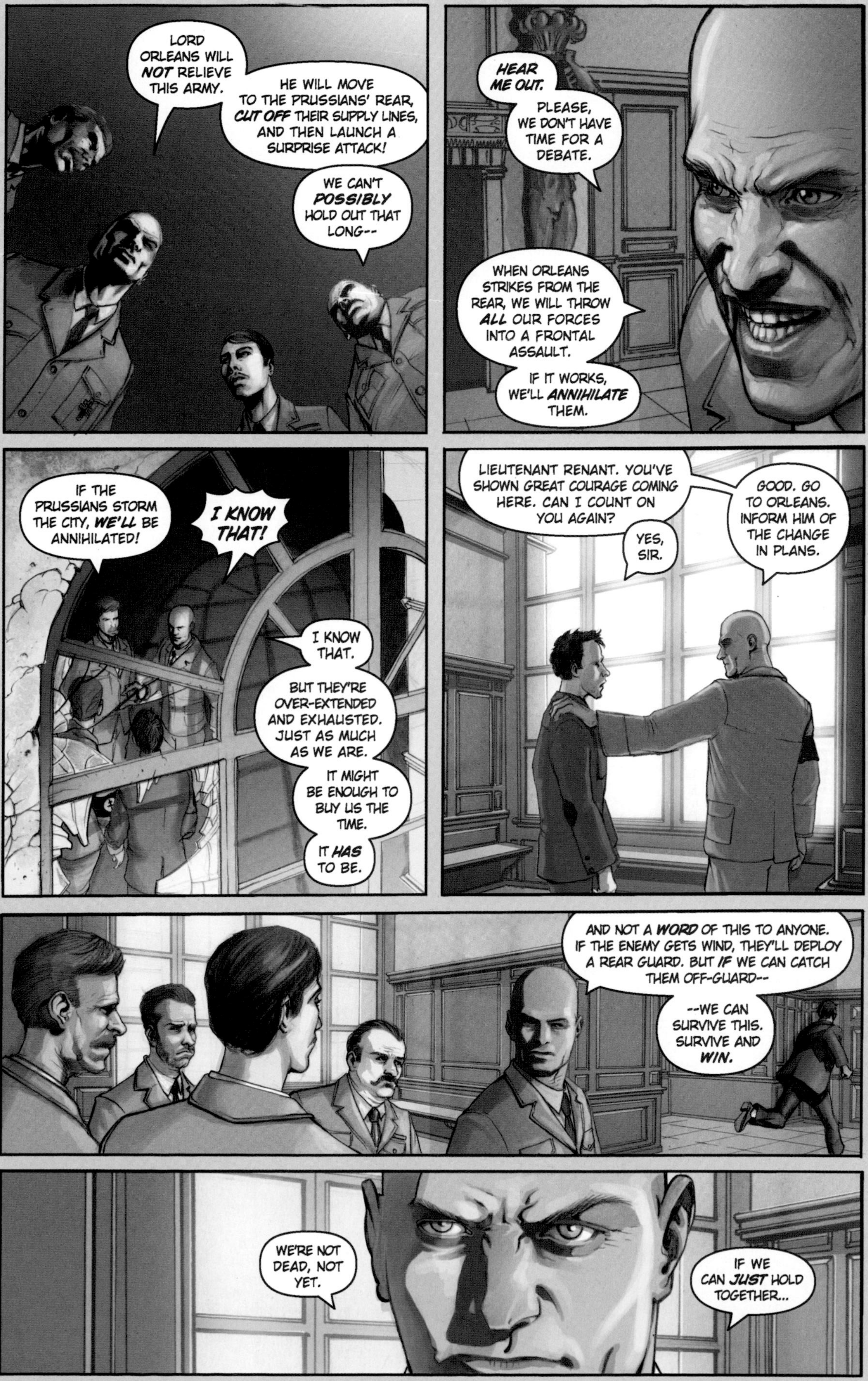
LORD ORLEANS WILL NOT RELIEVE THIS ARMY.
HE WILL MOVE TO THE PRUSSIANS' REAR, CUT OFF THEIR SUPPLY LINES, AND THEN LAUNCH A SURPRISE ATTACK!
WE CAN'T POSSIBLY HOLD OUT THAT LONG--
HEAR ME OUT.
PLEASE, WE DON'T HAVE TIME FOR A DEBATE.
WHEN ORLEANS STRIKES FROM THE REAR, WE WILL THROW ALL OUR FORCES INTO A FRONTAL ASSAULT.
IF IT WORKS, WE'LL ANNIHILATE THEM.
IF THE PRUSSIANS STORM THE CITY, WE'LL BE ANNIHILATED!
I KNOW THAT!
I KNOW THAT.
BUT THEY'RE OVER-EXTENDED AND EXHAUSTED. JUST AS MUCH AS WE ARE.
IT MIGHT BE ENOUGH TO BUY US THE TIME.
IT HAS TO BE.
LIEUTENANT RENANT. YOU'VE SHOWN GREAT COURAGE COMING HERE. CAN I COUNT ON YOU AGAIN?
YES, SIR.
GOOD. GO TO ORLEANS. INFORM HIM OF THE CHANGE IN PLANS.
AND NOT A WORD OF THIS TO ANYONE. IF THE ENEMY GETS WIND, THEY'LL DEPLOY A REAR GUARD. BUT IF WE CAN CATCH THEM OFF-GUARD--
--WE CAN SURVIVE THIS. SURVIVE AND WIN.
WE'RE NOT DEAD, NOT YET.
IF WE CAN JUST HOLD TOGETHER...

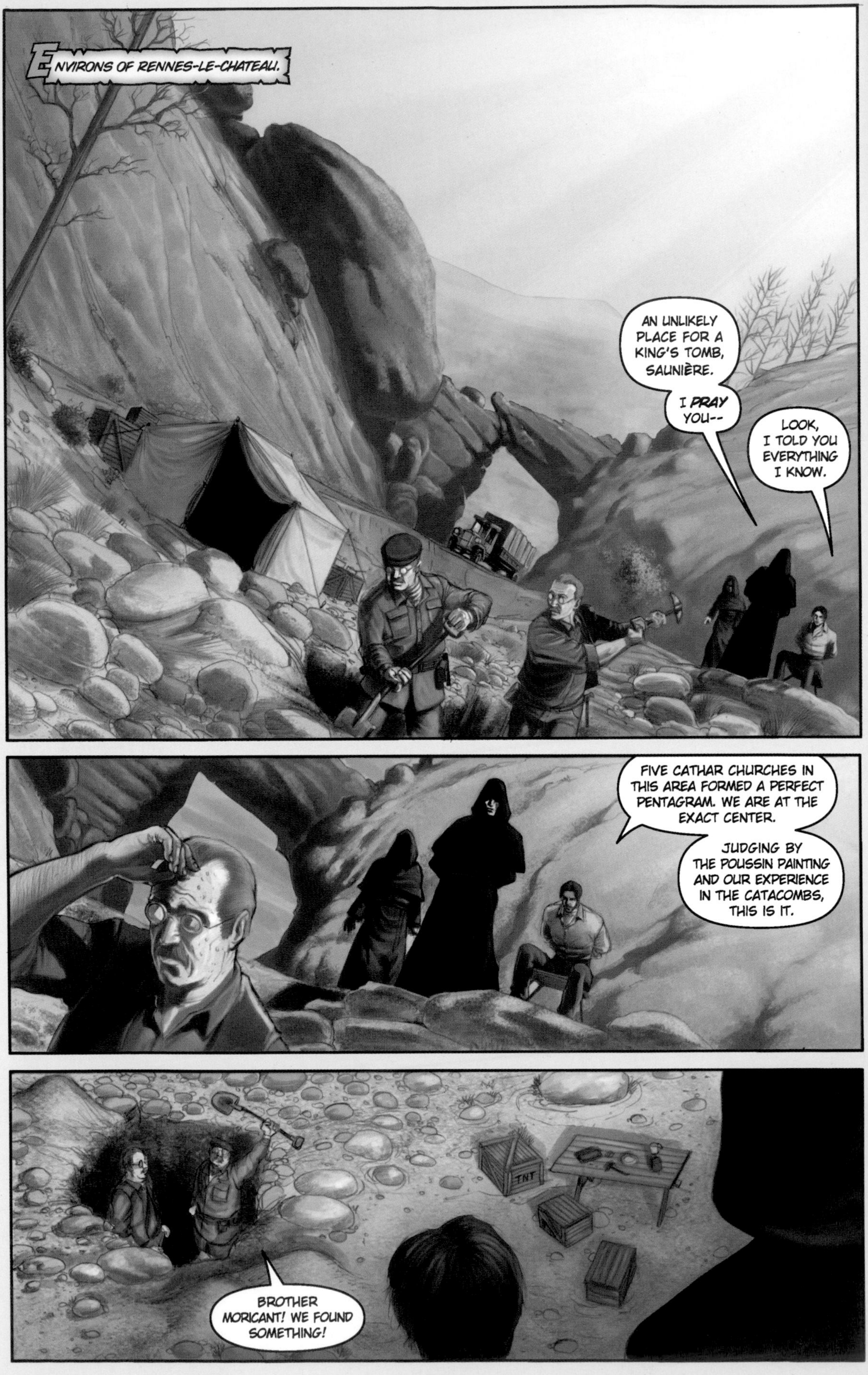
ENVIRONS OF RENNES-LE-CHATEAU.
AN UNLIKELY PLACE FOR A KING'S TOMB, SAUNIÈRE.
I *PRAY* YOU--
LOOK, I TOLD YOU EVERYTHING I KNOW.
FIVE CATHAR CHURCHES IN THIS AREA FORMED A PERFECT PENTAGRAM. WE ARE AT THE EXACT CENTER.
JUDGING BY THE POUSSIN PAINTING AND OUR EXPERIENCE IN THE CATACOMBS, THIS IS IT.
TNT
BROTHER MORICANT! WE FOUND SOMETHING!

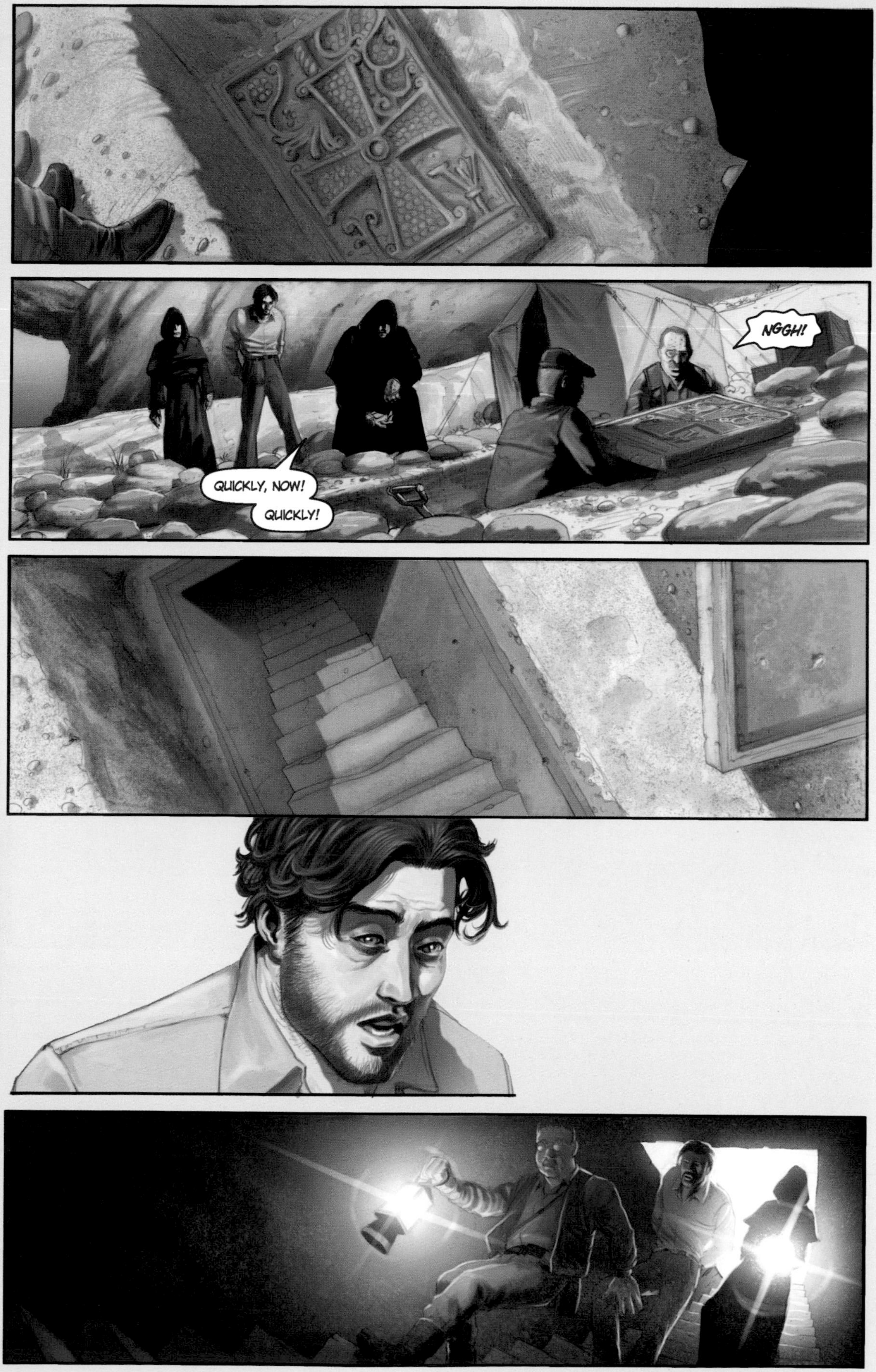
NGGH!
QUICKLY, NOW!
QUICKLY!

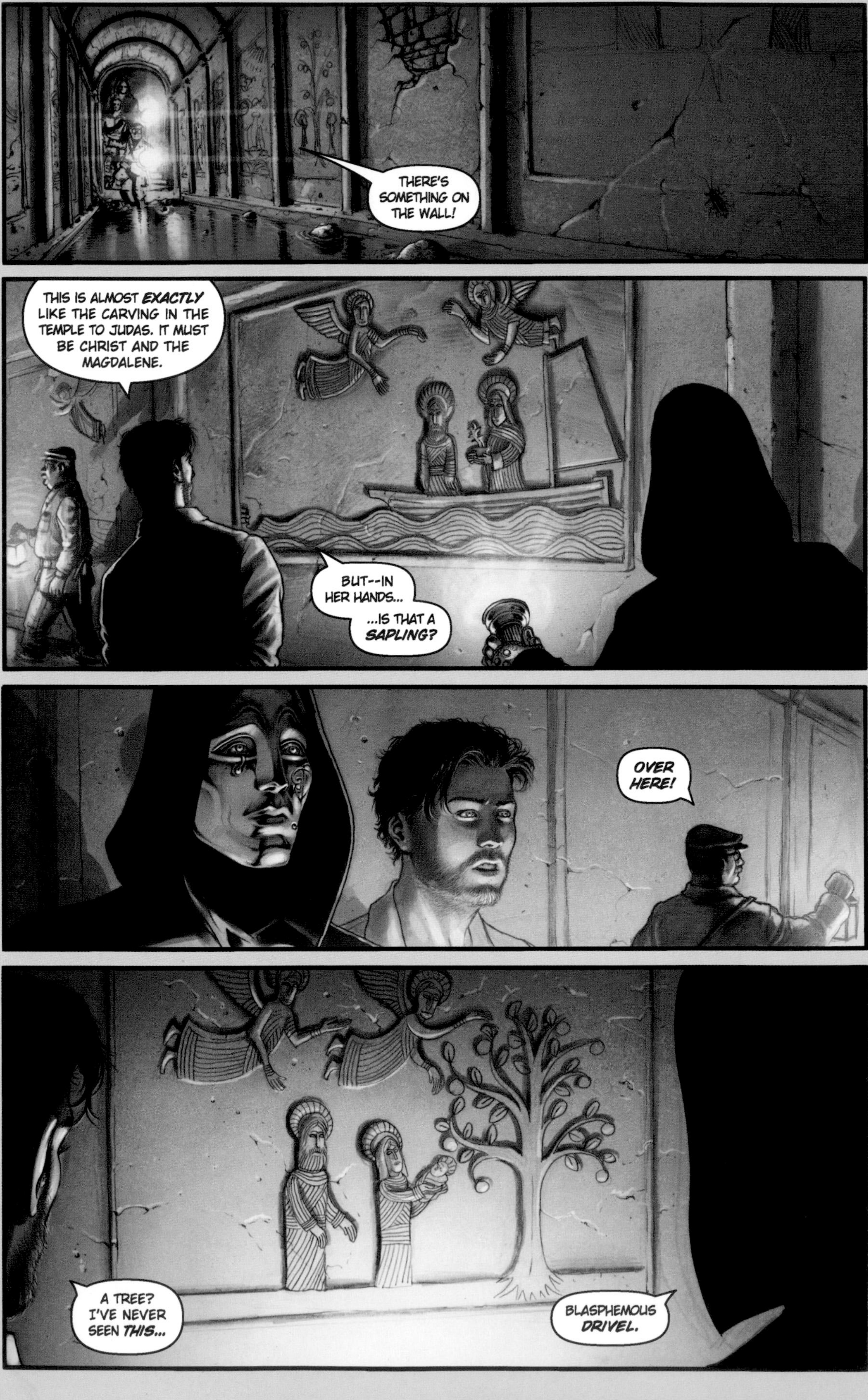
THERE'S SOMETHING ON THE WALL!
THIS IS ALMOST *EXACTLY* LIKE THE CARVING IN THE TEMPLE TO JUDAS. IT MUST BE CHRIST AND THE MAGDALENE.
BUT--IN HER HANDS... ...IS THAT A *SAPLING?*
OVER HERE!
A TREE? I'VE NEVER SEEN *THIS...*
BLASPHEMOUS *DRIVEL.*

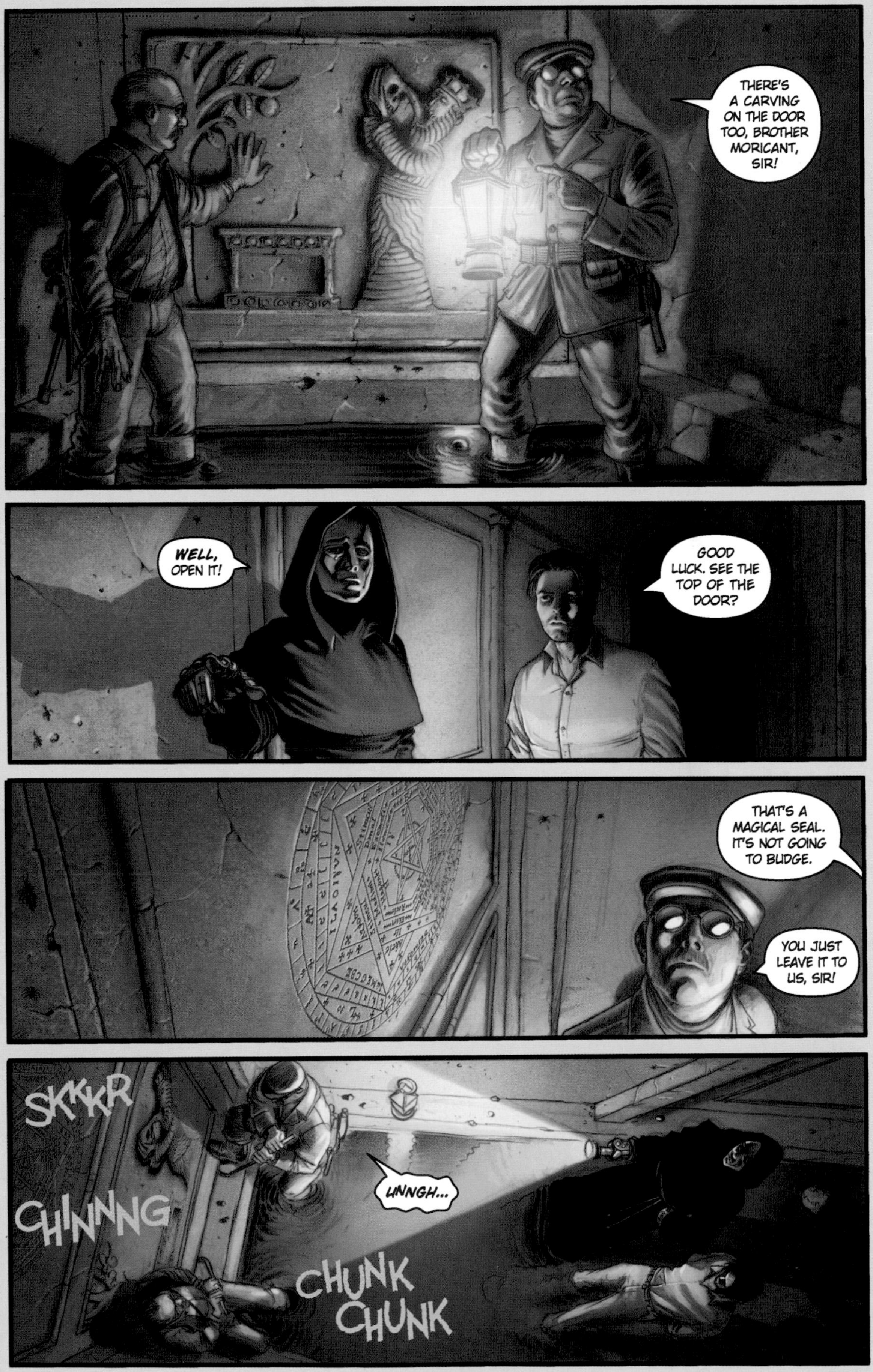
THERE'S A CARVING ON THE DOOR TOO, BROTHER MORICANT, SIR!
WELL, OPEN IT!
GOOD LUCK. SEE THE TOP OF THE DOOR?
THAT'S A MAGICAL SEAL. IT'S NOT GOING TO BUDGE.
YOU JUST LEAVE IT TO US, SIR!
SKKKR
CHINNNG
UNNGH...
CHUNK CHUNK

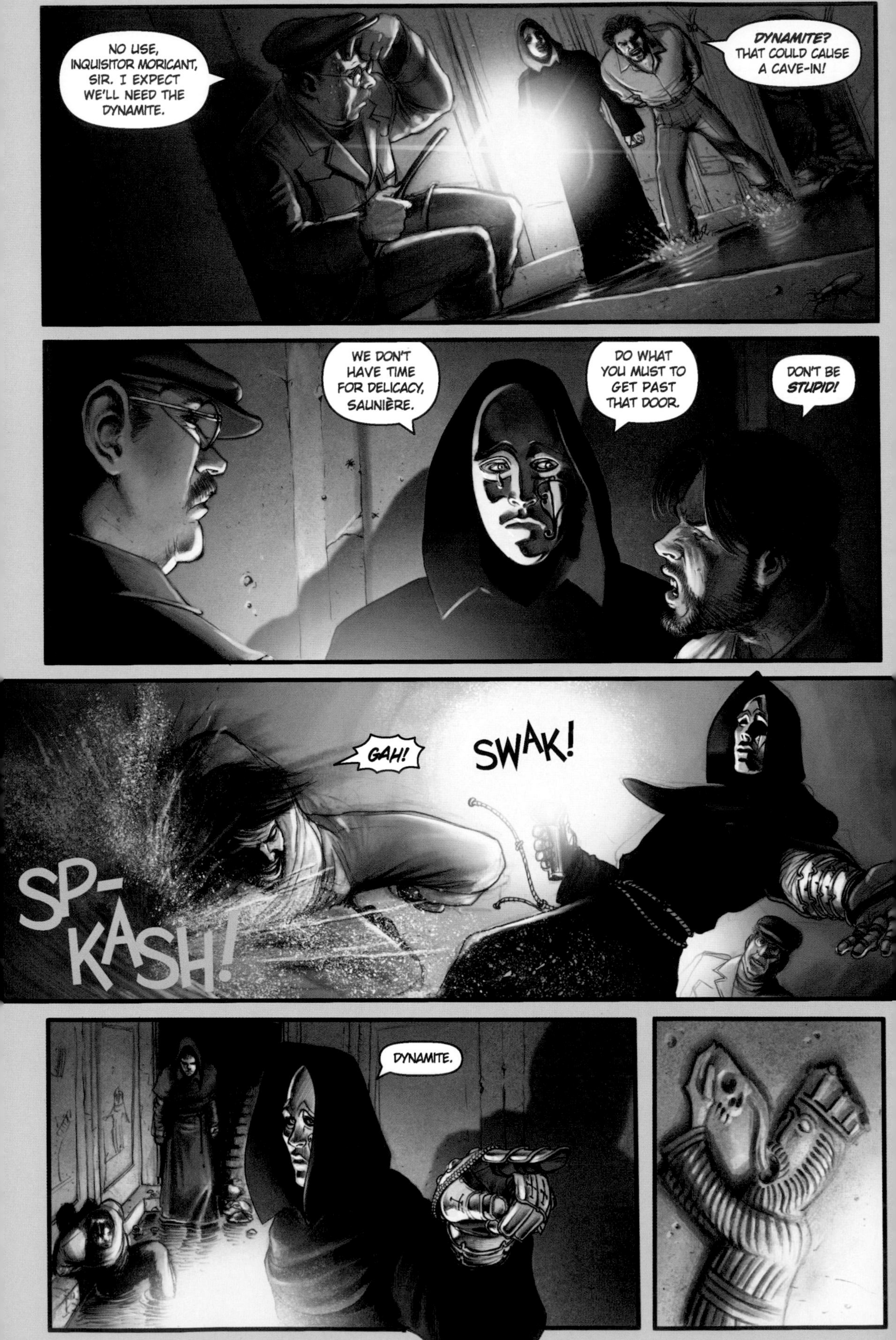
NO USE, INQUISITOR MORICANT, SIR. I EXPECT WE'LL NEED THE DYNAMITE.
DYNAMITE? THAT COULD CAUSE A CAVE-IN!
WE DON'T HAVE TIME FOR DELICACY, SAUNIÈRE.
DO WHAT YOU MUST TO GET PAST THAT DOOR.
DON'T BE STUPID!
GAH!
SWAK!
SP-KASH!
DYNAMITE.

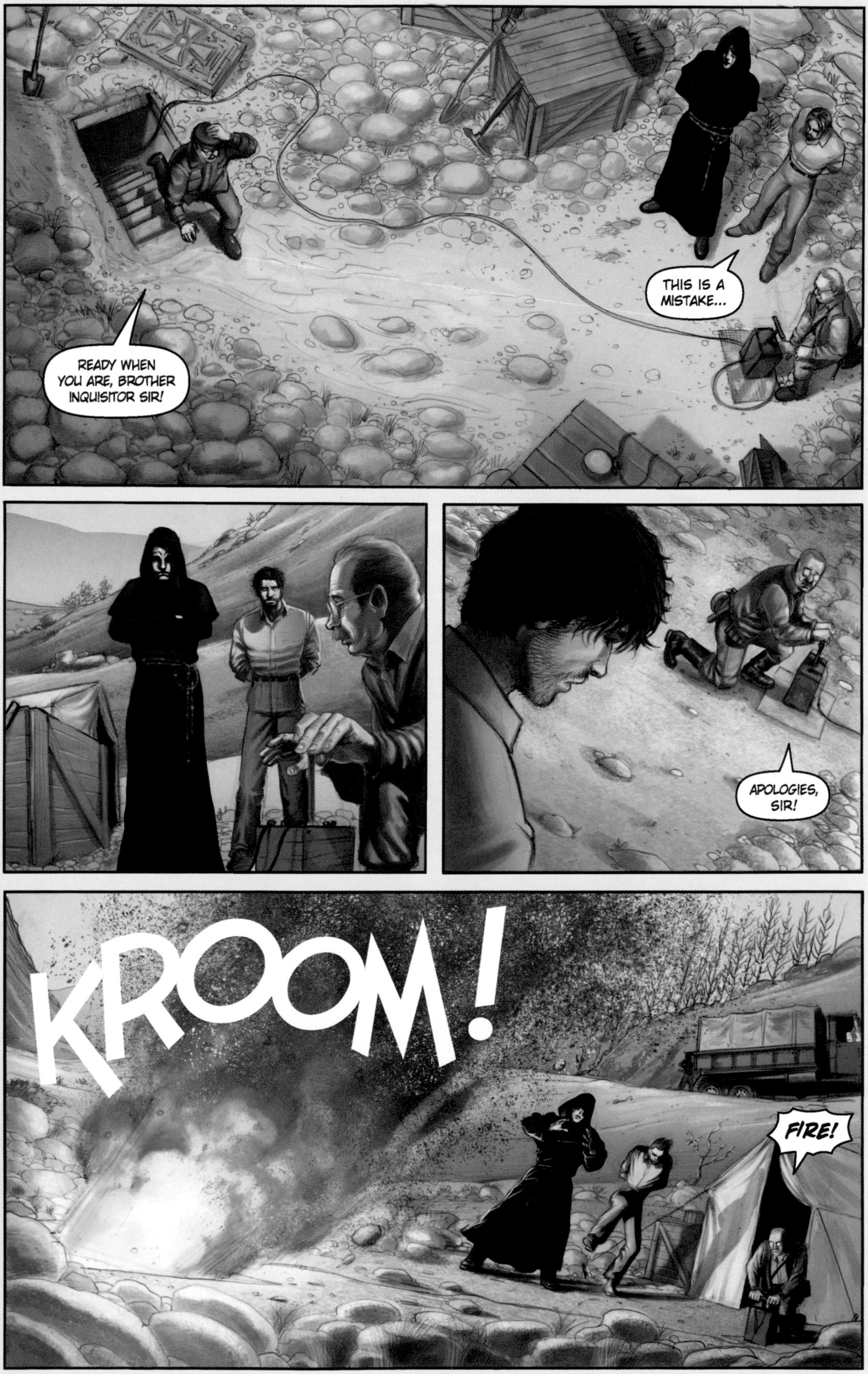

THIS IS A MISTAKE...
READY WHEN YOU ARE, BROTHER INQUISITOR SIR!
APOLOGIES, SIR!
KROOM!
FIRE!

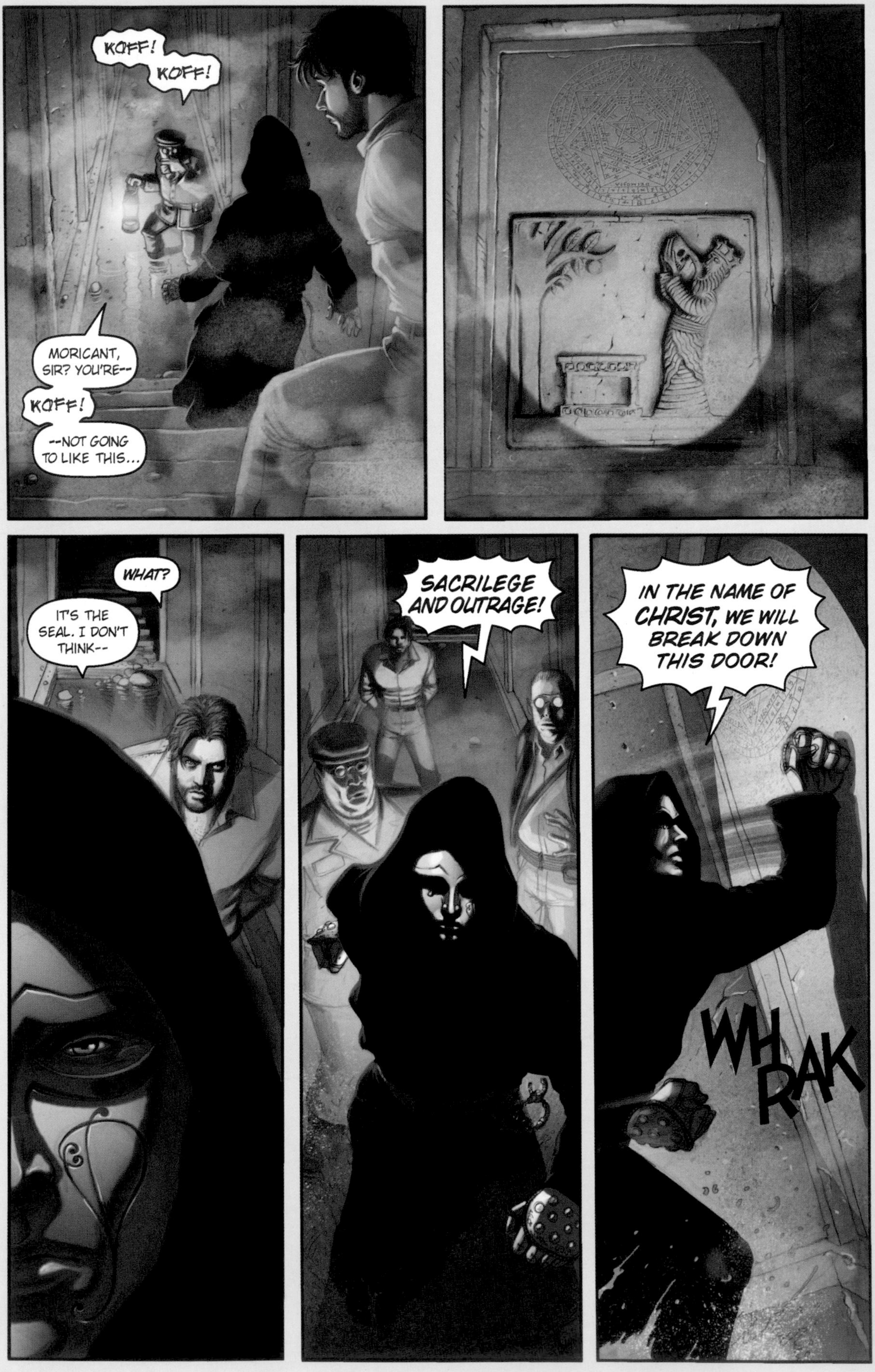
KOFF!
KOFF!
MORICANT, SIR? YOU'RE--
KOFF!
--NOT GOING TO LIKE THIS...
WHAT?
IT'S THE SEAL. I DON'T THINK--
SACRILEGE AND OUTRAGE!
IN THE NAME OF CHRIST, WE WILL BREAK DOWN THIS DOOR!
WHRAK

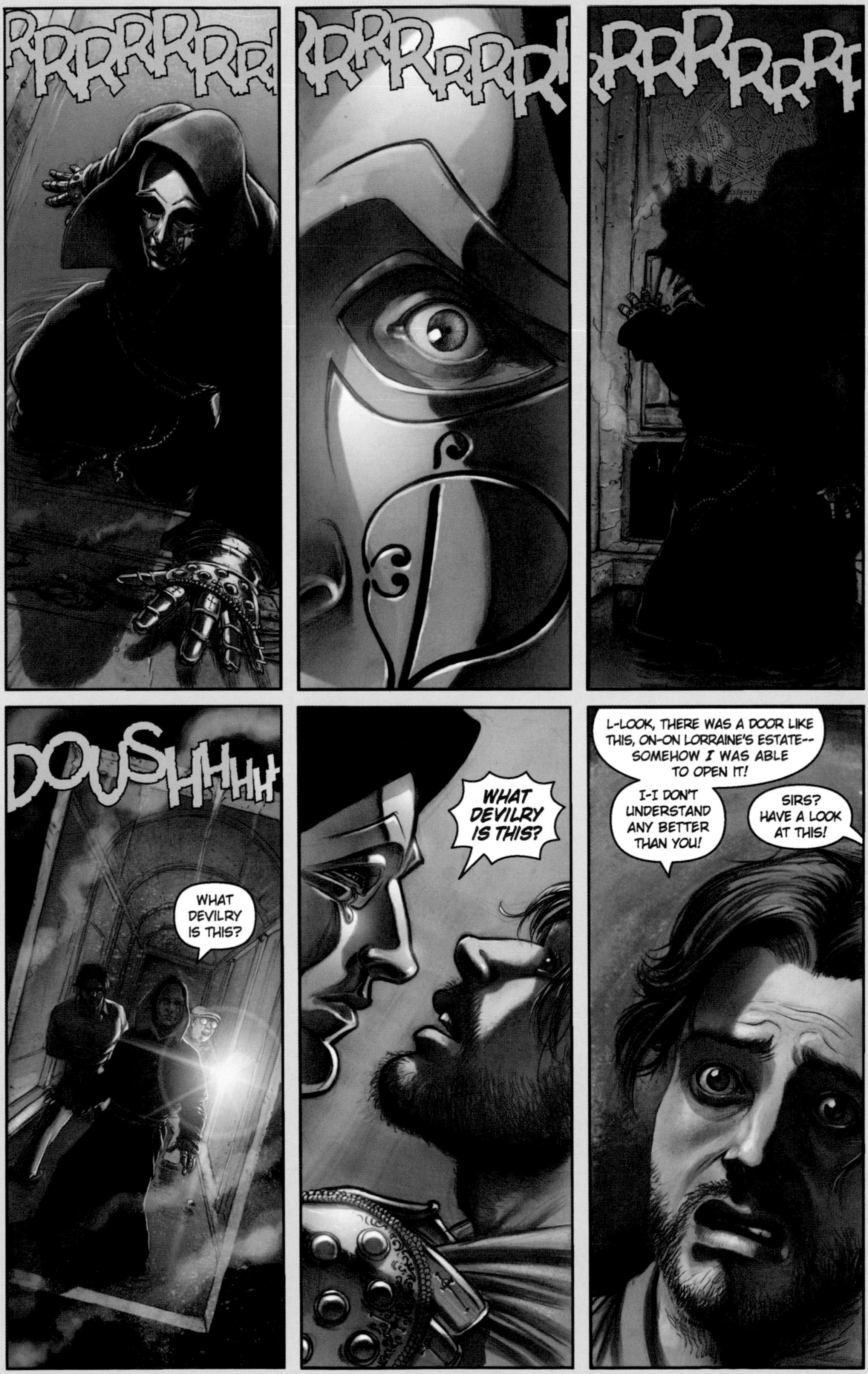
RRRRRRRR
RRRRRRRR
RRRRRRRR
DOUSHHHH
WHAT DEVILRY IS THIS?
WHAT DEVILRY IS THIS?
L-LOOK, THERE WAS A DOOR LIKE THIS, ON-ON LORRAINE'S ESTATE-- SOMEHOW I WAS ABLE TO OPEN IT!
I-I DON'T UNDERSTAND ANY BETTER THAN YOU!
SIRS? HAVE A LOOK AT THIS!

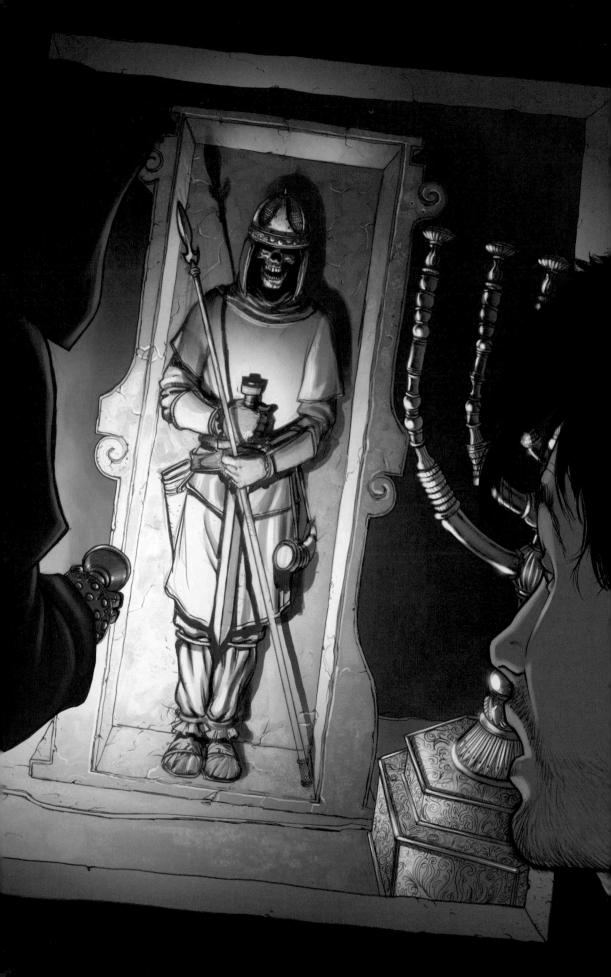

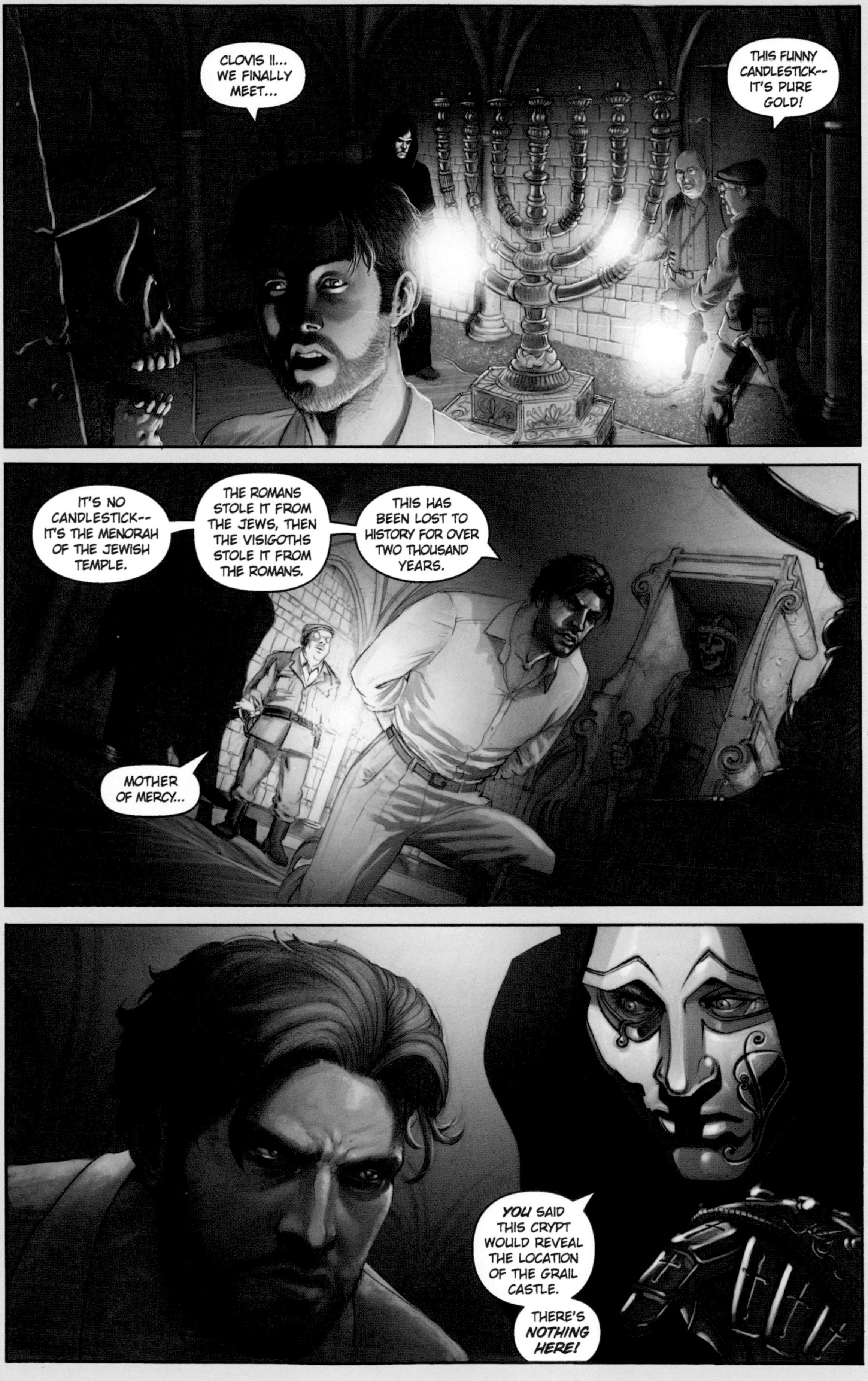
CLOVIS II... WE FINALLY MEET...
THIS FUNNY CANDLESTICK-- IT'S PURE GOLD!
IT'S NO CANDLESTICK-- IT'S THE MENORAH OF THE JEWISH TEMPLE.
THE ROMANS STOLE IT FROM THE JEWS, THEN THE VISIGOTHS STOLE IT FROM THE ROMANS.
THIS HAS BEEN LOST TO HISTORY FOR OVER TWO THOUSAND YEARS.
MOTHER OF MERCY...
YOU SAID THIS CRYPT WOULD REVEAL THE LOCATION OF THE GRAIL CASTLE.
THERE'S NOTHING HERE!

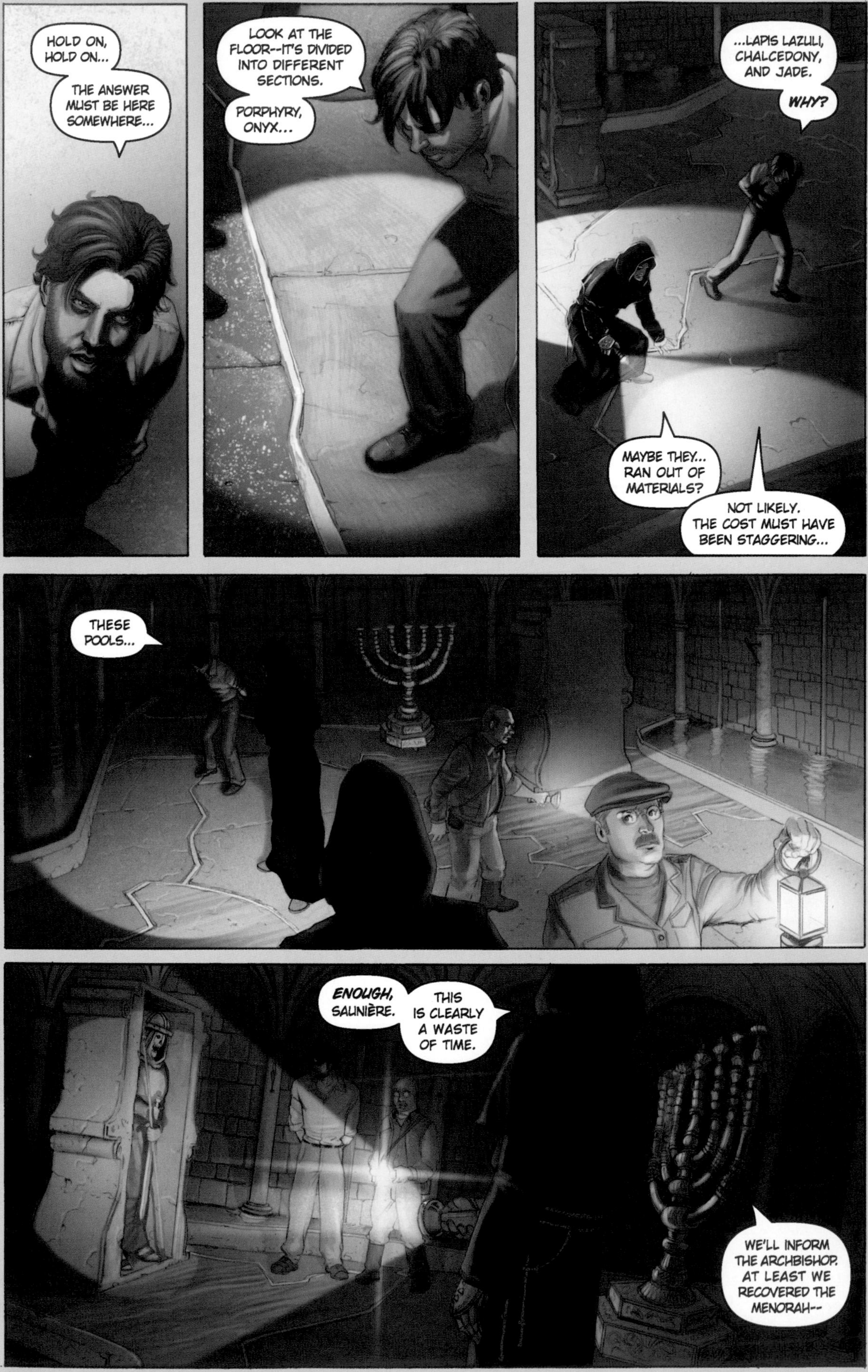
HOLD ON, HOLD ON...
THE ANSWER MUST BE HERE SOMEWHERE...
LOOK AT THE FLOOR--IT'S DIVIDED INTO DIFFERENT SECTIONS.
PORPHYRY, ONYX...
...LAPIS LAZULI, CHALCEDONY, AND JADE.
WHY?
MAYBE THEY... RAN OUT OF MATERIALS?
NOT LIKELY. THE COST MUST HAVE BEEN STAGGERING...
THESE POOLS...
ENOUGH, SAUNIÈRE.
THIS IS CLEARLY A WASTE OF TIME.
WE'LL INFORM THE ARCHBISHOP. AT LEAST WE RECOVERED THE MENORAH--

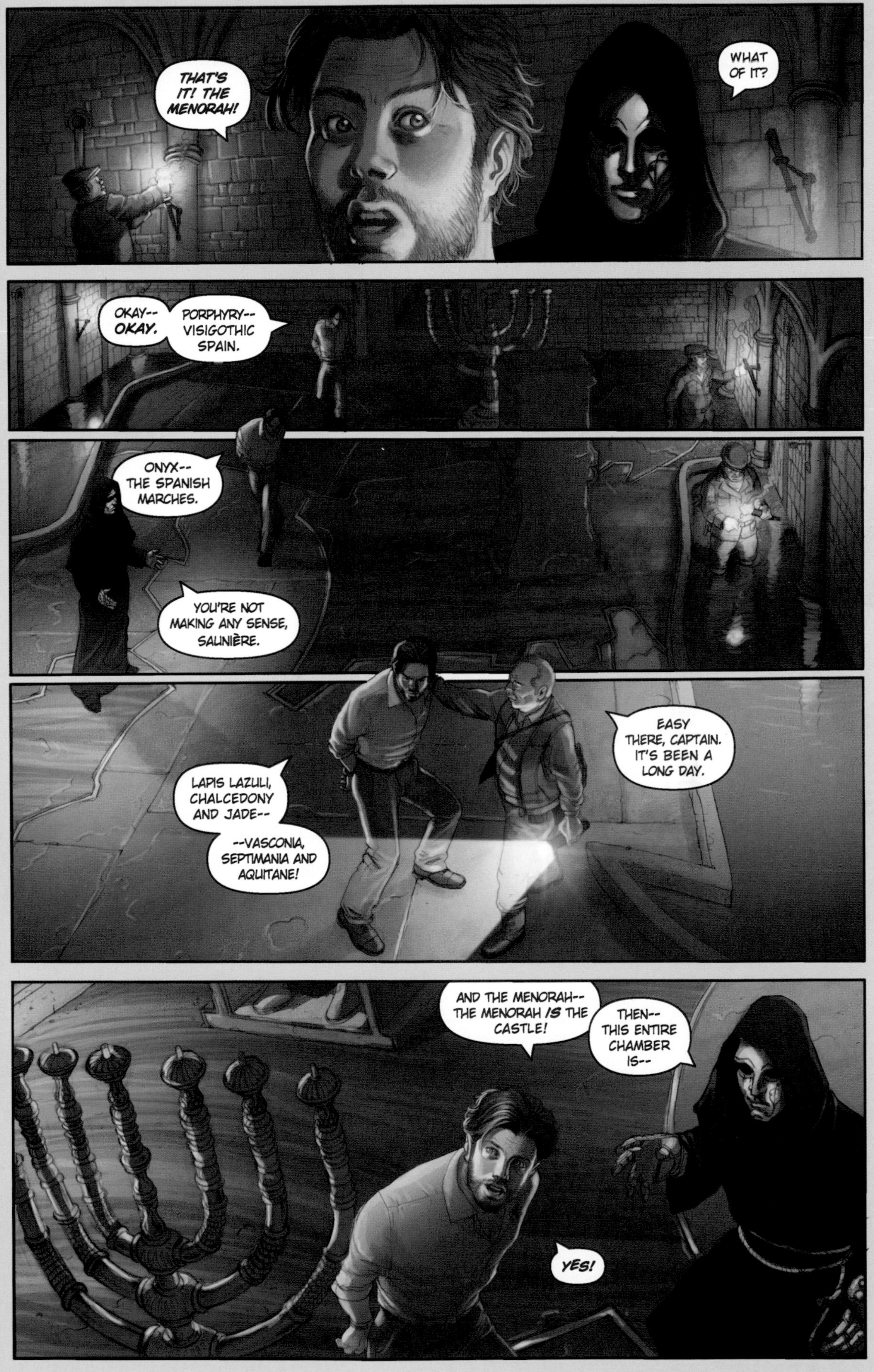
THAT'S IT! THE MENORAH!
WHAT OF IT?
OKAY-- OKAY.
PORPHYRY-- VISIGOTHIC SPAIN.
ONYX-- THE SPANISH MARCHES.
YOU'RE NOT MAKING ANY SENSE, SAUNIÈRE.
EASY THERE, CAPTAIN. IT'S BEEN A LONG DAY.
LAPIS LAZULI, CHALCEDONY AND JADE--
--VASCONIA, SEPTIMANIA AND AQUITANE!
AND THE MENORAH-- THE MENORAH IS THE CASTLE!
THEN-- THIS ENTIRE CHAMBER IS--
YES!

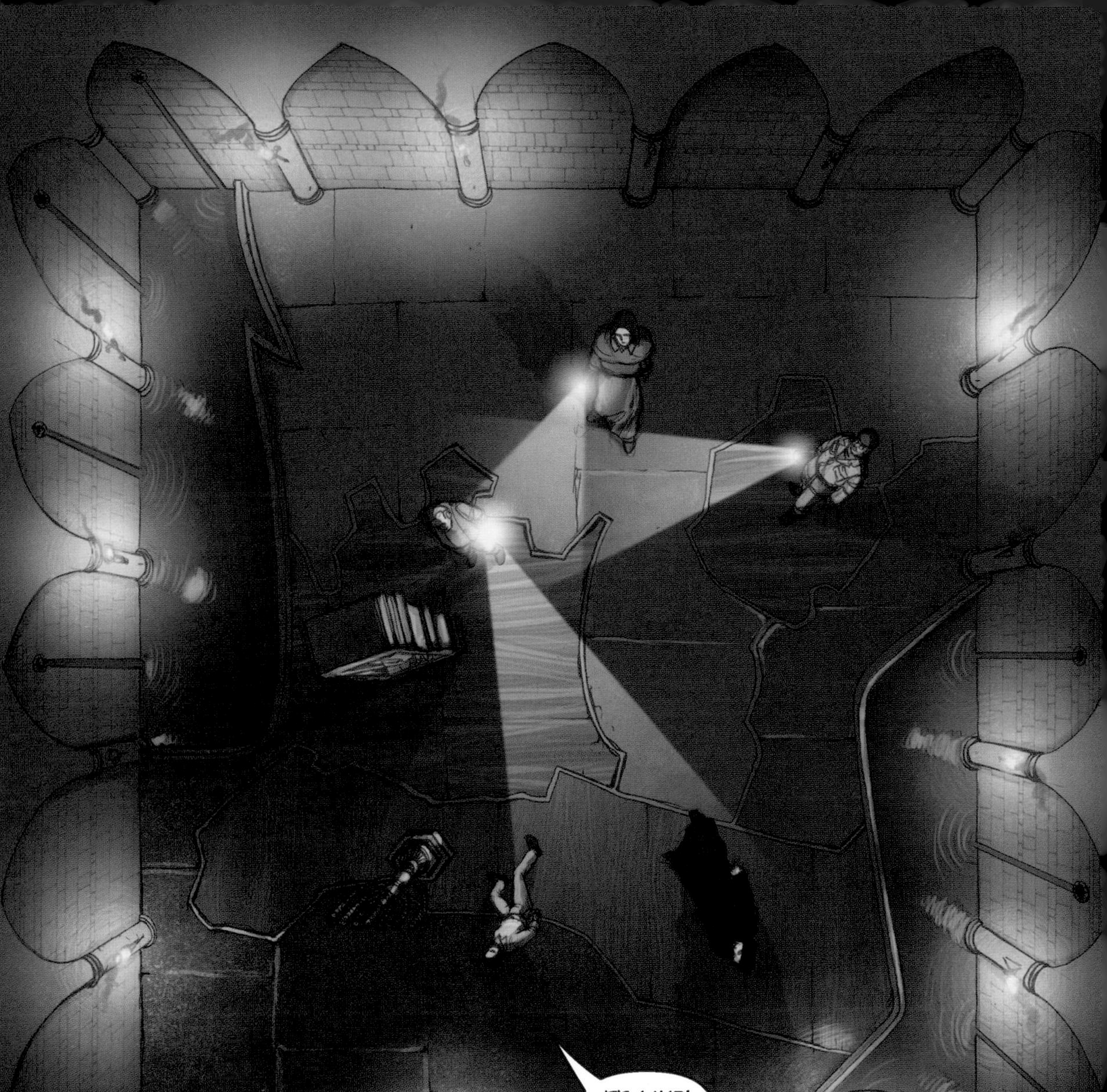
IT'S A MAP! A MAP OF THE DOMAINS OF CLOVIS II.
AND THE MENORAH--IT'S IN PRESENT-DAY CATALONIA.
THAT'S IT!

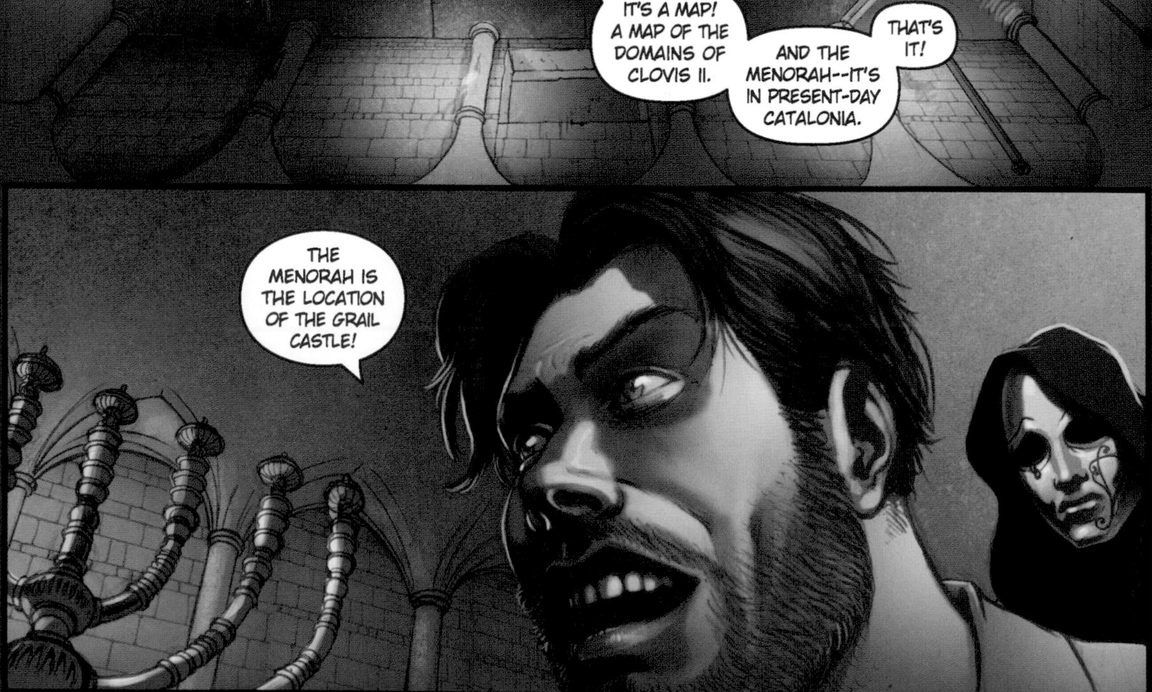
THE MENORAH IS THE LOCATION OF THE GRAIL CASTLE!

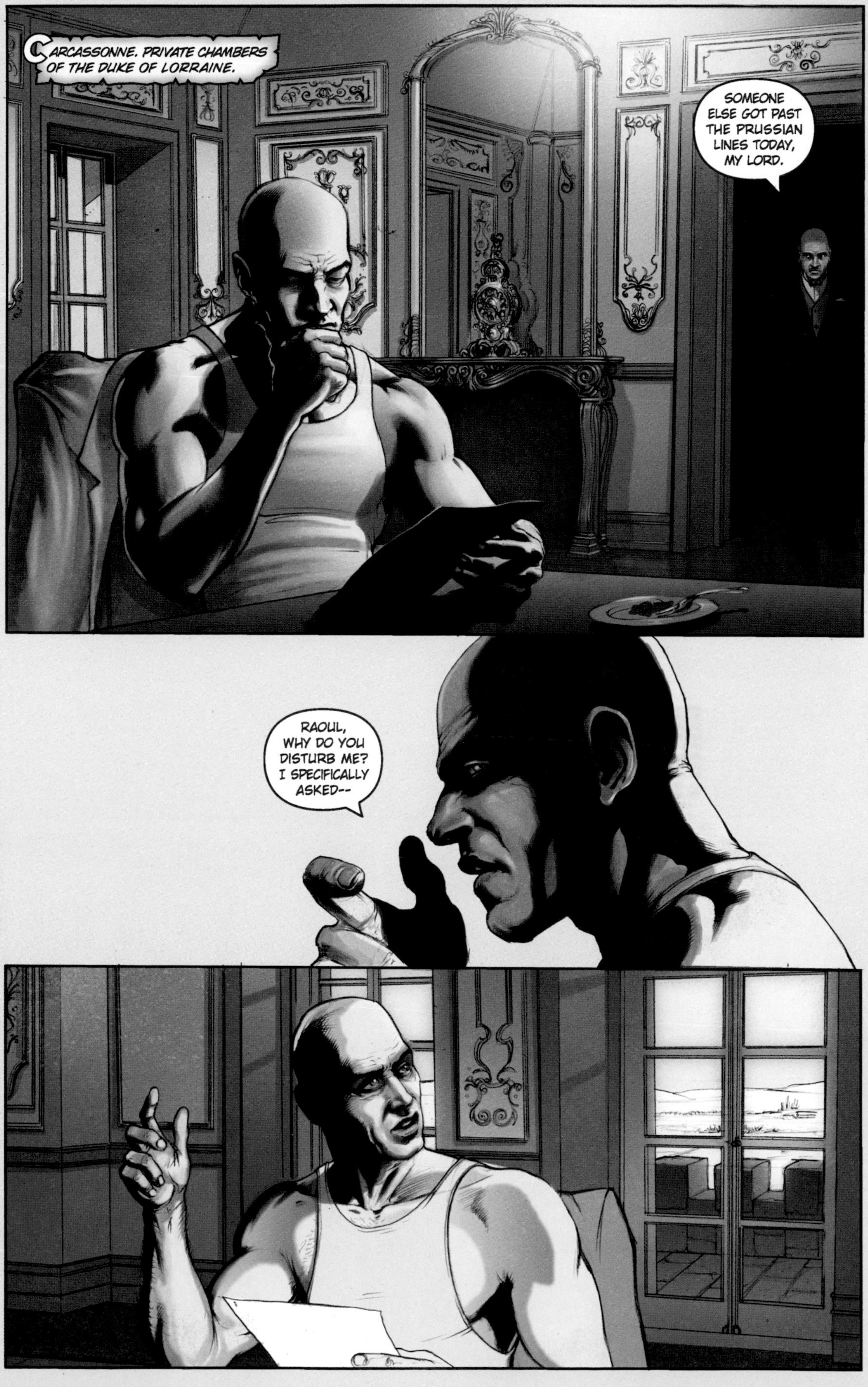
CARCASSONNE. PRIVATE CHAMBERS OF THE DUKE OF LORRAINE.
SOMEONE ELSE GOT PAST THE PRUSSIAN LINES TODAY, MY LORD.
RAOUL, WHY DO YOU DISTURB ME? I SPECIFICALLY ASKED--

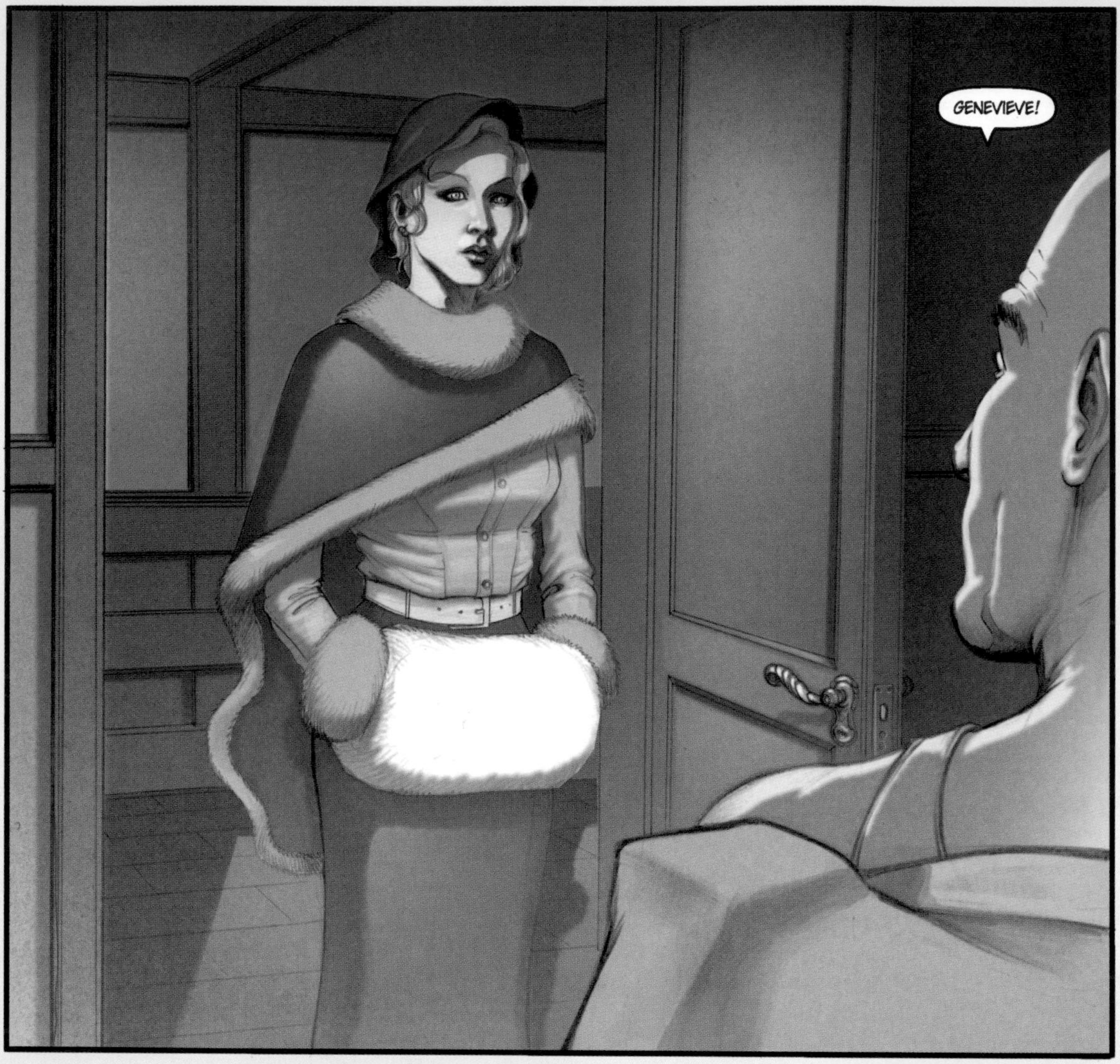
GENEVIEVE!

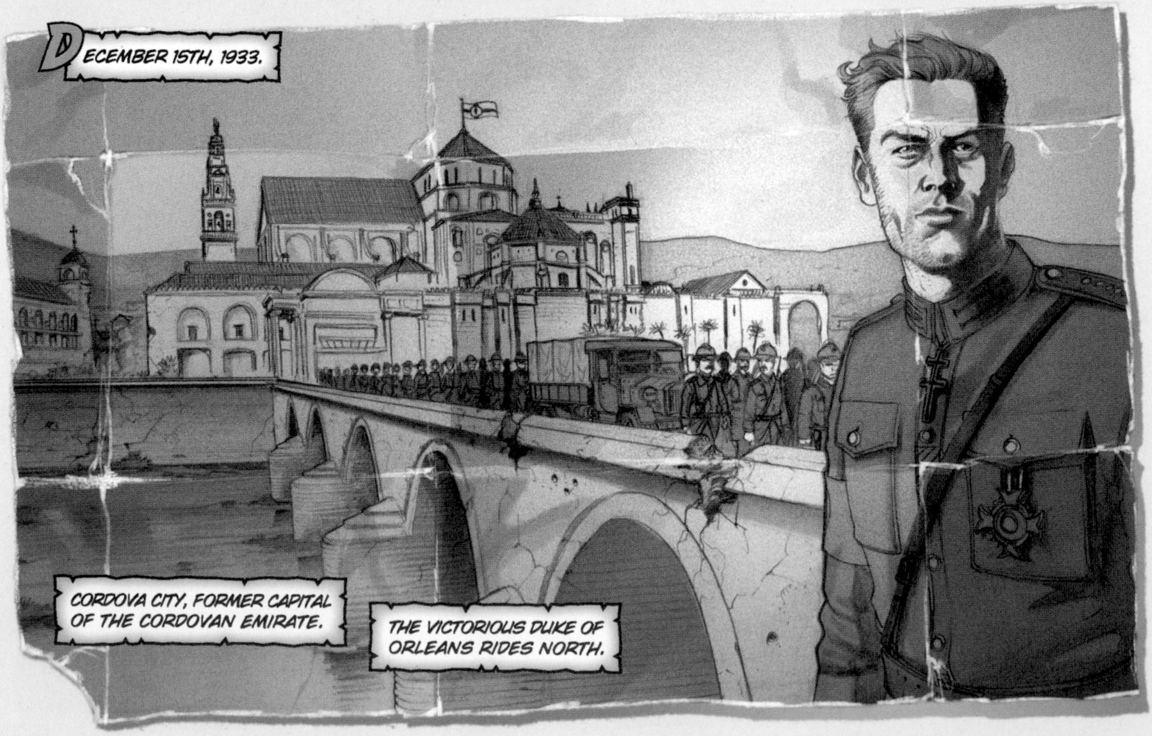
DECEMBER 15TH, 1933.
CORDOVA CITY, FORMER CAPITAL OF THE CORDOVAN EMIRATE.
THE VICTORIOUS DUKE OF ORLEANS RIDES NORTH.

Le Journal de la Liberté

Paris's leading anglophone newspaper • vol. 205, no. 131 • Dec. 15, MCMXXXIII

Editors in Chief: M. Tait Bergstrom, M. Matthew Pasteris. **Story Editor:** M. Arvid Nelson. **Art Editor:** M. Juan Ferreyra. **Photography Editor:** M. Alexander Waldman. **Layout Supervisor:** M. William Kartalopoulos. **Editors Emeritus:** M. Clark A. Smith, M. Howard P. Lovecraft, M. Robert E. Howard. Redacted under the direction of His Excellency Archbishop Emile-Jean Ireneaux. *Le Journal de la Liberté* is printed under the benign auspices of his Imperial Majesty Kaiser Wilhelm II of Prussia.

God Save the Kaiser

PRUSSIAN FORCES TRAP LORRAINE, FRENCH ARMY IN CARCASSONNE

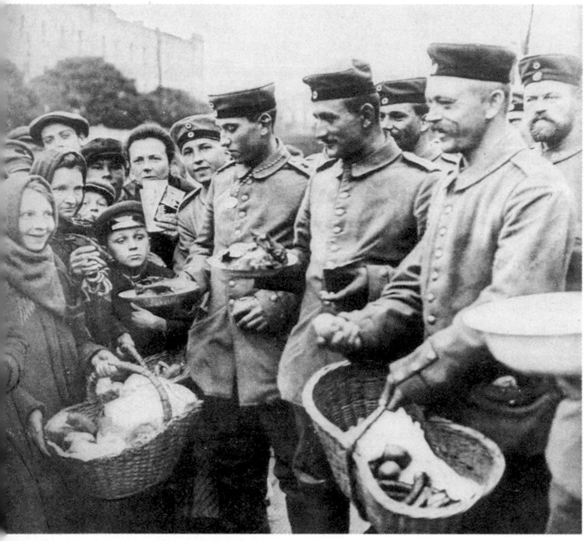

Prussian soldiers distribute food to grateful Paris citizens. We trust and hope the items in the rightmost soldier's basket are, in fact, sausages.

Carcassonne – Following a catastrophic defeat and the loss of Paris, the Anglo-French forces under the Duke of Lorraine have fled southward, harried all the way by the relentlessly pursuing Prussian invaders.

Lorraine's severely depleted army has holed up in the walled city of Carcassonne, giving the Prussians complete dominance over most of France.

"About 95 percent of the French homeland is now in the hands of the Kaiser," General Erich von Falkenhayn, commander of the Prussian expeditionary force, said. "It's only a matter of time before Lorraine is forced to capitulate." He did not speculate on what would become of France under Prussian occupation, saying it was "at the sole discretion of the Kaiser."

Most of the French territory still in Lorraine's hands consists of the Spanish Marches. The Duke of Lorraine forced the annexation of the Marches despite the objections of King Louis XXII almost two months ago.

Islamic extremists from the Cordovan Emirate assassinated a key political figure on the eve of the annexation, leading Lorraine to declare war on Cordova. That action led to declarations of war on France by Prussia, the Holy Roman Empire and the Ottoman Empire. Russia and England soon joined the war on the side of the French.

Shortly thereafter, Lorraine launched a coup and seized the French crown. King Louis' current whereabouts are unknown.

Lorraine was counting on halting the Prussian advance at Paris, while the Duke of Orleans led an expeditionary army south, against the Cordovan Emirate.

Lorraine badly underestimated the military might of the Prussians, and the current status of Orleans's army is unknown.

A victory against Cordova would free up huge reserves of troops to fortify Lorraine, but this seems unlikely. Reports from the Cordovan campaign are sparse, but the majority indicate Orleans's initially rapid advance has become mired down by stiff Cordovan resistance.

A few reports suggest just the opposite, that Cordova may have fallen. But von Falkenhayn dismissed this as "far-fetched."

Lorraine burned Paris to the ground to deny the Prussian army provender, but General von Falkenhayn denied that his forces were over-extended or under-supplied.

"It's true, we planned on re-equipping at Paris, but France is a large country," he said. "Lorraine ended up hurting his own people more than us."

Indeed, Prussian soldiers have been distributing provisions to the beleaguered denizens of Paris. Support in the city for Lorraine was high in the initial stages of the war, but is now in scarcer supply than food.

A large army from the Holy Roman Empire is moving south, across the conquered French territories, to aid in an eventual assault on Carcassonne. Von Falkenhayn did not specify when the attack would occur, but he said Lorraine faces two choices: "unconditional surrender or total annihilation."

Notice to Readers

The Prussian Reichsprotectorate of Lorraine and Northern France will assume publication of *Le Journal de la Liberté*, effective immediately. The editorial staff of *Le Journal* has decided to continue at the paper, under the supervision of the occupiers. They promise to deliver the same quality news coverage our readers have come to expect.

British to Withdraw from War?

Berlin – Queen Elizabeth II of Great Britain, faced with an increasingly bleak wartime situation, may be discussing terms for an armistice with the Kaiser. Neither British nor Prussian officials would confirm this, but if the British are removed from the conflict, it would be a potentially fatal blow to the Duke of Lorraine. British forces make up a large part of Lorraine's troops at Carcassonne.

Russians Begin E. Prussian Offensive

Königsberg – a massive Russian invasion force has begun an offensive into East Prussia. Estimates put their total strength at over 200,000 men. Prussian forces, combined with a corps of the Teutonic Knights, are tracking the movements of the invaders and will "intercept at a geographically advantageous location," Josias von Heeringen, Prussian War Minister, said.

Italian Provinces Rebel from Holy Roman Empire, Adding to Woes

Trieste – Following the revolt of its Serbian provinces, the Holy Roman Empire now faces another uprising, amongst its Italian subjects. Emperor Rudolph of the Holy Roman Empire denied that his hold on power was disintegrating. He said the various rebellions would have no effect on his troop commitments to the Prussian forces surrounding the Duke of Lorraine.

Achtung!

Paris residents are directed to obey orders from Prussian military personnel. Failure to comply may result in immediate imprisonment. Curfews are in effect until further notice. Civilians found outside their residences after sundown will be shot. Have identification papers ready at all times.

By order of Obergruppenführer Ernst von Ulrichs, Military

Latest Wartime Developments

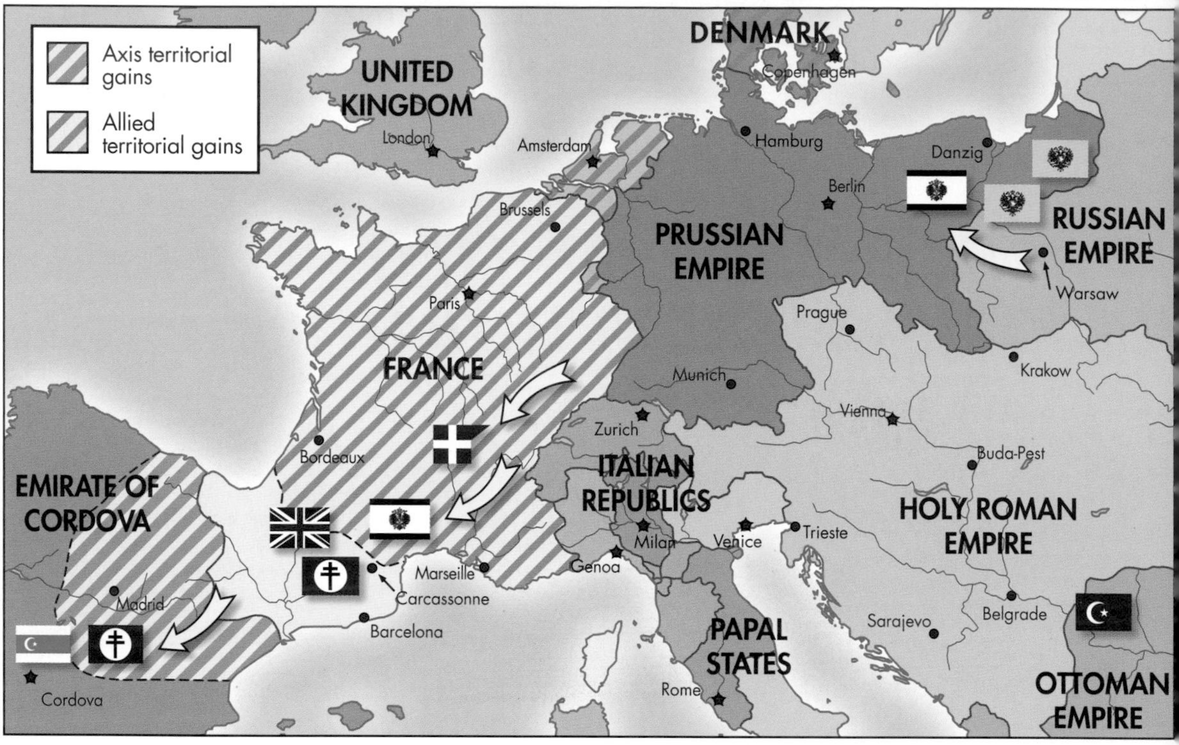
Axis territorial gains
Allied territorial gains
UNITED KINGDOM
London
Amsterdam
DENMARK
Copenhagen
Hamburg
Danzig
Berlin
RUSSIAN EMPIRE
Warsaw
Brussels
PRUSSIAN EMPIRE
Paris
Prague
FRANCE
Munich
Krakow
Zurich
Vienna
Bordeaux
ITALIAN REPUBLICS
Buda-Pest
EMIRATE OF CORDOVA
HOLY ROMAN EMPIRE
Milan
Venice
Trieste
Genoa
Marseille
Carcassonne
Madrid
Barcelona
Sarajevo
Belgrade
PAPAL STATES
Rome
OTTOMAN EMPIRE
Cordova

The Western Front

In the west, the Duke of Orleans commands a French invasion of the Cordovan Emirate. The architect of France's war strategy, the Duke of Lorraine, has called it "a crusade to drive Islam from Western Europe."

At first, Orleans made rapid progress, capturing the strategically important city of Madrid in a single day. But it has been more than two weeks since the last confirmed report. Prussian commanders believe Orleans might be encountering stiffer opposition as he closes in on Cordova City, the capital.

The Eastern Front

France's declaration of war on Cordova prompted Prussia to declare war on France. The first French province to fall to the subsequent invasion was the Duchy of Lorraine, the Duke of Lorraine's ancestral estates.

Lorraine has said he expected the initial loss of his duchy, but he planned on halting the Prussians at Paris, ultimately driving them out with the combined might of Orleans's troops once they returned from a lightning victory over the Cordovans.

That didn't happen.

A series of spectacular Prussian victories have left most of France in German control, and Lorraine's demoralized forces are currently trapped in the city of Carcassonne. An Austrian army is marching southwest through France to join the Prussians surrounding Lorraine and deal him the *coup de grace*.

The Far East

A potential complication for the Prussian and Austrian forces exists with the unfolding of yet another front. The Russian Tzar has declared war on Prussia and the Holy Roman Empire. Reports indicate a massive Russian incursion into East Prussia has begun.

The Prussian war ministry is confident about defenses in the east. Prussia's longtime ally the Teutonic Knights, are poised to declare war on Russia. The Knights are descendants of a military religious order founded during the Crusades. They control the Baltic ports through which Russia receives much of the imported goods critical to its war effort.

But matters for the German powers are further confounded by uprisings across the Holy Roman Empire. Emperor Rudolph's Serbian and Italian subjects are in open revolt, and there is growing discontent among the peoples of Bohemia and Galicia.

THE AXIS:

- Greater France
- The Russian Empire
- The United Kingdom

THE ALLIES:

- The Prussian Empire
- The Holy Roman Empire
- The Emirate of Cordova
- The Ottoman Empire

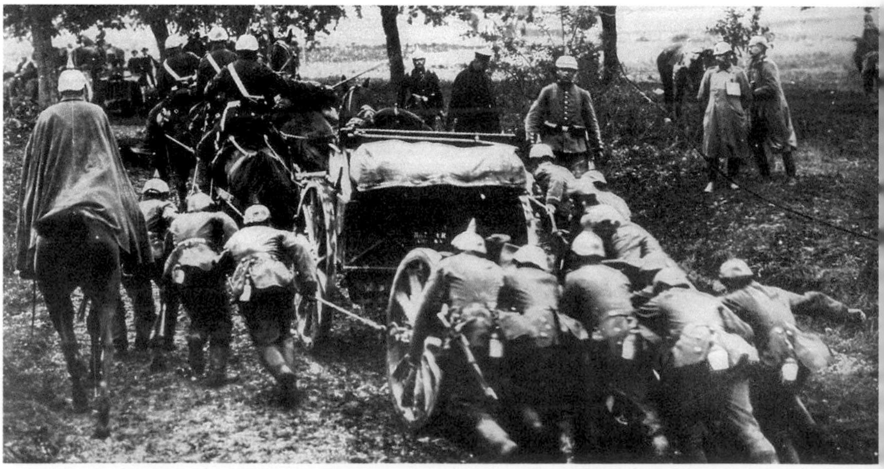

Prussian soldiers rush artillery into position for impending assault on Carcassonne.

CHAPTER TWO

THE BATTLE OF THE THREE EMPERORS

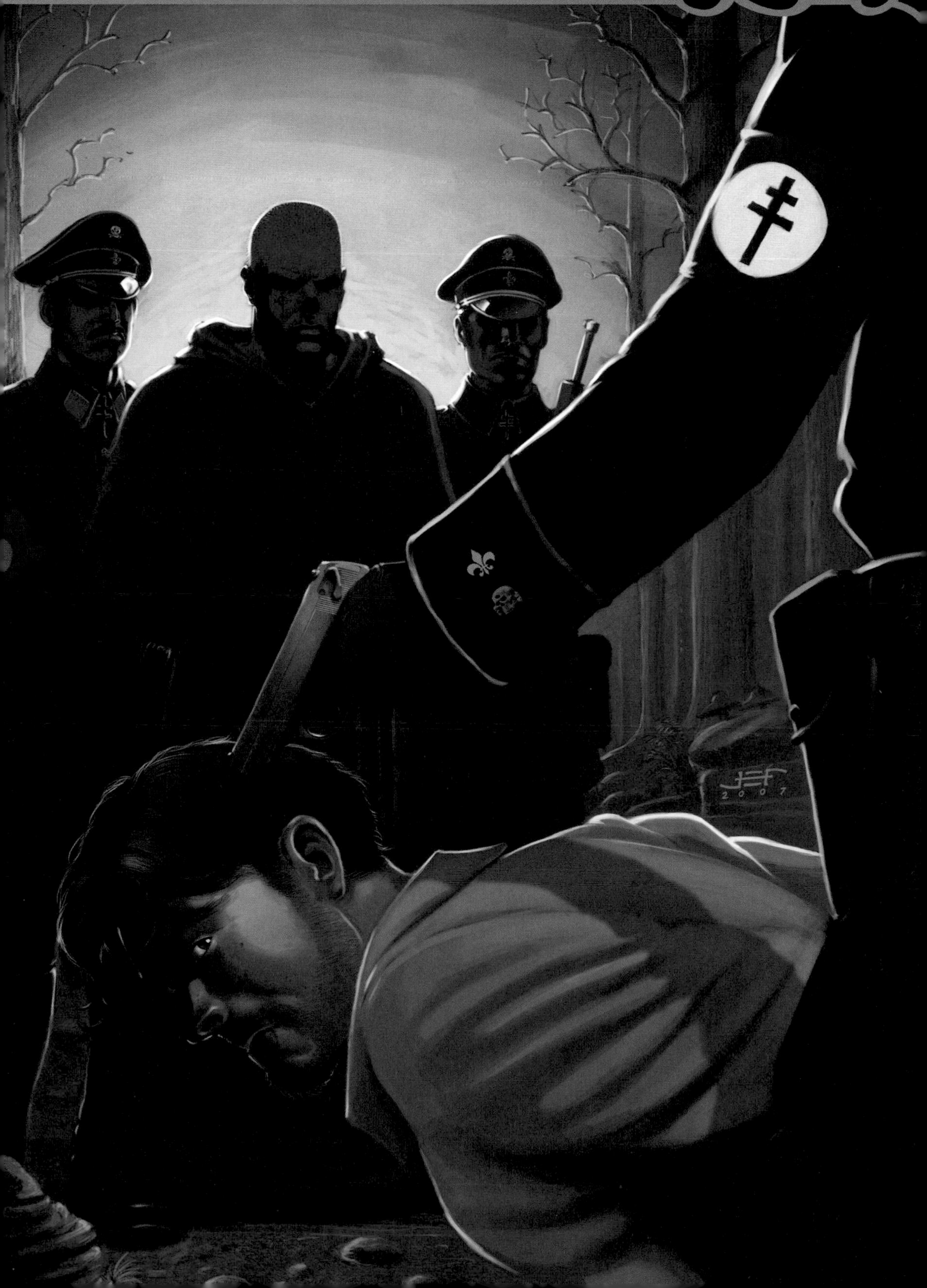

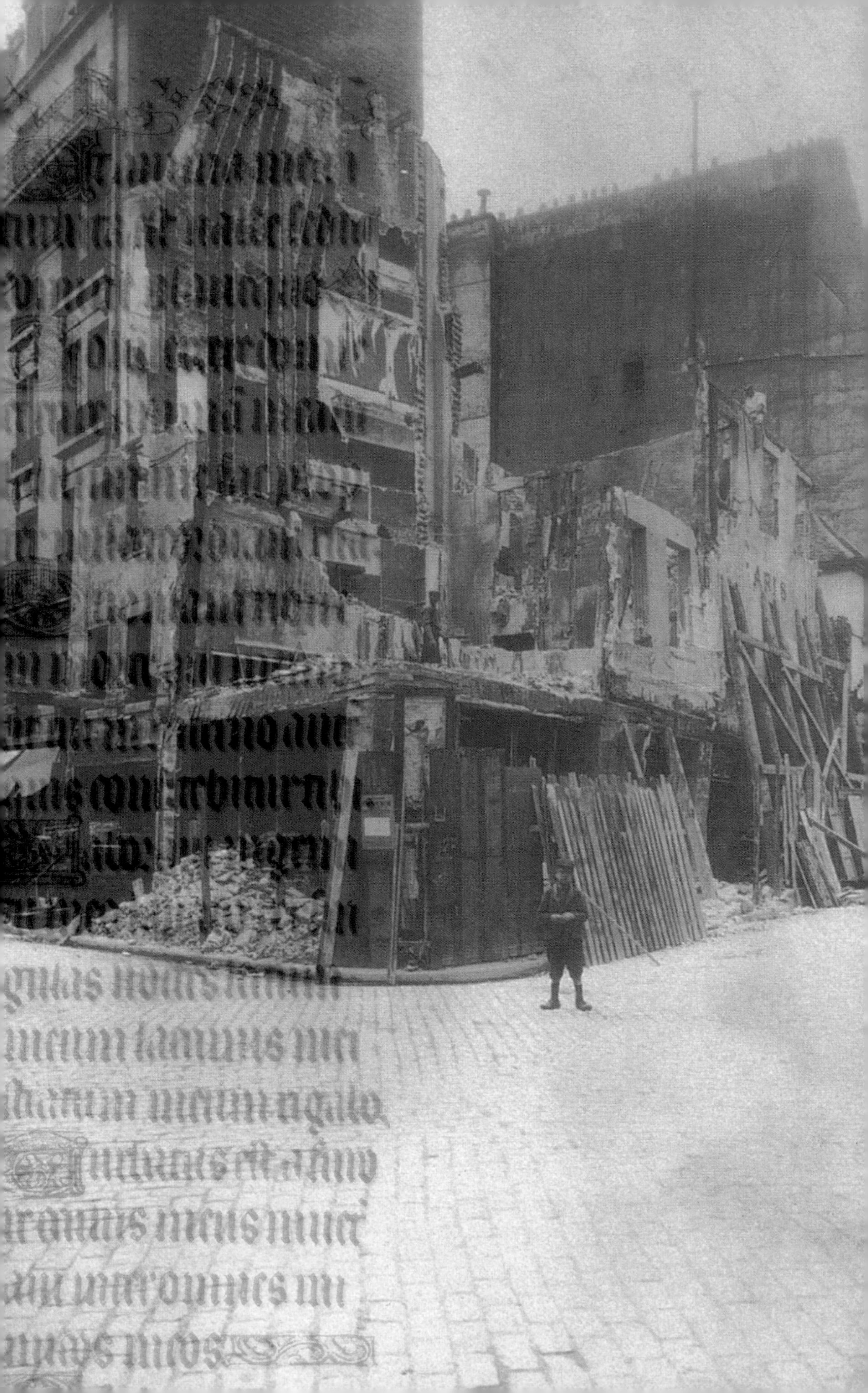

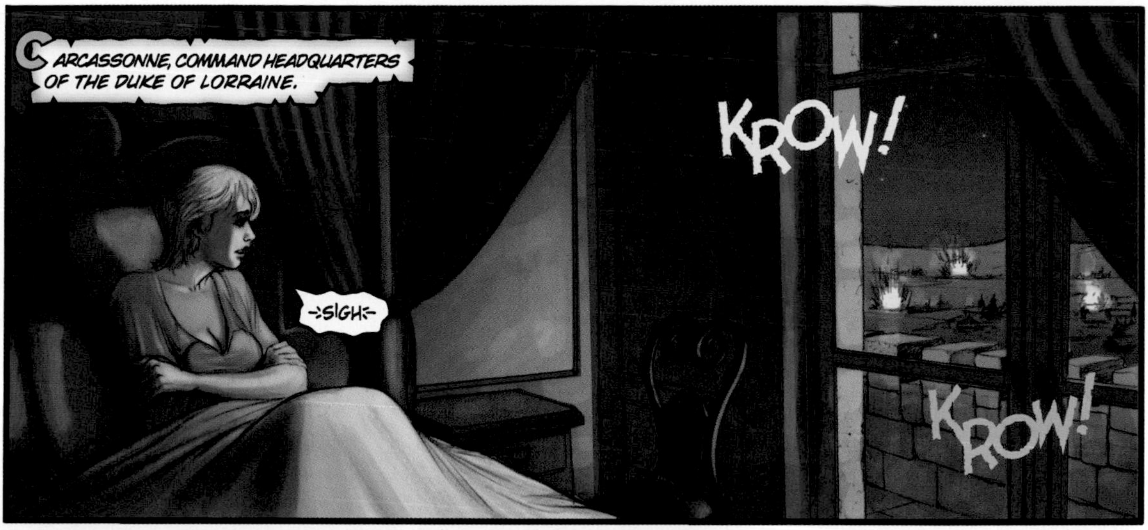
CARCASSONNE, COMMAND HEADQUARTERS OF THE DUKE OF LORRAINE.
KROW!
-SIGH-
KROW!

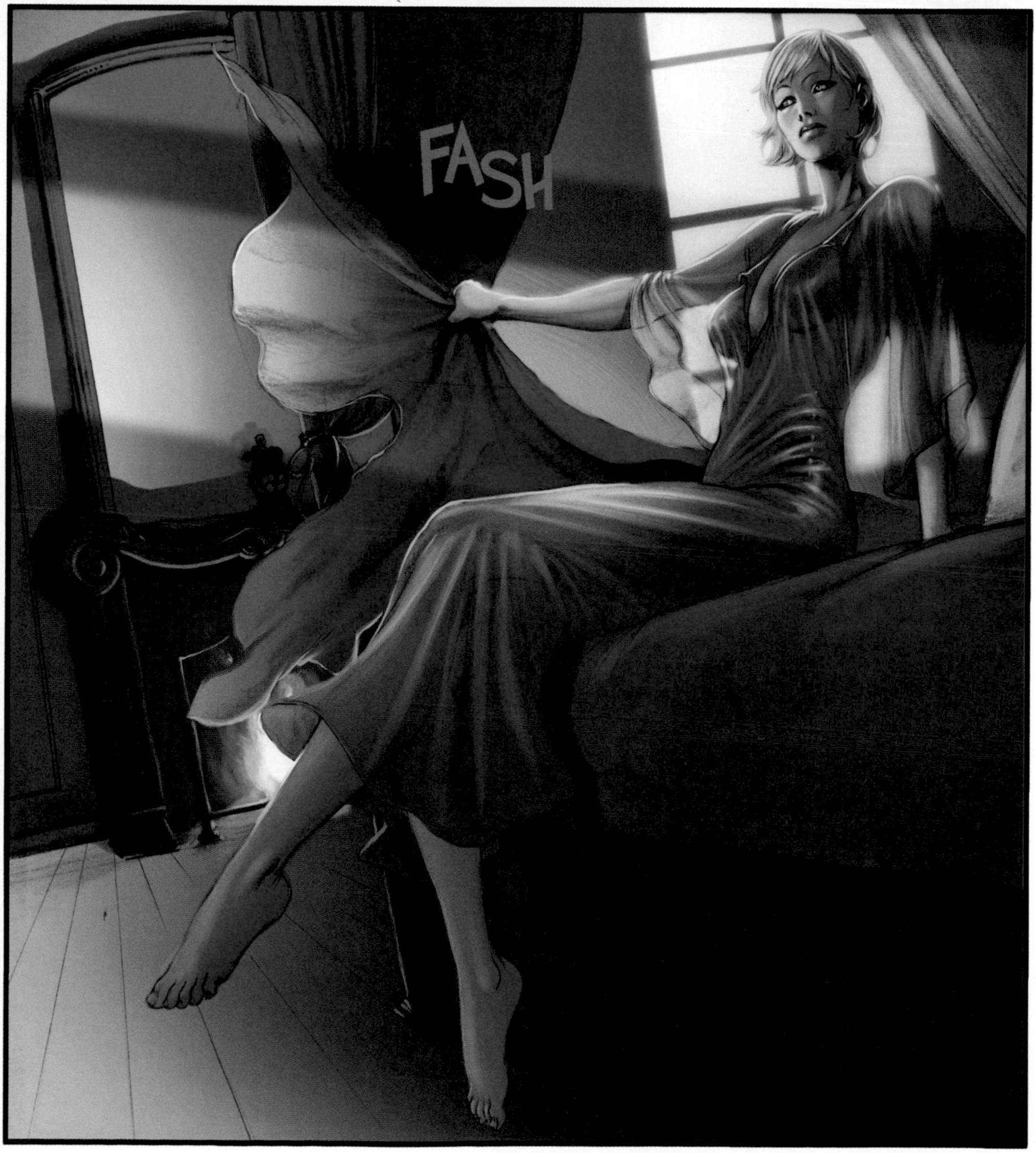
FASH

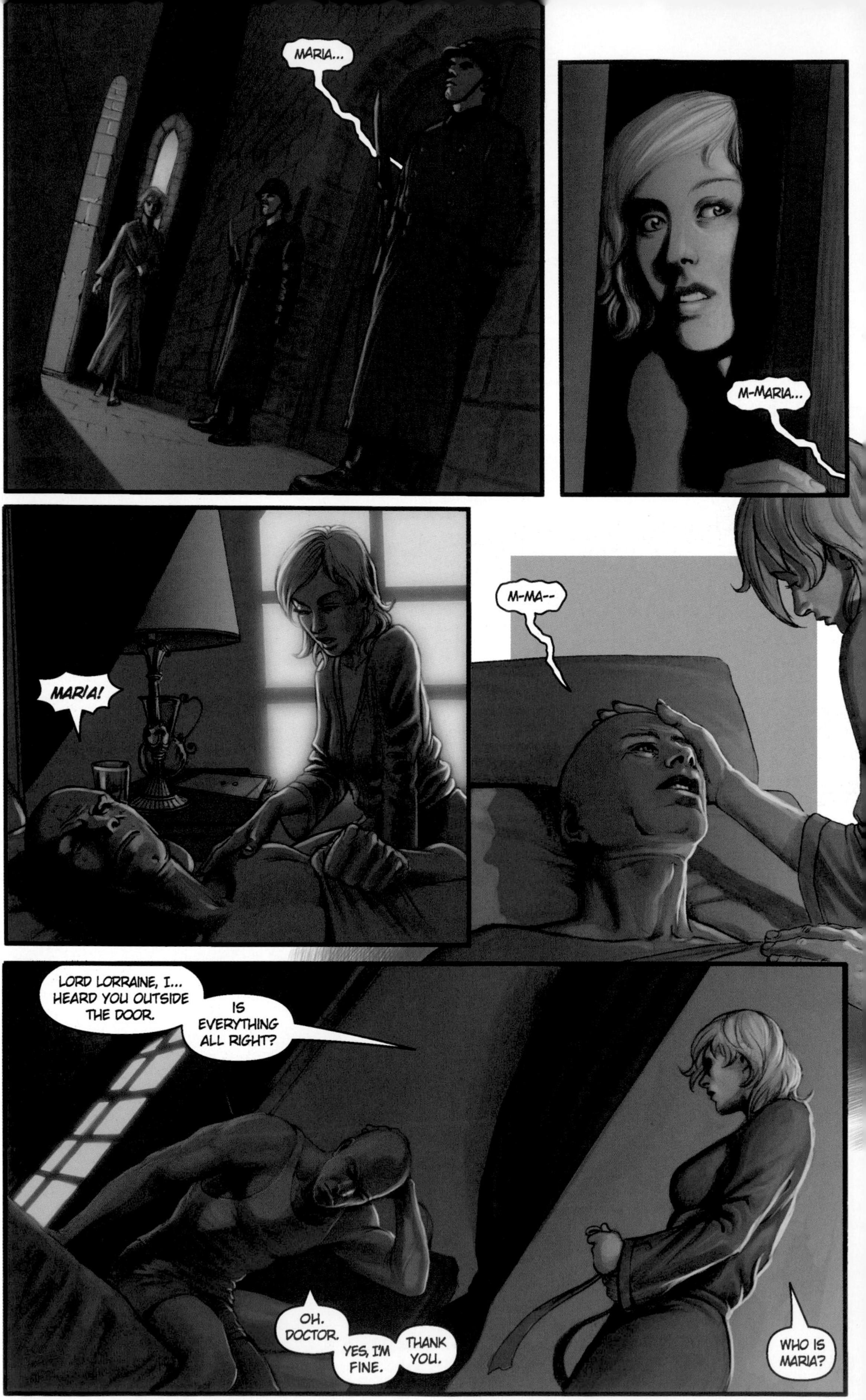
MARIA...
M-MARIA...
MARIA!
M-MA--
LORD LORRAINE, I... HEARD YOU OUTSIDE THE DOOR.
IS EVERYTHING ALL RIGHT?
OH. DOCTOR.
YES, I'M FINE.
THANK YOU.
WHO IS MARIA?

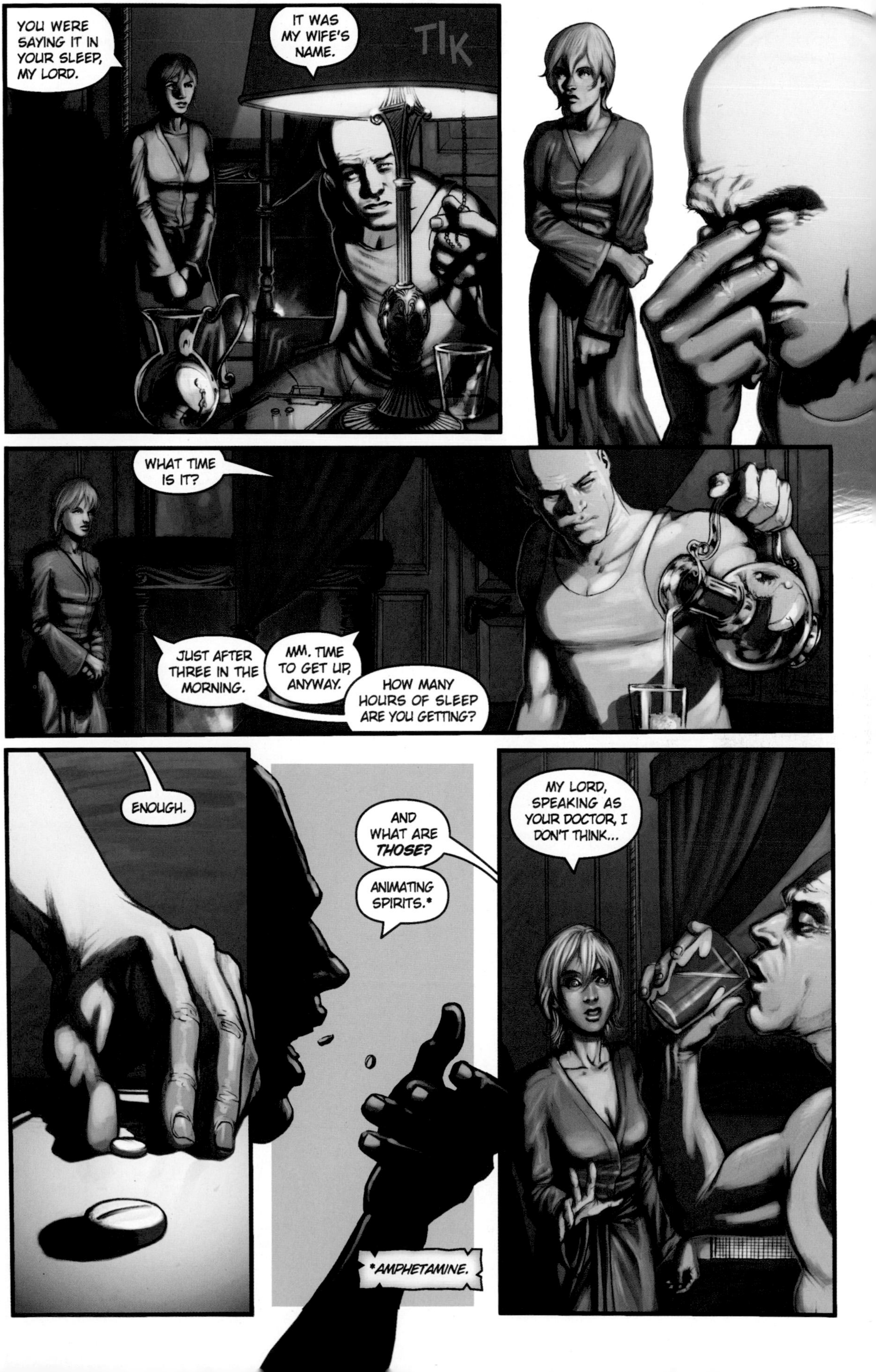
YOU WERE SAYING IT IN YOUR SLEEP, MY LORD.
IT WAS MY WIFE'S NAME.
TIK
WHAT TIME IS IT?
JUST AFTER THREE IN THE MORNING.
MM. TIME TO GET UP, ANYWAY.
HOW MANY HOURS OF SLEEP ARE YOU GETTING?
ENOUGH.
AND WHAT ARE *THOSE?*
ANIMATING SPIRITS.*
MY LORD, SPEAKING AS YOUR DOCTOR, I DON'T THINK...
*AMPHETAMINE.

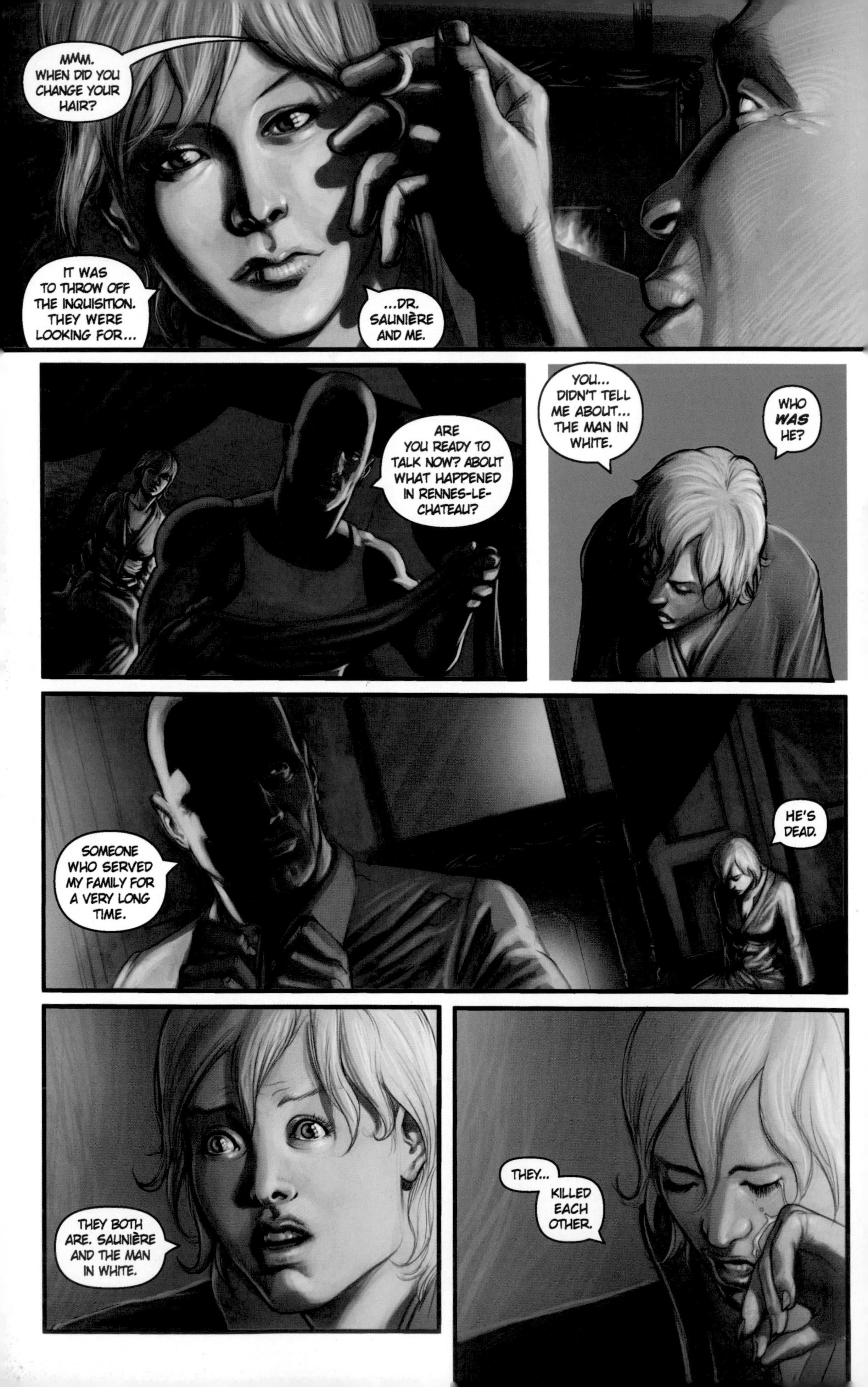
MMM. WHEN DID YOU CHANGE YOUR HAIR?
IT WAS TO THROW OFF THE INQUISITION. THEY WERE LOOKING FOR...
...DR. SAUNIÈRE AND ME.
ARE YOU READY TO TALK NOW? ABOUT WHAT HAPPENED IN RENNES-LE-CHATEAU?
YOU... DIDN'T TELL ME ABOUT... THE MAN IN WHITE.
WHO *WAS* HE?
SOMEONE WHO SERVED MY FAMILY FOR A VERY LONG TIME.
HE'S DEAD.
THEY BOTH ARE. SAUNIÈRE AND THE MAN IN WHITE.
THEY... KILLED EACH OTHER.

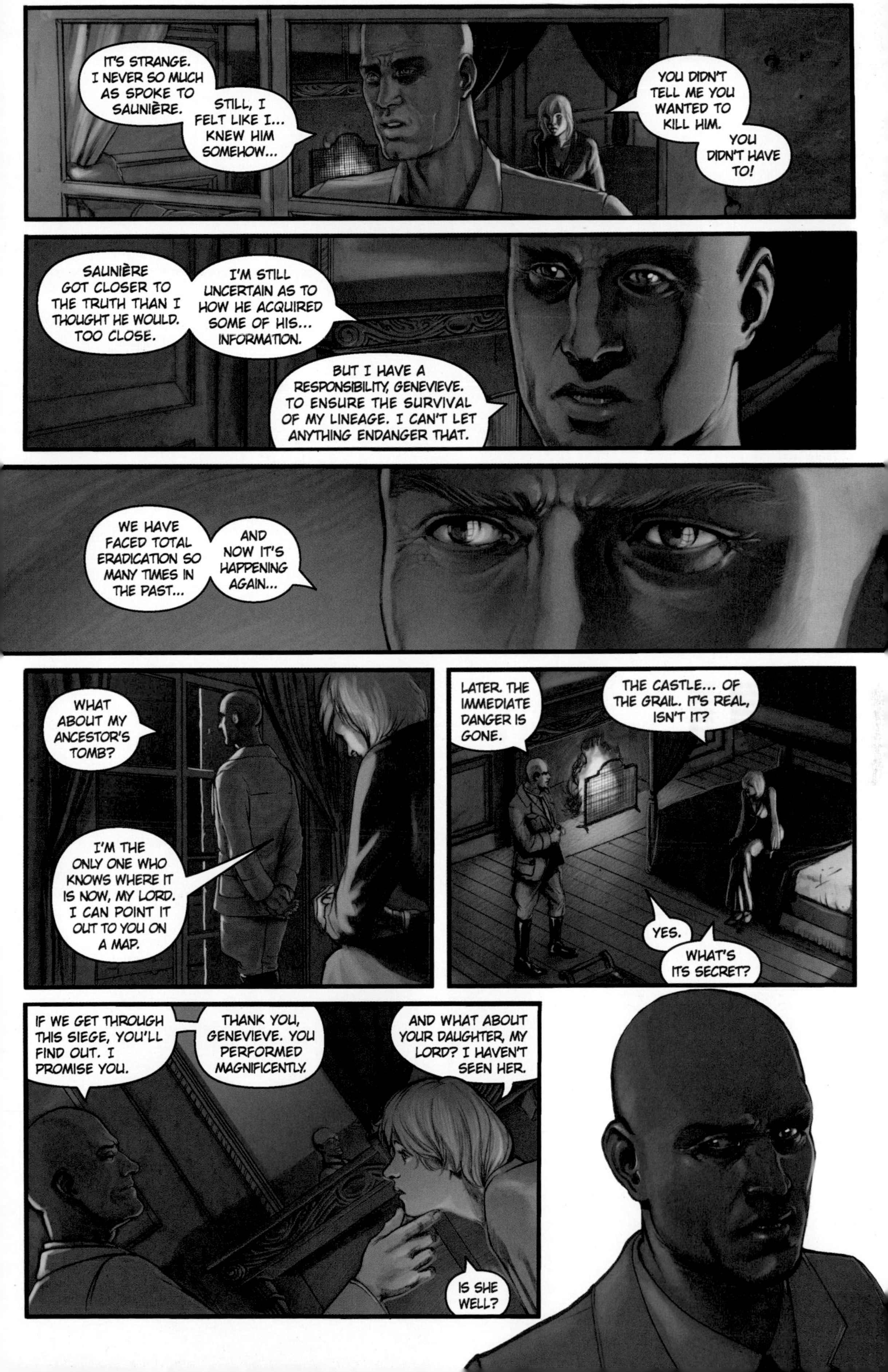
IT'S STRANGE. I NEVER SO MUCH AS SPOKE TO SAUNIÈRE.
STILL, I FELT LIKE I... KNEW HIM SOMEHOW...
YOU DIDN'T TELL ME YOU WANTED TO KILL HIM.
YOU DIDN'T HAVE TO!
SAUNIÈRE GOT CLOSER TO THE TRUTH THAN I THOUGHT HE WOULD. TOO CLOSE.
I'M STILL UNCERTAIN AS TO HOW HE ACQUIRED SOME OF HIS... INFORMATION.
BUT I HAVE A RESPONSIBILITY, GENEVIEVE. TO ENSURE THE SURVIVAL OF MY LINEAGE. I CAN'T LET ANYTHING ENDANGER THAT.
WE HAVE FACED TOTAL ERADICATION SO MANY TIMES IN THE PAST...
AND NOW IT'S HAPPENING AGAIN...
WHAT ABOUT MY ANCESTOR'S TOMB?
I'M THE ONLY ONE WHO KNOWS WHERE IT IS NOW, MY LORD. I CAN POINT IT OUT TO YOU ON A MAP.
LATER. THE IMMEDIATE DANGER IS GONE.
THE CASTLE... OF THE GRAIL. IT'S REAL, ISN'T IT?
YES.
WHAT'S ITS SECRET?
IF WE GET THROUGH THIS SIEGE, YOU'LL FIND OUT. I PROMISE YOU.
THANK YOU, GENEVIEVE. YOU PERFORMED MAGNIFICENTLY.
AND WHAT ABOUT YOUR DAUGHTER, MY LORD? I HAVEN'T SEEN HER.
IS SHE WELL?

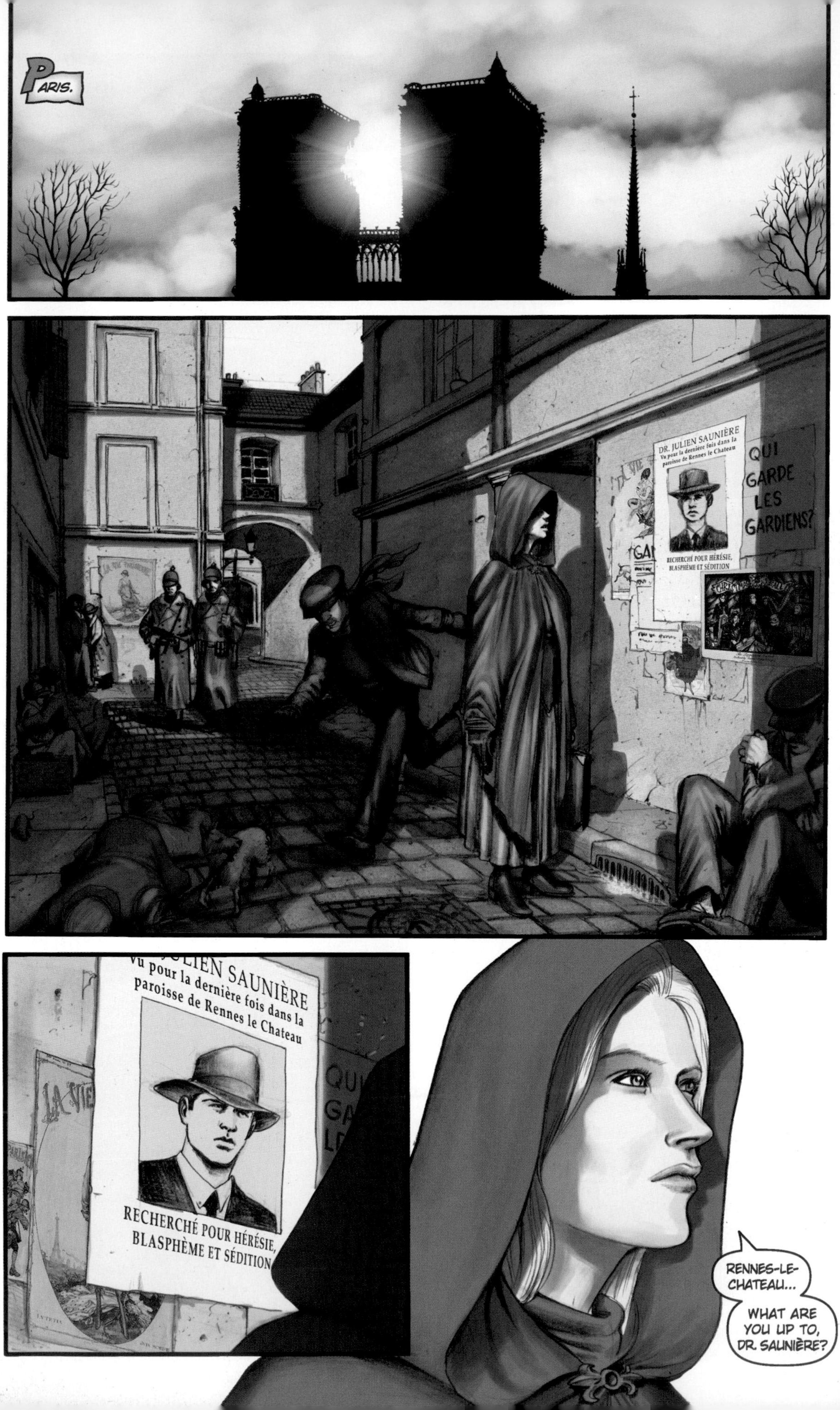
PARIS.
DR. JULIEN SAUNIÈRE
Vu pour la dernière fois dans la paroisse de Rennes le Chateau
RECHERCHÉ POUR HÉRÉSIE, BLASPHÈME ET SÉDITION
QUI GARDE LES GARDIENS?
JULIEN SAUNIÈRE
Vu pour la dernière fois dans la paroisse de Rennes le Chateau
RECHERCHÉ POUR HÉRÉSIE, BLASPHÈME ET SÉDITION
RENNES-LE-CHATEAU...
WHAT ARE YOU UP TO, DR. SAUNIÈRE?

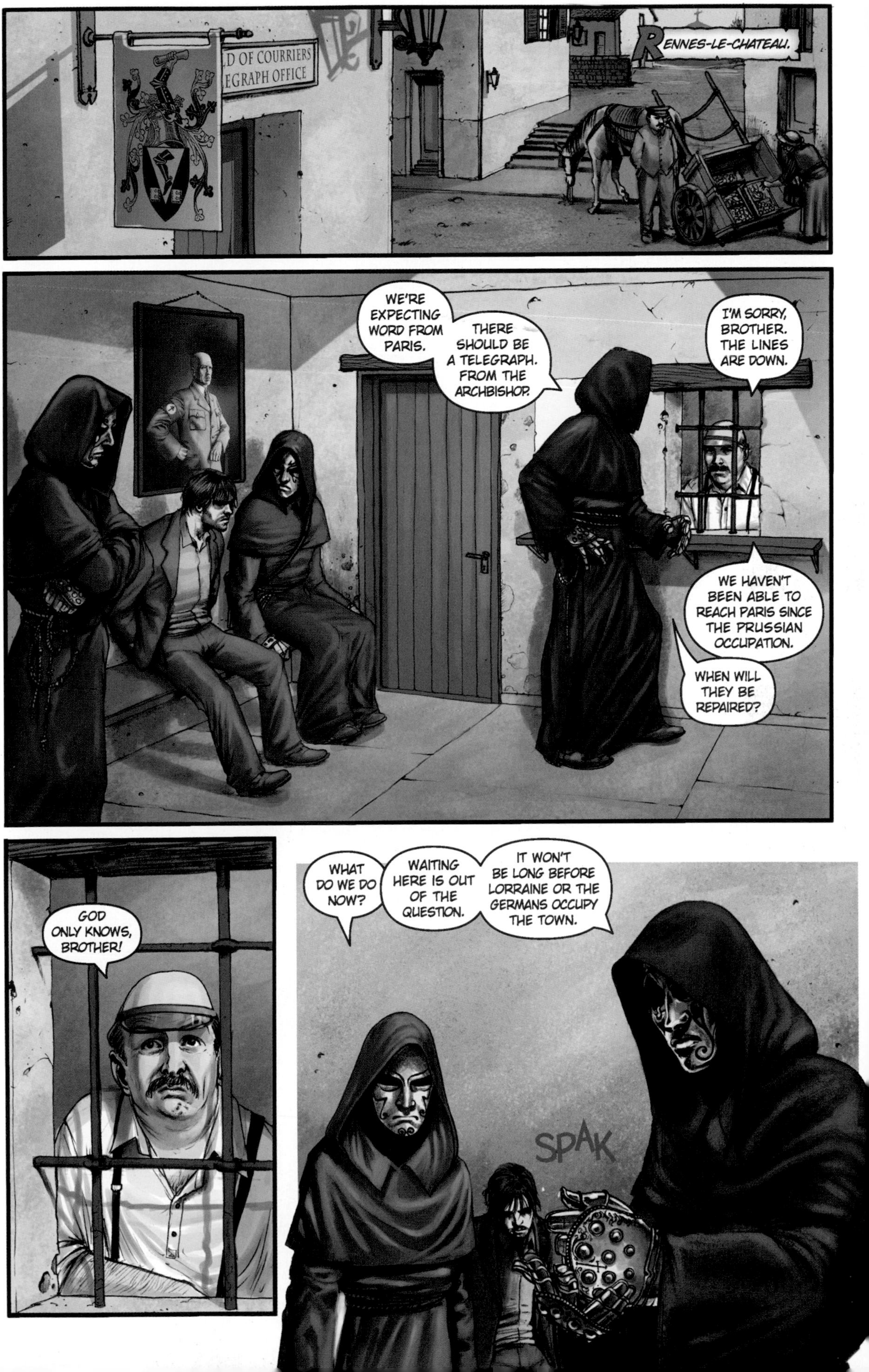
LD OF COURRIERS
EGRAPH OFFICE
RENNES-LE-CHATEAU.
WE'RE EXPECTING WORD FROM PARIS.
THERE SHOULD BE A TELEGRAPH. FROM THE ARCHBISHOP.
I'M SORRY, BROTHER. THE LINES ARE DOWN.
WE HAVEN'T BEEN ABLE TO REACH PARIS SINCE THE PRUSSIAN OCCUPATION.
WHEN WILL THEY BE REPAIRED?
GOD ONLY KNOWS, BROTHER!
WHAT DO WE DO NOW?
WAITING HERE IS OUT OF THE QUESTION.
IT WON'T BE LONG BEFORE LORRAINE OR THE GERMANS OCCUPY THE TOWN.
SPAK

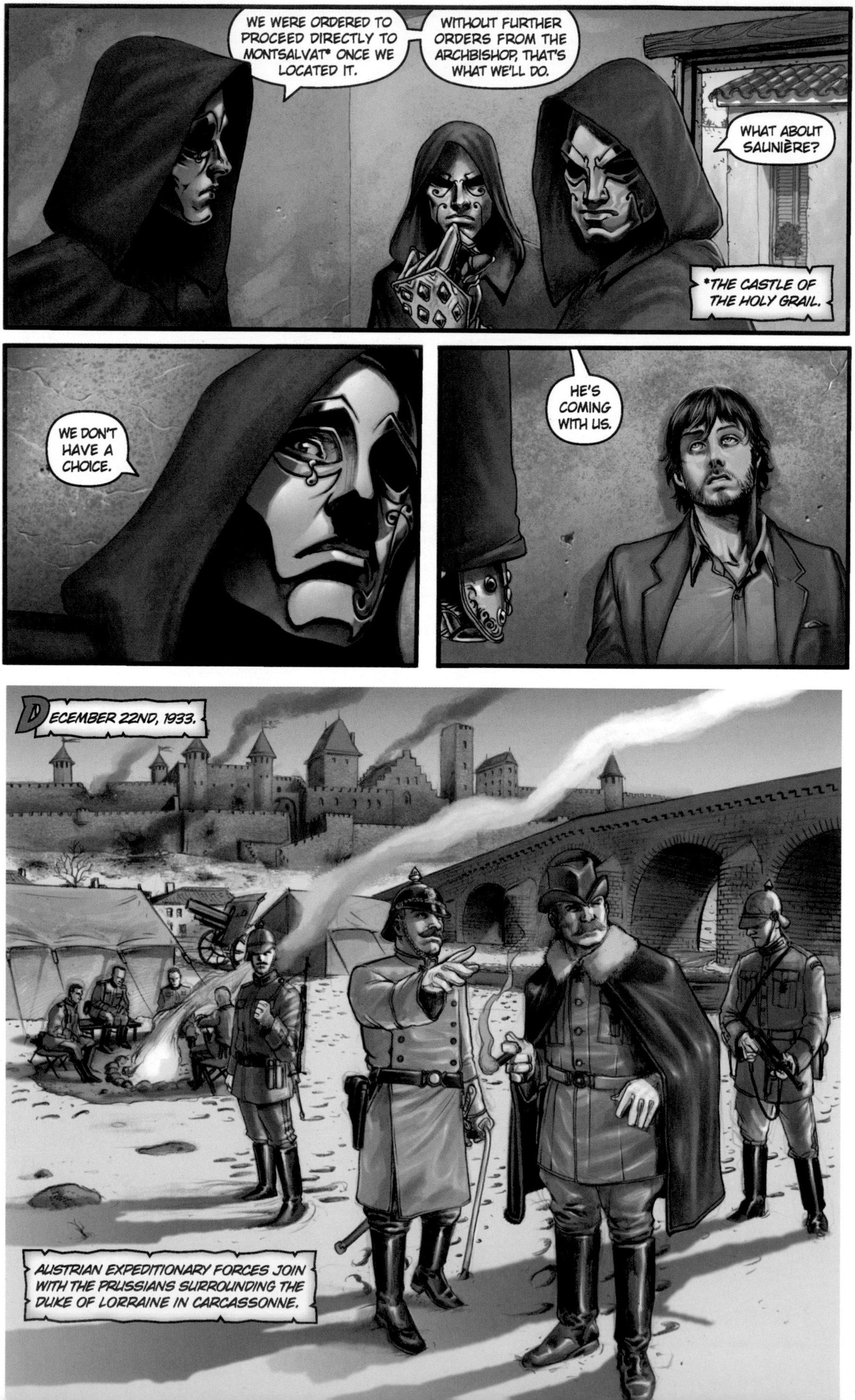
WE WERE ORDERED TO PROCEED DIRECTLY TO MONTSALVAT* ONCE WE LOCATED IT.
WITHOUT FURTHER ORDERS FROM THE ARCHBISHOP, THAT'S WHAT WE'LL DO.
WHAT ABOUT SAUNIÈRE?
*THE CASTLE OF THE HOLY GRAIL.
WE DON'T HAVE A CHOICE.
HE'S COMING WITH US.
DECEMBER 22ND, 1933.
AUSTRIAN EXPEDITIONARY FORCES JOIN WITH THE PRUSSIANS SURROUNDING THE DUKE OF LORRAINE IN CARCASSONNE.

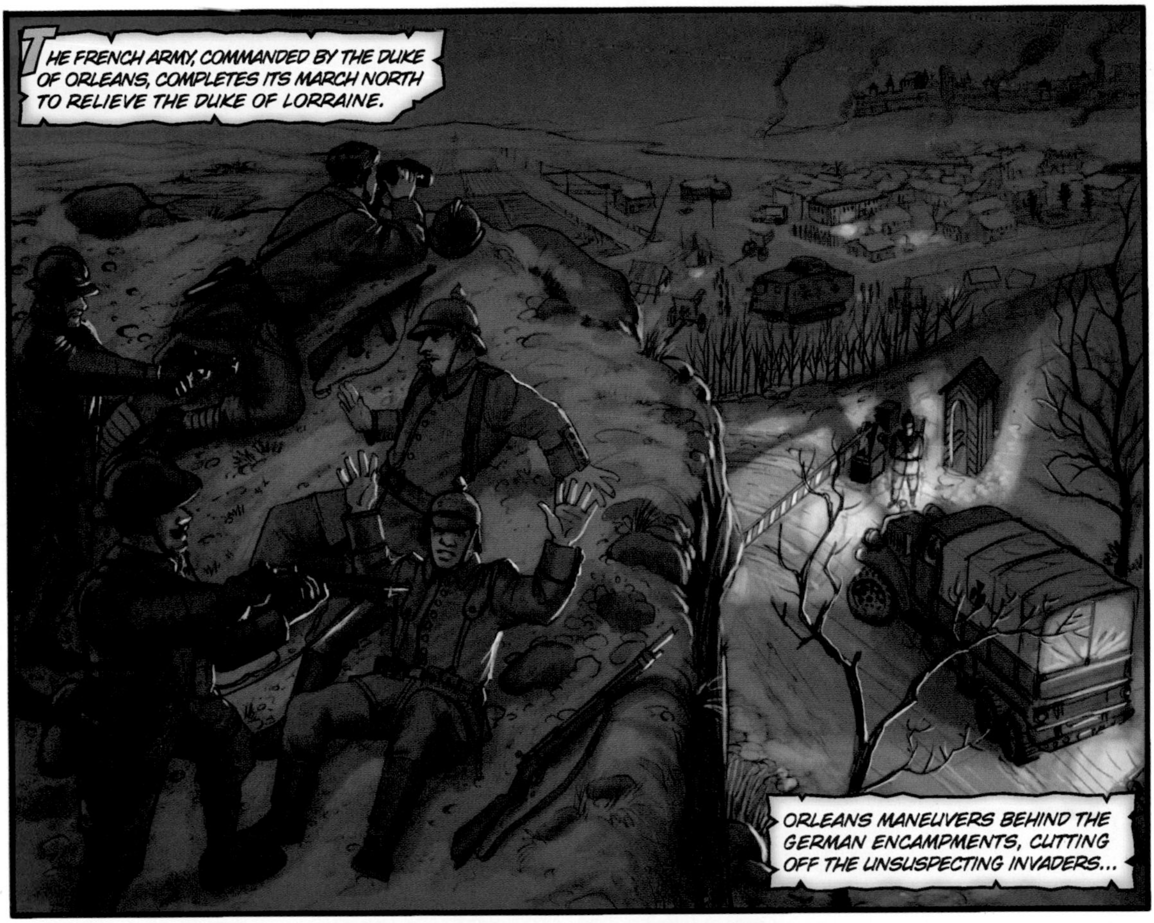
THE FRENCH ARMY, COMMANDED BY THE DUKE OF ORLEANS, COMPLETES ITS MARCH NORTH TO RELIEVE THE DUKE OF LORRAINE.
ORLEANS MANEUVERS BEHIND THE GERMAN ENCAMPMENTS, CUTTING OFF THE UNSUSPECTING INVADERS...

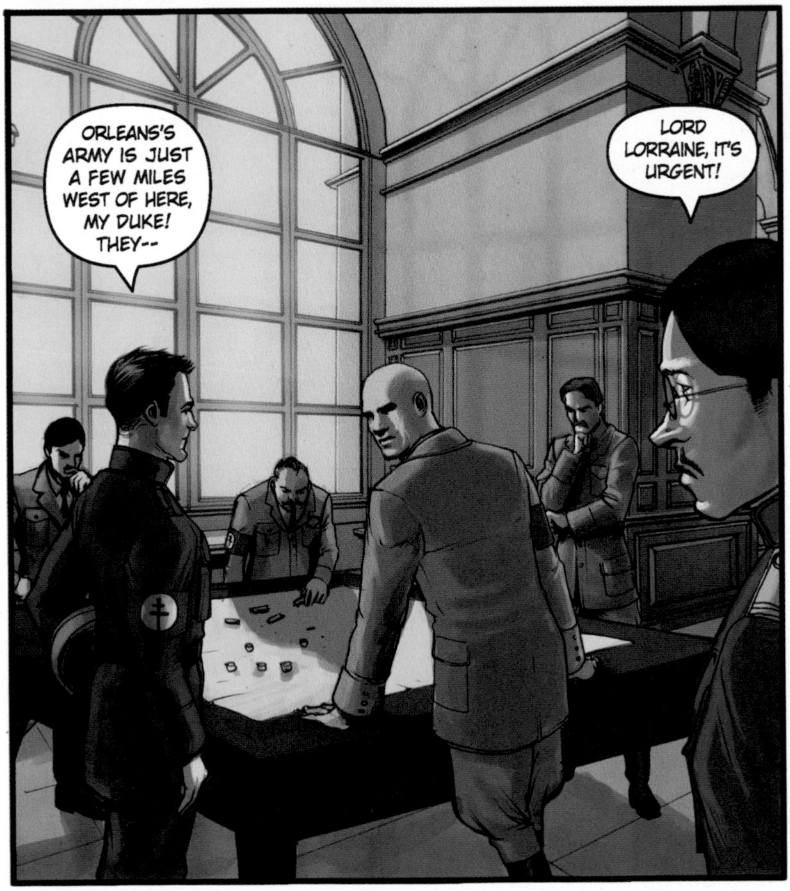
LORD LORRAINE, IT'S URGENT!
ORLEANS'S ARMY IS JUST A FEW MILES WEST OF HERE, MY DUKE! THEY--

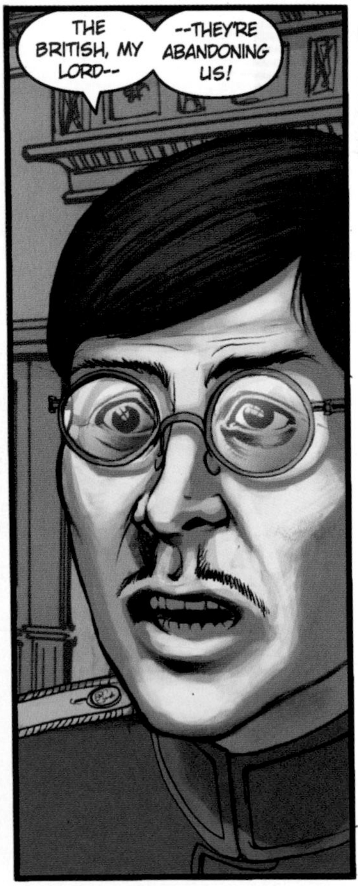
THE BRITISH, MY LORD--
--THEY'RE ABANDONING US!

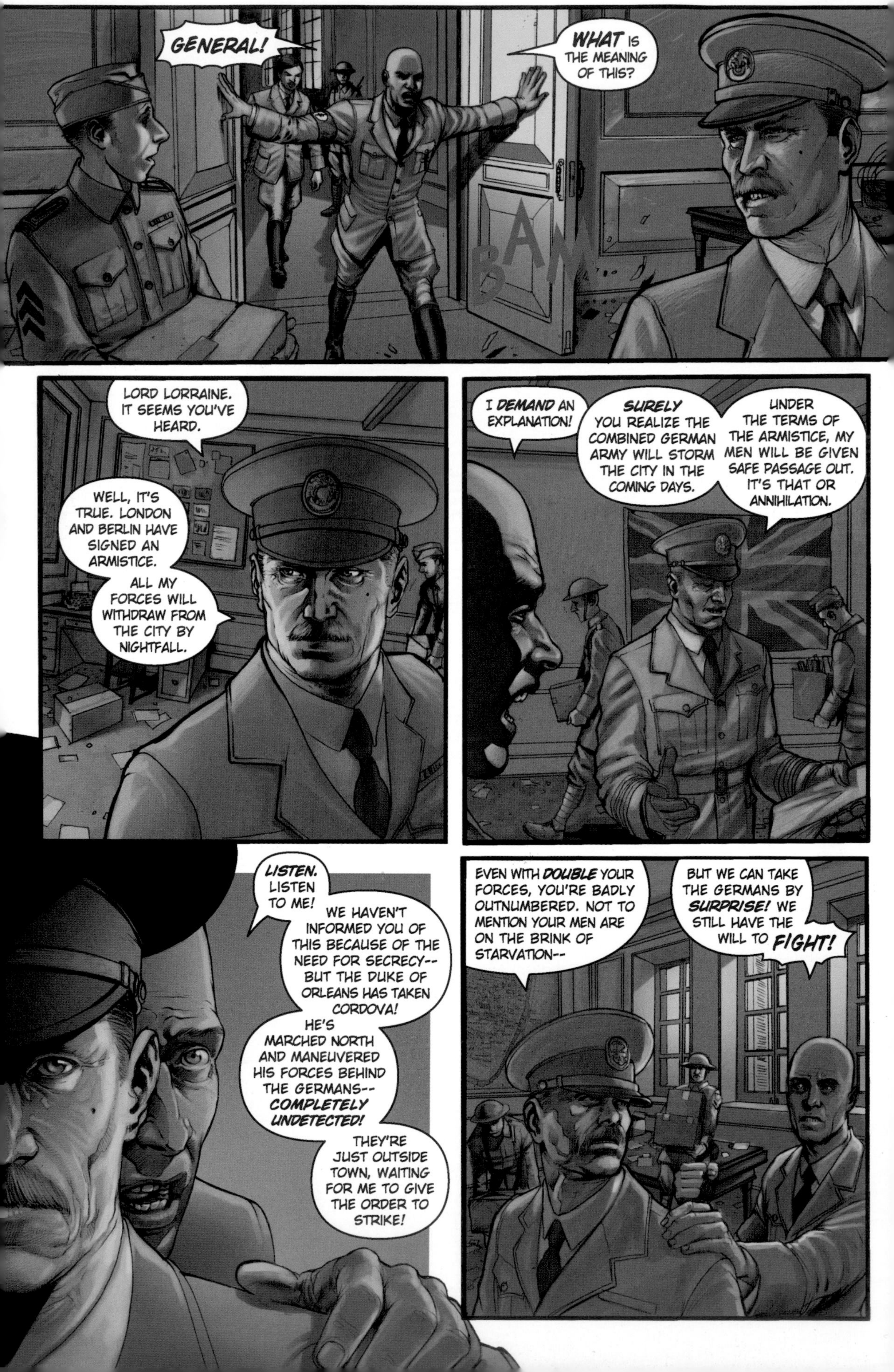
GENERAL!
WHAT IS THE MEANING OF THIS?
BAM
LORD LORRAINE. IT SEEMS YOU'VE HEARD.
WELL, IT'S TRUE. LONDON AND BERLIN HAVE SIGNED AN ARMISTICE.
ALL MY FORCES WILL WITHDRAW FROM THE CITY BY NIGHTFALL.
I DEMAND AN EXPLANATION!
SURELY YOU REALIZE THE COMBINED GERMAN ARMY WILL STORM THE CITY IN THE COMING DAYS.
UNDER THE TERMS OF THE ARMISTICE, MY MEN WILL BE GIVEN SAFE PASSAGE OUT. IT'S THAT OR ANNIHILATION.
LISTEN. LISTEN TO ME!
WE HAVEN'T INFORMED YOU OF THIS BECAUSE OF THE NEED FOR SECRECY-- BUT THE DUKE OF ORLEANS HAS TAKEN CORDOVA!
HE'S MARCHED NORTH AND MANEUVERED HIS FORCES BEHIND THE GERMANS-- COMPLETELY UNDETECTED!
THEY'RE JUST OUTSIDE TOWN, WAITING FOR ME TO GIVE THE ORDER TO STRIKE!
EVEN WITH DOUBLE YOUR FORCES, YOU'RE BADLY OUTNUMBERED. NOT TO MENTION YOUR MEN ARE ON THE BRINK OF STARVATION--
BUT WE CAN TAKE THE GERMANS BY SURPRISE! WE STILL HAVE THE WILL TO FIGHT!

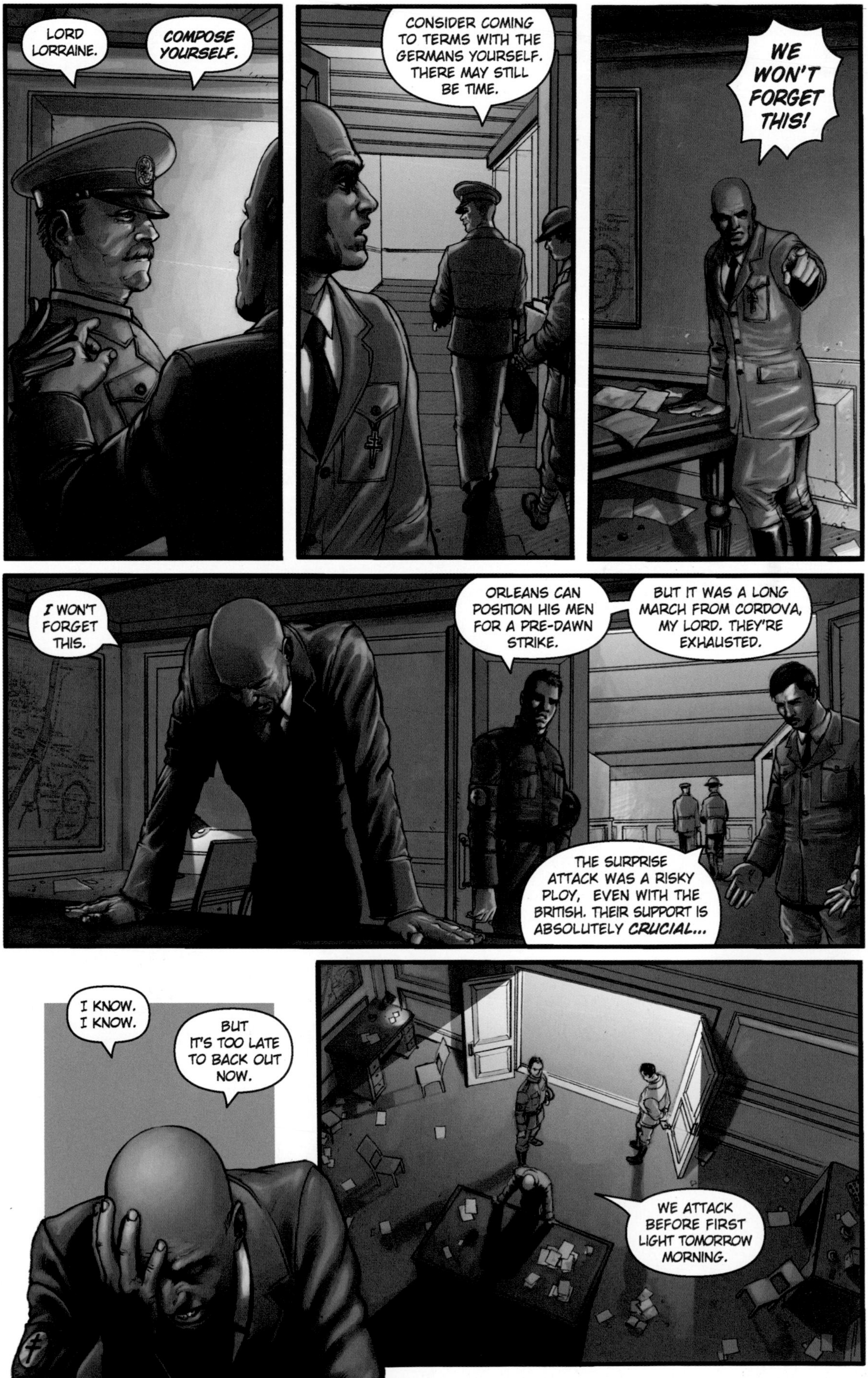
LORD LORRAINE.
COMPOSE YOURSELF.
CONSIDER COMING TO TERMS WITH THE GERMANS YOURSELF. THERE MAY STILL BE TIME.
WE WON'T FORGET THIS!
I WON'T FORGET THIS.
ORLEANS CAN POSITION HIS MEN FOR A PRE-DAWN STRIKE.
BUT IT WAS A LONG MARCH FROM CORDOVA, MY LORD. THEY'RE EXHAUSTED.
THE SURPRISE ATTACK WAS A RISKY PLOY, EVEN WITH THE BRITISH. THEIR SUPPORT IS ABSOLUTELY CRUCIAL...
I KNOW. I KNOW.
BUT IT'S TOO LATE TO BACK OUT NOW.
WE ATTACK BEFORE FIRST LIGHT TOMORROW MORNING.

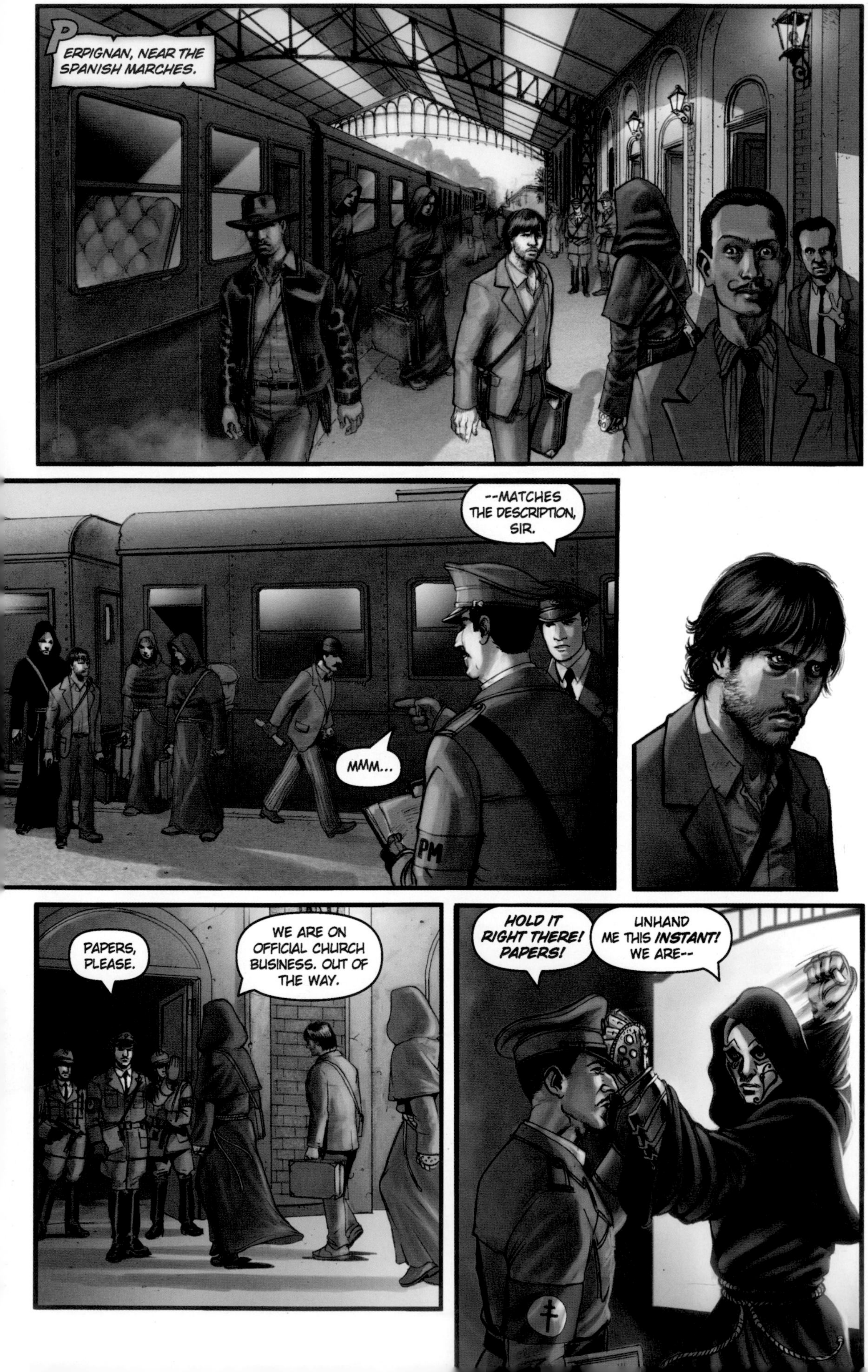
PERPIGNAN, NEAR THE SPANISH MARCHES.
--MATCHES THE DESCRIPTION, SIR.
MMM...
PAPERS, PLEASE.
WE ARE ON OFFICIAL CHURCH BUSINESS. OUT OF THE WAY.
HOLD IT RIGHT THERE! PAPERS!
UNHAND ME THIS INSTANT! WE ARE--
PM

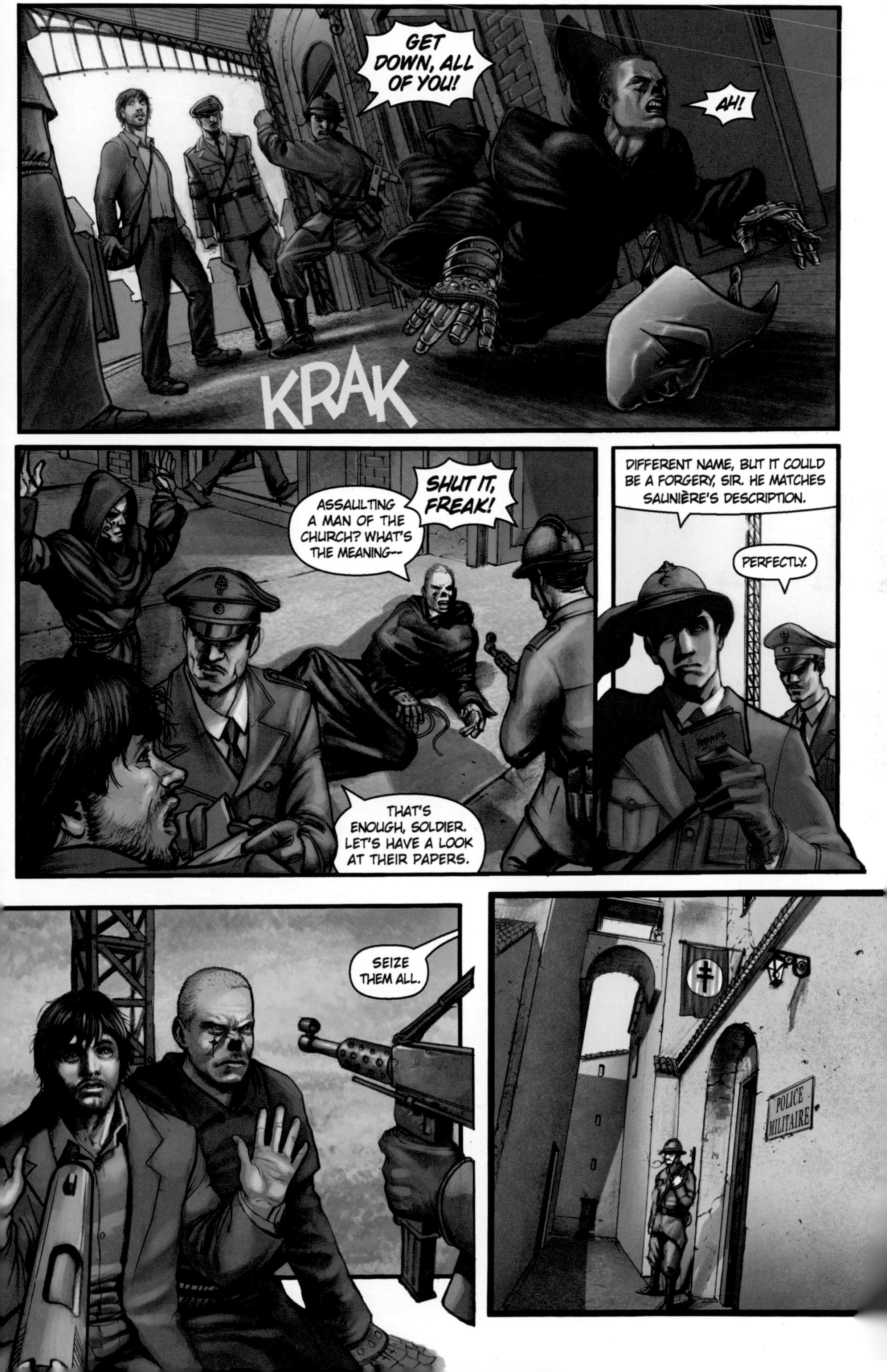
GET DOWN, ALL OF YOU!
AH!
KRAK
SHUT IT, FREAK!
ASSAULTING A MAN OF THE CHURCH? WHAT'S THE MEANING--
THAT'S ENOUGH, SOLDIER. LET'S HAVE A LOOK AT THEIR PAPERS.
DIFFERENT NAME, BUT IT COULD BE A FORGERY, SIR. HE MATCHES SAUNIÈRE'S DESCRIPTION.
PERFECTLY.
SEIZE THEM ALL.
POLICE MILITAIRE

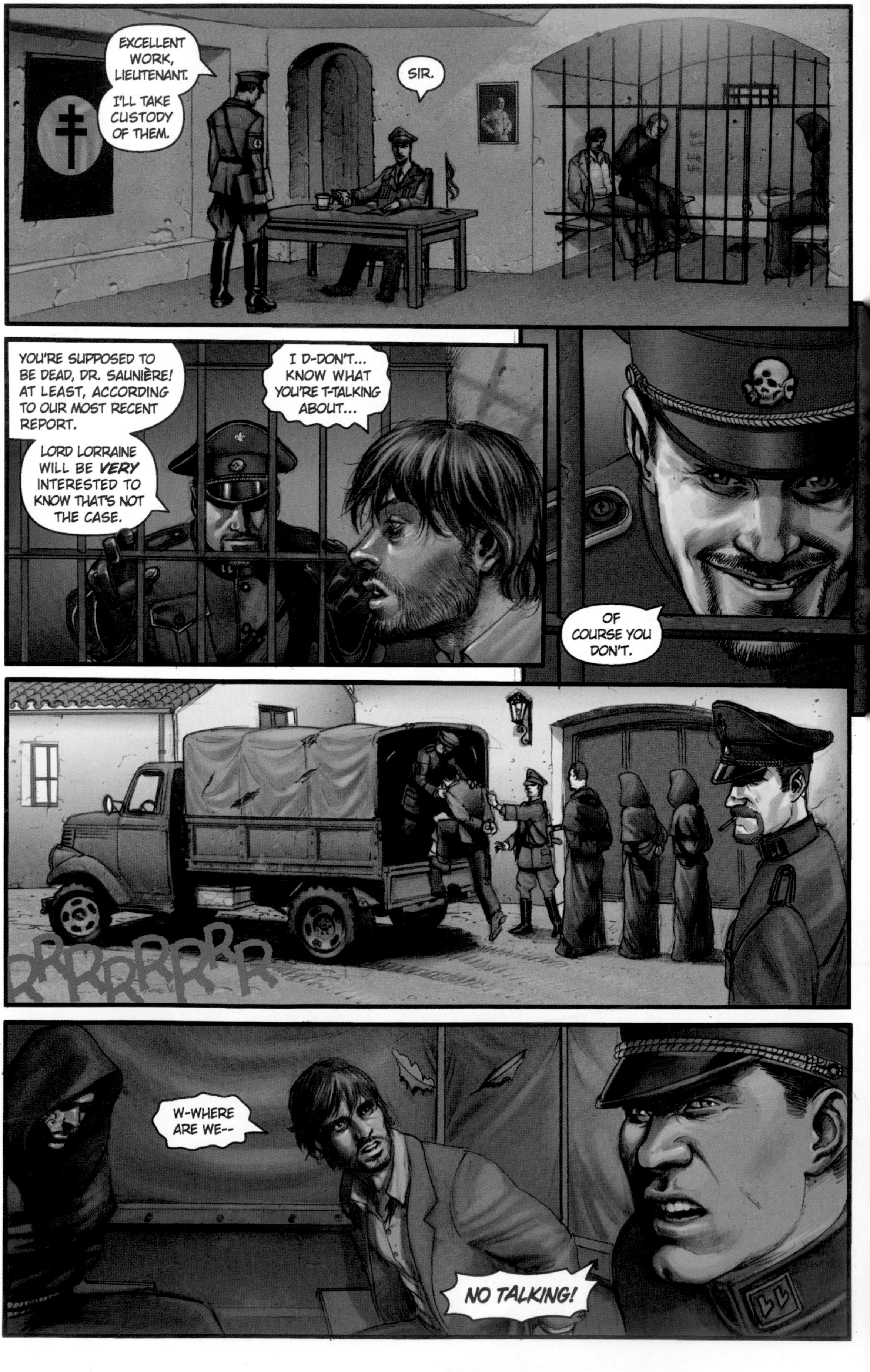
EXCELLENT WORK, LIEUTENANT.
I'LL TAKE CUSTODY OF THEM.
SIR.
YOU'RE SUPPOSED TO BE DEAD, DR. SAUNIÈRE! AT LEAST, ACCORDING TO OUR MOST RECENT REPORT.
LORD LORRAINE WILL BE VERY INTERESTED TO KNOW THAT'S NOT THE CASE.
I D-DON'T... KNOW WHAT YOU'RE T-TALKING ABOUT...
OF COURSE YOU DON'T.
RRRRRRRR
W-WHERE ARE WE--
NO TALKING!

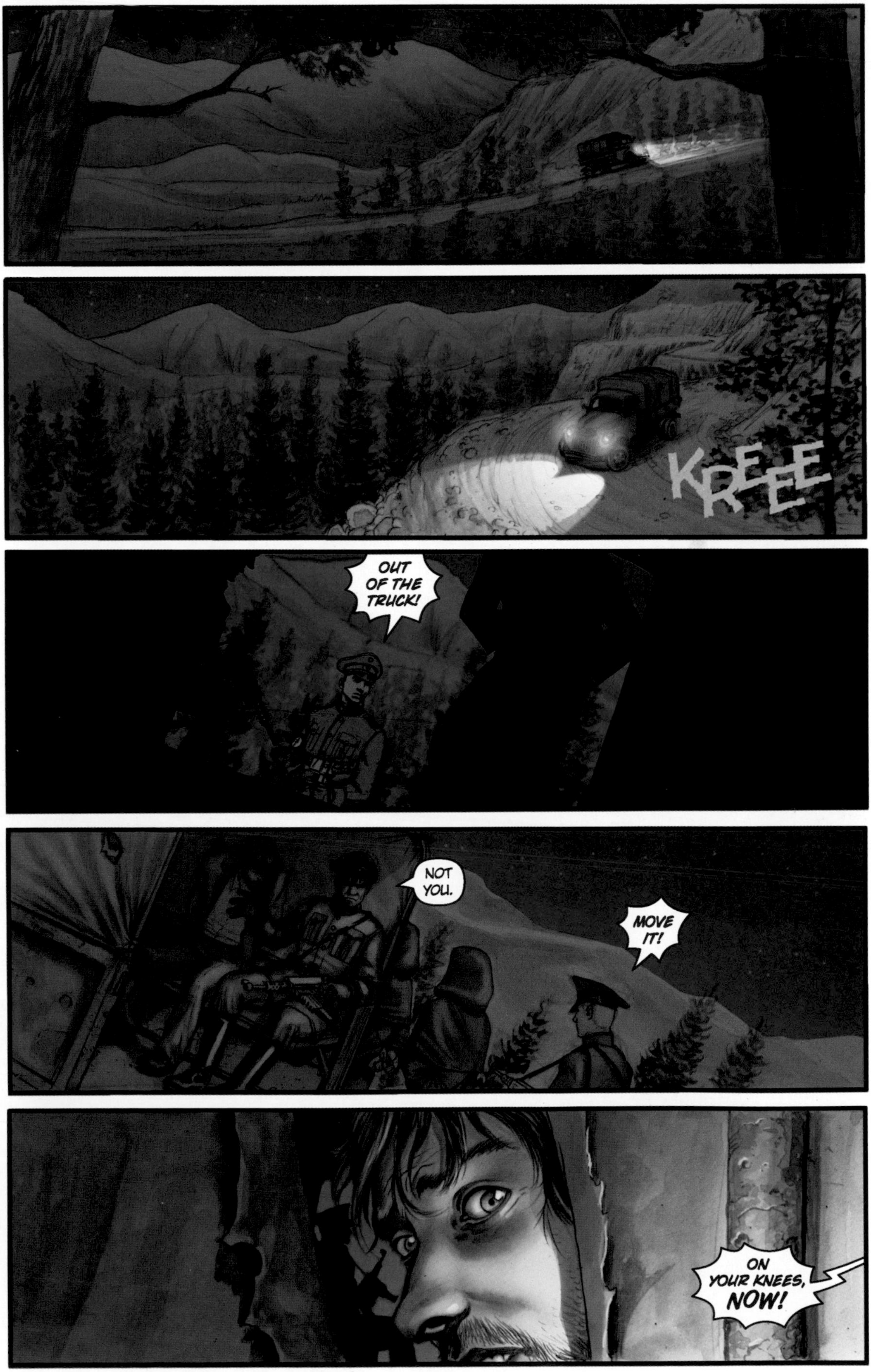
KREEE
OUT OF THE TRUCK!
NOT YOU.
MOVE IT!
ON YOUR KNEES, NOW!

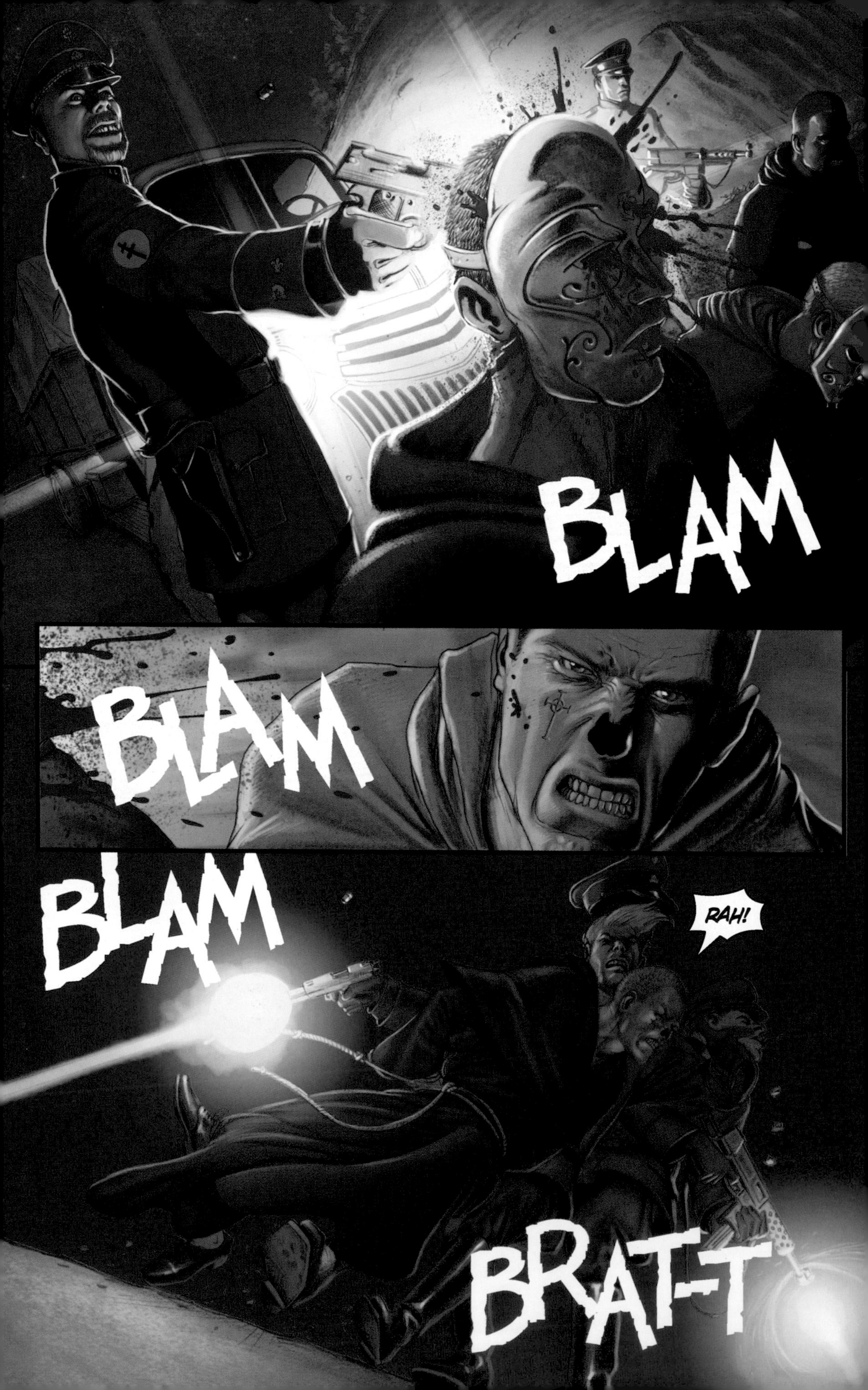
BLAM
BLAM
BLAM
RAH!
BRAT-T

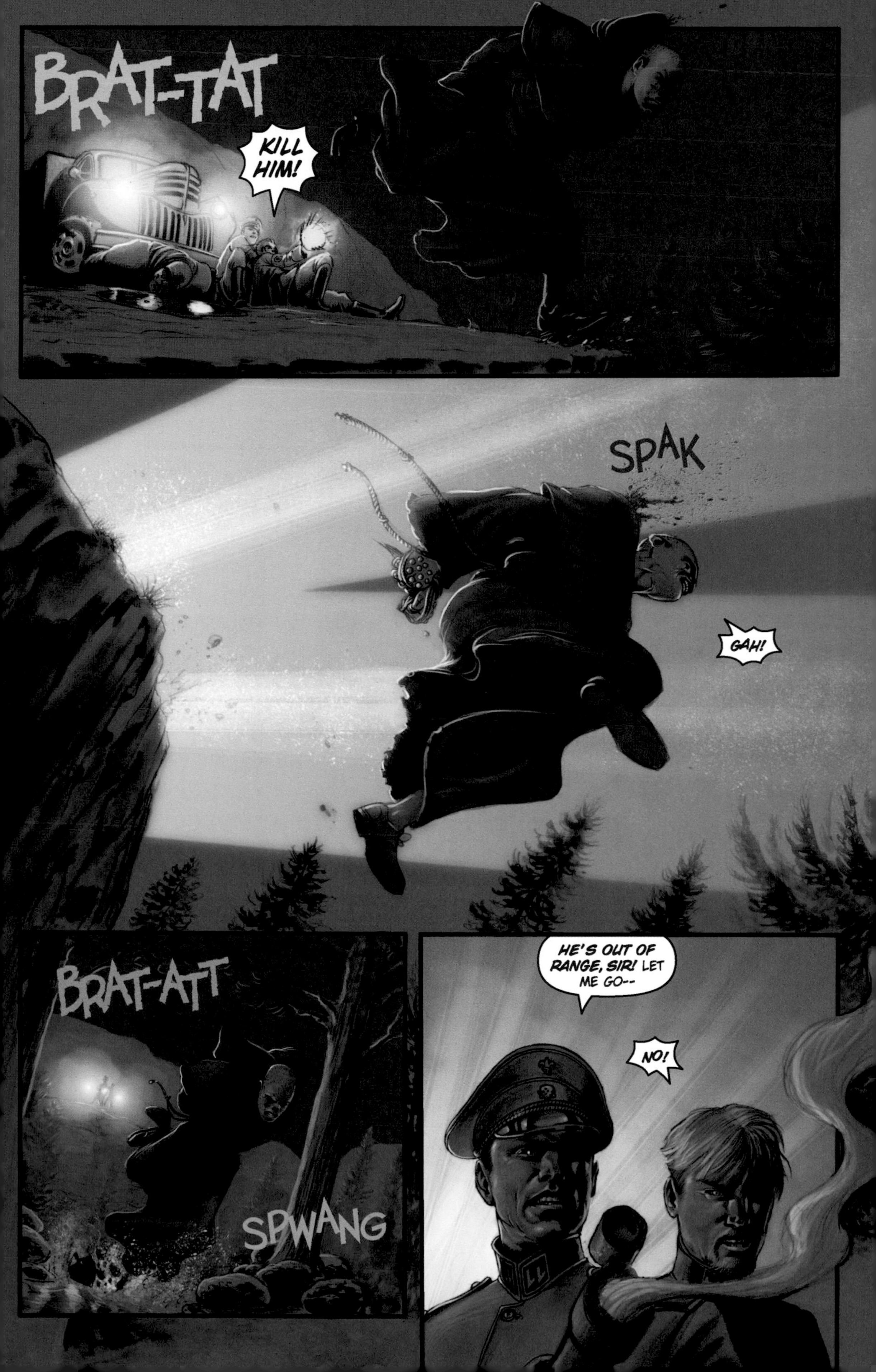
BRAT-TAT
KILL HIM!
SPAK
GAH!
BRAT-ATT
SPWANG
HE'S OUT OF RANGE, SIR! LET ME GO--
NO!

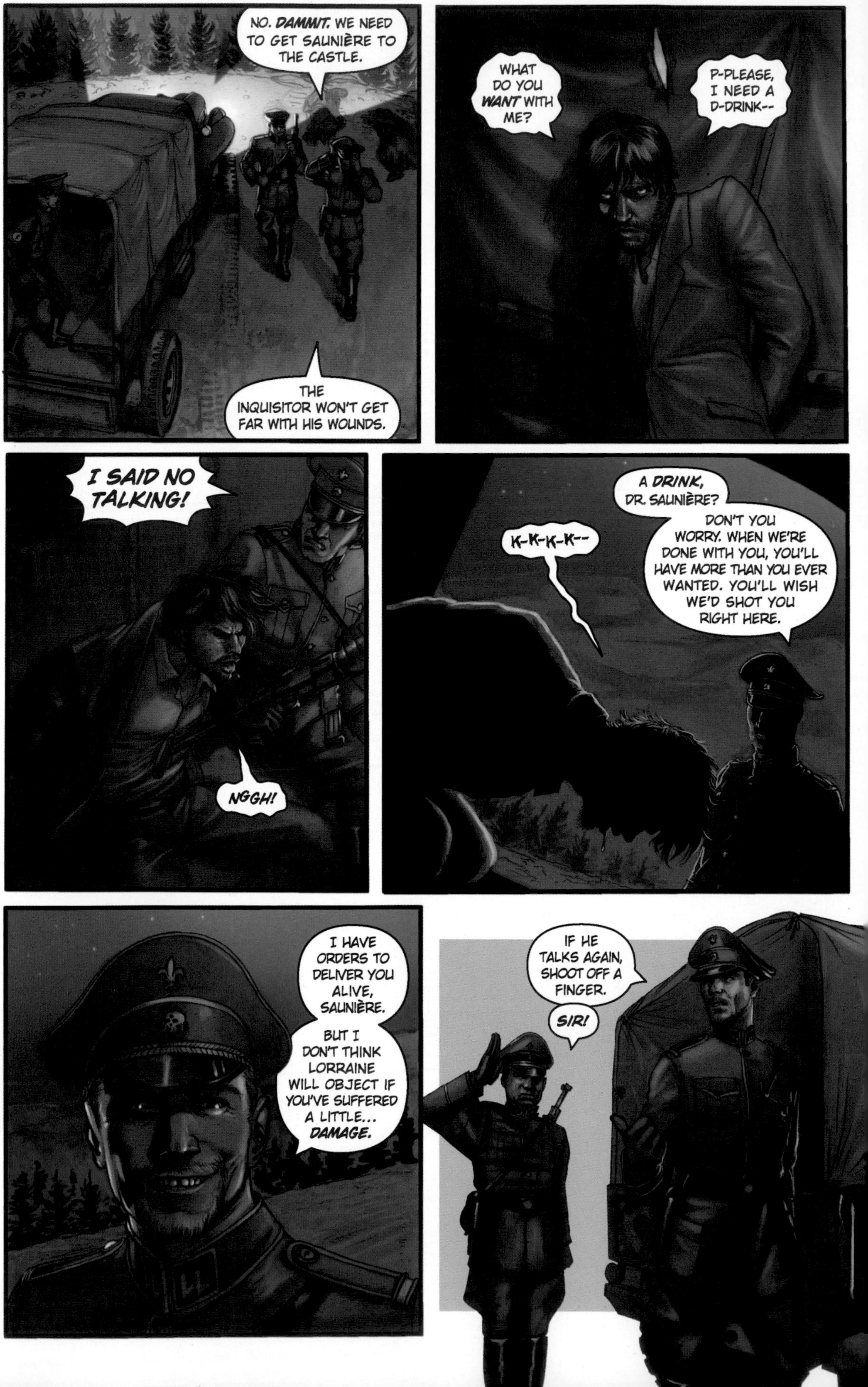
NO. DAMMIT. WE NEED TO GET SAUNIÈRE TO THE CASTLE.
THE INQUISITOR WON'T GET FAR WITH HIS WOUNDS.
WHAT DO YOU WANT WITH ME?
P-PLEASE, I NEED A D-DRINK--
I SAID NO TALKING!
NGGH!
A DRINK, DR. SAUNIÈRE?
K-K-K-K--
DON'T YOU WORRY. WHEN WE'RE DONE WITH YOU, YOU'LL HAVE MORE THAN YOU EVER WANTED. YOU'LL WISH WE'D SHOT YOU RIGHT HERE.
I HAVE ORDERS TO DELIVER YOU ALIVE, SAUNIÈRE.
BUT I DON'T THINK LORRAINE WILL OBJECT IF YOU'VE SUFFERED A LITTLE... DAMAGE.
IF HE TALKS AGAIN, SHOOT OFF A FINGER.
SIR!

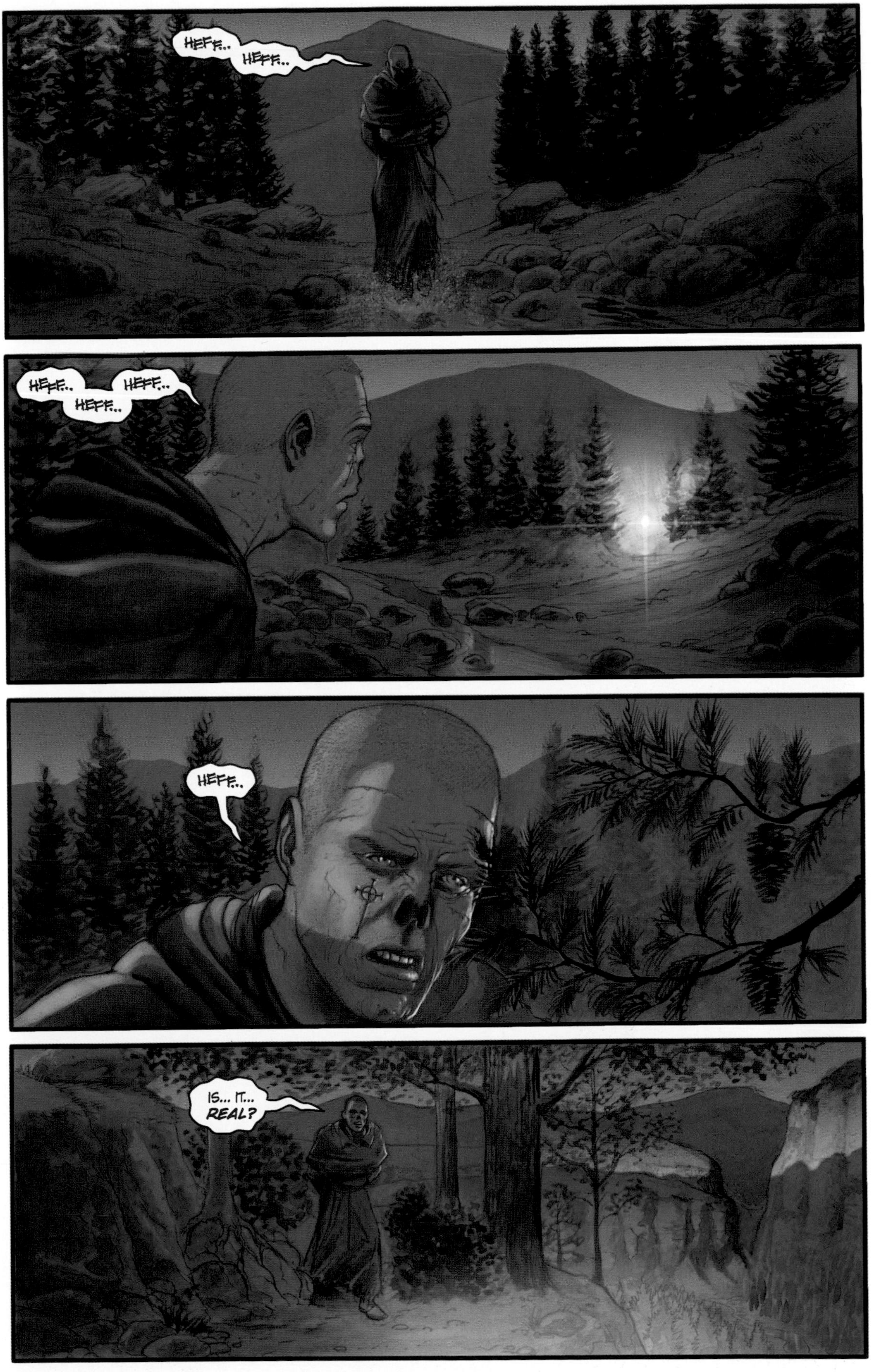
HEFF.. HEFF..
HEFF.. HEFF.. HEFF..
HEFF..
IS... IT... REAL?

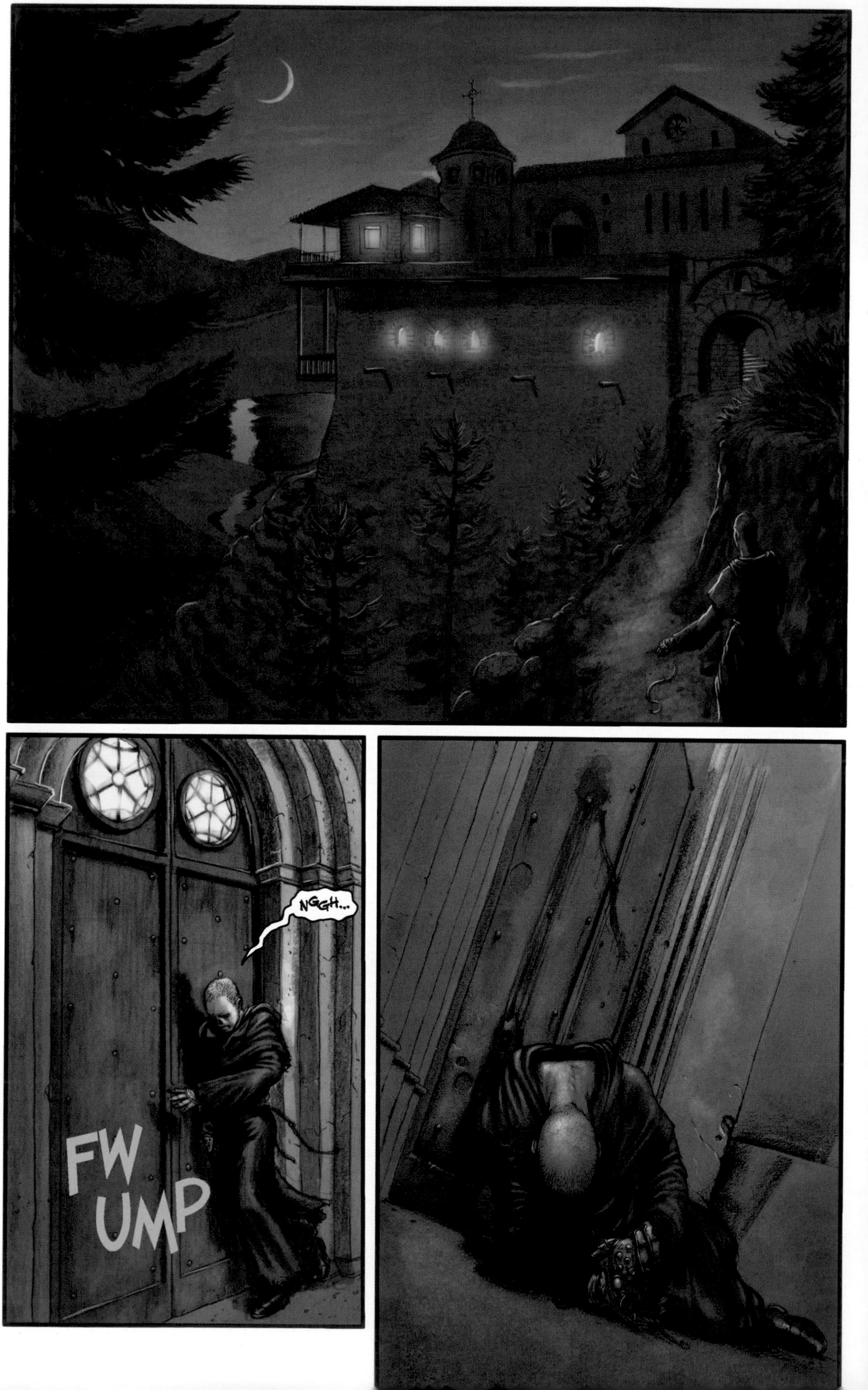
NGGH...
FW UMP

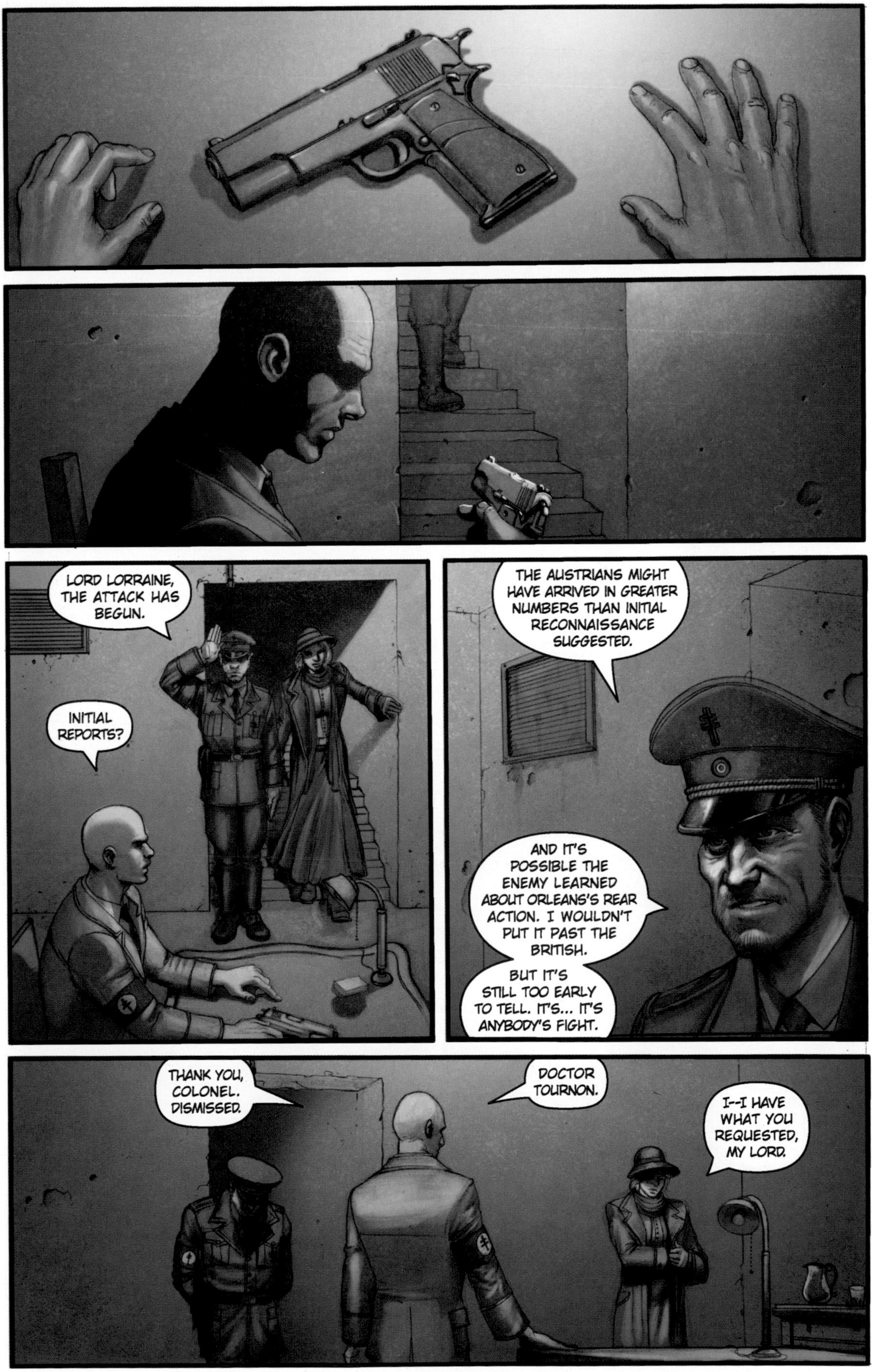
LORD LORRAINE, THE ATTACK HAS BEGUN.
INITIAL REPORTS?
THE AUSTRIANS MIGHT HAVE ARRIVED IN GREATER NUMBERS THAN INITIAL RECONNAISSANCE SUGGESTED.
AND IT'S POSSIBLE THE ENEMY LEARNED ABOUT ORLEANS'S REAR ACTION. I WOULDN'T PUT IT PAST THE BRITISH.
BUT IT'S STILL TOO EARLY TO TELL. IT'S... IT'S ANYBODY'S FIGHT.
THANK YOU, COLONEL. DISMISSED.
DOCTOR TOURNON.
I--I HAVE WHAT YOU REQUESTED, MY LORD.

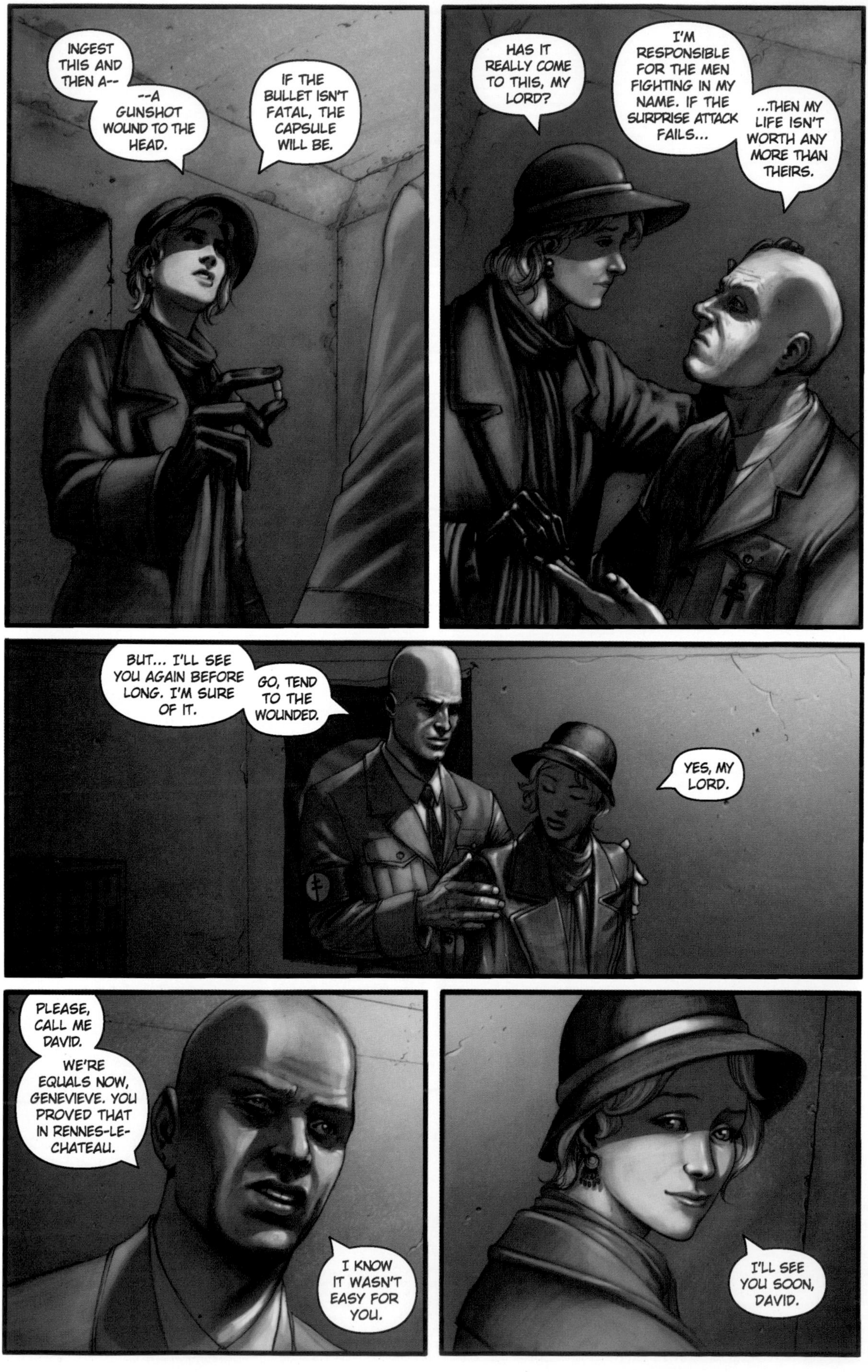
INGEST THIS AND THEN A--
--A GUNSHOT WOUND TO THE HEAD.
IF THE BULLET ISN'T FATAL, THE CAPSULE WILL BE.
HAS IT REALLY COME TO THIS, MY LORD?
I'M RESPONSIBLE FOR THE MEN FIGHTING IN MY NAME. IF THE SURPRISE ATTACK FAILS...
...THEN MY LIFE ISN'T WORTH ANY MORE THAN THEIRS.
BUT... I'LL SEE YOU AGAIN BEFORE LONG. I'M SURE OF IT.
GO, TEND TO THE WOUNDED.
YES, MY LORD.
PLEASE, CALL ME DAVID.
WE'RE EQUALS NOW, GENEVIEVE. YOU PROVED THAT IN RENNES-LE-CHATEAU.
I KNOW IT WASN'T EASY FOR YOU.
I'LL SEE YOU SOON, DAVID.

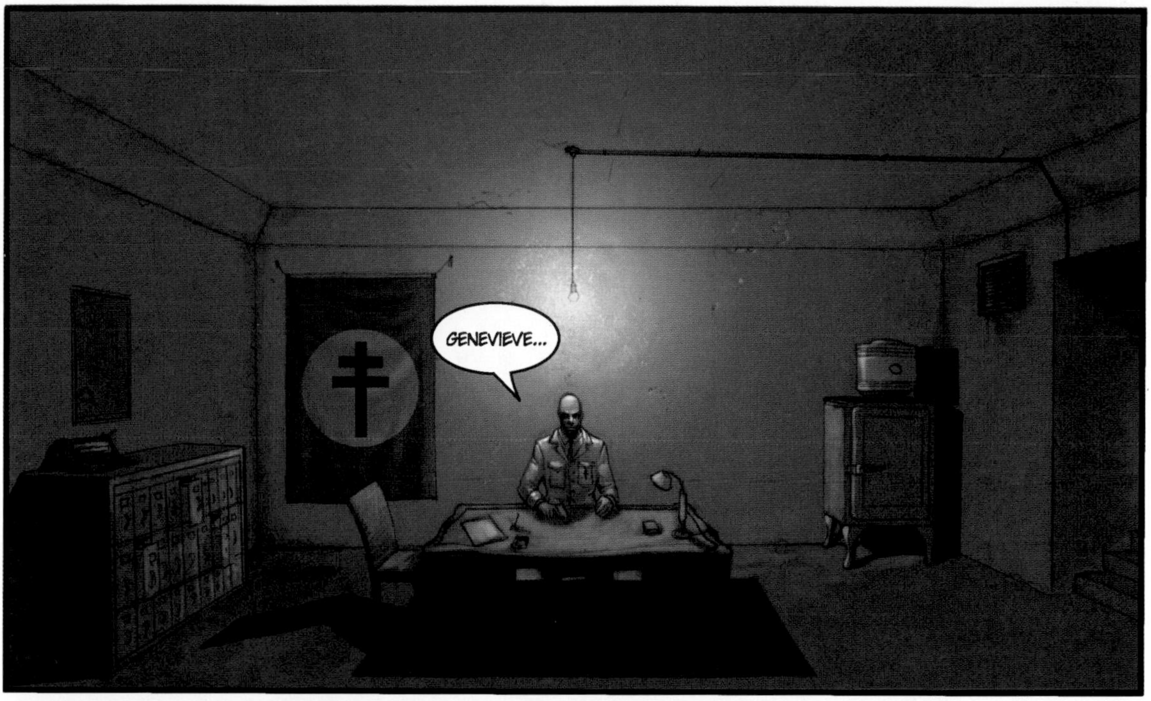
GENEVIEVE...

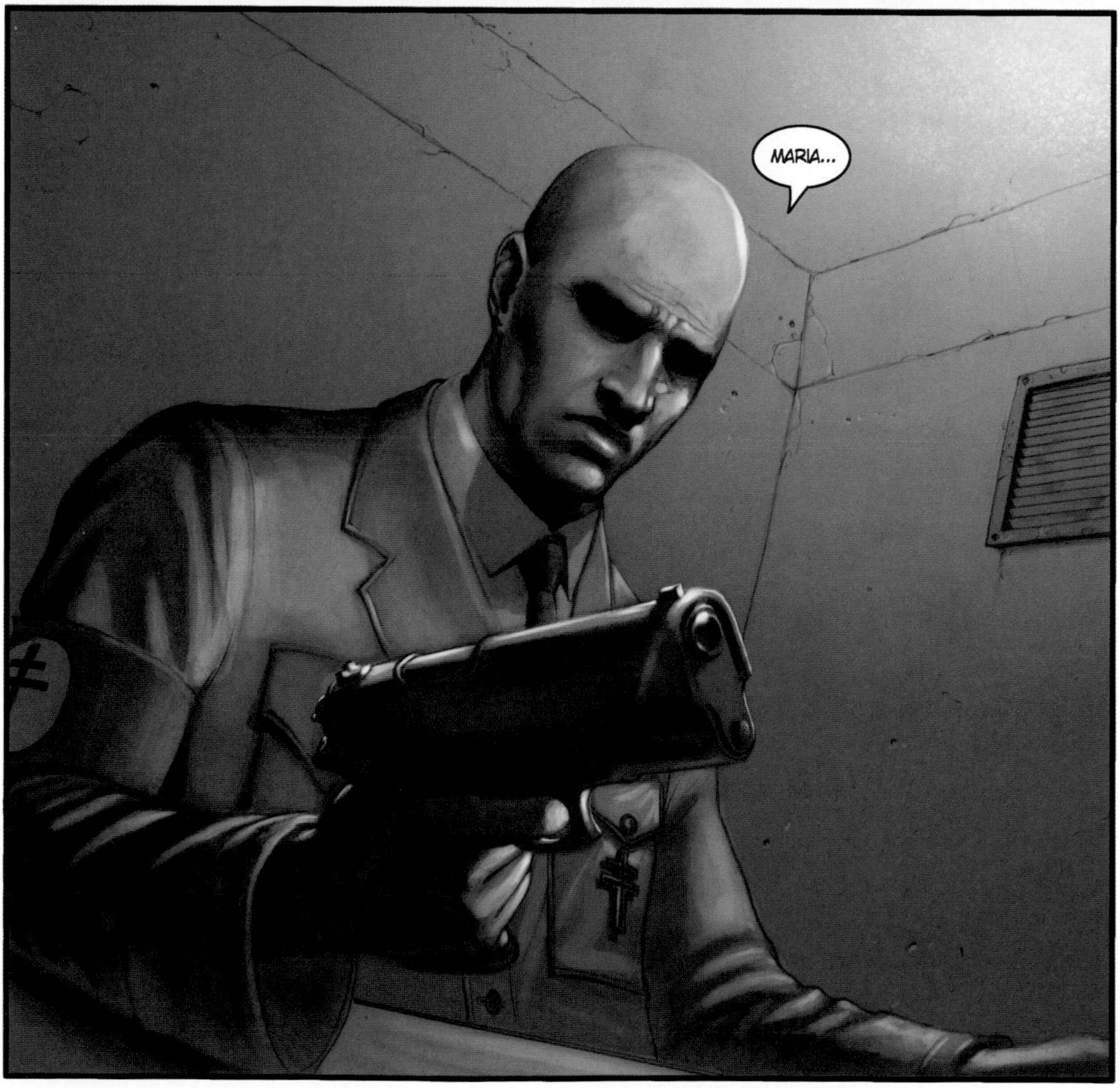
MARIA...

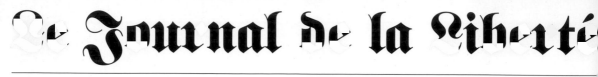

Le Journal de la Liberté

Paris's leading anglophone newspaper • vol. 205, no. 131 • Dec. 22, MCMXXXIII

Imperial Seal

Editors in Chief: M. Mike Richardson, M. Scott Allie. **Story Editor:** M. Arvid Nelson. **Art Editor:** M. Juan Ferreyra. **Photography Editor:** M. Eugène Atget. **Layout Supervisor:** M. Ryan Jorgensen. **Editors Emeritus:** M. Clark A. Smith, M. Howard P. Lovecraft, M. Robert E. Howard. Redacted under the direction of Obergruppenführer Ernst Von Ulrichs, protector of Paris. *Le Journal de la Liberté* is printed under the benign auspices of his Imperial Majesty Kaiser Wilhelm II of Prussia.

God Save the Kaiser

of Approval

SURRENDER IMMINENT?

British Withdraw From Conflict • Austrians Join Prussian Forces Surrounding French in Carcassonne • How Much Longer Can Lorraine Hold Out?

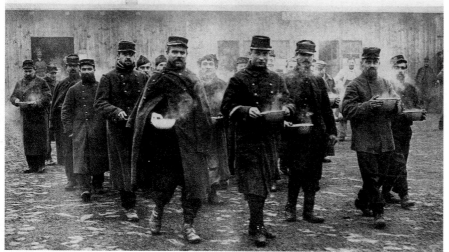

French prisoners of war interned in a camp outside Paris.

Carcassonne – The Duke of Lorraine was voted First Consul of France by Parliament shortly after the outbreak of war with Prussia. Long before then, he came to personify an imperialist foreign policy to expand France's domain in Europe and overseas.

Now, less than two months into the war he started, France's armies are in tatters and Lorraine's vision of Greater France is on the verge of total annihilation.

The duke and his shattered army are trapped inside the southern city of Carcassonne, surrounded by a much larger Prussian force. The French face eradication if Lorraine does not surrender soon, according to the Prussian military high command.

"There is no place Lorraine can run or hide," Gen. Erich von Falkenhayn, commander of the Prussian forces in France, said. "Our terms are simple: surrender unconditionally, or be destroyed."

To make matters worse for the French, a large Austrian contingent has joined the Prussians outside Carcassonne, bringing the total number of troops facing Lorraine to well over 150,000. The exact numbers of Lorraine's forces are unknown, but sources say the number cannot be higher than 30,000.

The French were rocked by another setback late yesterday: the withdrawal of their British allies from the conflict.

The British have long supported Lorraine in his cause of uprooting Islam from Europe. When Prussia and the Holy Roman Empire declared war on France following Lorraine's invasion of the Emirate of Cordova, Britain immediately came to France's aid.

But, faced with the deteriorating military situation and high casualties sustained during the failed defense of Paris, the British have sued for peace with the German powers.

"The conflict raging across the continent troubles Her Majesty, but She can no longer bear the costs of participation," a spokesman for Queen Elizabeth II of Great Britain and Ireland said.

By the time this article is printed, the British will already have begun their withdrawal from Carcassonne.

No word has come from inside the city, as the Duke of Lorraine is completely cut off from all outside communication.

Gen. von Falkenhayn said an assault on Lorraine's positions could occur "at any time."

Prussia, Holy Roman Empire Faced With Dilemmas of Their Own

But the Prussian army has itself been severely taxed in its hunt across France for Lorraine.

"The only reason we haven't stormed Lorraine's positions yet is that our supplies are so thin,' a source in the Prussian military command said.

Lorraine razed Paris to the ground before abandoning it to the Prussians, depriving them of much-needed provender.

"This is blitzkrieg," the source said. "We're supposed to strike fast and live off the land. Problem is, you can't live off the land if it's been burnt to a cinder."

Gen. von Falkenhayn dismissed these concerns.

"This isn't a stroll in the Black Forest. This is war," he said "Whatever the condition of our supply lines, the situation is far more dire for Lorraine."

He also discounted rumors the French Army of the South had triumphed over the Cordovan Emirate and was rushing north to aid Lorraine.

"Even supposing Cordova's been subjugated in this short time, which seems unlikely, Lorraine is completely cut off. The Army of the South cannot come to his defense."

No news has been heard from Cordova in several weeks.

Moreover, Prussian forces in Pomerania are facing a massive Russian offensive. Russia declared war on Prussia and the Holy Roman Empire soon after they declared war on France.

"The sooner we conclude the French campaign, the better," Gen. Paul von Hindenburg, commander of the Prussian forces fighting the Russians, said. "We're holding out for now, but it's only a matter of time."

Emperor Rudolf I of the Holy Roman Empire is facing widespread internal instability as a result of His decision to aid Prussia. His Serbian subjects have taken advantage of the outbreak of war to declare independence, and His Italian subjects are in open revolt.

Notice to Readers

Due to intractable contumacy and a pronounced lack of cheer, the entire editorial staff of *Le Journal de la Liberté* has been sacked. The only persons retaining their jobs are MM. Nelson and Ferreyra, who have proved most willing to comply with the dictates of their new masters. The Prussian Reichsprotectorate of Northern France thanks them for their service.

CHAPTER THREE
DELIRIUM TREMENS

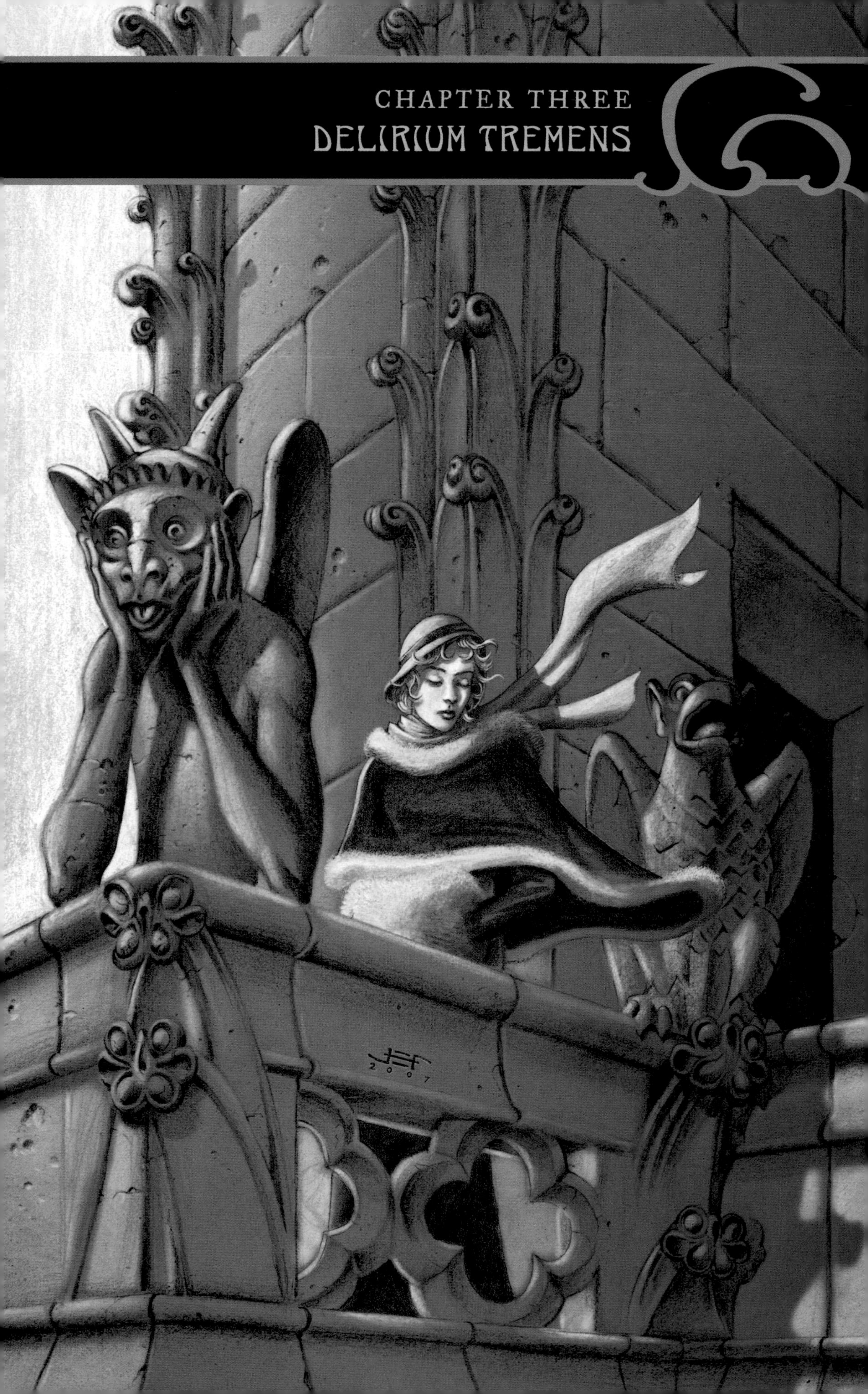

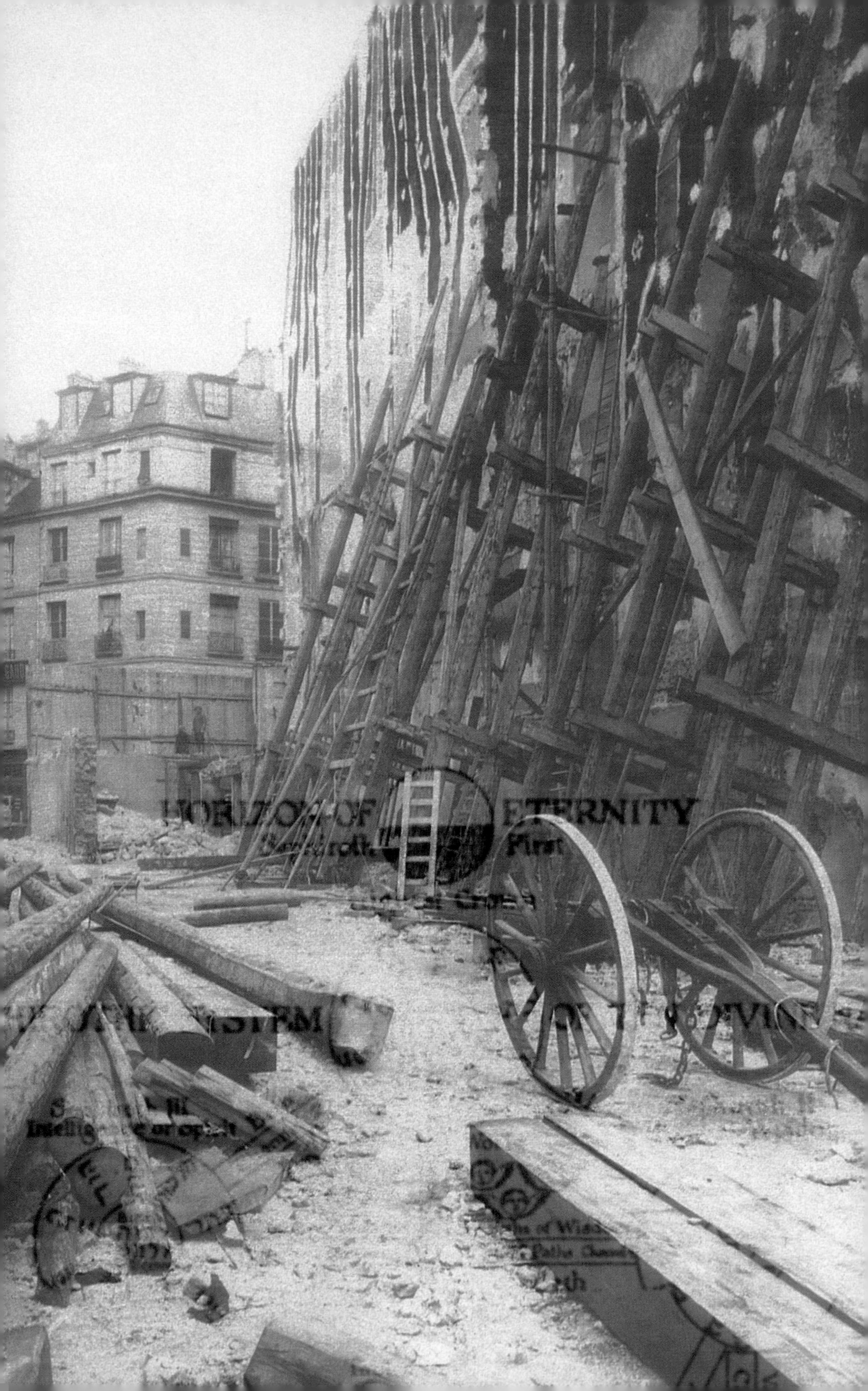
ETERNITY
First

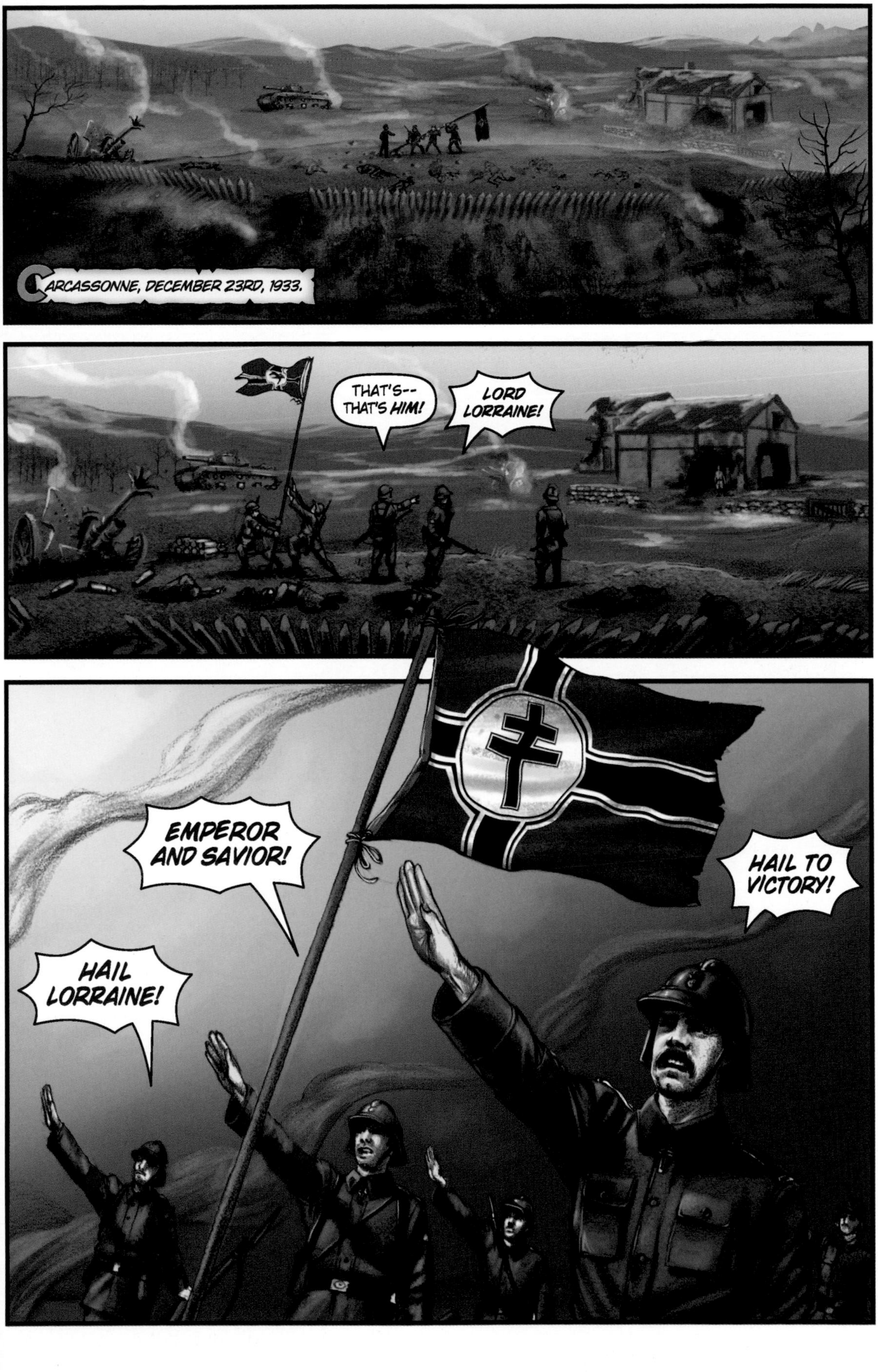
CARCASSONNE, DECEMBER 23RD, 1933.
THAT'S-- THAT'S HIM!
LORD LORRAINE!
EMPEROR AND SAVIOR!
HAIL TO VICTORY!
HAIL LORRAINE!

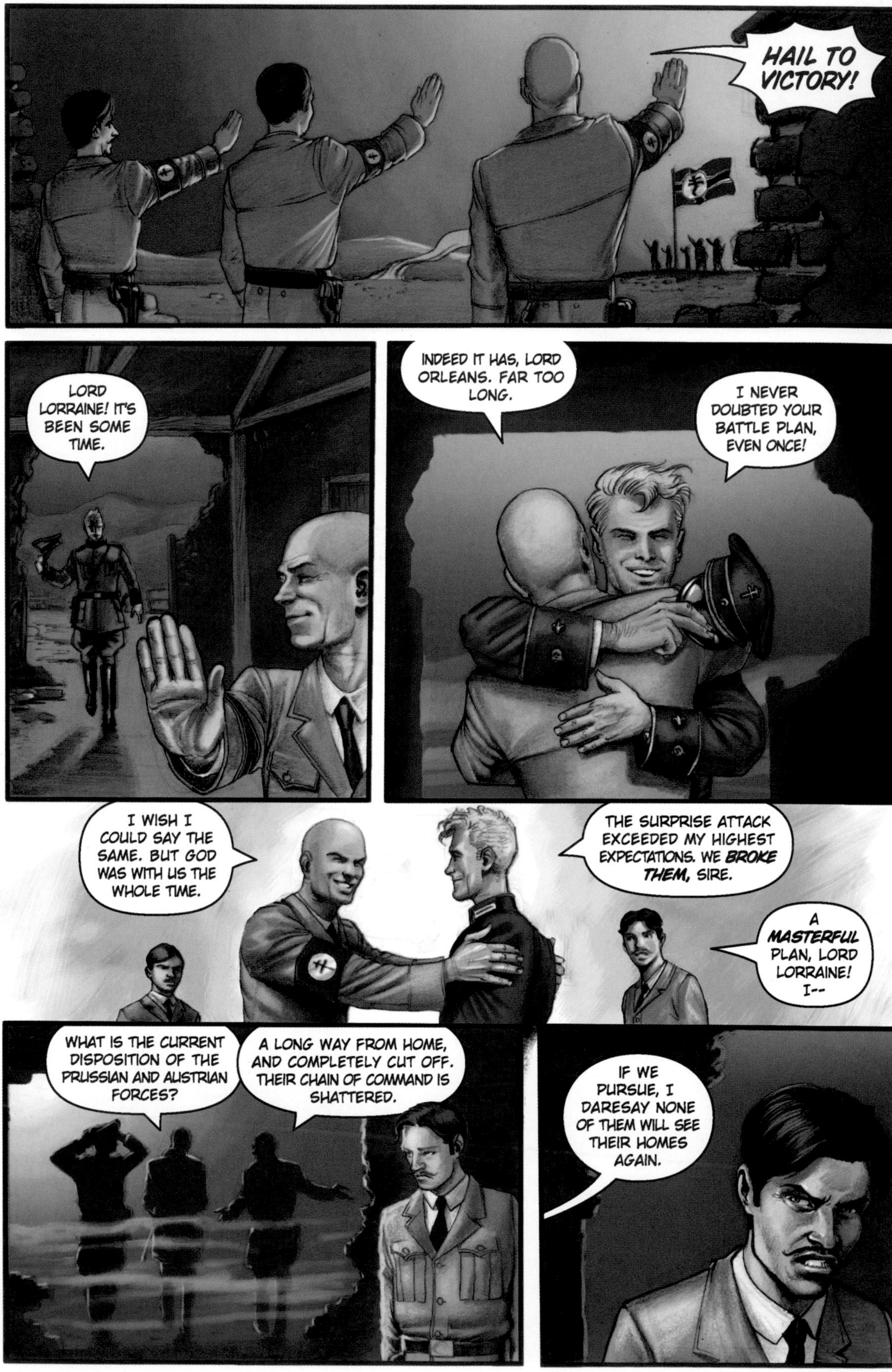
HAIL TO VICTORY!
LORD LORRAINE! IT'S BEEN SOME TIME.
INDEED IT HAS, LORD ORLEANS. FAR TOO LONG.
I NEVER DOUBTED YOUR BATTLE PLAN, EVEN ONCE!
I WISH I COULD SAY THE SAME. BUT GOD WAS WITH US THE WHOLE TIME.
THE SURPRISE ATTACK EXCEEDED MY HIGHEST EXPECTATIONS. WE BROKE THEM, SIRE.
A MASTERFUL PLAN, LORD LORRAINE! I--
WHAT IS THE CURRENT DISPOSITION OF THE PRUSSIAN AND AUSTRIAN FORCES?
A LONG WAY FROM HOME, AND COMPLETELY CUT OFF. THEIR CHAIN OF COMMAND IS SHATTERED.
IF WE PURSUE, I DARESAY NONE OF THEM WILL SEE THEIR HOMES AGAIN.

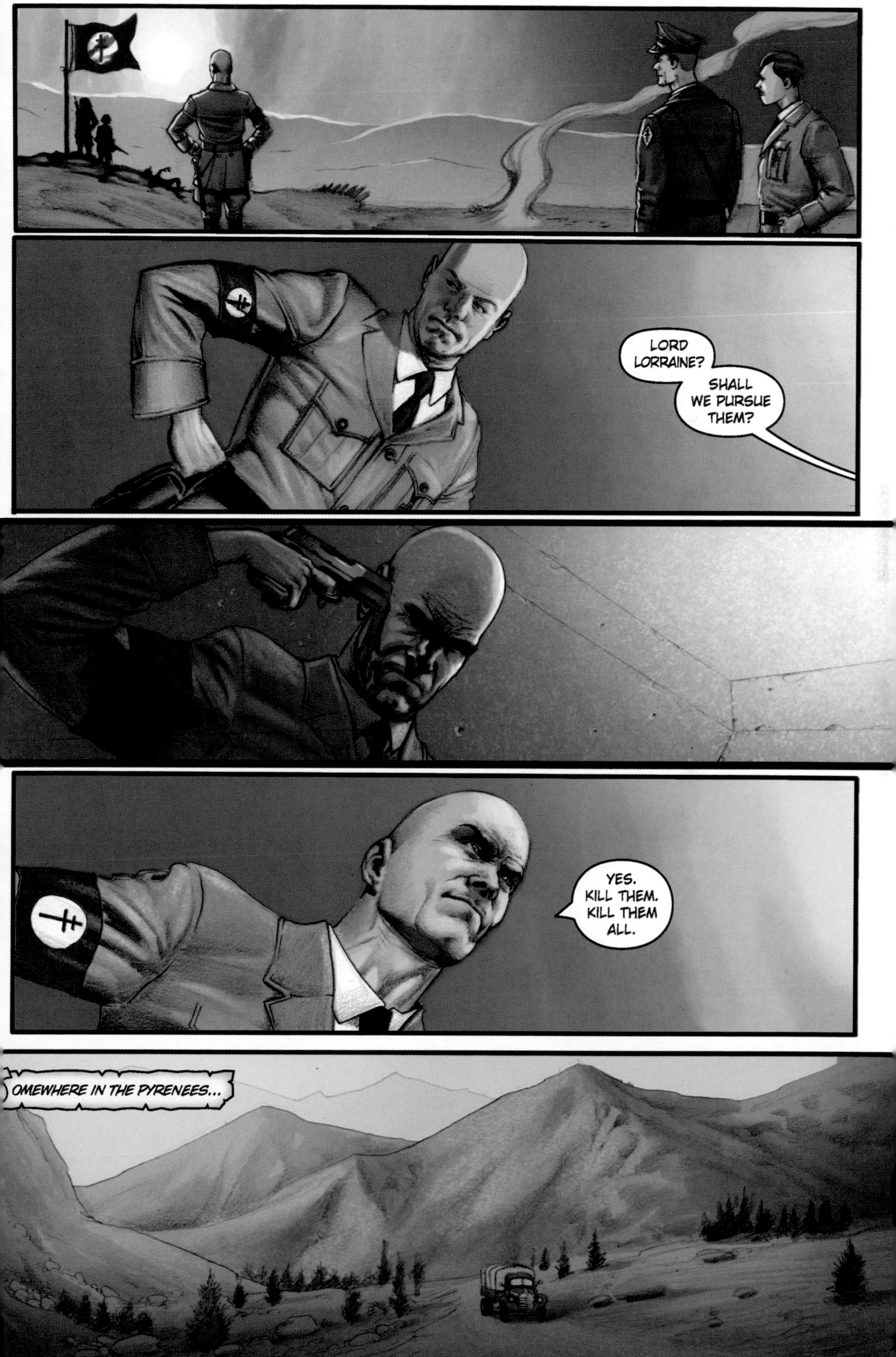
LORD LORRAINE?
SHALL WE PURSUE THEM?
YES. KILL THEM. KILL THEM ALL.
OMEWHERE IN THE PYRENEES...

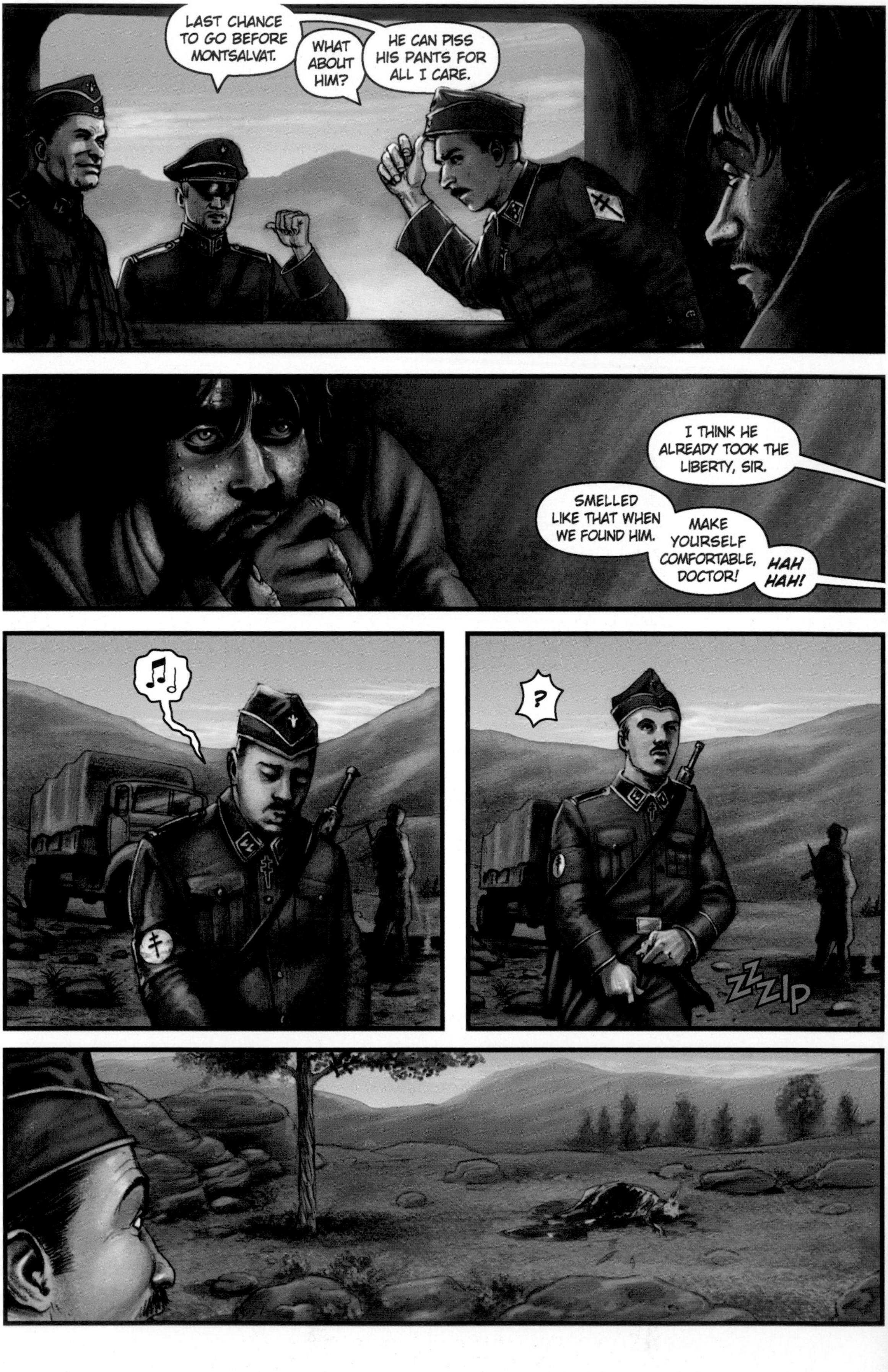
LAST CHANCE TO GO BEFORE MONTSALVAT.
WHAT ABOUT HIM?
HE CAN PISS HIS PANTS FOR ALL I CARE.
I THINK HE ALREADY TOOK THE LIBERTY, SIR.
SMELLED LIKE THAT WHEN WE FOUND HIM.
MAKE YOURSELF COMFORTABLE, DOCTOR!
HAH HAH!
?
ZZZIP

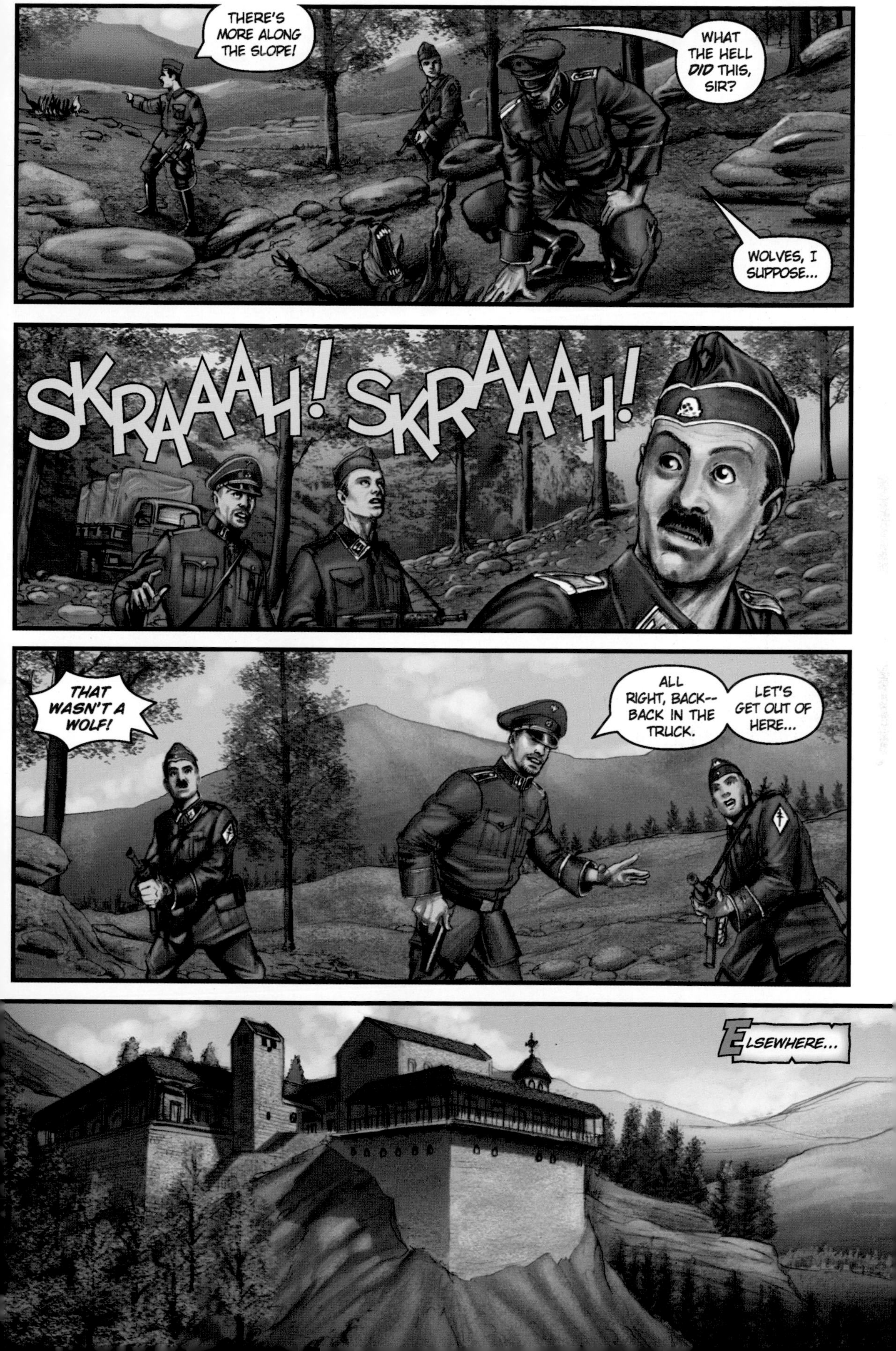
THERE'S MORE ALONG THE SLOPE!
WHAT THE HELL DID THIS, SIR?
WOLVES, I SUPPOSE...
SKRAAAH! SKRAAAH!
THAT WASN'T A WOLF!
ALL RIGHT, BACK--BACK IN THE TRUCK.
LET'S GET OUT OF HERE...
ELSEWHERE...

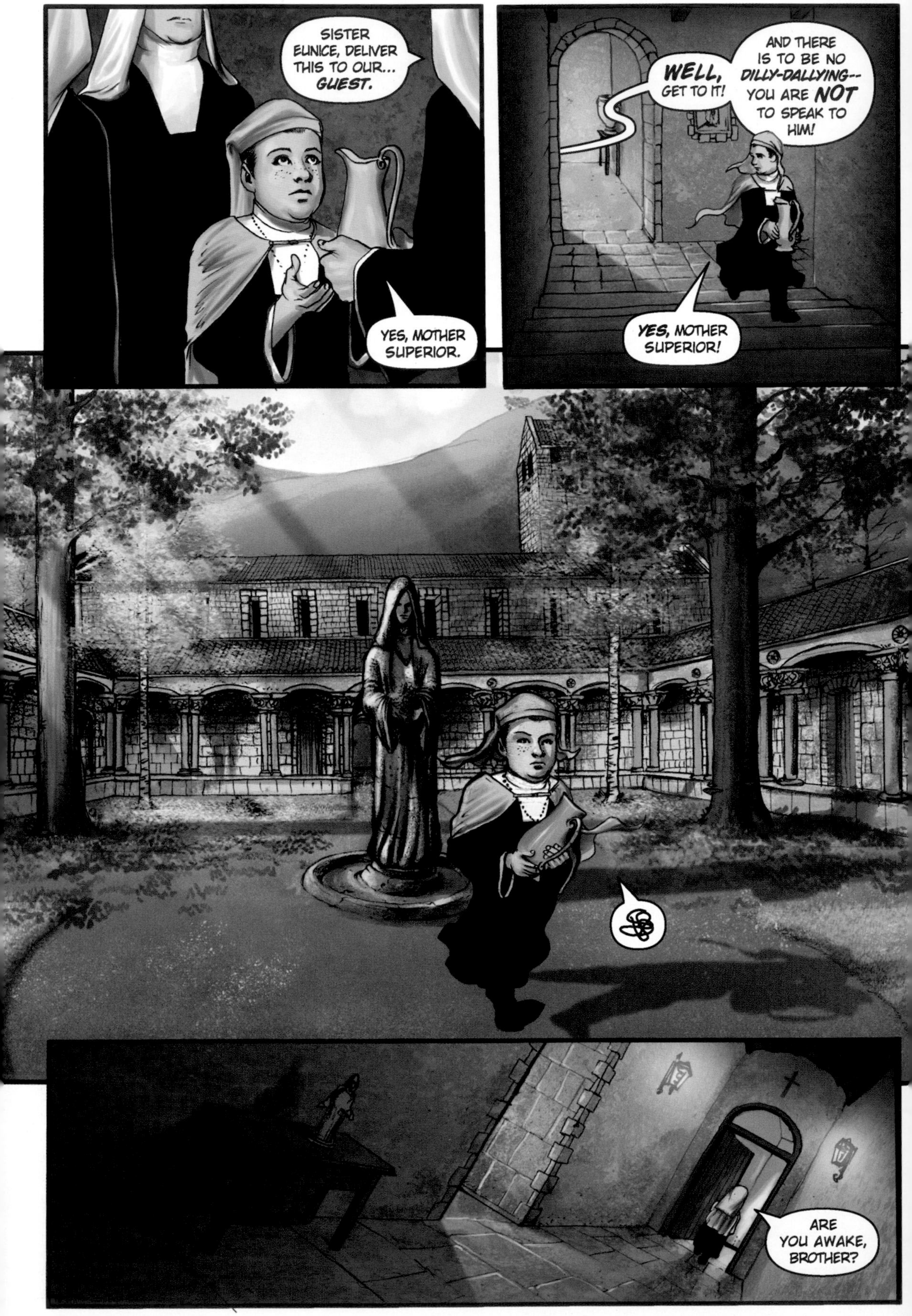
SISTER EUNICE, DELIVER THIS TO OUR... GUEST.
YES, MOTHER SUPERIOR.
WELL, GET TO IT!
AND THERE IS TO BE NO DILLY-DALLYING-- YOU ARE NOT TO SPEAK TO HIM!
YES, MOTHER SUPERIOR!
ARE YOU AWAKE, BROTHER?

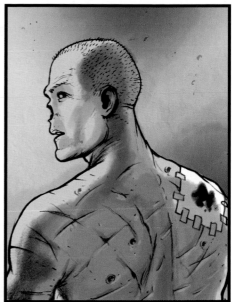

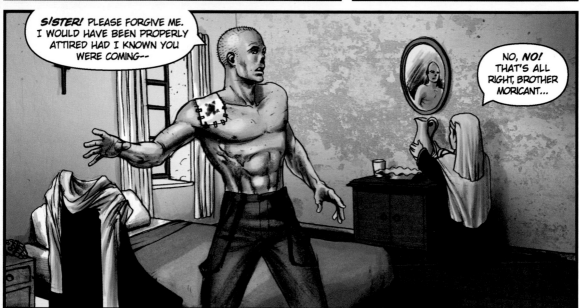

SISTER! PLEASE FORGIVE ME. I WOULD HAVE BEEN PROPERLY ATTIRED HAD I KNOWN YOU WERE COMING--

NO, NO! THAT'S ALL RIGHT, BROTHER MORICANT...

I ADMIT WE'RE NOT USED TO HAVING MEN HERE, ESPECIALLY NOT ONE AS...

...PHYSICALLY ENDOWED AS YOU.

AHH... YES. WELL...

I REALIZE YOU'RE TAKING AN ENORMOUS RISK, HIDING ME.

I WILL LEAVE AS SOON AS I'M ABLE.

YOU NEEDN'T CONCERN YOURSELF!

YOU HAVE TAKEN HOLY ORDERS, YOU ARE... DOING THE LORD'S WORK.

WE SISTERS HAVE A SACRED OBLIGATION TO AID OUR BROTHER IN CHRIST!

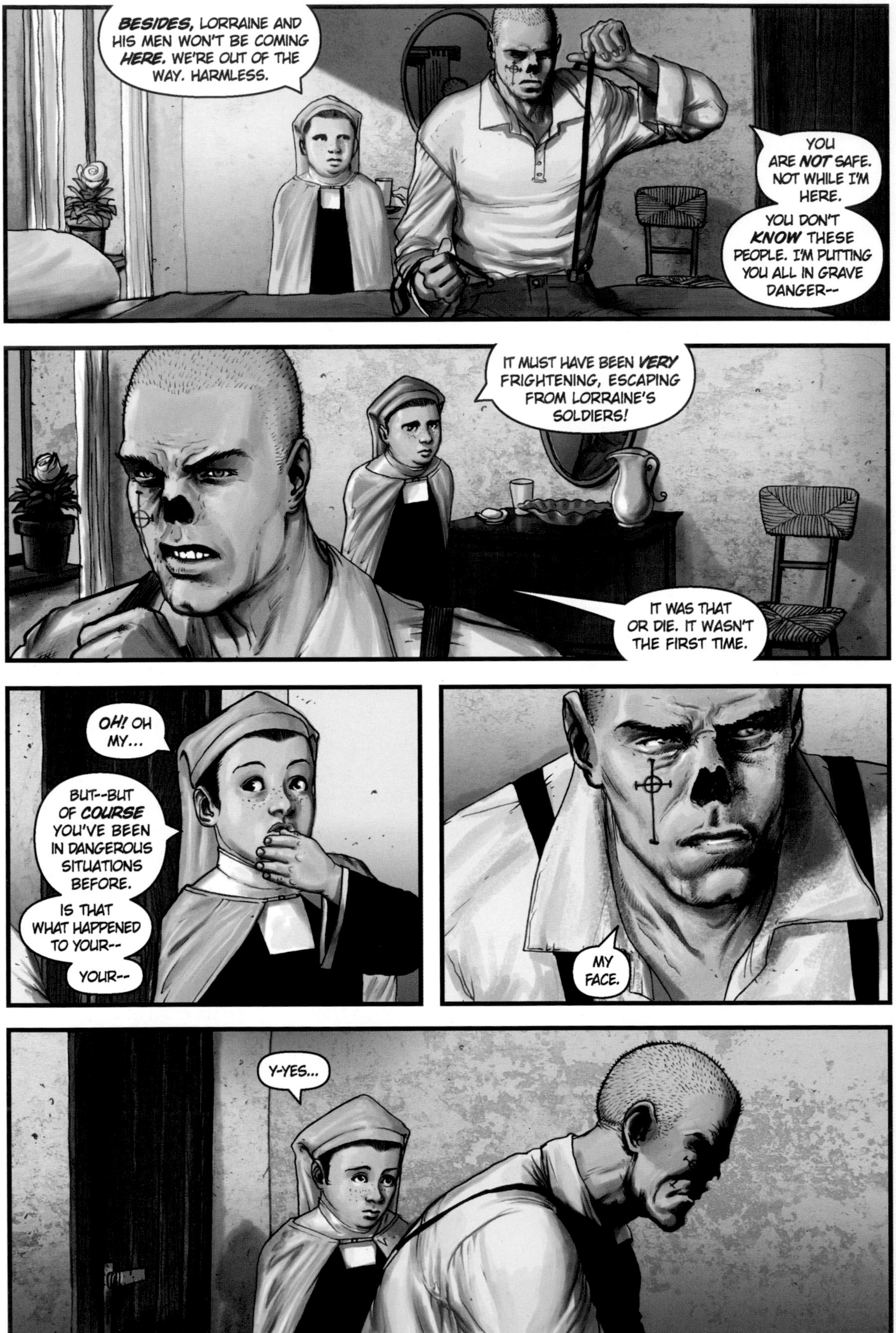
BESIDES, LORRAINE AND HIS MEN WON'T BE COMING HERE. WE'RE OUT OF THE WAY. HARMLESS.
YOU ARE NOT SAFE. NOT WHILE I'M HERE.
YOU DON'T KNOW THESE PEOPLE. I'M PUTTING YOU ALL IN GRAVE DANGER--
IT MUST HAVE BEEN VERY FRIGHTENING, ESCAPING FROM LORRAINE'S SOLDIERS!
IT WAS THAT OR DIE. IT WASN'T THE FIRST TIME.
OH! OH MY...
BUT--BUT OF COURSE YOU'VE BEEN IN DANGEROUS SITUATIONS BEFORE.
IS THAT WHAT HAPPENED TO YOUR--
YOUR--
MY FACE.
Y-YES...

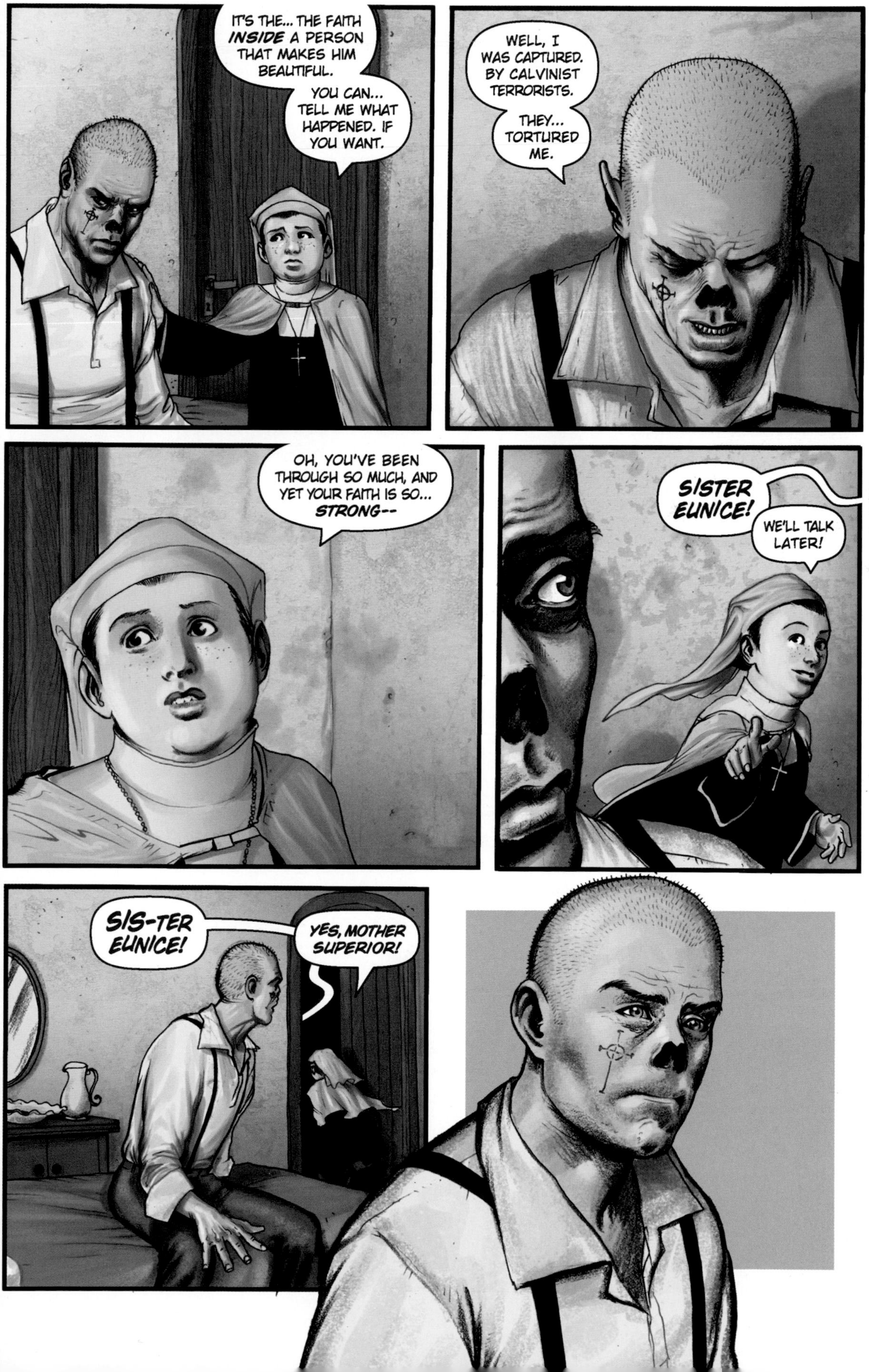
IT'S THE... THE FAITH INSIDE A PERSON THAT MAKES HIM BEAUTIFUL.
YOU CAN... TELL ME WHAT HAPPENED. IF YOU WANT.
WELL, I WAS CAPTURED. BY CALVINIST TERRORISTS.
THEY... TORTURED ME.
OH, YOU'VE BEEN THROUGH SO MUCH, AND YET YOUR FAITH IS SO... STRONG--
SISTER EUNICE!
WE'LL TALK LATER!
SIS-TER EUNICE!
YES, MOTHER SUPERIOR!

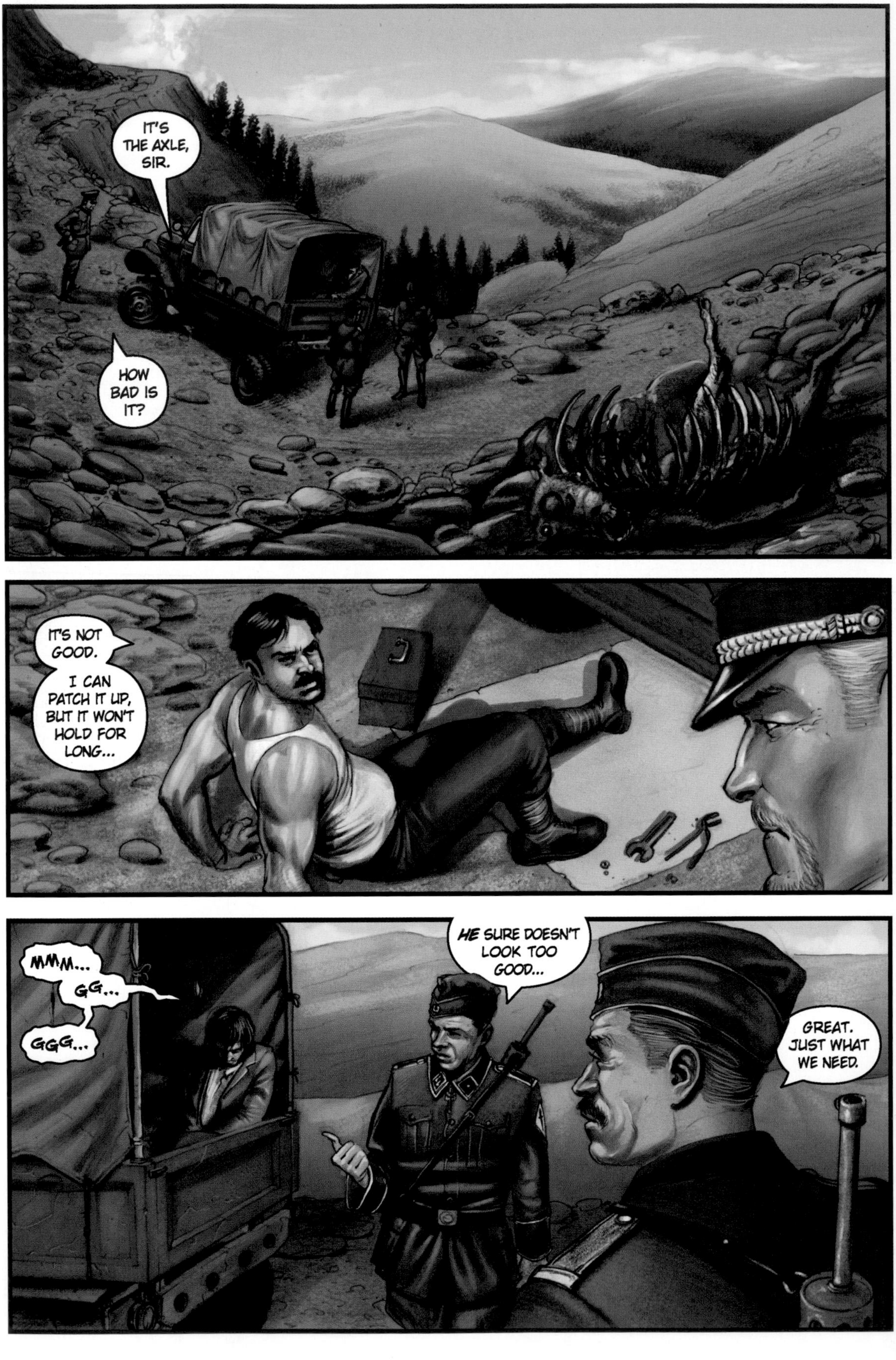
IT'S THE AXLE, SIR.
HOW BAD IS IT?
IT'S NOT GOOD.
I CAN PATCH IT UP, BUT IT WON'T HOLD FOR LONG...
MMM... GG... GGG...
HE SURE DOESN'T LOOK TOO GOOD...
GREAT. JUST WHAT WE NEED.

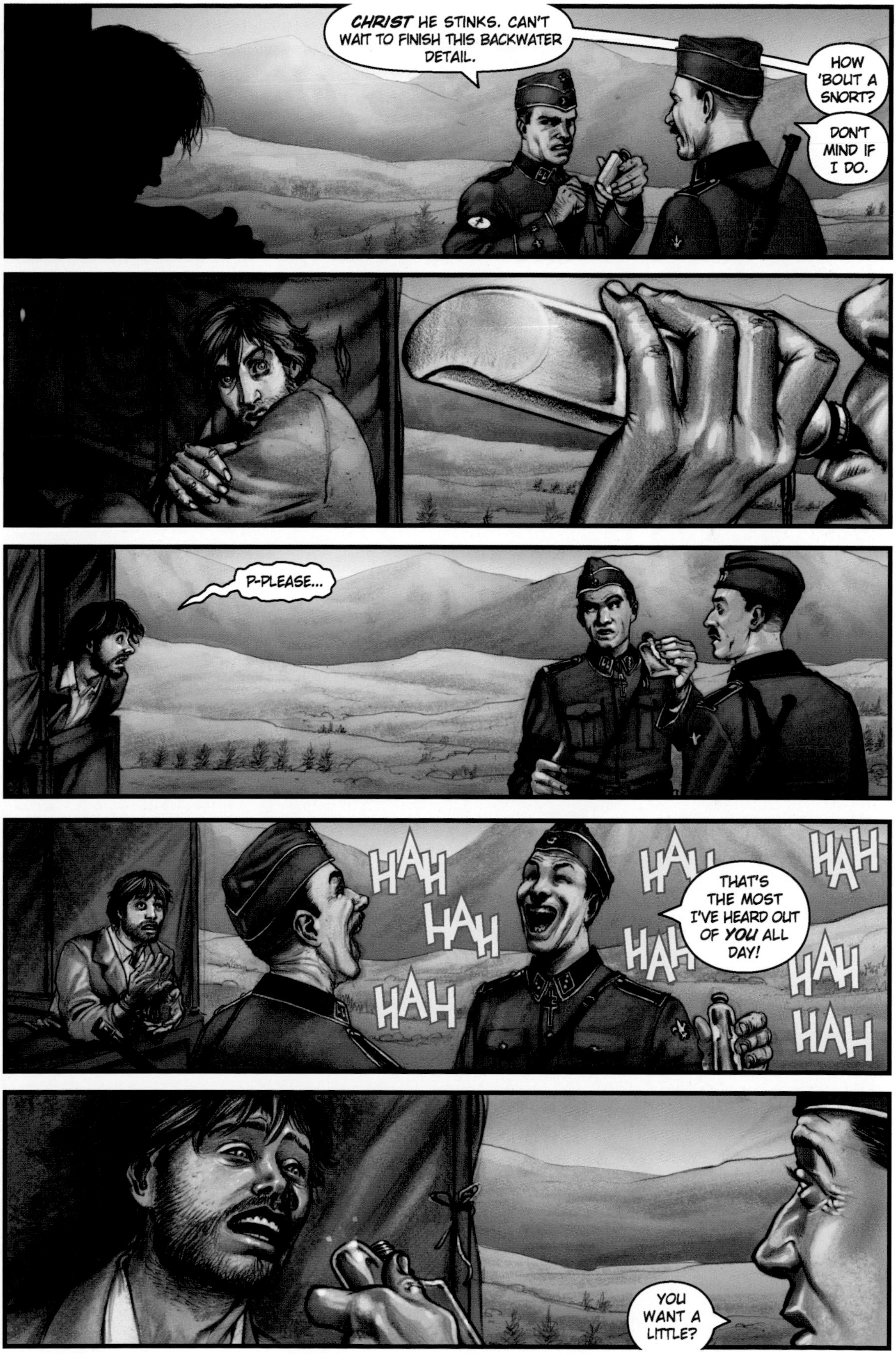
CHRIST HE STINKS. CAN'T WAIT TO FINISH THIS BACKWATER DETAIL.
HOW 'BOUT A SNORT?
DON'T MIND IF I DO.
P-PLEASE...
HAH HAH HAH
HAH HAH HAH HAH HAH HAH
THAT'S THE MOST I'VE HEARD OUT OF YOU ALL DAY!
YOU WANT A LITTLE?

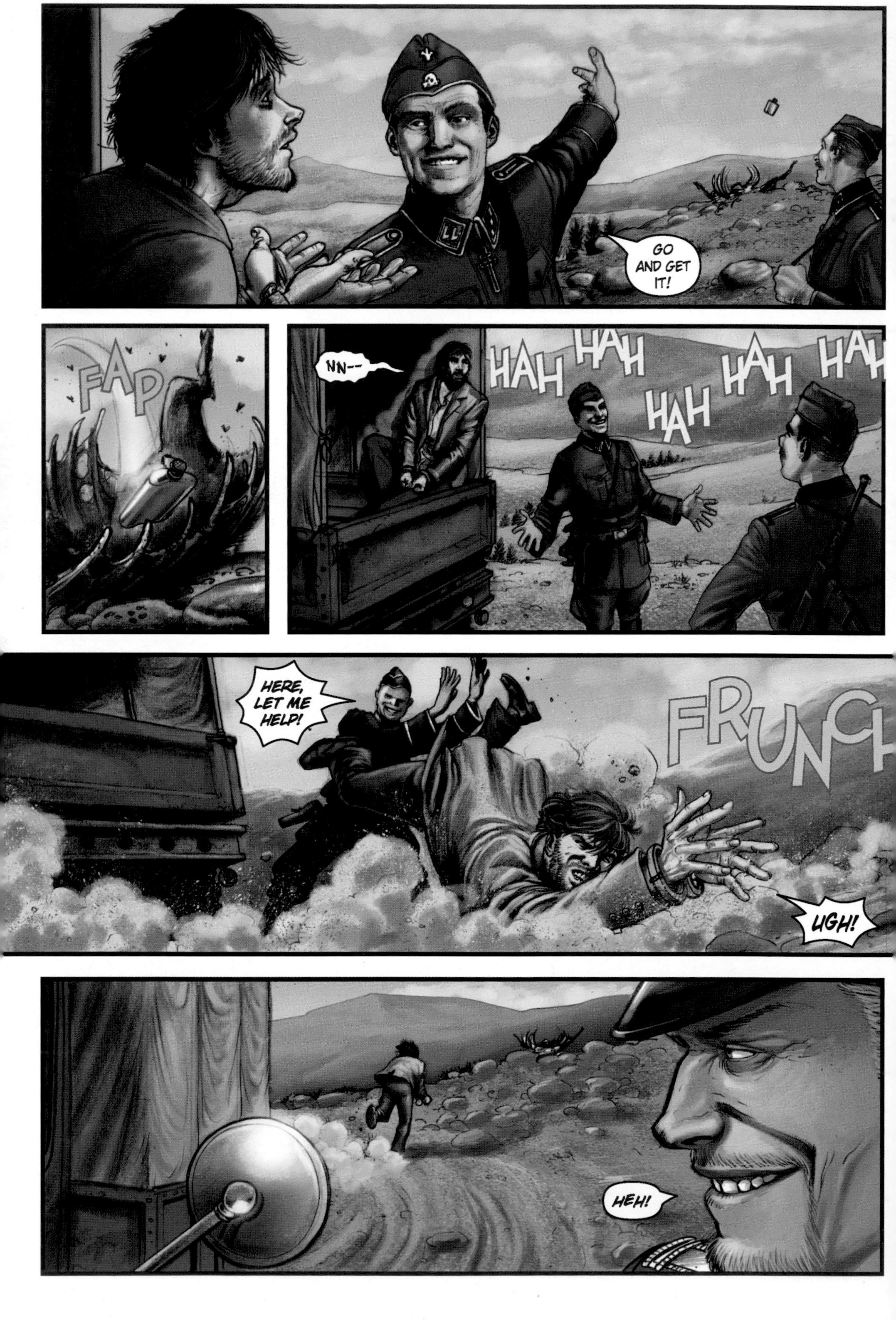
GO AND GET IT!
FAP
NN--
HAH HAH HAH HAH HAH HAH
HERE, LET ME HELP!
FRUNCH
UGH!
HEH!

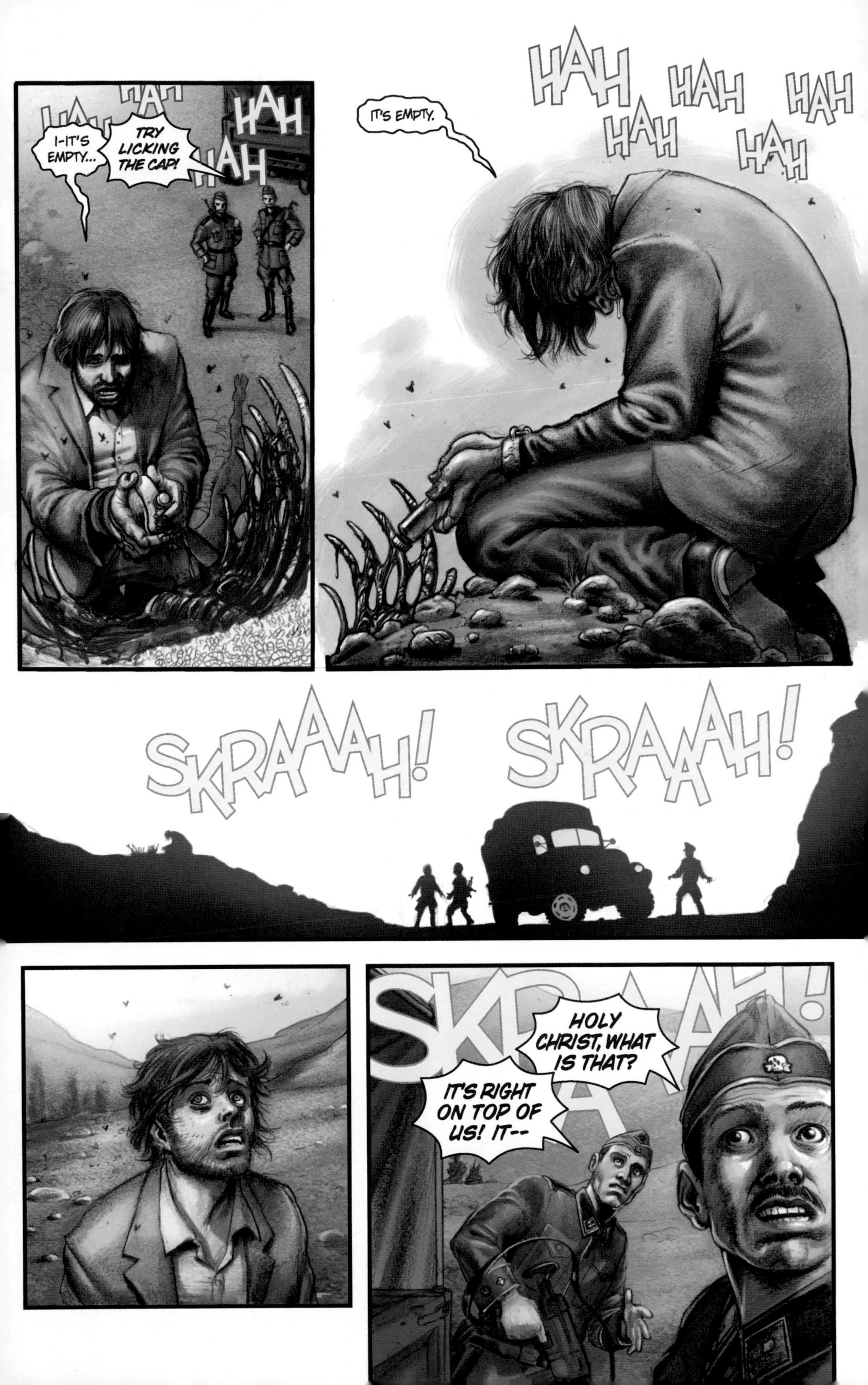
HAH
HAH
HAH
HAH
I-IT'S EMPTY...
TRY LICKING THE CAP!
IT'S EMPTY.
HAH HAH HAH
HAH HAH
SKRAAAH! SKRAAAH!
SKRAAAH!
HOLY CHRIST, WHAT IS THAT?
IT'S RIGHT ON TOP OF US! IT--

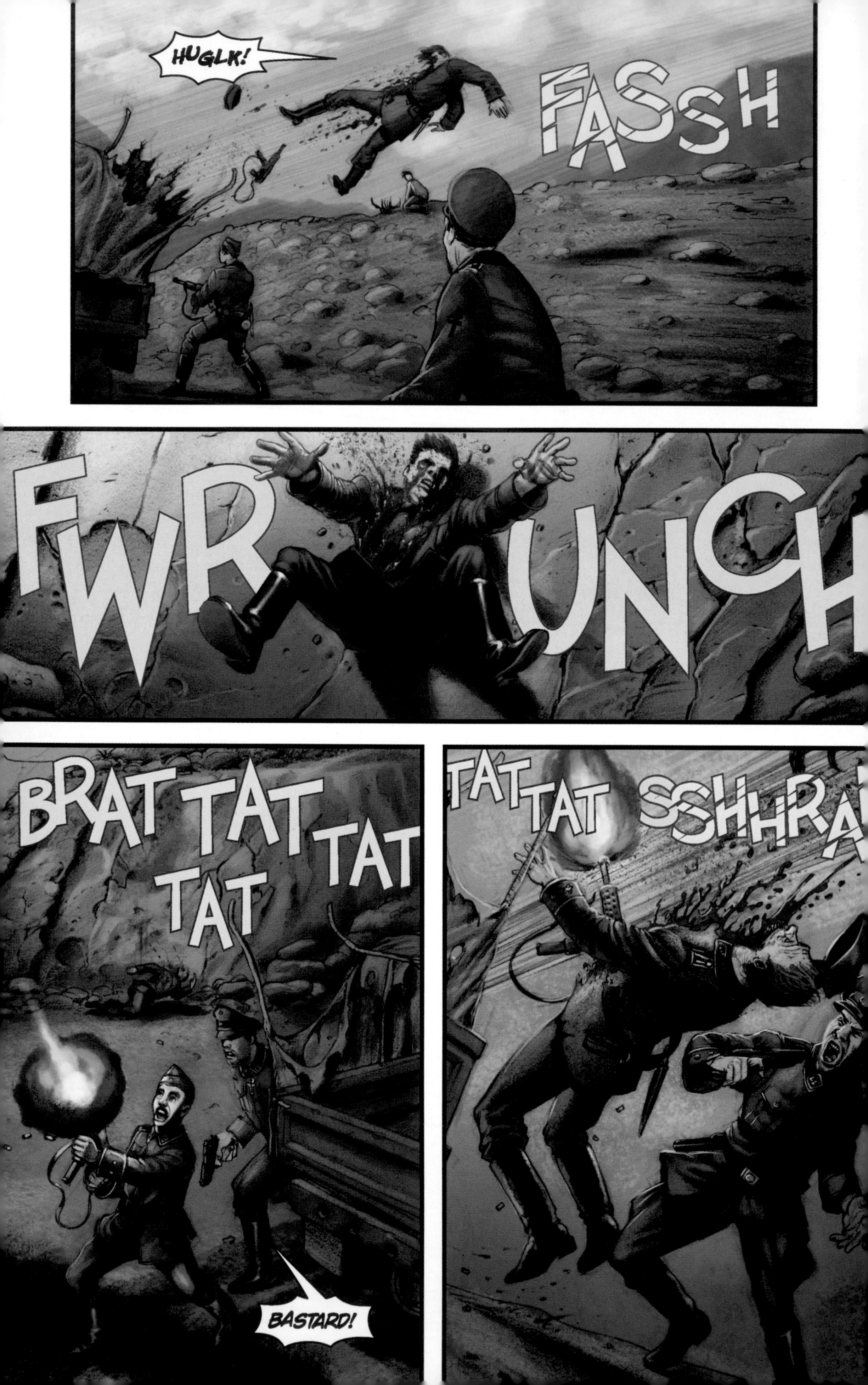
HUGLK!
FASSH
FWRUNCH
BRAT TAT TAT TAT
BASTARD!
TAT TAT SSHHRA

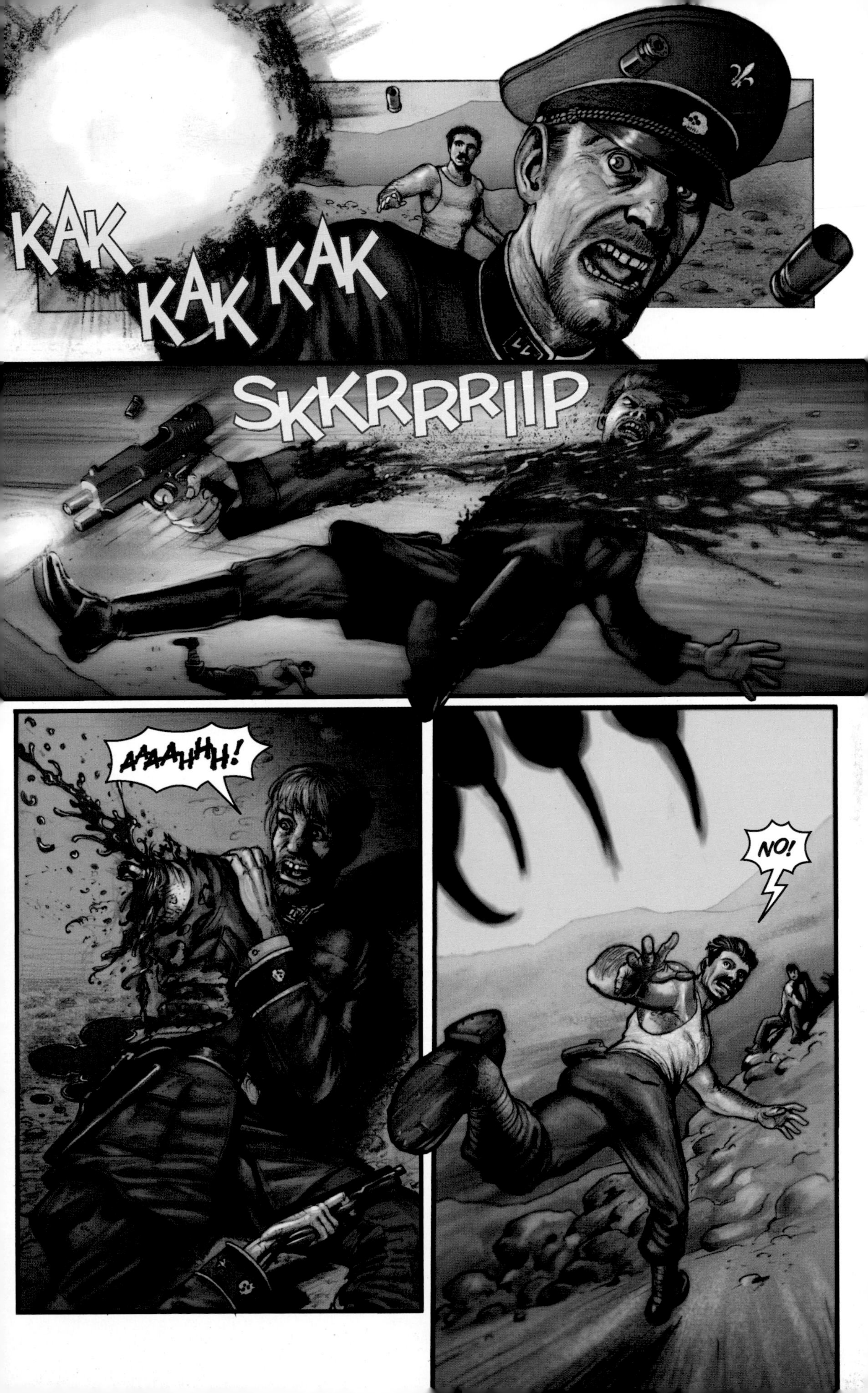
KAK
KAK KAK
SKKRRRIIP
AAAAHHH!
NO!

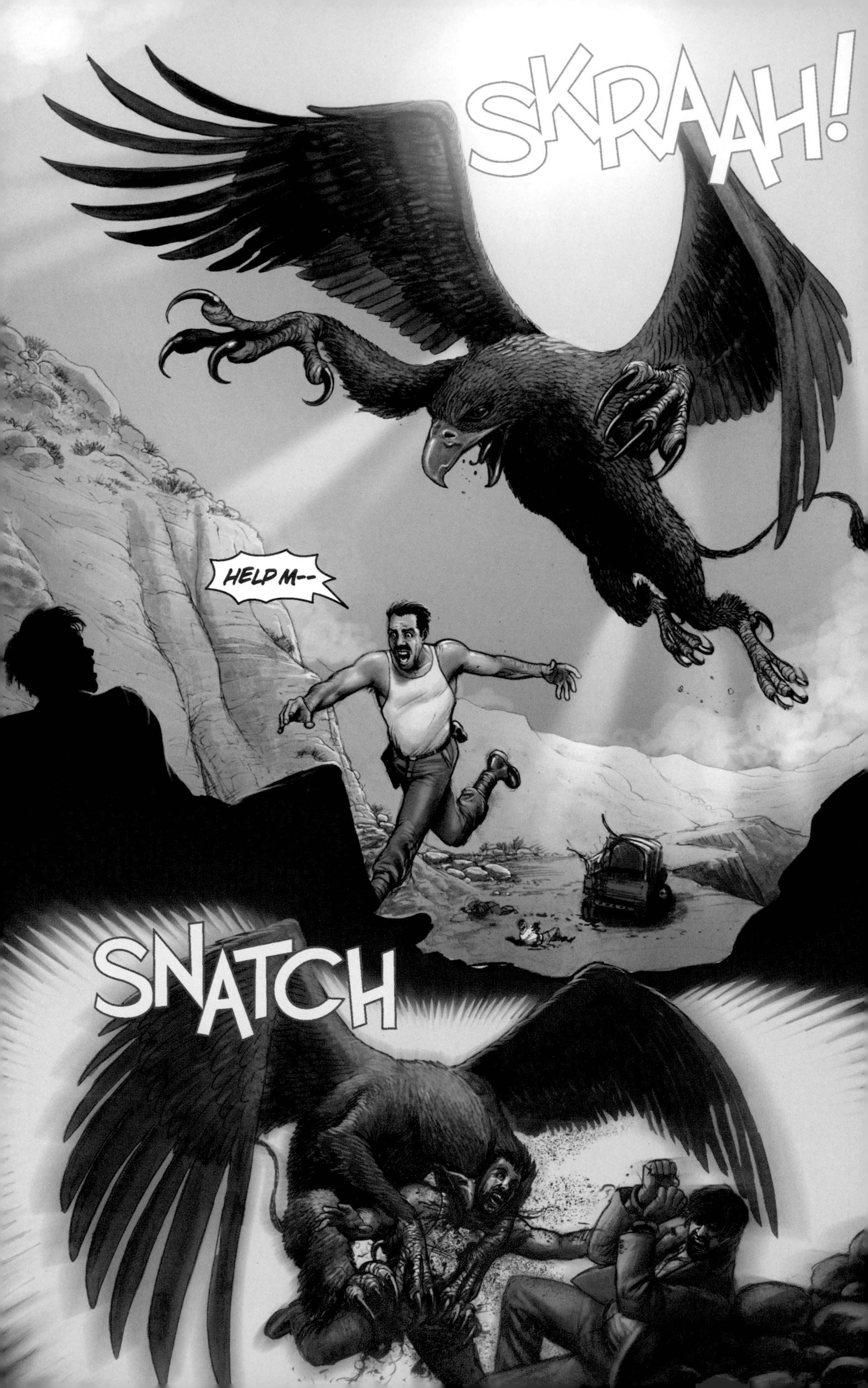
SKRAAH!
HELP M--
SNATCH

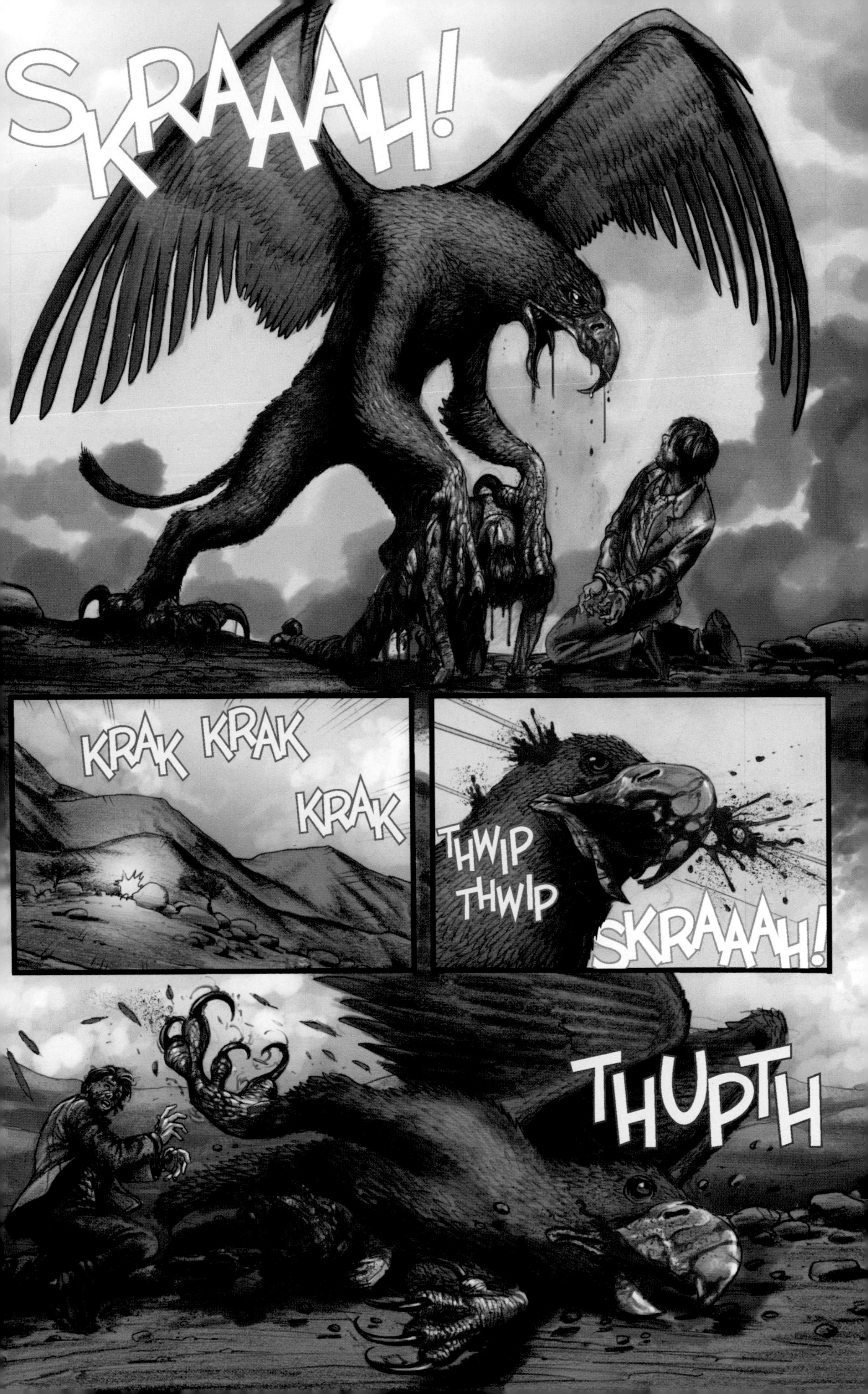
SKRAAAH!
KRAK KRAK
KRAK
THWIP
THWIP
SKRAAAH!
THUPTH

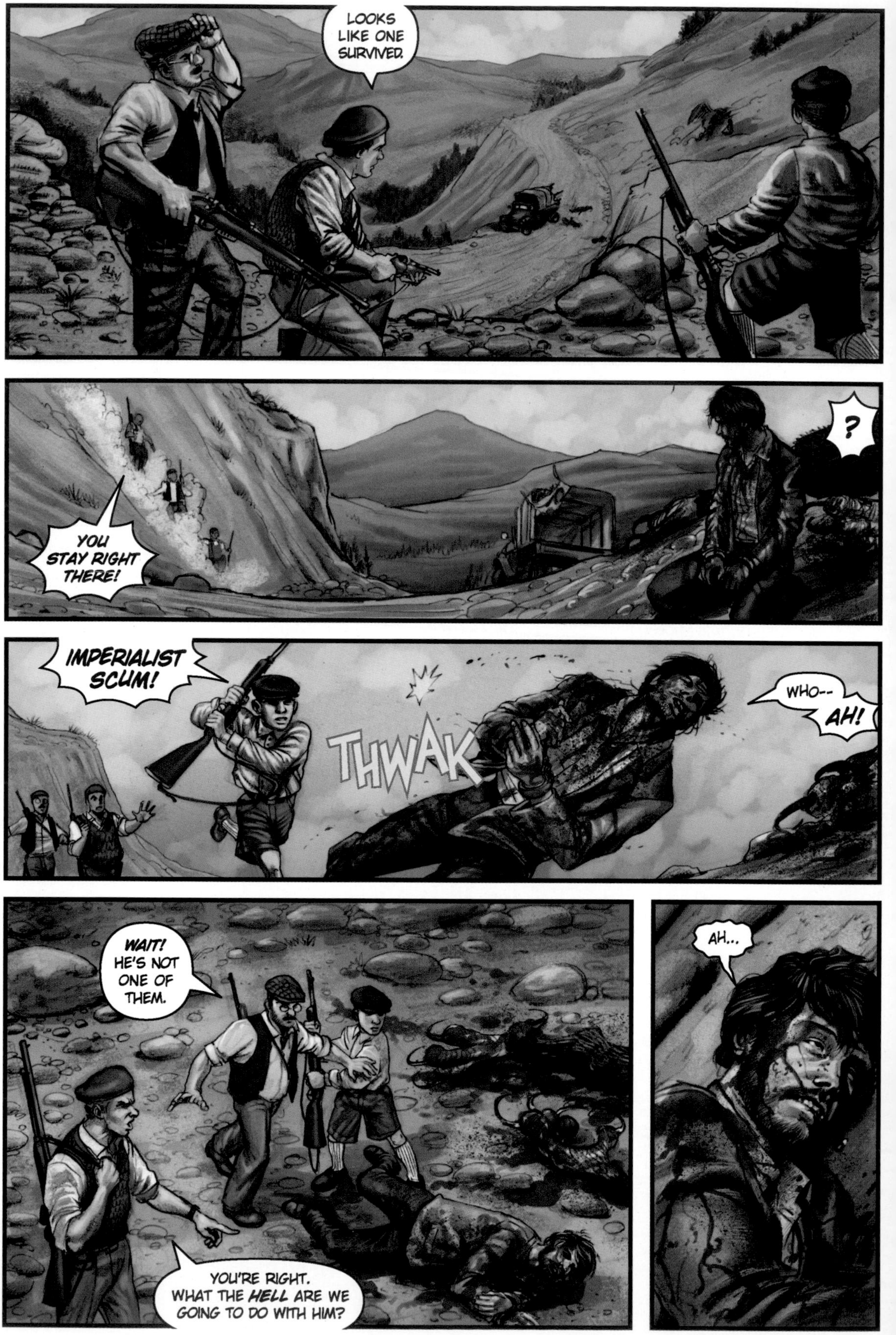
LOOKS LIKE ONE SURVIVED.
YOU STAY RIGHT THERE!
?
IMPERIALIST SCUM!
THWAK
WHO-- AH!
WAIT! HE'S NOT ONE OF THEM.
YOU'RE RIGHT. WHAT THE HELL ARE WE GOING TO DO WITH HIM?
AH...

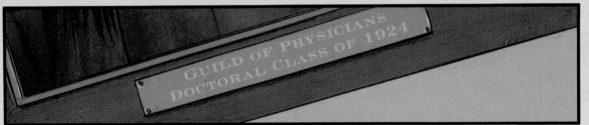

GUILD OF PHYSICIANS
DOCTORAL CLASS OF 1924

WE'RE DEPARTING WITHIN AN HOUR, DR. TOURNON.

I'LL BE READY!

JULIEN...

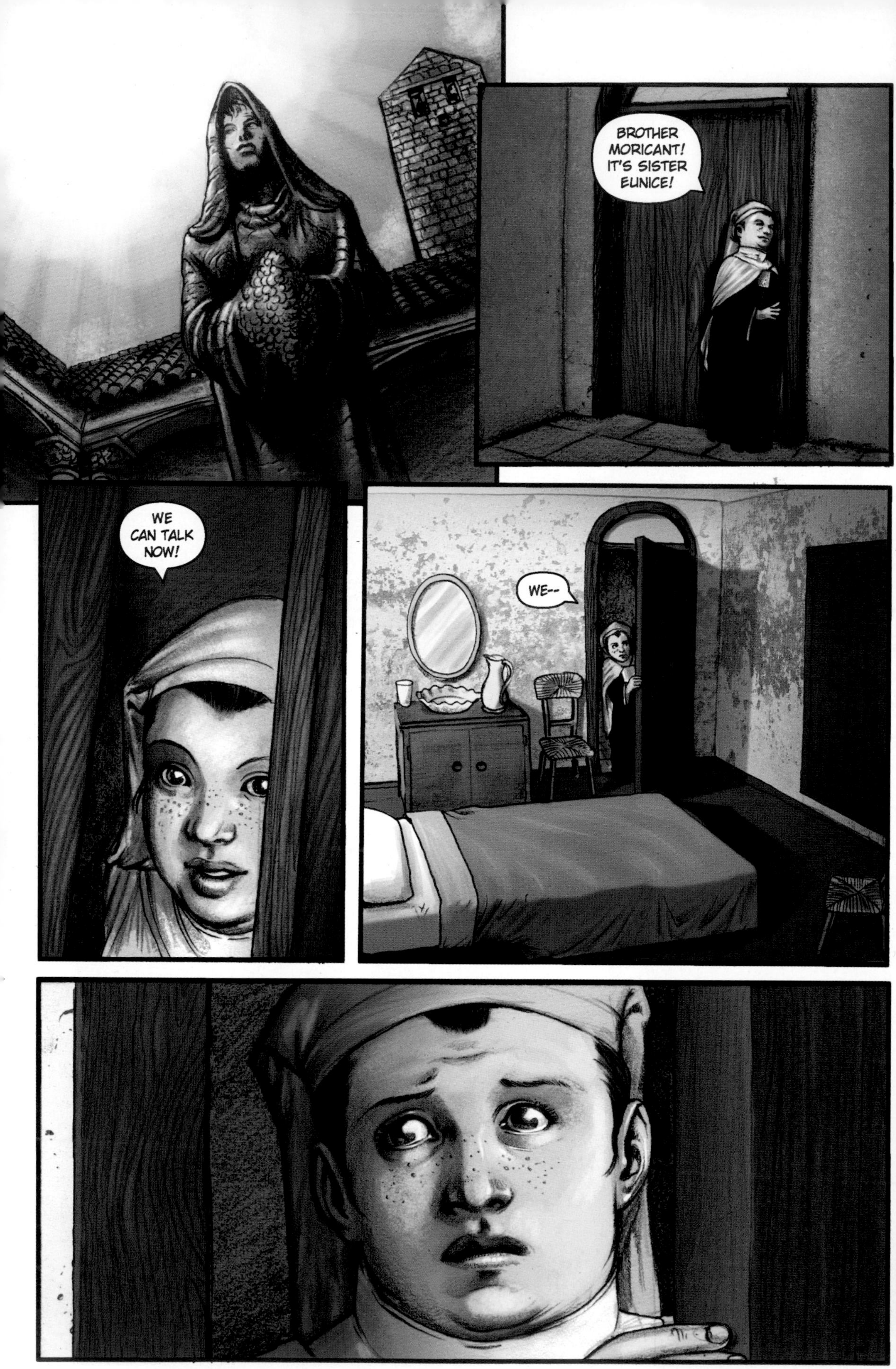
BROTHER MORICANT! IT'S SISTER EUNICE!
WE CAN TALK NOW!
WE--

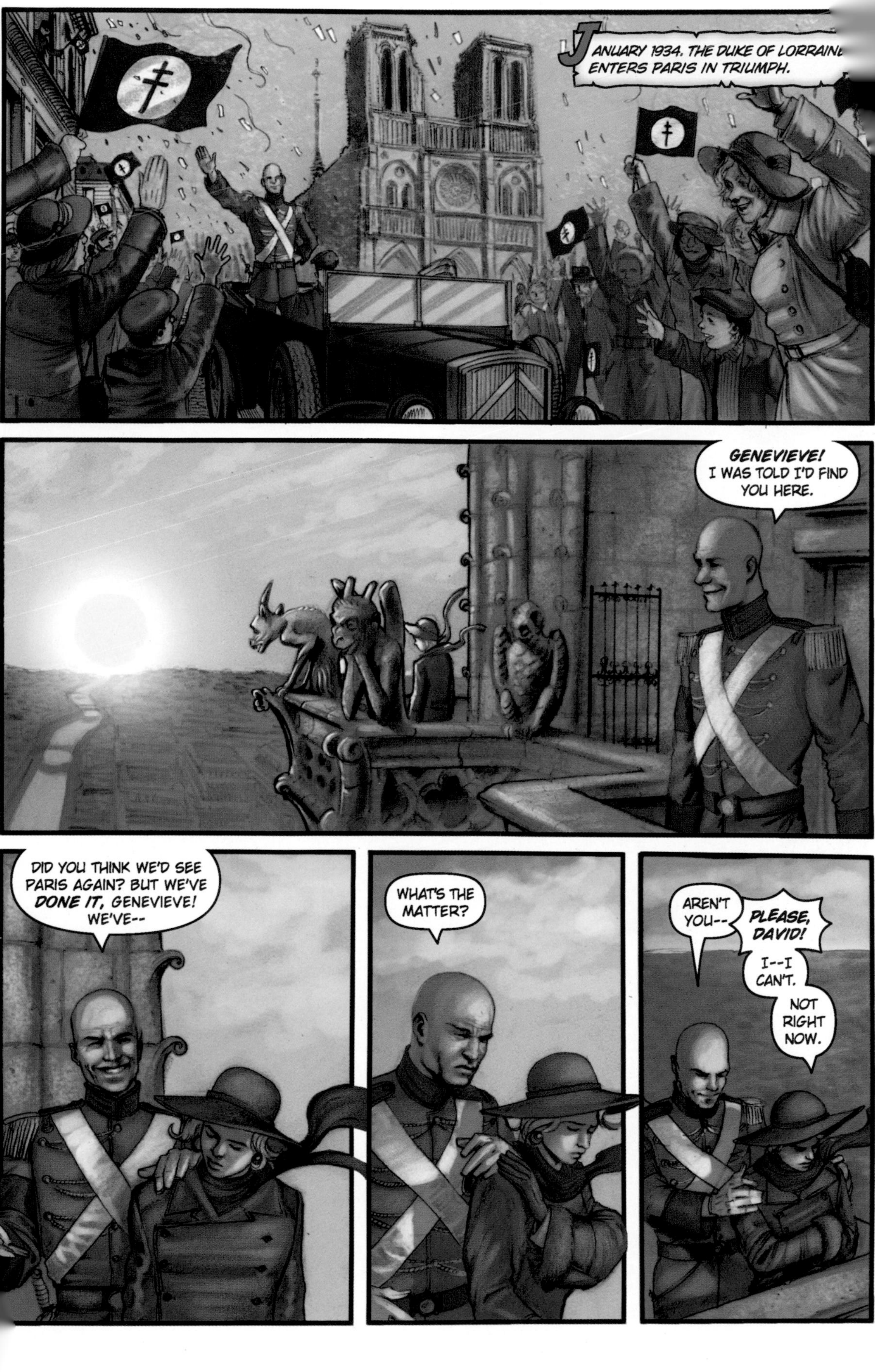
JANUARY 1934. THE DUKE OF LORRAINE ENTERS PARIS IN TRIUMPH.
GENEVIEVE! I WAS TOLD I'D FIND YOU HERE.
DID YOU THINK WE'D SEE PARIS AGAIN? BUT WE'VE DONE IT, GENEVIEVE! WE'VE--
WHAT'S THE MATTER?
AREN'T YOU--
PLEASE, DAVID!
I--I CAN'T.
NOT RIGHT NOW.

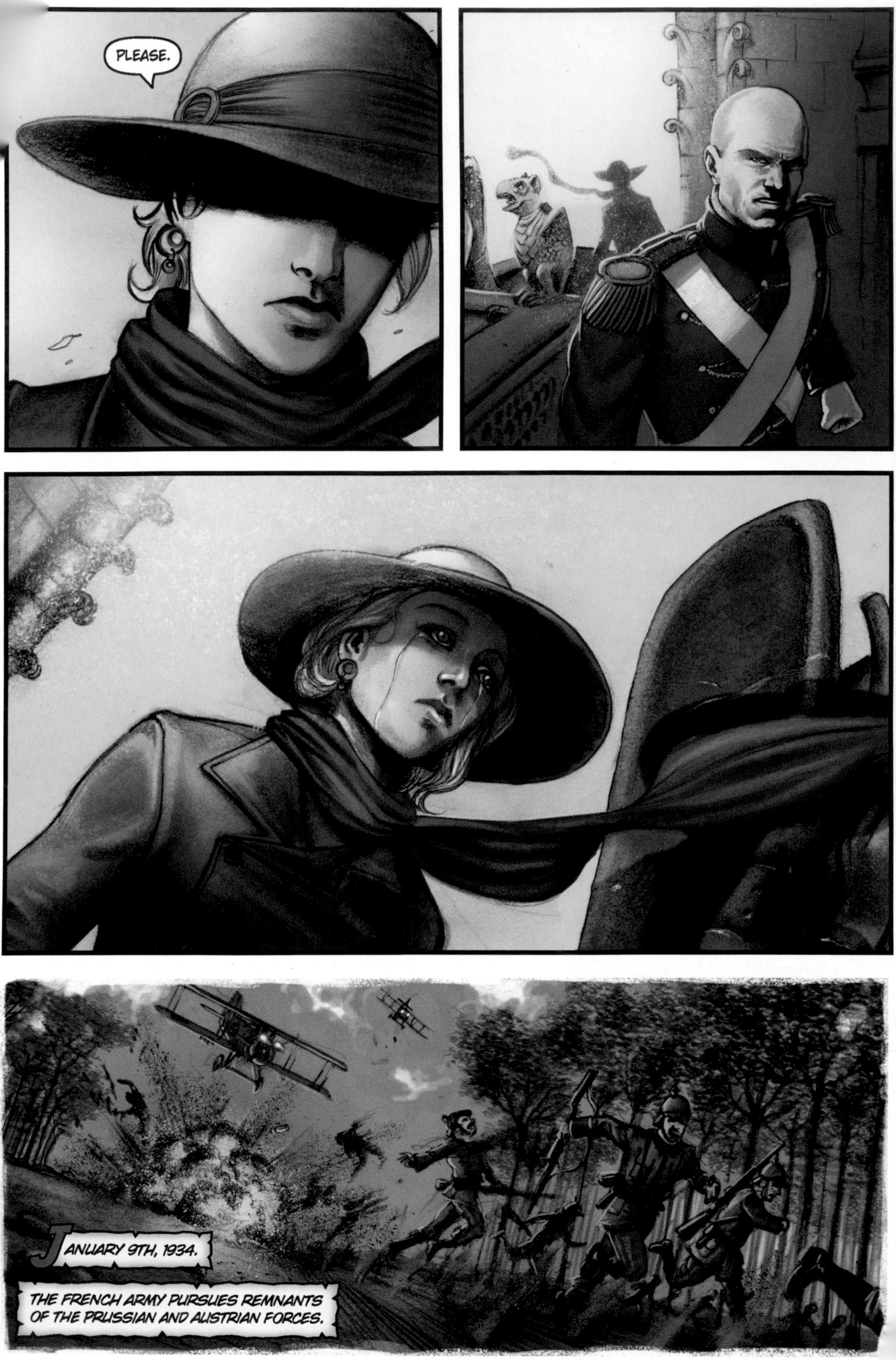
PLEASE.
JANUARY 9TH, 1934.
THE FRENCH ARMY PURSUES REMNANTS OF THE PRUSSIAN AND AUSTRIAN FORCES.

Le Journal de la Liberté

Paris's leading anglophone newspaper • vol. 205, no. 146 • Jan. 6, MCMXXXIII

Editors in Chief: M. Michael Richardson, M. Scott Allie, M. Ryan Jorgensen. **Story Editor:** M. Arvid Nelson. **Art Editor:** M. Juan Ferreyra. **Photography Editor:** M. Eugène Atget. **Layout Supervisor:** M. Gary Grazzini. **Editors Emeritus:** M. Clark A. Smith, M. Howard P. Lovecraft, M. Robert E. Howard. *Le Journal de la Liberté* is printed under the benign auspices of his eminence David-Louis Plantard de St. Clair, Duke of Lorraine and First Consul of the Empire of France.

Official seal of the First Consul

⚜ GOD SAVE LORD LORRAINE ⚜

GERMANS IN DISARRAY AS FRENCH GIVE CHASE INTO FLANDERS, ALPS

Prussians Face Worsening Second Front in Pomerania • Revolutions Erupt in Holy Roman Empire

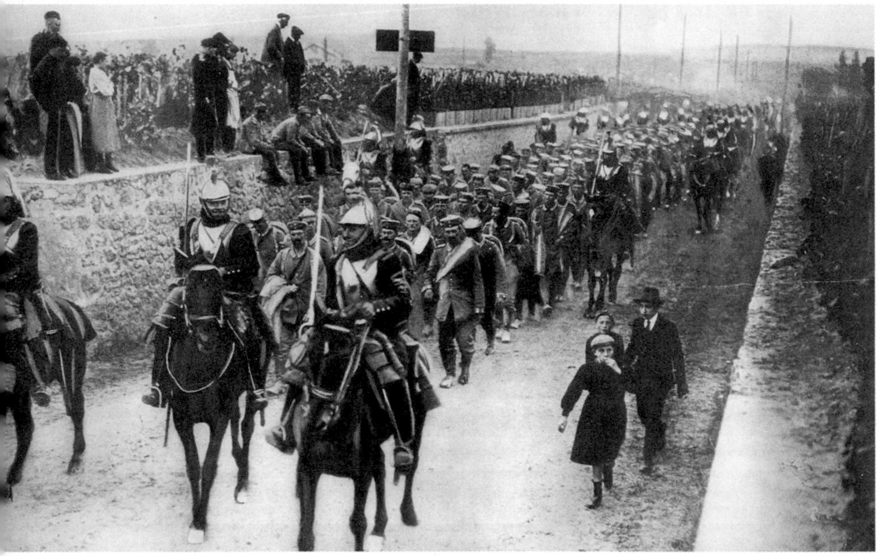

French cuirassiers escort Prussian prisoners of war near Lille.

The Western Front, Duchy of Lorraine – "We expect to take Brussels within days," the Duke of Orleans, commander of the French forces chasing the beleaguered Prussian army across France, said. "We'll keep pushing until we reach the Rhine."

Lord Orleans refused to comment on what he might do once on the threshold of the German homeland. "I wouldn't discount a push for Berlin itself," he said.

Such a statement would have been unthinkable a few weeks ago. Lord Lorraine, supreme commander of the French war effort, was huddled in the fortress-city of Carcassonne with his shattered army, awaiting what seemed like virtually guaranteed annihilation by a much larger combined Prussian and Austrian host surrounding him.

But a second French army, led by Orleans himself, was rushing from the south to launch a surprise attack on the Germans.

Orleans was flush with victory in the Iberian Peninsula. His army eradicated the Cordovan Emirate, ending over 1,200 years of Islamic rule in Western Europe.

Orleans arrived for the surprise attack against the Germans with little time to spare.

"A few more days, and we would have been done for," the Duke of Nevers, who was with Lorraine in Carcassonne, said. Lorraine's army was battered and demoralized after a devastating loss on the outskirts of Paris. But Lord Lorraine is known for his tenacity and surprise tactics.

"Lorraine's plan for the surprise attack was the last thing the Germans were expecting, a strategy worthy of Alexander himself," Orleans said.

However, the plan was thrown into disarray when British forces supporting Lord Lorraine pulled out of the fight.

"We were counting on the British. Without them, the surprise attack was a desperate ploy," a source close to Lorraine said.

Lord Orleans said the success of the surprise attack was "nothing short of a miracle."

"The odds just kept piling up against us," he said. "But what we lacked in numbers, we made up for in morale, discipline, and will to fight. Our soldiers are the best in Europe, in the world."

The combined armies of Prussia and the Holy Roman Empire, themselves depleted by a dogged march through France, were caught completely off guard by the assault on their poorly guarded rear.

"There are times when superior numbers can actually be a hindrance. The more massive an army, the more sluggish it is to respond to unexpected tactical developments," Gen. Batiste Millrand, one of Lorraine's top commanders, said.

"We smashed them."

The Prussian and Austrian armies now find themselves in much the same position Lorraine was in only weeks earlier – on the run, and completely disorganized.

"The Prussians are desperately trying to reorganize themselves for a push back through the Flanders Plain, but we're hounding them relentlessly," Orleans said.

"We're chasing the Austrians into the Alps. Soon we'll quite literally have them between a rock and a hard place," The Duke of Nevers said.

Elizabeth II, the British monarch, dispatched an envoy to Paris to congratulate Lord Lorraine.

"Her Majesty trusts Lord Lorraine understands armistice with the Prussians was the only salient course of action for Britain," Sir Winston Churchill, a spokesman for the British Crown, said.

But prospects for reconciliation seem remote. "The abandonment of the British at Carcassonne was extremely unfortunate," a spokesperson for Lorraine said. "We're exploring all our options to determine the appropriate response."

Lord Lorraine refused to see the English envoy. ⚜

Notice to Readers

The editorial staff of *Le Journal de la Liberté* imposed by the Prussian occupiers will retain their positions, as they have elected to comply with all of Lord Lorraine's editorial dictates. Lord Lorraine thanks the editors for their political complicity. This newspaper will resume publication with the highest standards of journalistic integrity.

Latest Wartime Developments

Troubles Multiply for Prussia, Holy Roman Empire

Prussia and Austria-Hungary's military and political fortunes hemorrhage daily, with no end in sight.

While French troops "vigorously pursue" what remains of Prussia's western forces, Russian troops have occupied much of East Prussia, including the vital Baltic port of Danzig, in the east.

"They're getting squeezed on both ends," the Duke of Nevers, a close confidant of the Duke of Lorraine, said.

"The Russian army is like a locomotive – slow to get going, but impossible to halt once it's underway. And now it's gathering speed," said Col. Ferand Sabouret, a Russian specialist at the École Militaire in Fontainebleau.

Prussian military planners had relied on the Teutonic Knights to blunt the Russian offensive, but the medieval order, responsible for much of the Baltic coastline in the eastern hinterlands of the Prussian Empire, has crumbled in the face of the Russian advance.

"They were also counting on a quick knockout blow in France, but the tables have really turned," Sabouret said.

"If the situation doesn't change dramatically in the coming weeks, they may well consider armistice negotiations with us," a source within Lord Lorraine's senior advisory said.

If Prussia is being crushed by outside forces, the Holy Roman Empire is being torn apart from within.

Emperor Rudolph of the Holy Roman Empire (HRE) is faced with widespread internal disorder. Revolts are flaring everywhere from Bohemia to Italy to Serbia.

Russian forces are reportedly aiding Serbian rebels, while Italian nationalists receive military support from the French.

"France supports the rights of the Holy Roman Empire's Italian subjects to self-determination," a spokesperson for the Duke of Lorraine said.

The HRE's decision to go to war with its longtime ally Prussia against Russia and France was unpopular with its ethnically diverse subjects.

"Many of the HRE's constituents view the Habsburg emperors as foreign tyrants," Lord Nevers said.

The devastating rout of Austrian forces outside Carcassonne caused a mass exodus of support for Emperor Rudolf amongst the HRE's restless populations.

Whether Emperor Rudolf still has the military might to force his sprawling, polyglot empire together is an open question. Members of the provincial Hungarian and Bohemian legislators have passed resolutions calling for his abdication.

"It's entirely possible we're looking at the end of the Habsburg dynasty," Lord Nevers said.

It would only be one in a growing list of casualties wrought by the ever-expanding war.

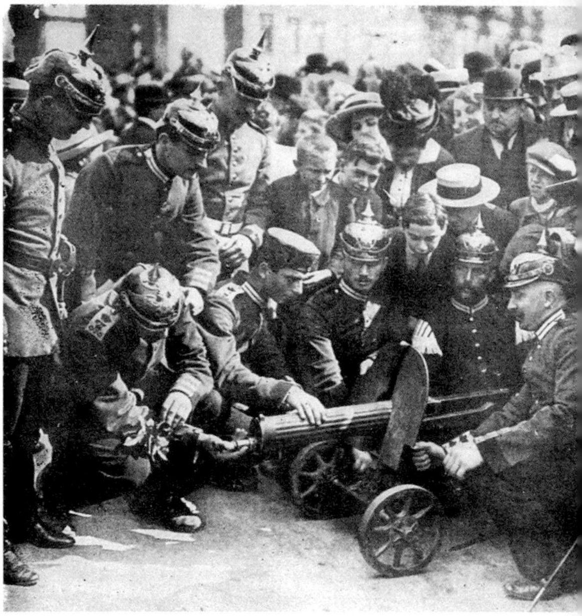

Prussian soldiers inspect a Russian machine gun captured during fighting in Pomerania. Prussian defenses are buckling under the Russian onslaught.

THE AXIS: Greater France · The Russian Empire

THE ALLIES: The Prussian Empire · The Holy Roman Empire · The Ottoman Empire

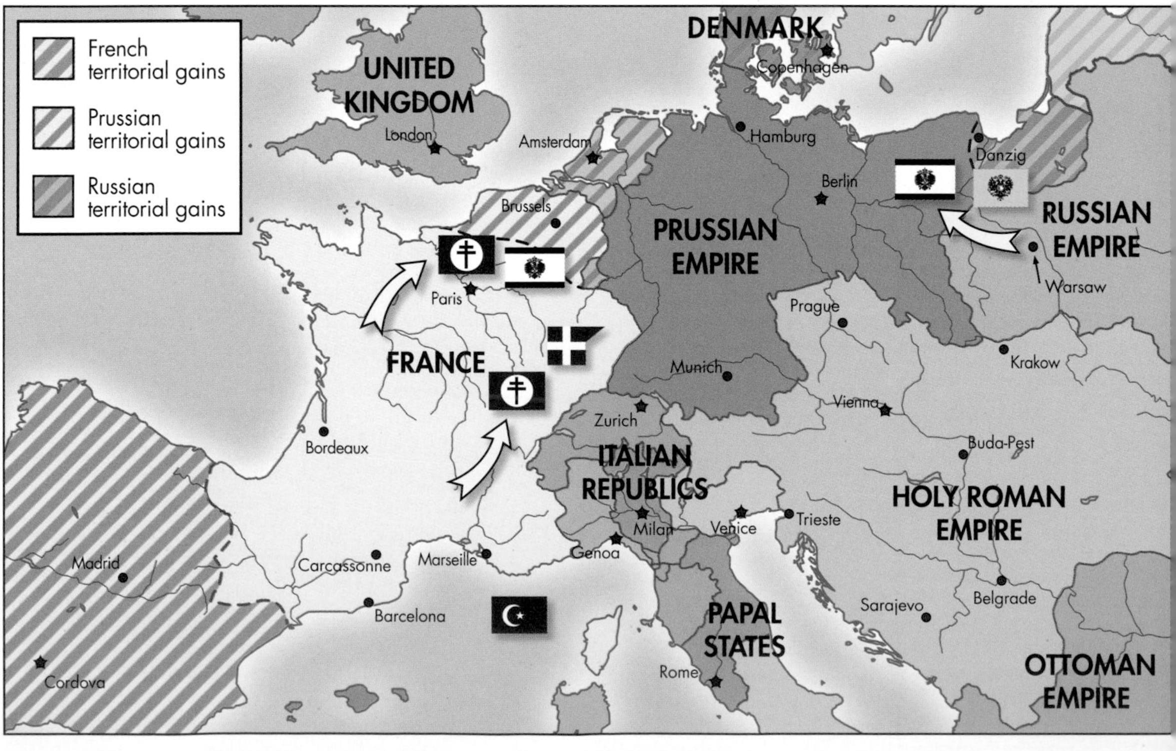
French territorial gains
Prussian territorial gains
Russian territorial gains
DENMARK
Copenhagen
UNITED KINGDOM
London
Amsterdam
Hamburg
Danzig
Berlin
Brussels
RUSSIAN EMPIRE
PRUSSIAN EMPIRE
Warsaw
Paris
Prague
Krakow
FRANCE
Munich
Vienna
Zurich
Bordeaux
Buda-Pest
ITALIAN REPUBLICS
HOLY ROMAN EMPIRE
Milan
Venice
Trieste
Madrid
Carcassonne
Marseille
Genoa
Belgrade
Sarajevo
Barcelona
PAPAL STATES
Rome
Cordova
OTTOMAN EMPIRE

CHAPTER FOUR
THE SECRET VALLEY

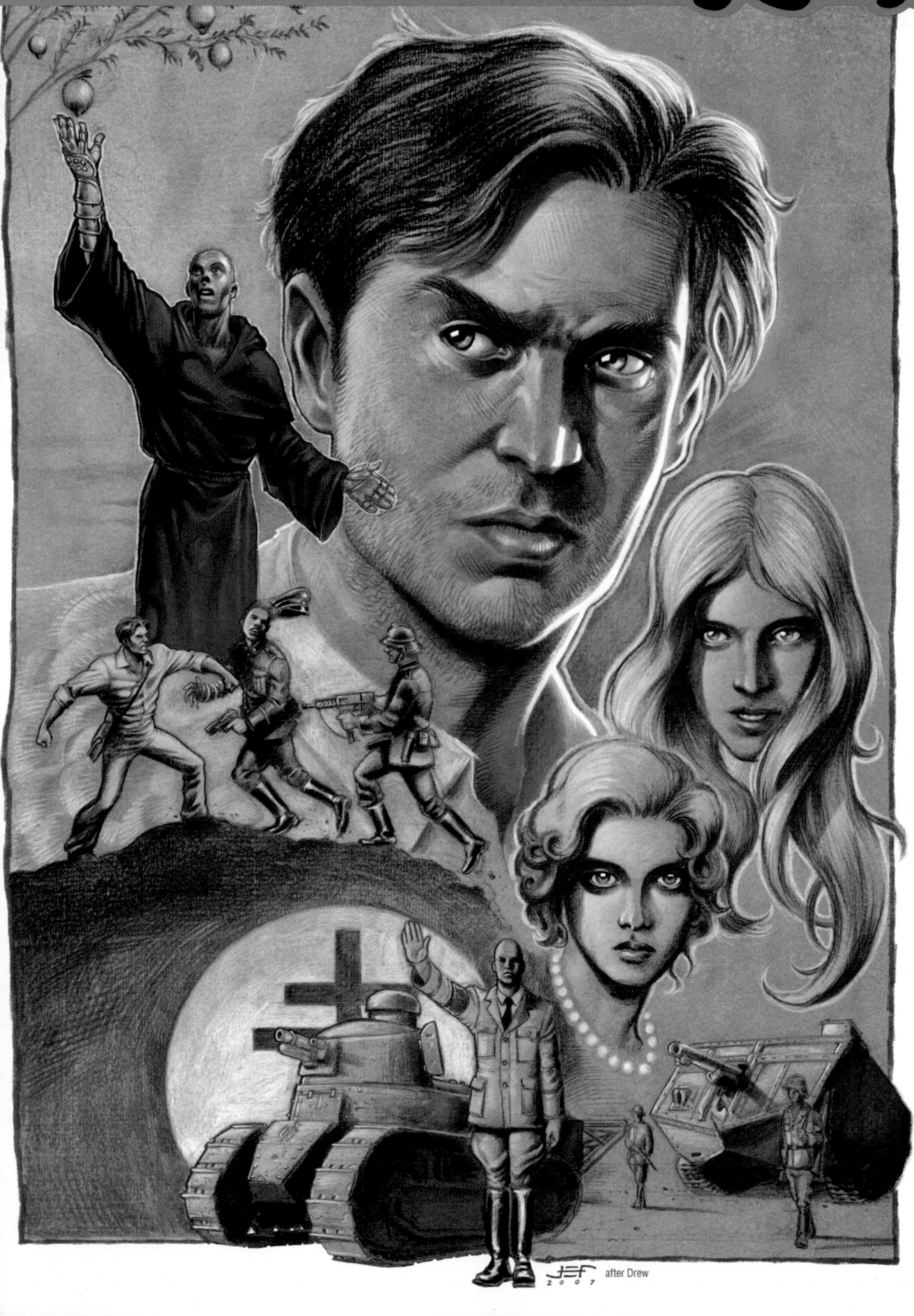
JEF 2007 after Drew

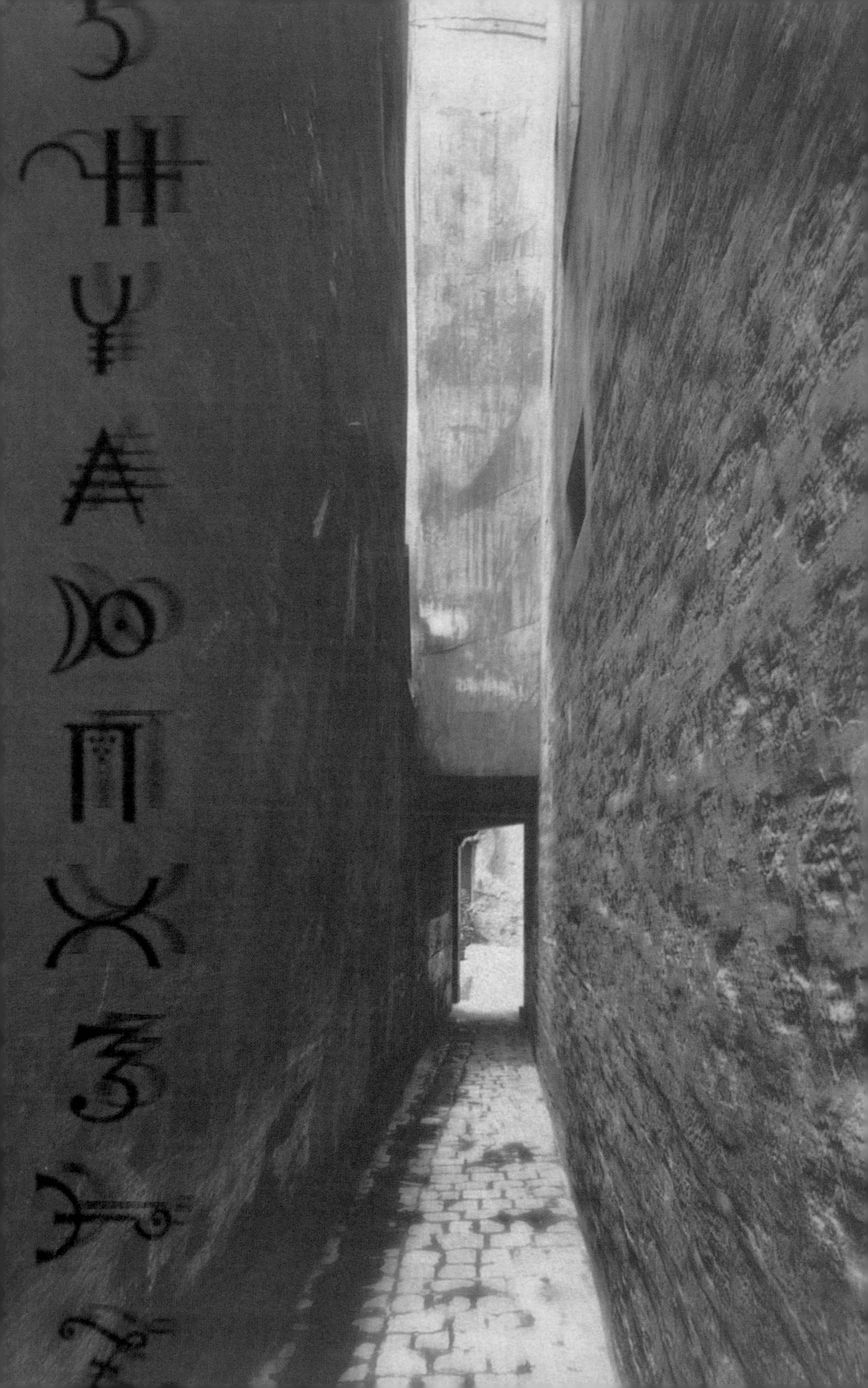

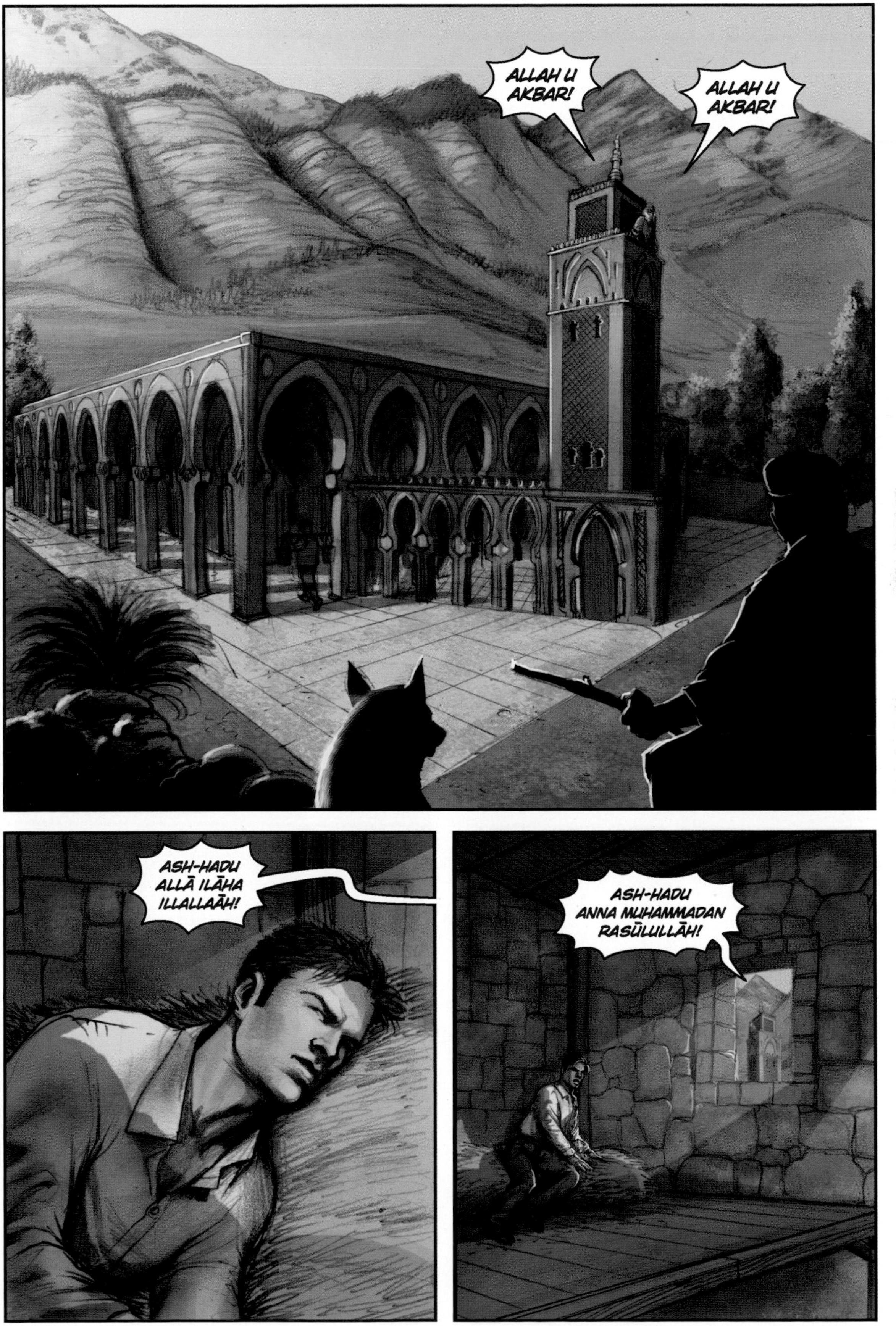
ALLAH U AKBAR!
ALLAH U AKBAR!
ASH-HADU ALLĀ ILĀHA ILLALLAĀH!
ASH-HADU ANNA MUHAMMADAN RASŪLULLĀH!

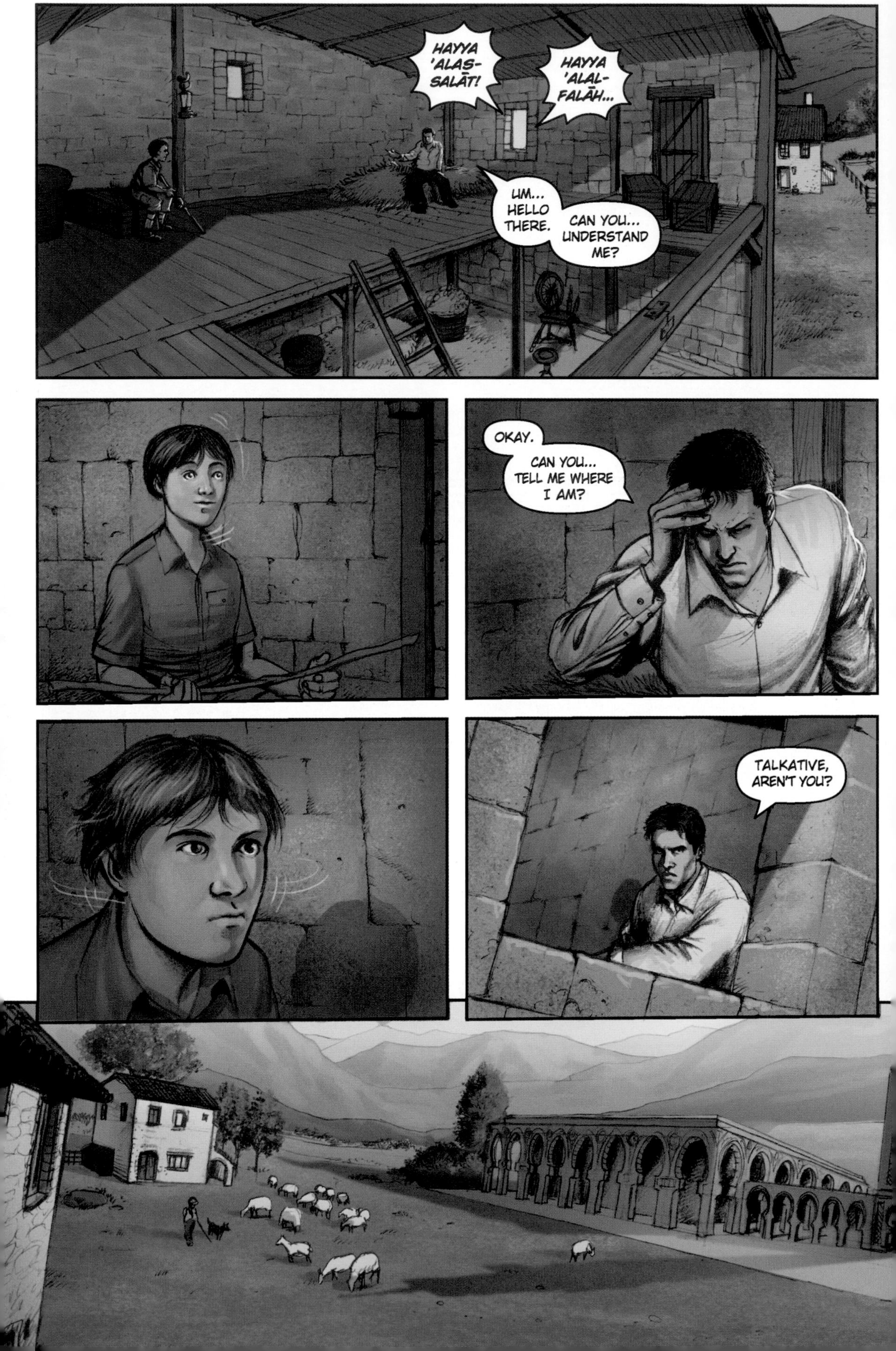
HAYYA 'ALAS-SALĀT!
HAYYA 'ALAL-FALĀH...
UM... HELLO THERE.
CAN YOU... UNDERSTAND ME?
OKAY.
CAN YOU... TELL ME WHERE I AM?
TALKATIVE, AREN'T YOU?

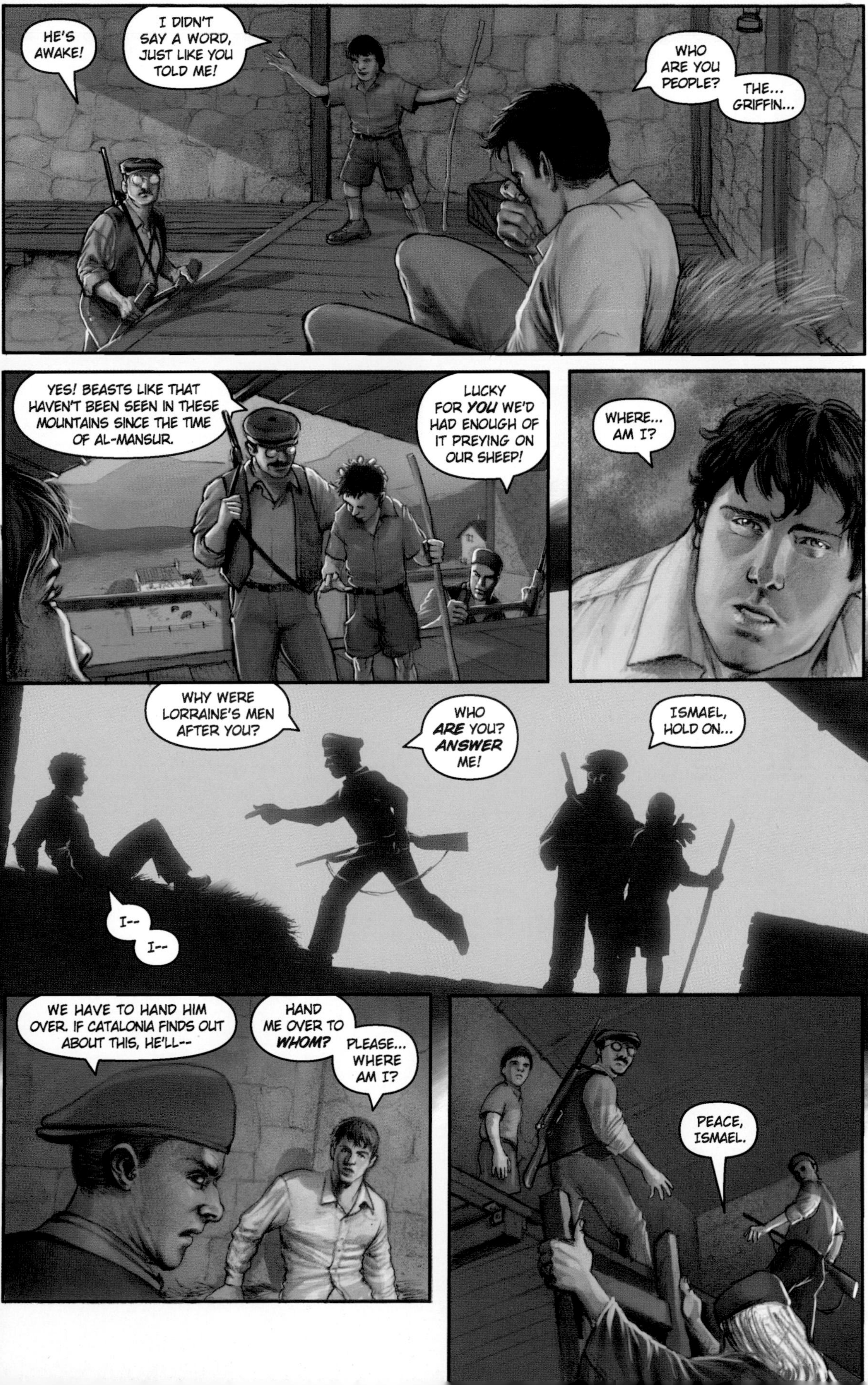
HE'S AWAKE!
I DIDN'T SAY A WORD, JUST LIKE YOU TOLD ME!
WHO ARE YOU PEOPLE?
THE... GRIFFIN...
YES! BEASTS LIKE THAT HAVEN'T BEEN SEEN IN THESE MOUNTAINS SINCE THE TIME OF AL-MANSUR.
LUCKY FOR *YOU* WE'D HAD ENOUGH OF IT PREYING ON OUR SHEEP!
WHERE... AM I?
WHY WERE LORRAINE'S MEN AFTER YOU?
WHO *ARE* YOU? *ANSWER* ME!
ISMAEL, HOLD ON...
I--
I--
WE HAVE TO HAND HIM OVER. IF CATALONIA FINDS OUT ABOUT THIS, HE'LL--
HAND ME OVER TO *WHOM?*
PLEASE... WHERE AM I?
PEACE, ISMAEL.

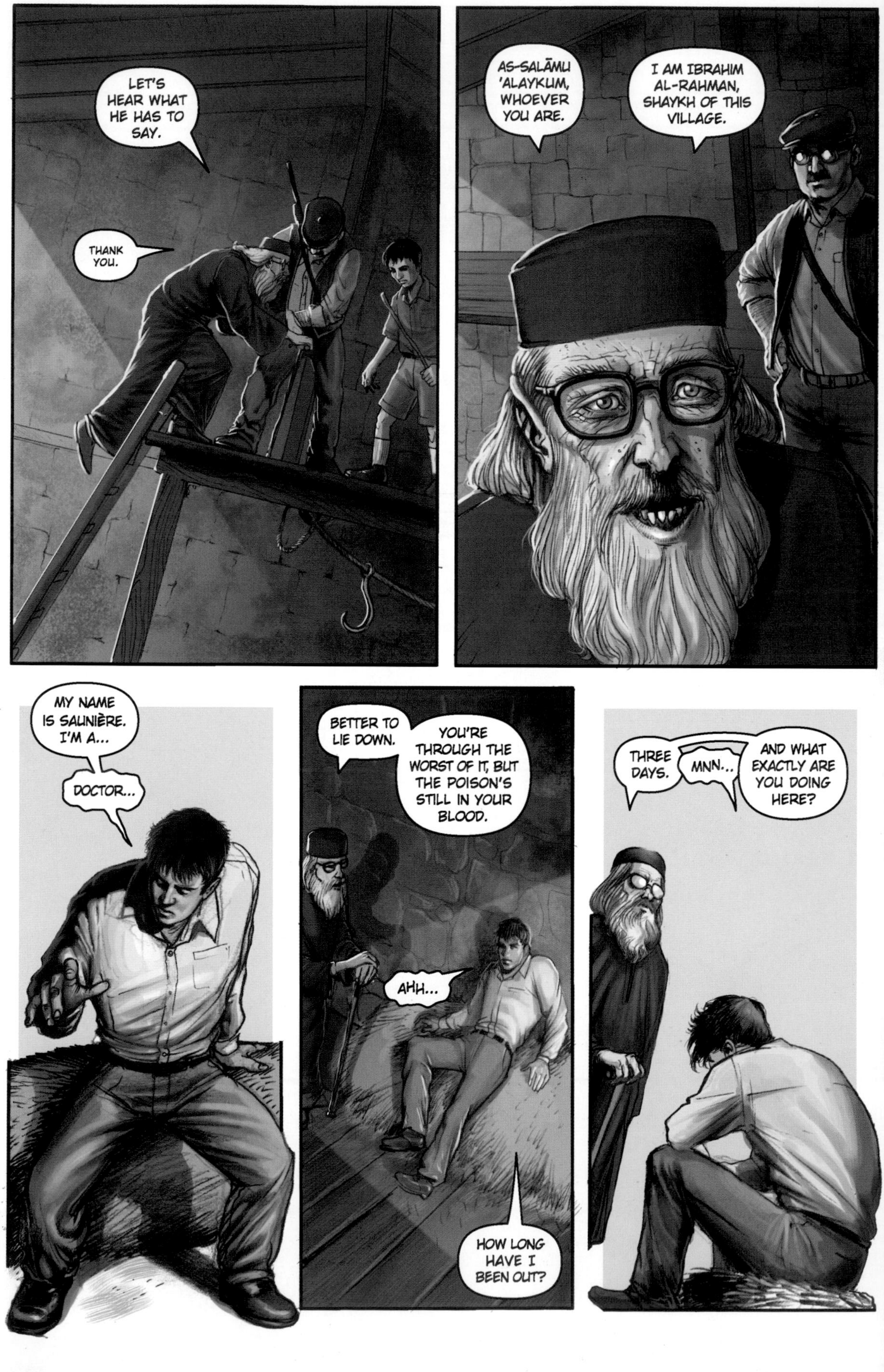
LET'S HEAR WHAT HE HAS TO SAY.
THANK YOU.
AS-SALĀMU 'ALAYKUM, WHOEVER YOU ARE.
I AM IBRAHIM AL-RAHMAN, SHAYKH OF THIS VILLAGE.
MY NAME IS SAUNIÈRE. I'M A...
DOCTOR...
BETTER TO LIE DOWN.
YOU'RE THROUGH THE WORST OF IT, BUT THE POISON'S STILL IN YOUR BLOOD.
AHH...
HOW LONG HAVE I BEEN OUT?
THREE DAYS.
MNN...
AND WHAT EXACTLY ARE YOU DOING HERE?

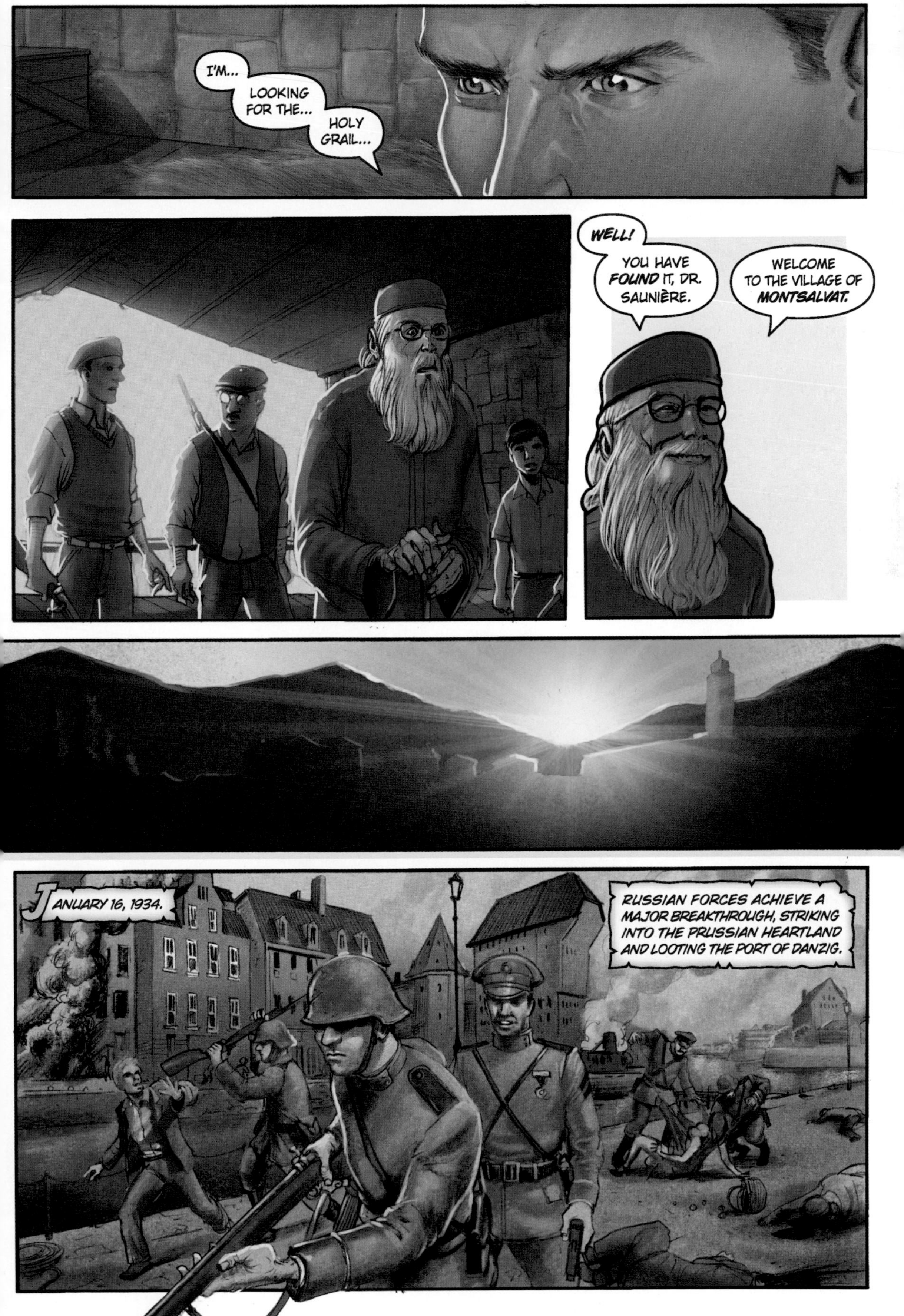
I'M... LOOKING FOR THE... HOLY GRAIL...
WELL!
YOU HAVE FOUND IT, DR. SAUNIÈRE.
WELCOME TO THE VILLAGE OF MONTSALVAT.
JANUARY 16, 1934.
RUSSIAN FORCES ACHIEVE A MAJOR BREAKTHROUGH, STRIKING INTO THE PRUSSIAN HEARTLAND AND LOOTING THE PORT OF DANZIG.

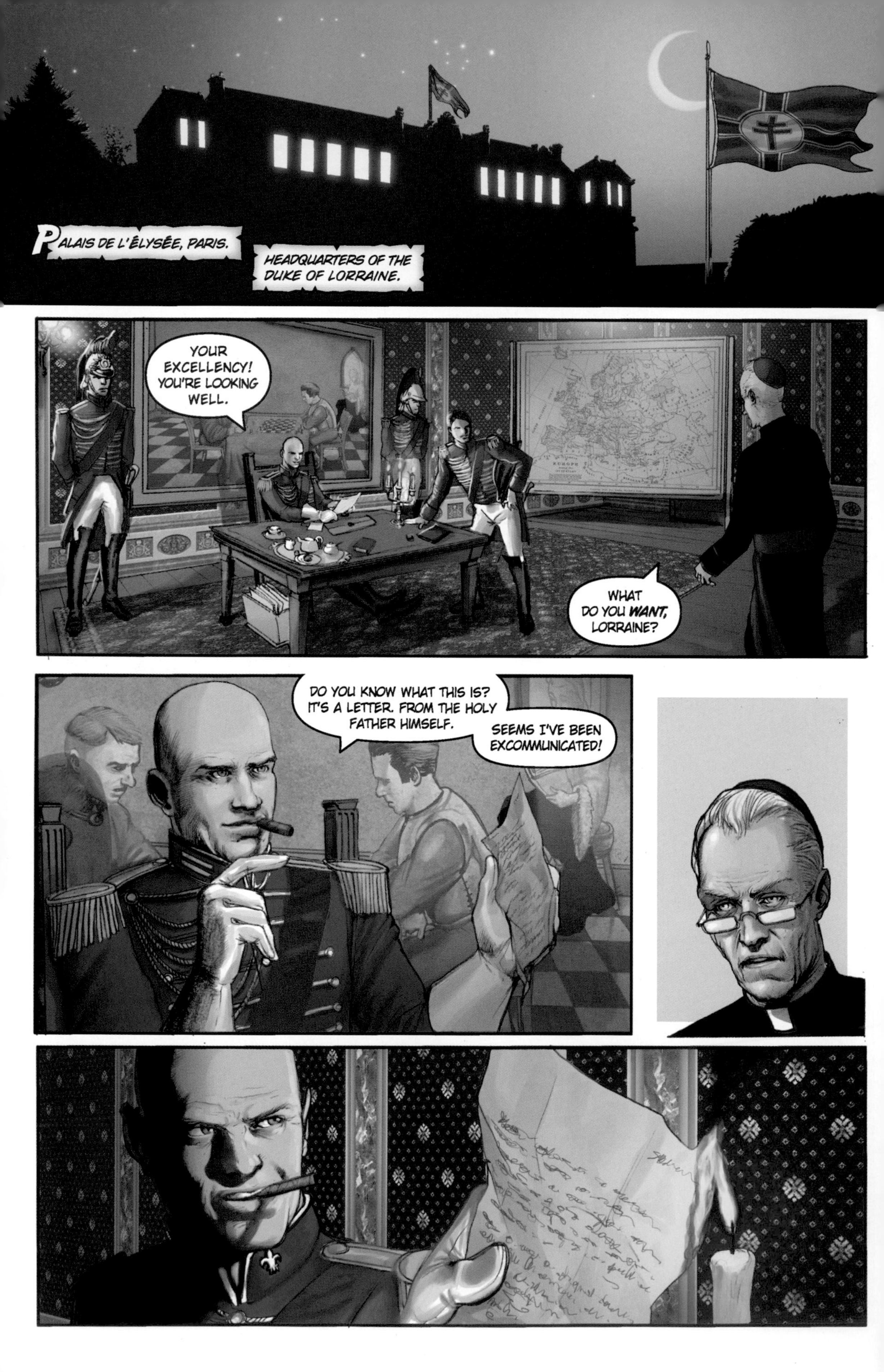
PALAIS DE L'ÉLYSÉE, PARIS.
HEADQUARTERS OF THE DUKE OF LORRAINE.
YOUR EXCELLENCY! YOU'RE LOOKING WELL.
WHAT DO YOU *WANT,* LORRAINE?
DO YOU KNOW WHAT THIS IS? IT'S A LETTER. FROM THE HOLY FATHER HIMSELF.
SEEMS I'VE BEEN EXCOMMUNICATED!

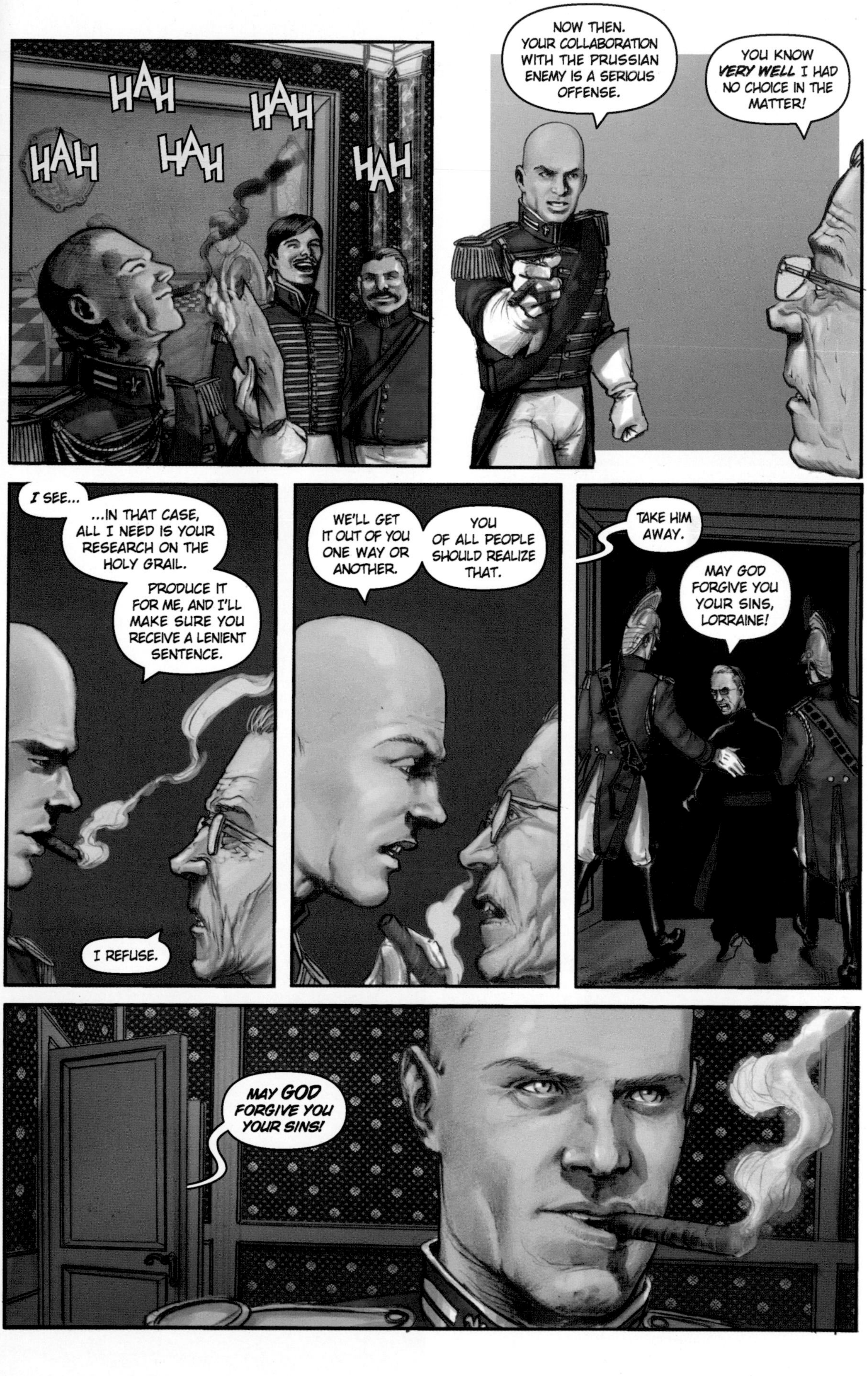
HAH
HAH
HAH
HAH
HAH
NOW THEN. YOUR COLLABORATION WITH THE PRUSSIAN ENEMY IS A SERIOUS OFFENSE.
YOU KNOW VERY WELL I HAD NO CHOICE IN THE MATTER!
I SEE...
...IN THAT CASE, ALL I NEED IS YOUR RESEARCH ON THE HOLY GRAIL.
PRODUCE IT FOR ME, AND I'LL MAKE SURE YOU RECEIVE A LENIENT SENTENCE.
I REFUSE.
WE'LL GET IT OUT OF YOU ONE WAY OR ANOTHER.
YOU OF ALL PEOPLE SHOULD REALIZE THAT.
TAKE HIM AWAY.
MAY GOD FORGIVE YOU YOUR SINS, LORRAINE!
MAY GOD FORGIVE YOU YOUR SINS!

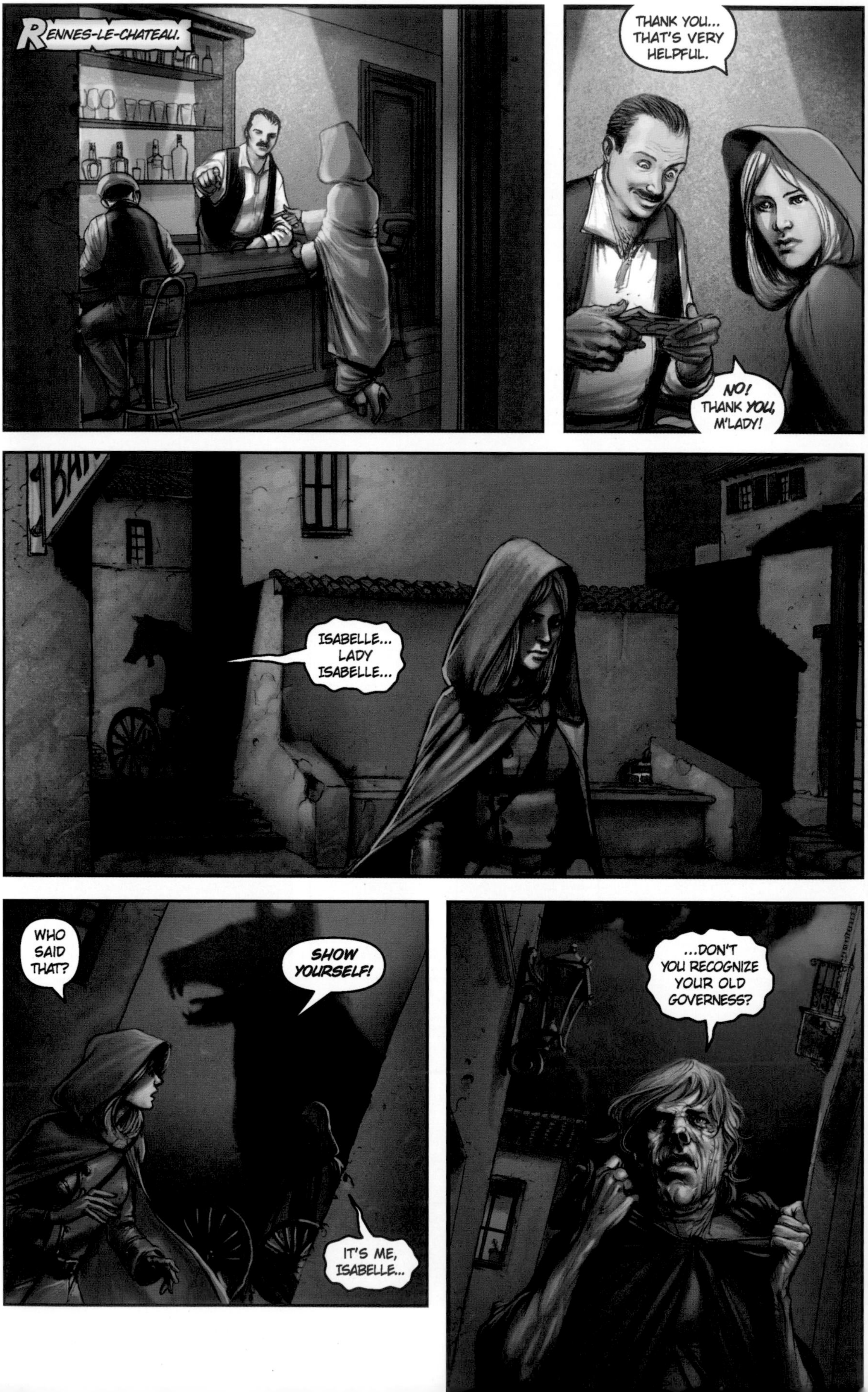
RENNES-LE-CHATEAU.
THANK YOU... THAT'S VERY HELPFUL.
NO! THANK YOU, M'LADY!
ISABELLE... LADY ISABELLE...
WHO SAID THAT?
SHOW YOURSELF!
IT'S ME, ISABELLE...
...DON'T YOU RECOGNIZE YOUR OLD GOVERNESS?

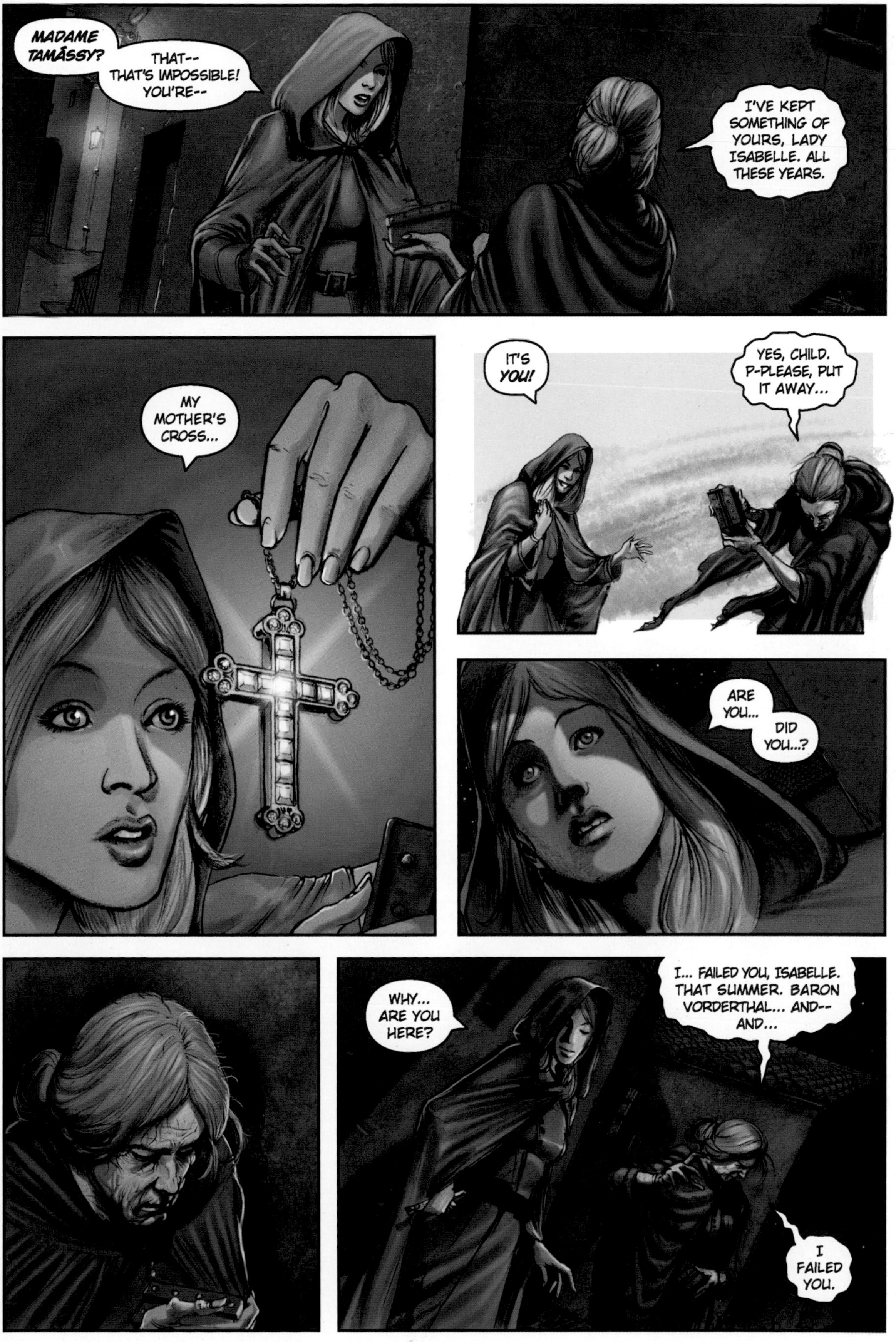
MADAME TAMÂSSY?
THAT-- THAT'S IMPOSSIBLE! YOU'RE--
I'VE KEPT SOMETHING OF YOURS, LADY ISABELLE. ALL THESE YEARS.
MY MOTHER'S CROSS...
IT'S YOU!
YES, CHILD. P-PLEASE, PUT IT AWAY...
ARE YOU...
DID YOU...?
WHY... ARE YOU HERE?
I... FAILED YOU, ISABELLE. THAT SUMMER. BARON VORDERTHAL... AND-- AND...
I FAILED YOU.

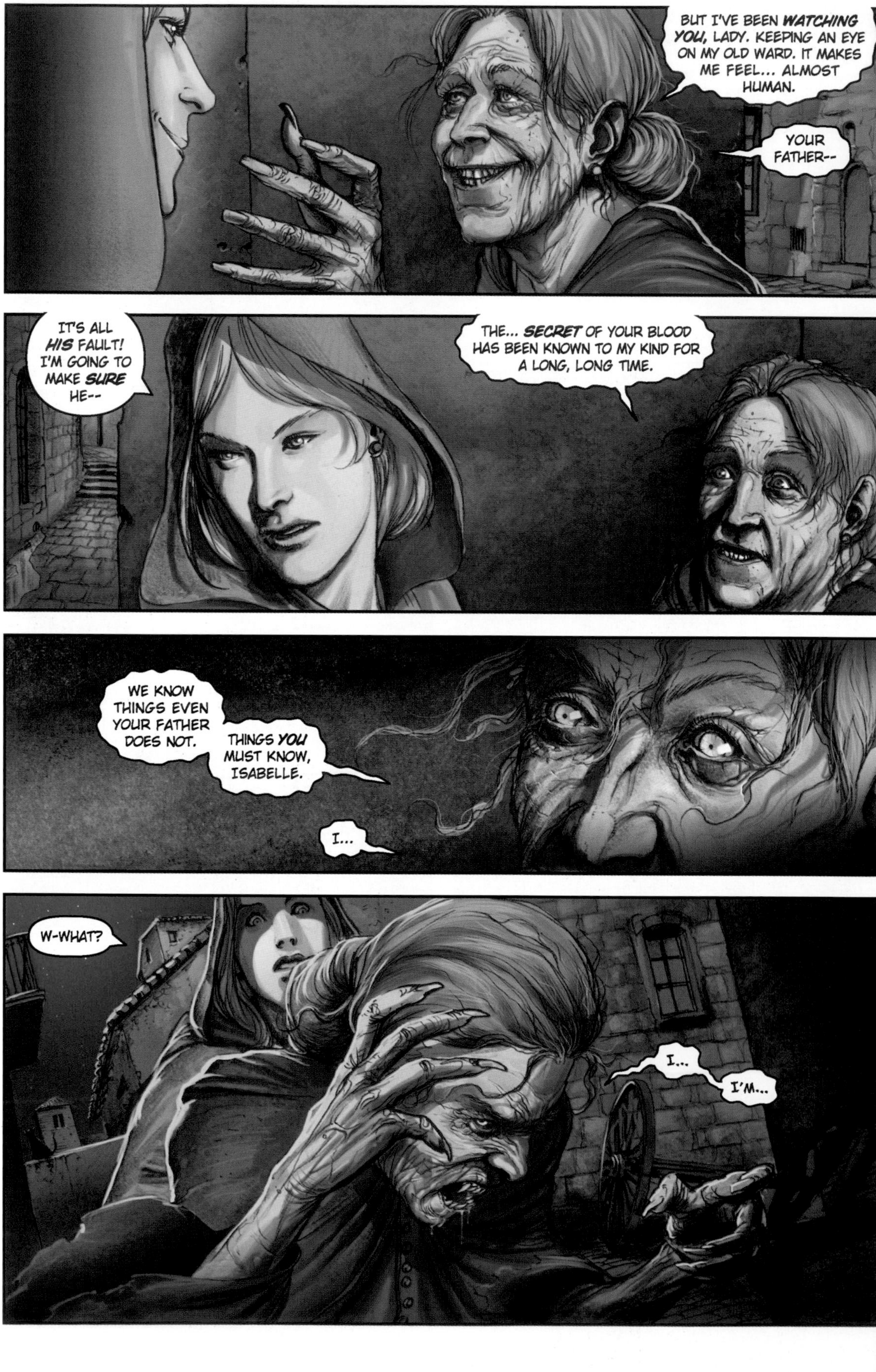
BUT I'VE BEEN WATCHING YOU, LADY. KEEPING AN EYE ON MY OLD WARD. IT MAKES ME FEEL... ALMOST HUMAN.
YOUR FATHER--
IT'S ALL HIS FAULT! I'M GOING TO MAKE SURE HE--
THE... SECRET OF YOUR BLOOD HAS BEEN KNOWN TO MY KIND FOR A LONG, LONG TIME.
WE KNOW THINGS EVEN YOUR FATHER DOES NOT.
THINGS YOU MUST KNOW, ISABELLE.
I...
W-WHAT?
I...
I'M...

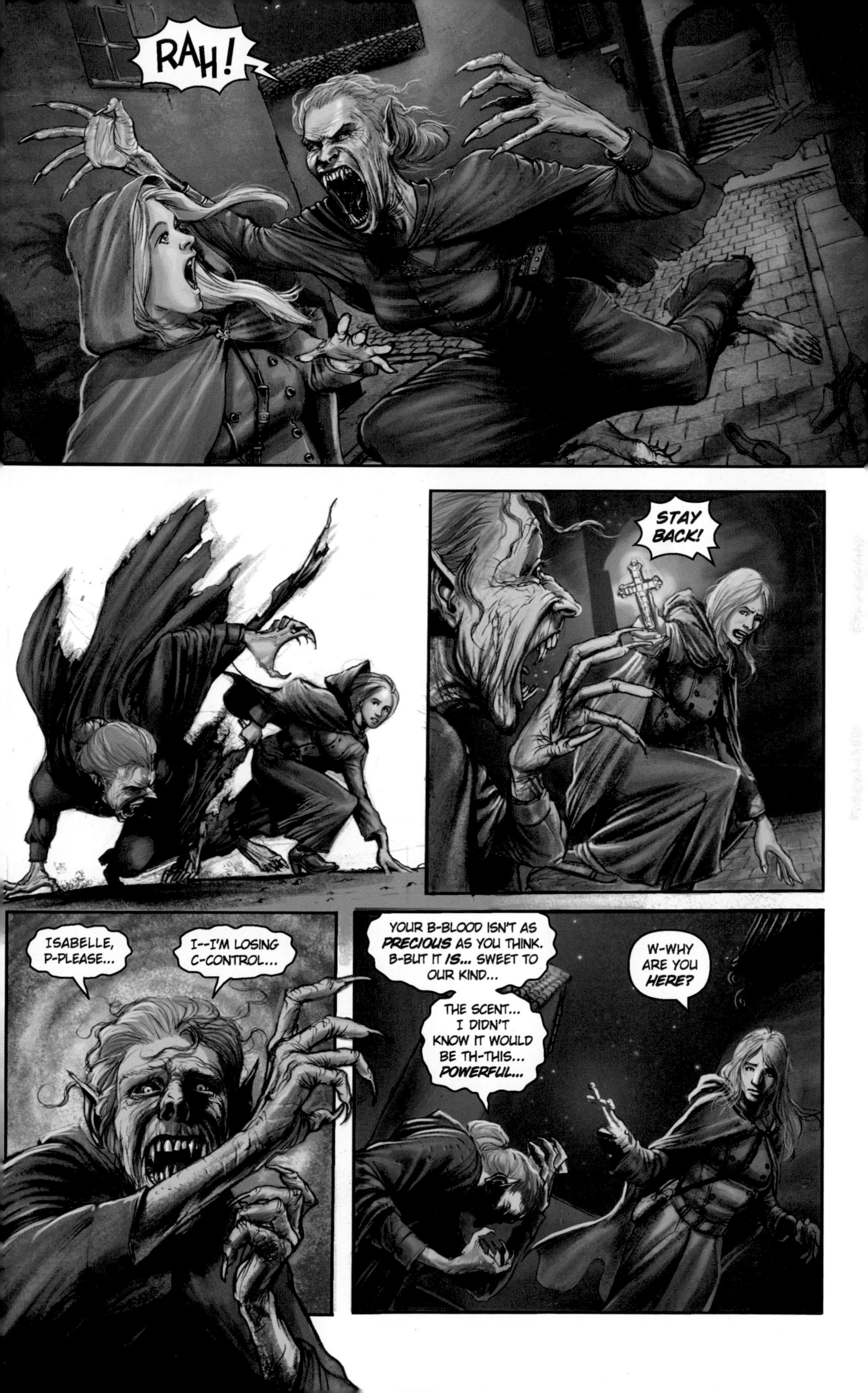
RAH!
STAY BACK!
ISABELLE, P-PLEASE...
I--I'M LOSING C-CONTROL...
YOUR B-BLOOD ISN'T AS PRECIOUS AS YOU THINK. B-BUT IT IS... SWEET TO OUR KIND...
THE SCENT... I DIDN'T KNOW IT WOULD BE TH-THIS... POWERFUL...
W-WHY ARE YOU HERE?

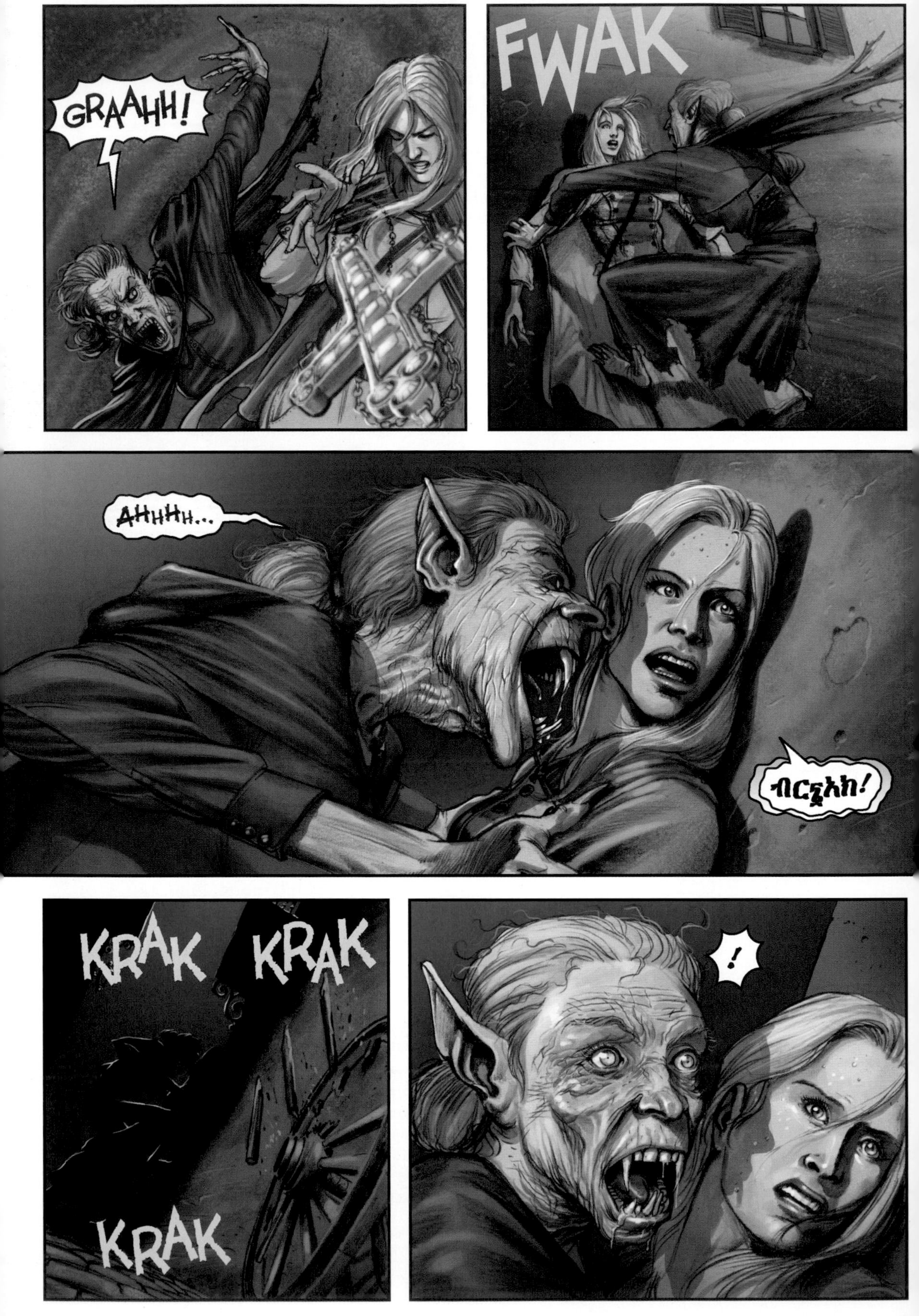
GRAAHH!
FWAK
AHHHH...
ብርኗአክ!
KRAK KRAK
KRAK
!

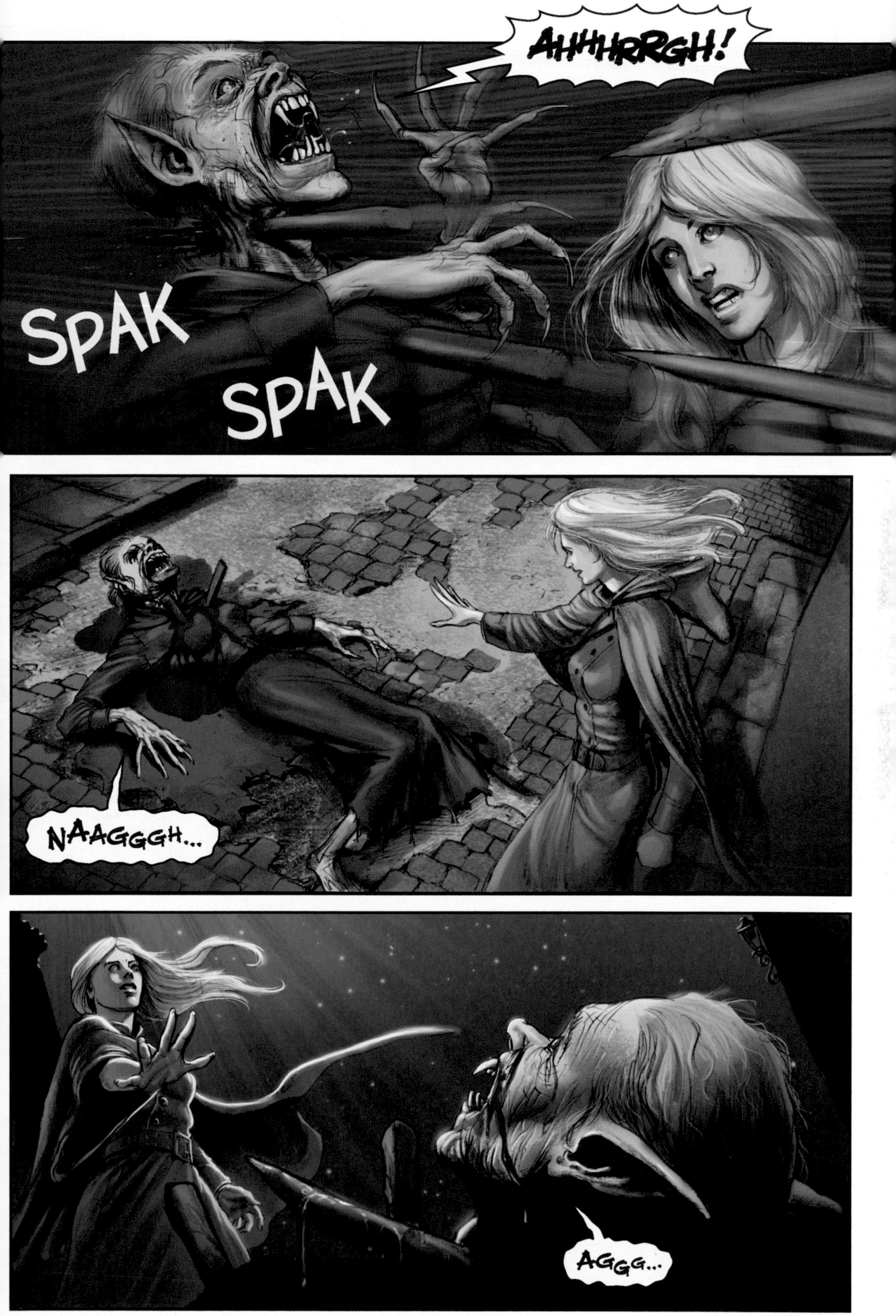
AHHHRRGH!
SPAK
SPAK
NAAGGGH...
AGGG...

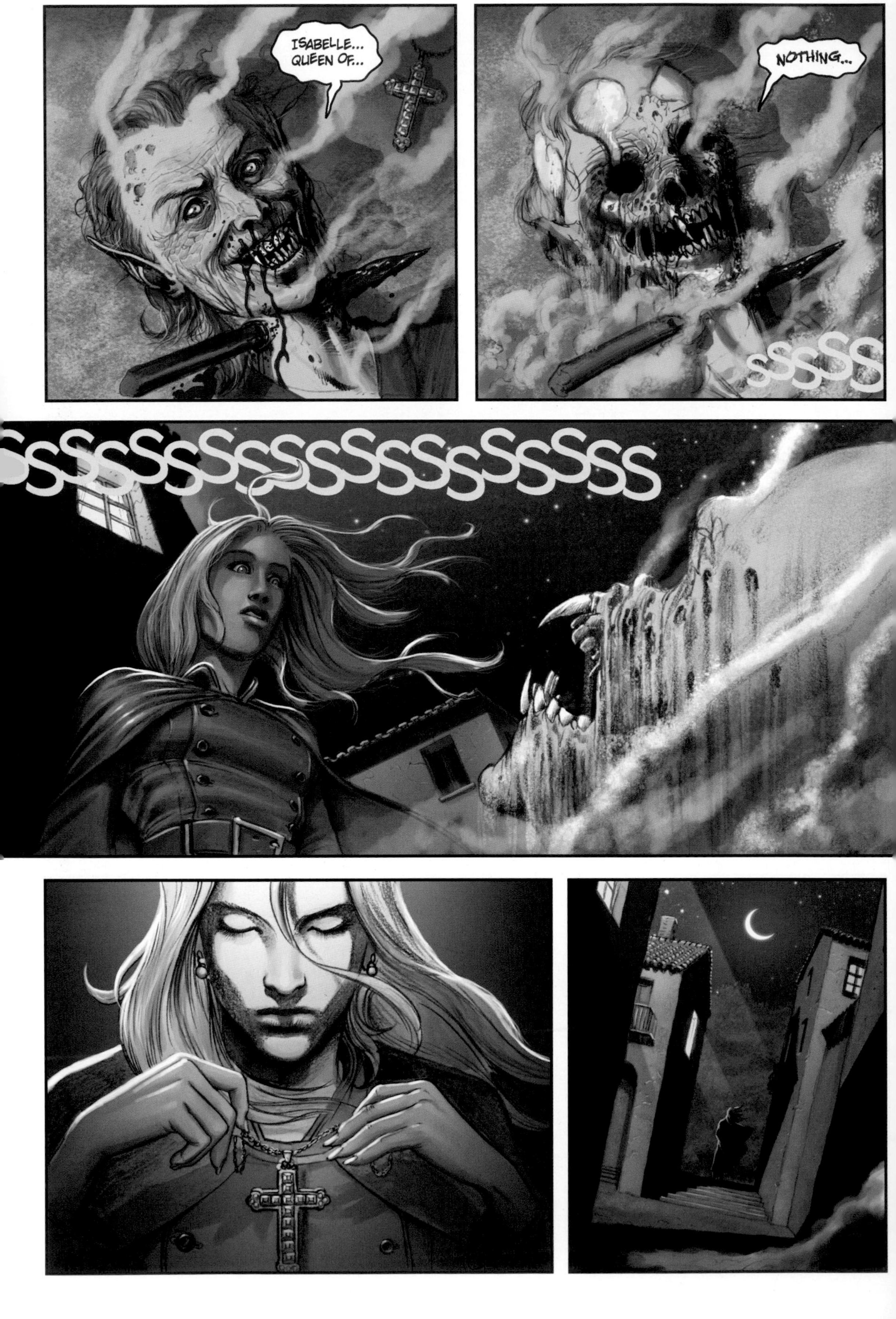
ISABELLE... QUEEN OF...
NOTHING...
SSSSS
SSSSSSSSSSSSSSSSSSSSS

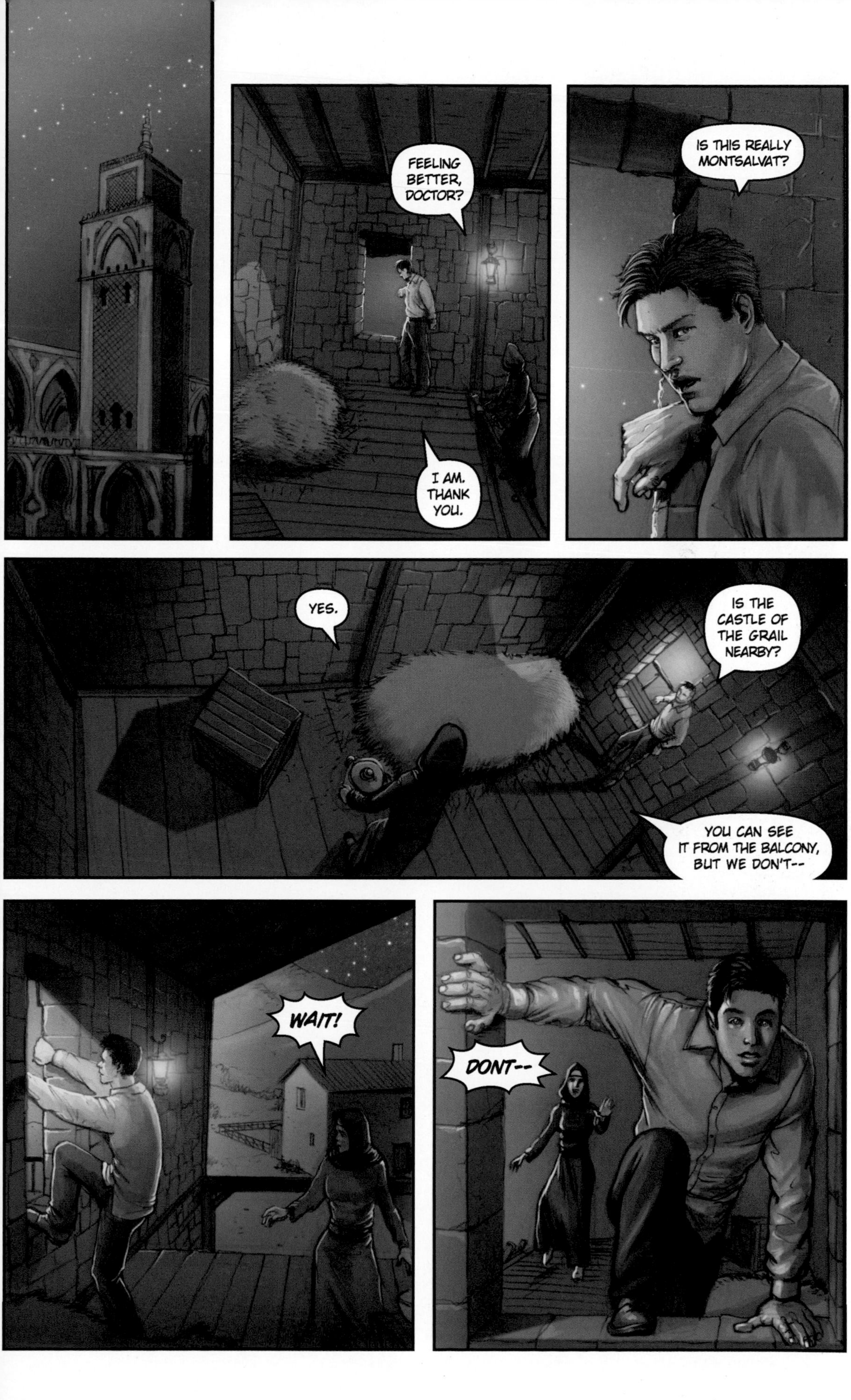
FEELING BETTER, DOCTOR?
I AM. THANK YOU.
IS THIS REALLY MONTSALVAT?
YES.
IS THE CASTLE OF THE GRAIL NEARBY?
YOU CAN SEE IT FROM THE BALCONY, BUT WE DON'T--
WAIT!
DONT--

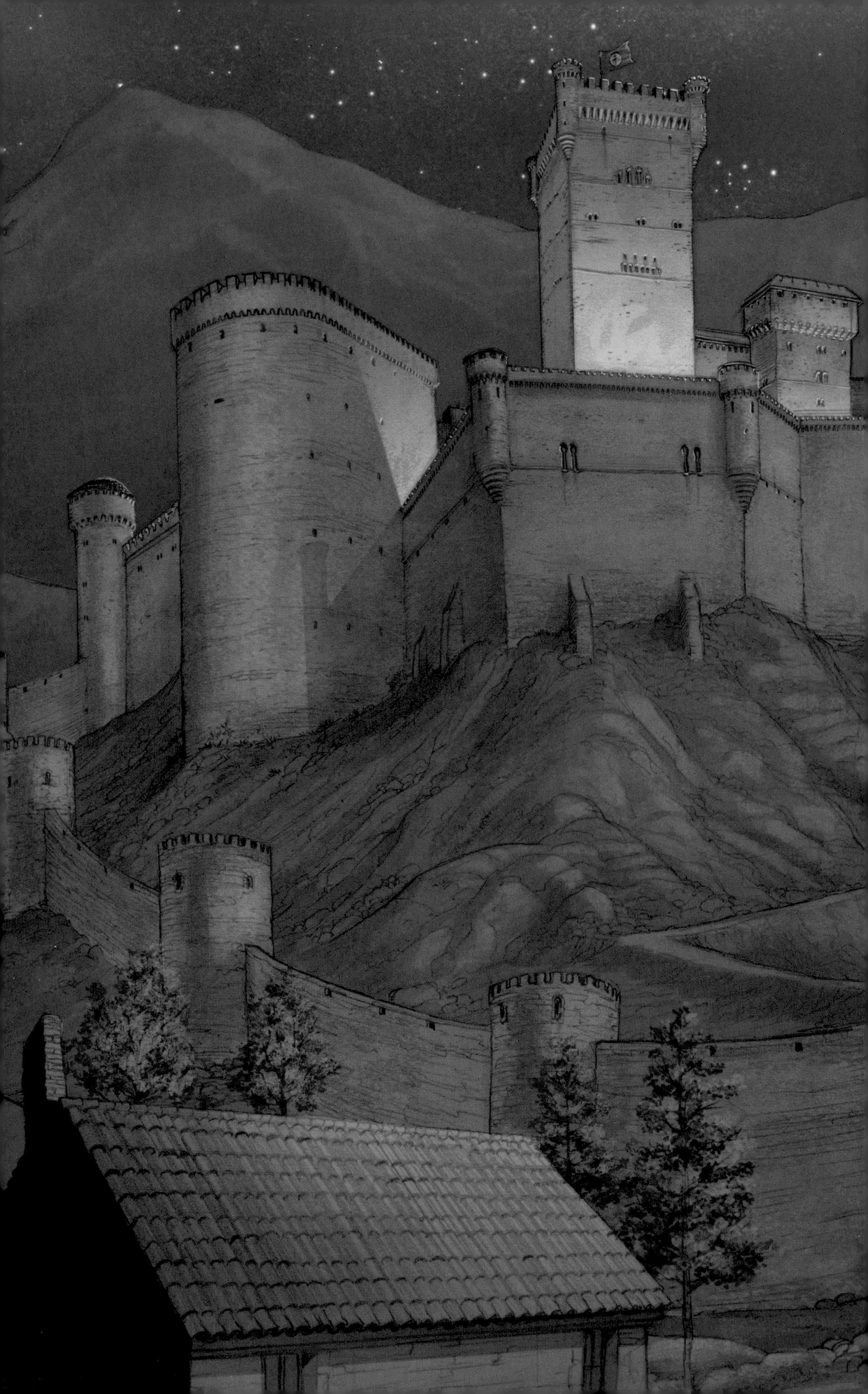

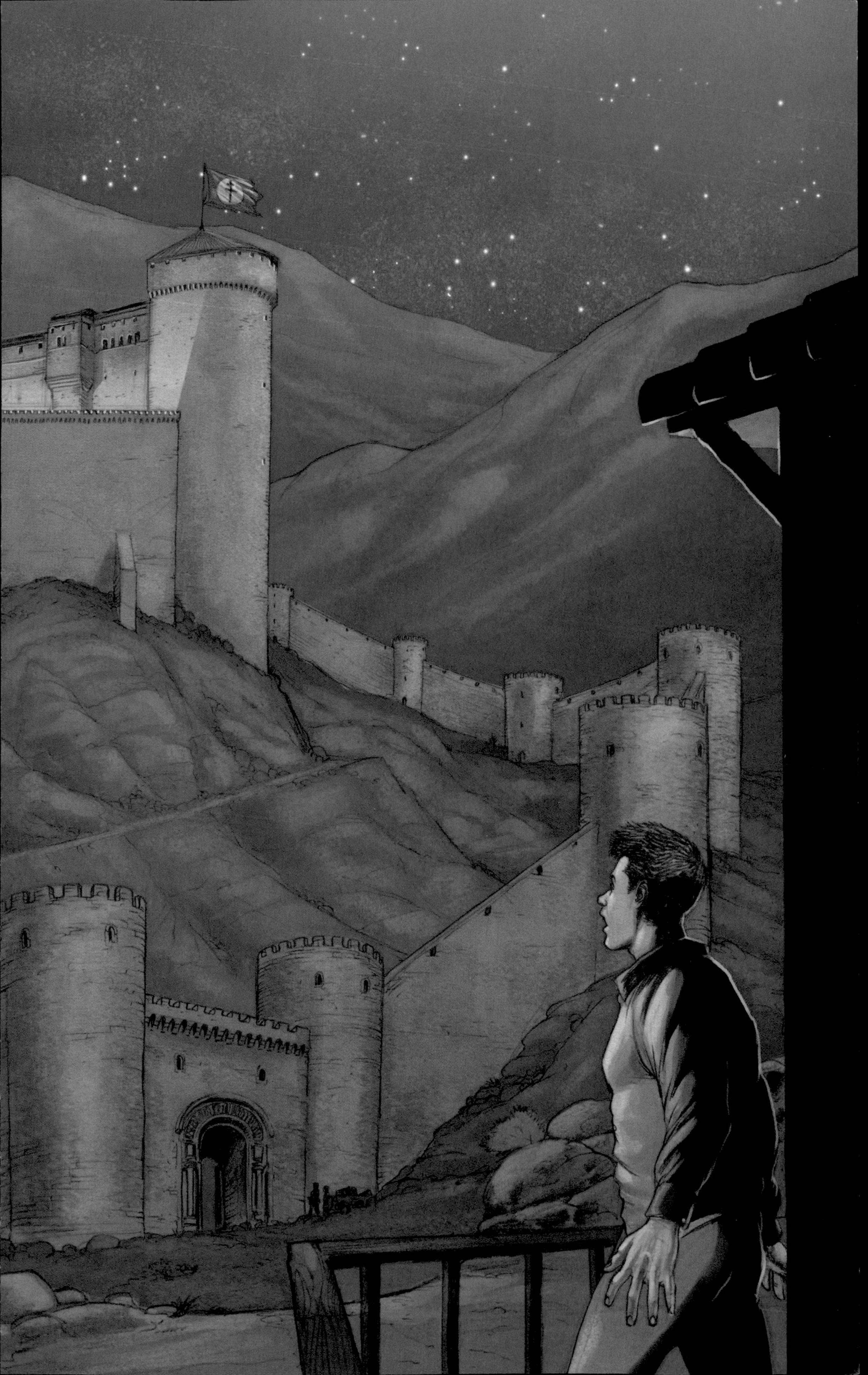

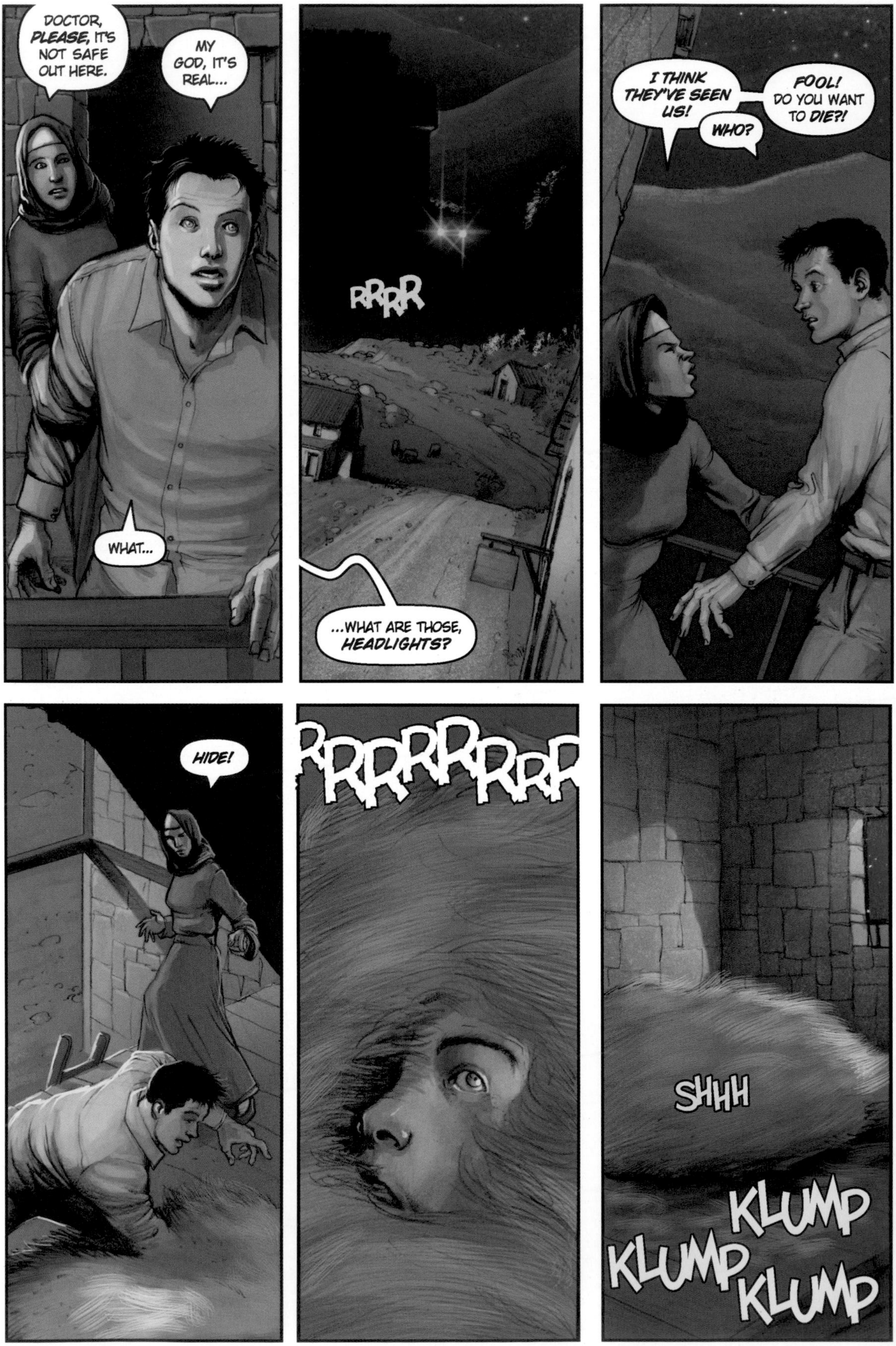
DOCTOR, PLEASE, IT'S NOT SAFE OUT HERE.
MY GOD, IT'S REAL...
WHAT...
RRRR
...WHAT ARE THOSE, HEADLIGHTS?
I THINK THEY'VE SEEN US!
WHO?
FOOL! DO YOU WANT TO DIE?!
HIDE!
RRRRRRRRRR
SHHH
KLUMP
KLUMP
KLUMP

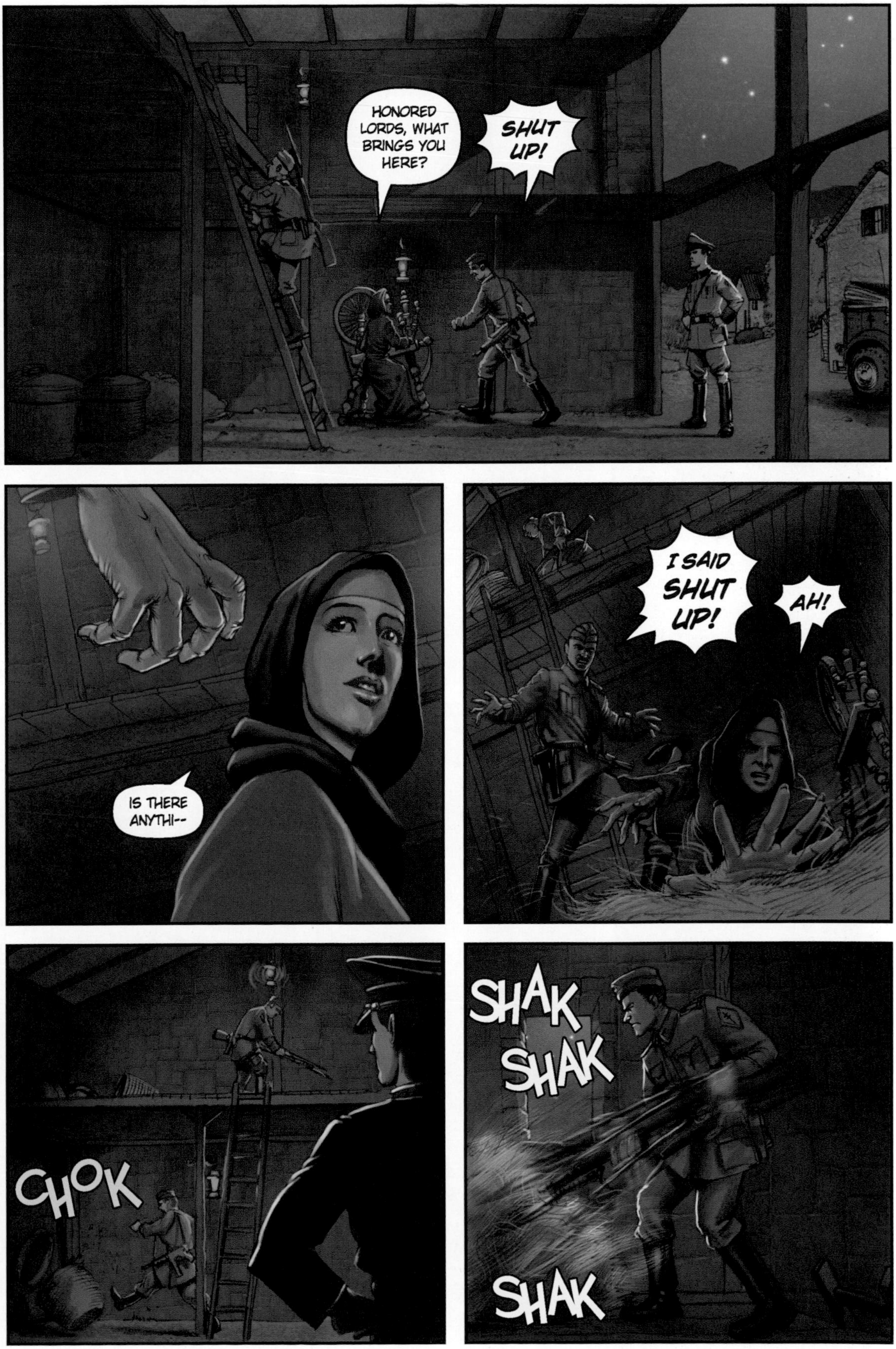
HONORED LORDS, WHAT BRINGS YOU HERE?
SHUT UP!
IS THERE ANYTHI--
I SAID SHUT UP!
AH!
CHOK
SHAK
SHAK
SHAK

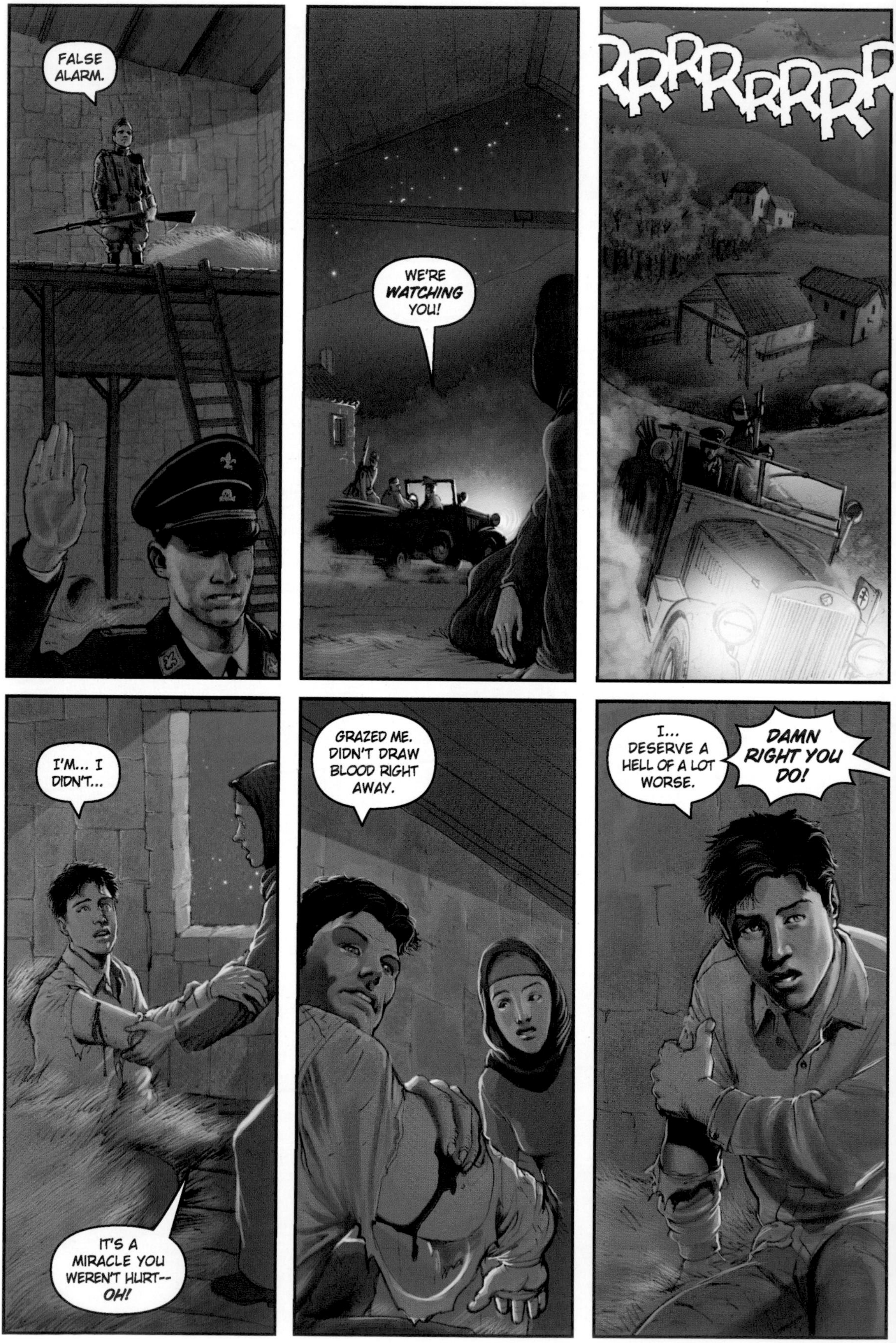
FALSE ALARM.
WE'RE *WATCHING* YOU!
RRRRRRRR
I'M... I DIDN'T...
IT'S A MIRACLE YOU WEREN'T HURT-- *OH!*
GRAZED ME. DIDN'T DRAW BLOOD RIGHT AWAY.
I... DESERVE A HELL OF A LOT WORSE.
DAMN RIGHT YOU DO!

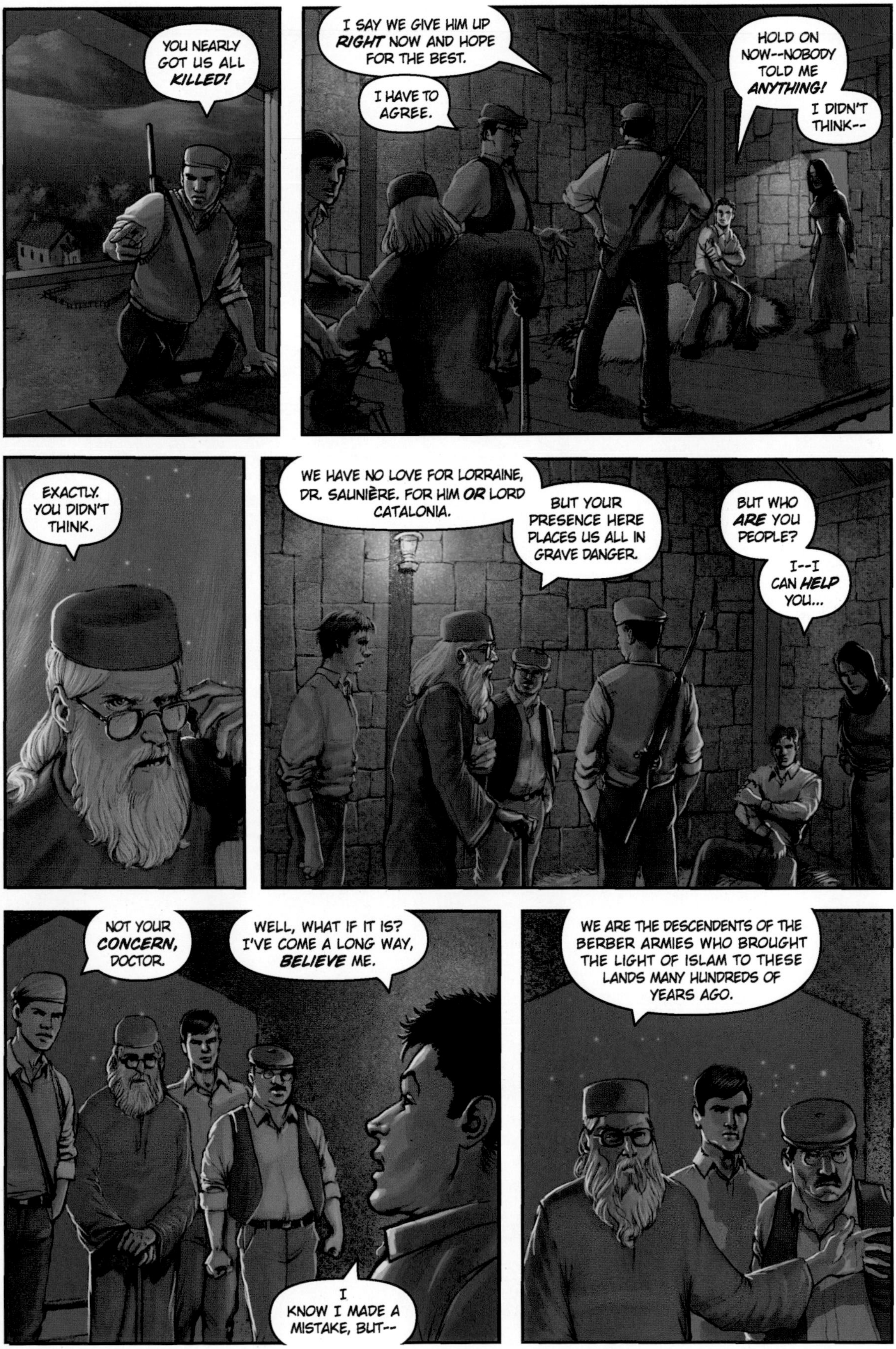
YOU NEARLY GOT US ALL KILLED!
I SAY WE GIVE HIM UP RIGHT NOW AND HOPE FOR THE BEST.
I HAVE TO AGREE.
HOLD ON NOW--NOBODY TOLD ME ANYTHING!
I DIDN'T THINK--
EXACTLY. YOU DIDN'T THINK.
WE HAVE NO LOVE FOR LORRAINE, DR. SAUNIÈRE. FOR HIM OR LORD CATALONIA.
BUT YOUR PRESENCE HERE PLACES US ALL IN GRAVE DANGER.
BUT WHO ARE YOU PEOPLE?
I--I CAN HELP YOU...
NOT YOUR CONCERN, DOCTOR.
WELL, WHAT IF IT IS? I'VE COME A LONG WAY, BELIEVE ME.
I KNOW I MADE A MISTAKE, BUT--
WE ARE THE DESCENDENTS OF THE BERBER ARMIES WHO BROUGHT THE LIGHT OF ISLAM TO THESE LANDS MANY HUNDREDS OF YEARS AGO.

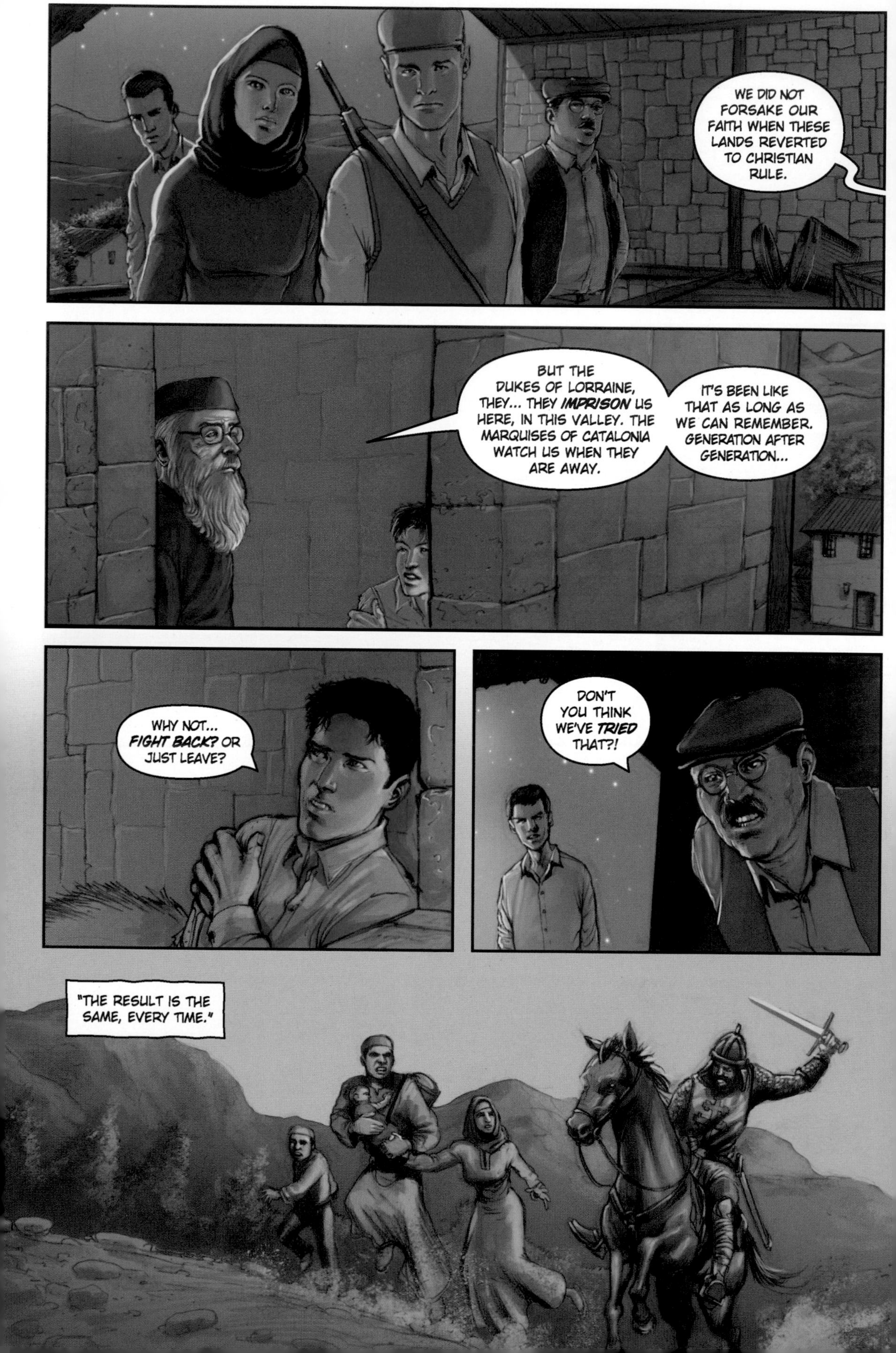
WE DID NOT FORSAKE OUR FAITH WHEN THESE LANDS REVERTED TO CHRISTIAN RULE.
BUT THE DUKES OF LORRAINE, THEY... THEY *IMPRISON* US HERE, IN THIS VALLEY. THE MARQUISES OF CATALONIA WATCH US WHEN THEY ARE AWAY.
IT'S BEEN LIKE THAT AS LONG AS WE CAN REMEMBER. GENERATION AFTER GENERATION...
WHY NOT... *FIGHT BACK?* OR JUST LEAVE?
DON'T YOU THINK WE'VE *TRIED* THAT?!
"THE RESULT IS THE SAME, EVERY TIME."

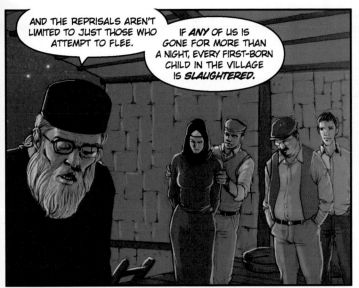

AND THE REPRISALS AREN'T LIMITED TO JUST THOSE WHO ATTEMPT TO FLEE.

IF *ANY* OF US IS GONE FOR MORE THAN A NIGHT, EVERY FIRST-BORN CHILD IN THE VILLAGE IS *SLAUGHTERED*.

BUT--WHY IMPRISON YOU IN THE FIRST PLACE? IT SEEMS *SENSELESS*...

WE WON'T HAND YOU OVER, BUT YOU *WILL* LEAVE THIS PLACE TOMORROW.

LEAVE, AND NEVER RETURN.

I'M SORRY, DOCTOR. THERE ARE--

THERE IS MORE TO THIS PLACE THAN YOU REALIZE, AND WE HAVE OUR CHILDREN TO THINK ABOUT.

THIS IS THE BEST WE CAN DO FOR YOU.

Le Journal de la Liberté

Paris's leading anglophone newspaper • vol. 205, no. 157 • Jan. 17, MCMXXXIV

Editors in Chief: M. Michael Richardson, M. Scott Allie, M. Ryan Jorgensen. **Story Editor:** M. Arvid Nelson. **Art Editor:** M. Juan Ferreyra. **Photography Editor:** M. Eugène Atget. **Layout Supervisor:** M. Gary Grazzini. **Editors Emeritus:** M. Clark A. Smith, M. Howard P. Lovecraft, M. Robert E. Howard. *Le Journal de la Liberté* is printed under the benign auspices of his eminence David-Louis Plantard de St. Clair, Duke of Lorraine and First Consul of the Empire of France.

Official seal of

the First Consul

⚜ **GOD SAVE LORD LORRAINE** ⚜

FRENCH RETAKE DUCHY OF LORRAINE; VINDICATION FOR FIRST CONSUL

Lorraine Confiscates Church Property in France, Pope Excommunicates

Paris, France – The Duke of Lorraine seized all Church property in Greater France early yesterday morning. Such a daring move against the Church hasn't been seen in France since the turbulent reign of Philip IV in the Middle Ages.

French troops met little resistance as they moved into the monasteries and churches. The takeover means Lord Lorraine now has complete control of all ecclesiastical property in France's ever-expanding empire.

Pope Pius XI condemned the appropriation and issued a writ of excommunication for Lorraine.

"We pray Lord Lorraine will repent of his sins and return to the Church its rightful holdings," Papal Nuncio Adolfo Bastianich said. But Lorraine doesn't seem prepared to return to the altar for wine and wafers any time soon.

Baron Robert Teniers, a spokesman for Lorraine, downplayed the importance of the seizure, saying the confiscated property was being held "in trusteeship."

Teniers said the first consul would return the property "at such a time as he deems appropriate." He said Lorraine would not commit to a timetable.

Church officials in France were reluctant to talk about the dramatic turn of events, but those who did expressed grave concern over the future of Christian civilization.

"When the sanctity of the Church is violated, all social order will break down," a priest who asked not to be mentioned by name said.

continued on page A5

French soldiers in the Duchy of Lorraine pause for a brief (and chilly) repast before returning to the fight. "Now that the Huns are out of our homeland, why not continue on into theirs?" a French colonel said.

The Western Front, Duchy of Lorraine – French forces are reclaiming territory from the Prussians as quickly as they lost it in the opening weeks of the war. In what was surely a sweet personal triumph for the Duke of Lorraine, his feudal homeland is once more under French sovereignty.

Citizens of Brussels and Antwerp greeted French soldiers with cheers and flowers as they paraded through the streets of the newly liberated cities.

Several weeks ago, absolute victory for the allied Prusso-Austrian powers seemed inevitable. But all that changed when French forces rallied around the city of Carcassonne and delivered the invaders a stunning defeat.

Now the Duke of Orleans pursues the retreating Prussians across the Flanders Plain while the Duke of Nevers chases the remnants of the Austrian forces across the Alps.

Nor is France prepared to stop at expelling the invaders.

"Now that the Huns are out of our homeland, why not continue on into theirs?" Col. Philippe LeMay, a member of Lord Nevers's command staff, said. That sentiment is widely shared by members of Lorraine's military high command.

"We are not just on the verge of the Rhine. We are on the verge of fulfiling our destiny," the Duke of Orleans said. "We want nothing less than a unified, Christian Europe. One empire, one leader, one religion – that is the charge God has given us."

On the Eastern front, things also fare poorly for the Prussians. A massive Russian invasion force is slowly but inexorably gaining ground in the eastern hinterlands of Prussia itself.

The Tzar may soon be opening a second front for the Austrian Holy Roman Empire as well. Russia has long champion-

oned independence for Austria-Hungary's Serbian province. With Serbia in open revolt, and with the Austrian military in disarray, the timing may be perfect for Russia to launch an offensive.

"Make no mistake about it, this is a worst-case scenario for the Prussians and the Austrians," LeMay said. He predicted armistice, or even outright surrender, was "only a matter of time."

So confident are French military planners that they are already setting their sights beyond Europe. Lord Lorraine made his ambitions to launch a "new crusade" in the Holy Land a major platform of his political agenda from his days in French parliament as speaker of the Hall of the Sword.

"The unification of Europe is but the first step," Lorraine said. "France will usher in the Kingdom of God. But for that to happen, Christ must reign again in Jerusalem." ⬥

CHAPTER FIVE
BLUE APPLES

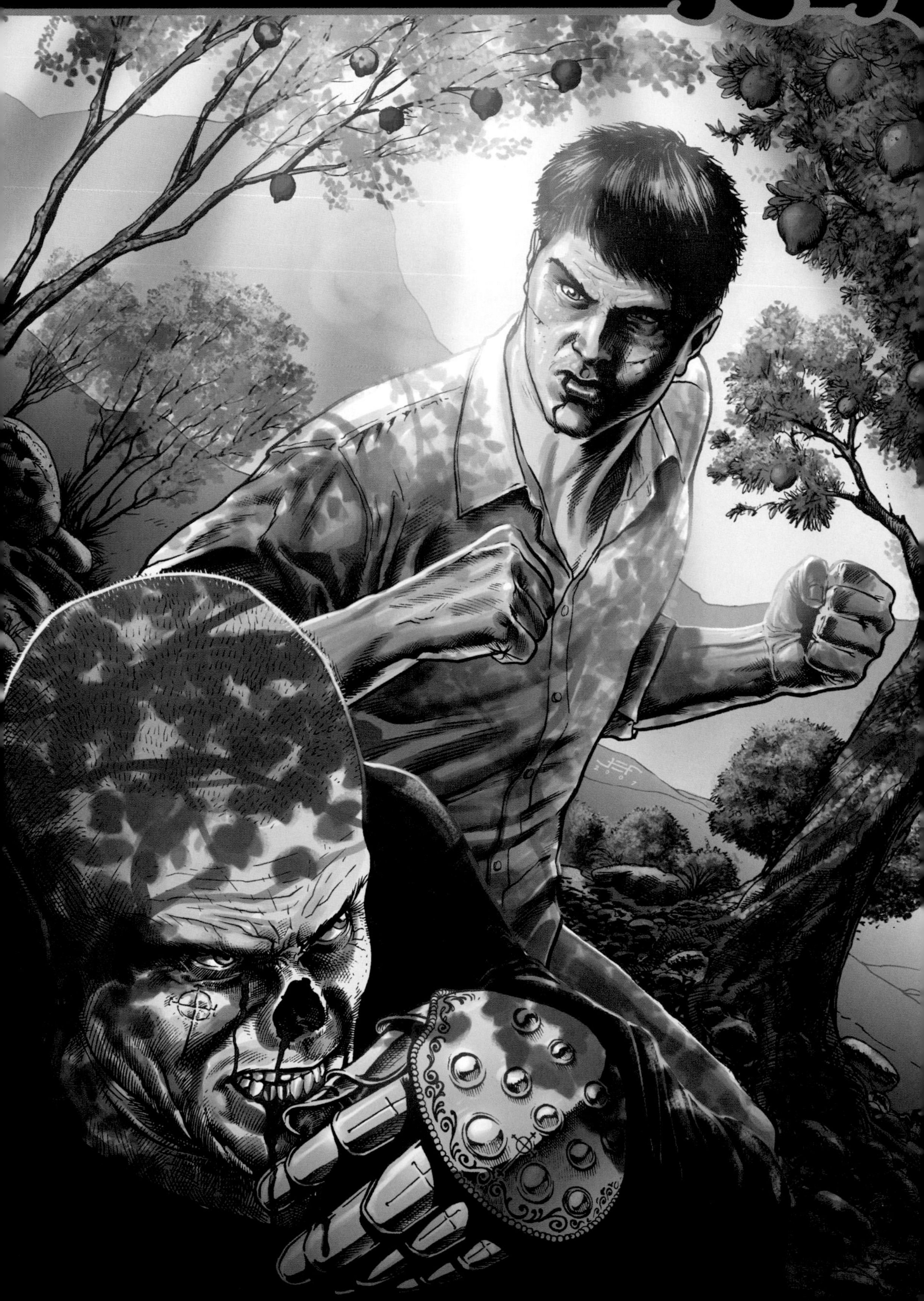

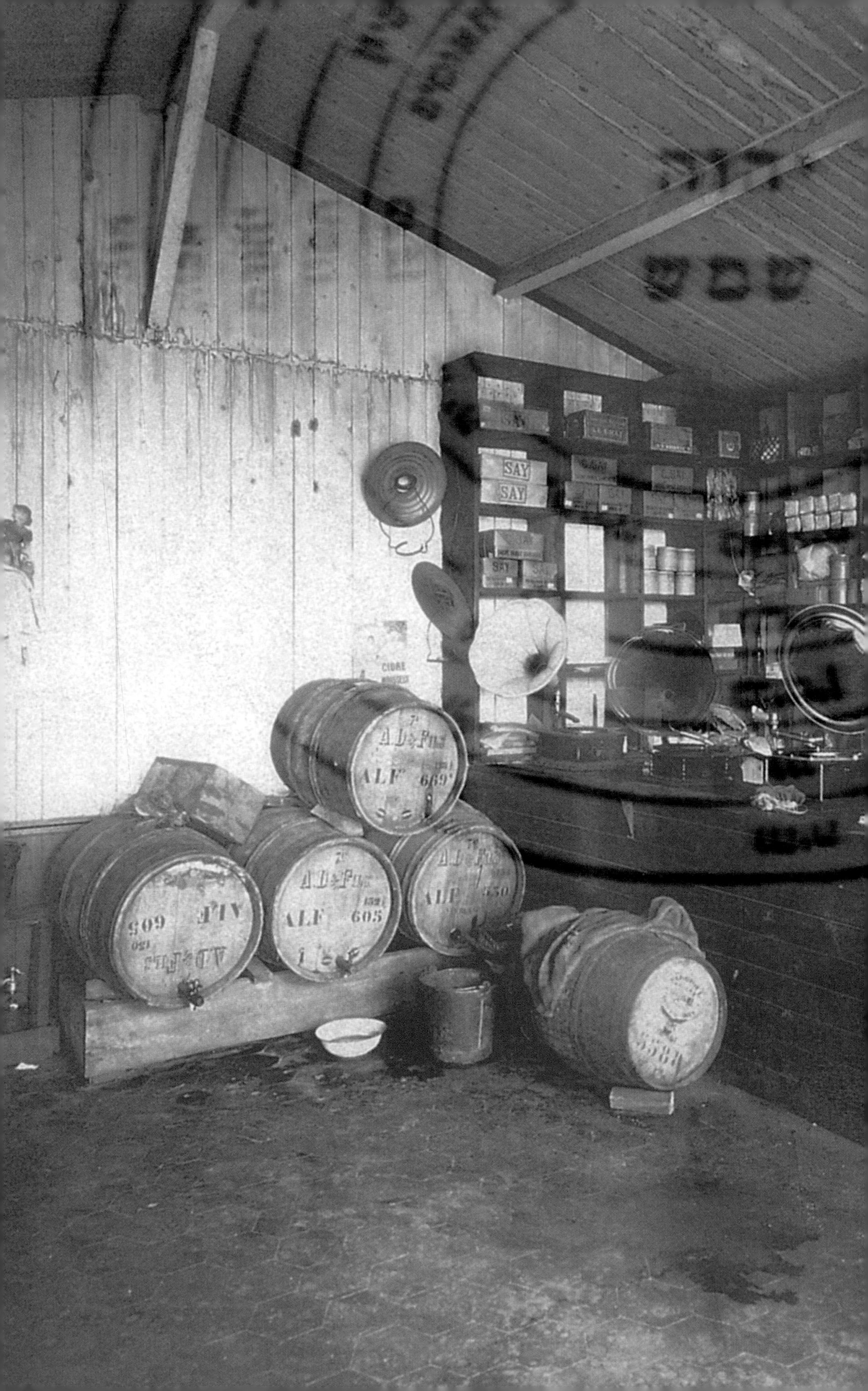
SAY
SAY
CIDRE
ALF 669
ALF 605

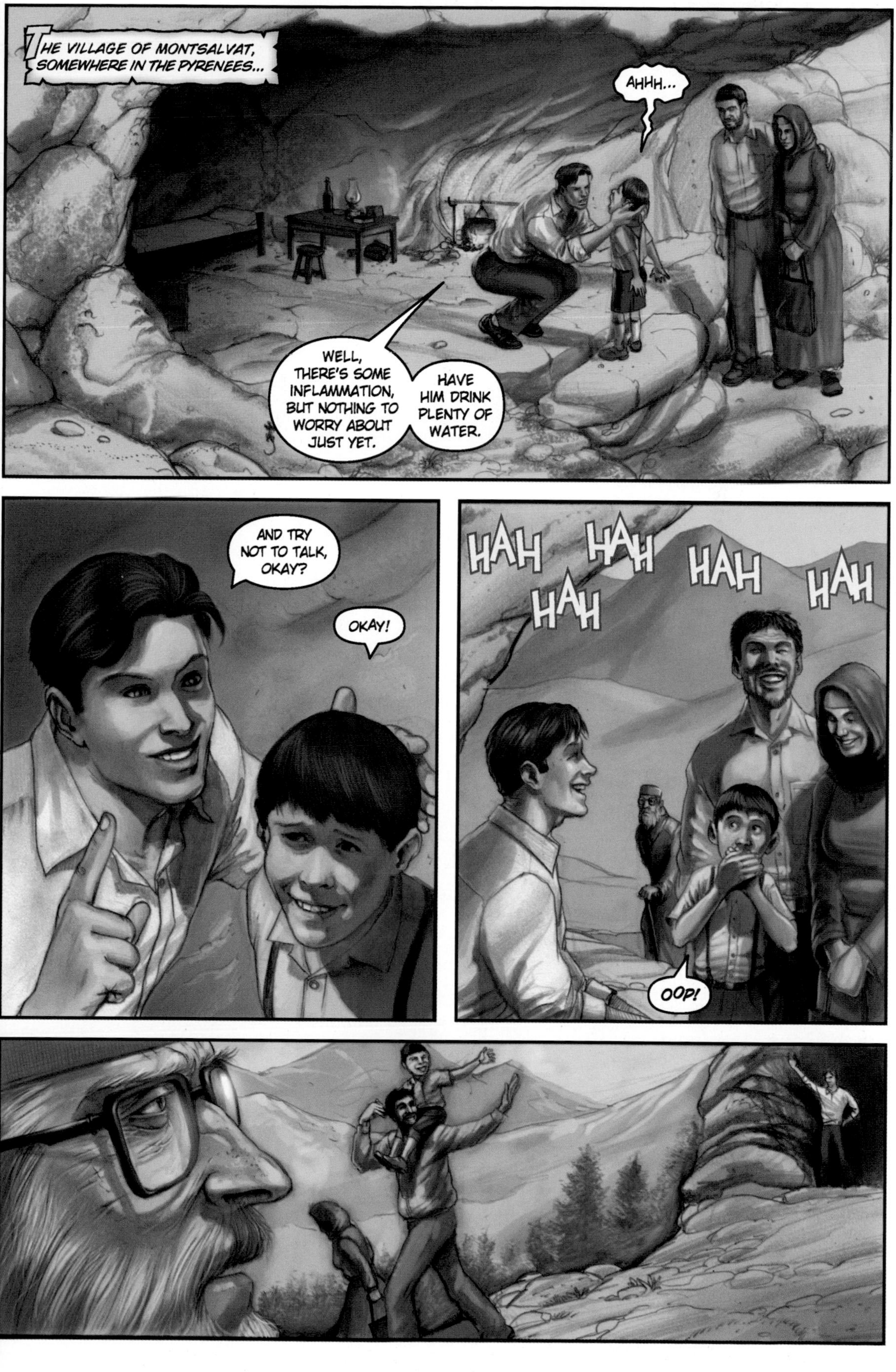
THE VILLAGE OF MONTSALVAT, SOMEWHERE IN THE PYRENEES...
AHHH...
WELL, THERE'S SOME INFLAMMATION, BUT NOTHING TO WORRY ABOUT JUST YET.
HAVE HIM DRINK PLENTY OF WATER.
AND TRY NOT TO TALK, OKAY?
OKAY!
HAH HAH HAH HAH HAH
OOP!

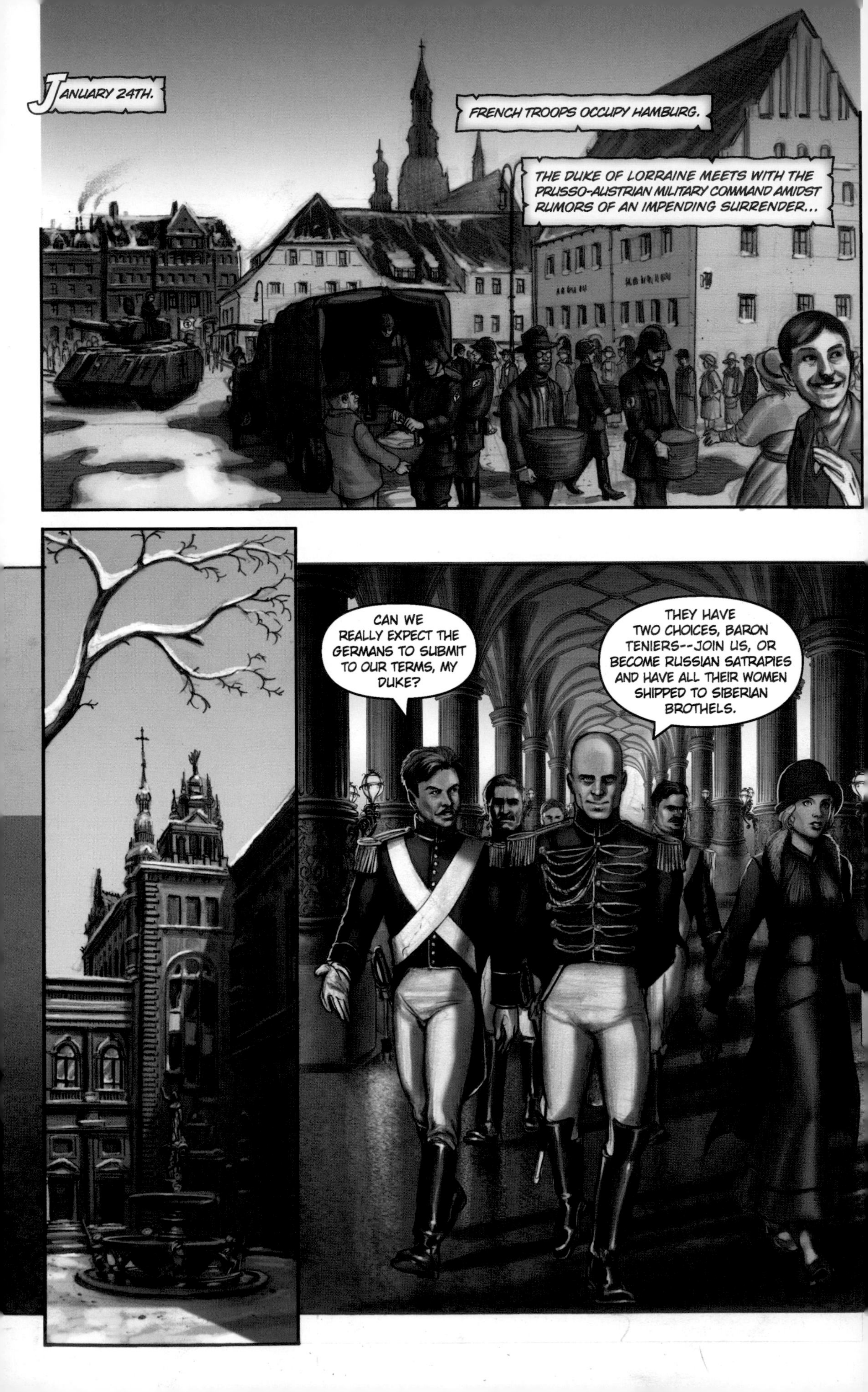
JANUARY 24TH.
FRENCH TROOPS OCCUPY HAMBURG.
THE DUKE OF LORRAINE MEETS WITH THE PRUSSO-AUSTRIAN MILITARY COMMAND AMIDST RUMORS OF AN IMPENDING SURRENDER...
CAN WE REALLY EXPECT THE GERMANS TO SUBMIT TO OUR TERMS, MY DUKE?
THEY HAVE TWO CHOICES, BARON TENIERS--JOIN US, OR BECOME RUSSIAN SATRAPIES AND HAVE ALL THEIR WOMEN SHIPPED TO SIBERIAN BROTHELS.

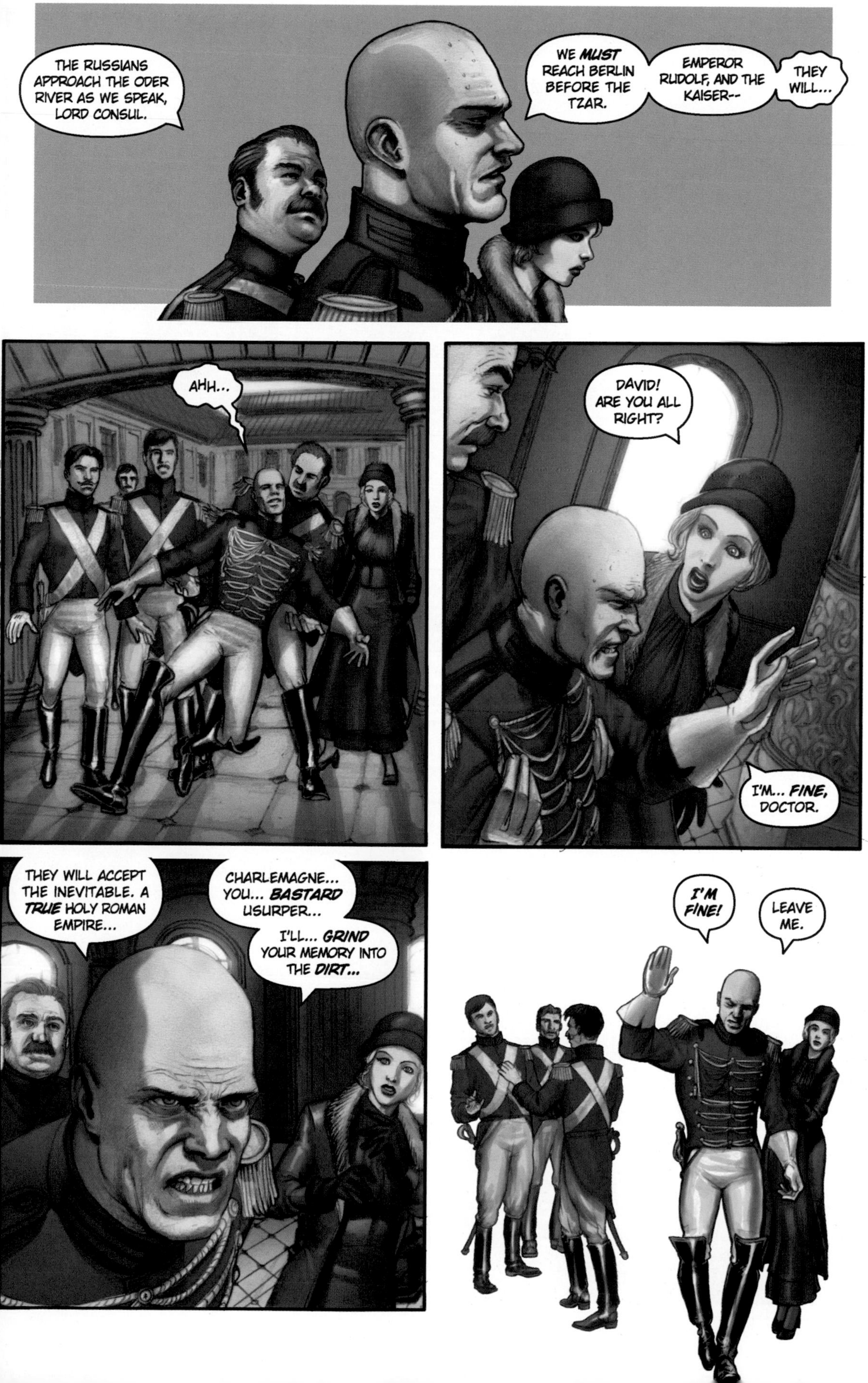
THE RUSSIANS APPROACH THE ODER RIVER AS WE SPEAK, LORD CONSUL.
WE MUST REACH BERLIN BEFORE THE TZAR.
EMPEROR RUDOLF, AND THE KAISER--
THEY WILL...
AHH...
DAVID! ARE YOU ALL RIGHT?
I'M... FINE, DOCTOR.
THEY WILL ACCEPT THE INEVITABLE. A TRUE HOLY ROMAN EMPIRE...
CHARLEMAGNE... YOU... BASTARD USURPER...
I'LL... GRIND YOUR MEMORY INTO THE DIRT...
I'M FINE!
LEAVE ME.

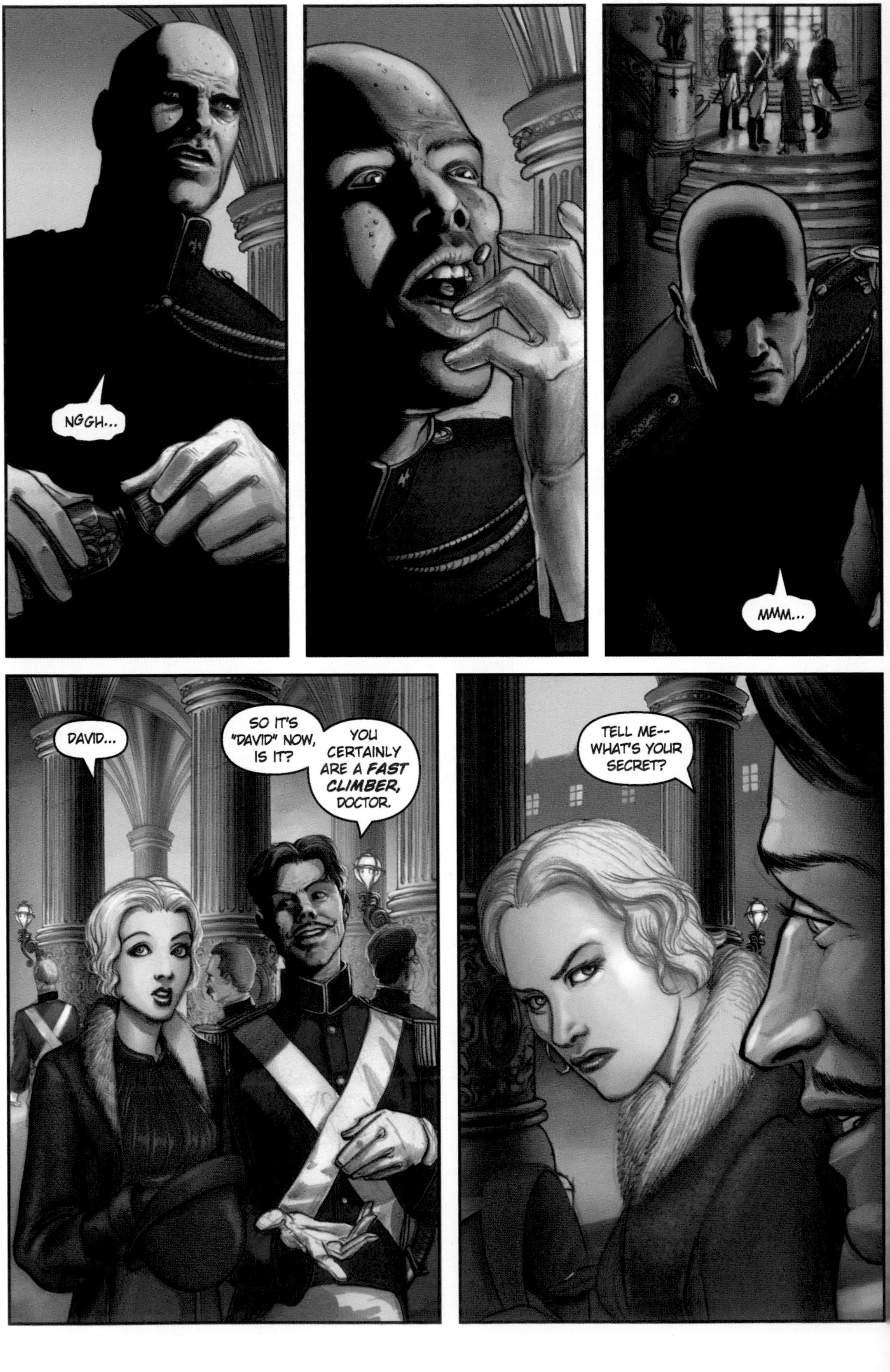
NGGH...
MMM...
DAVID...
SO IT'S "DAVID" NOW, IS IT?
YOU CERTAINLY ARE A FAST CLIMBER, DOCTOR.
TELL ME--WHAT'S YOUR SECRET?

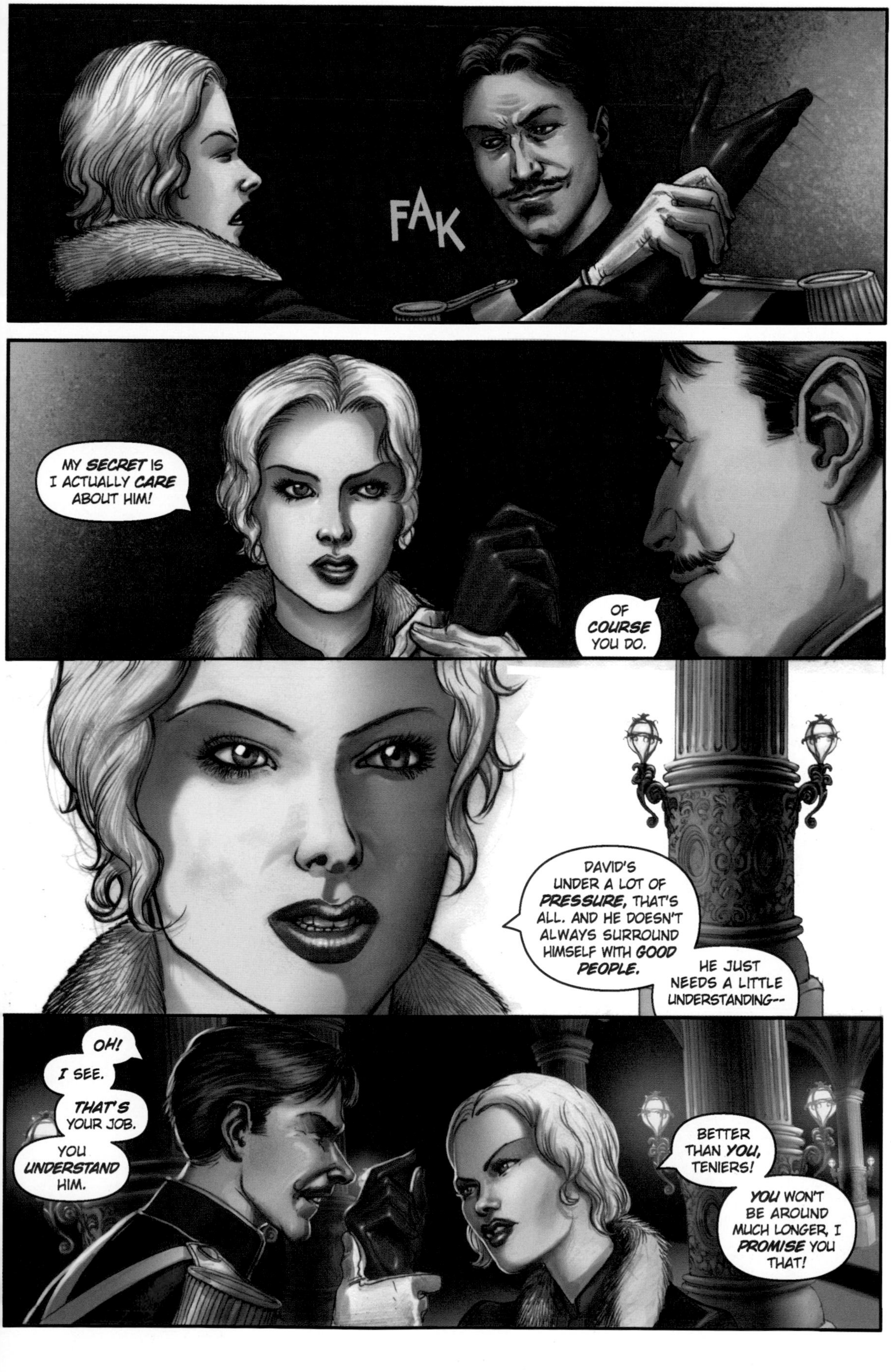
FAK
MY SECRET IS I ACTUALLY CARE ABOUT HIM!
OF COURSE YOU DO.
DAVID'S UNDER A LOT OF PRESSURE, THAT'S ALL. AND HE DOESN'T ALWAYS SURROUND HIMSELF WITH GOOD PEOPLE.
HE JUST NEEDS A LITTLE UNDERSTANDING--
OH!
I SEE.
THAT'S YOUR JOB.
YOU UNDERSTAND HIM.
BETTER THAN YOU, TENIERS!
YOU WON'T BE AROUND MUCH LONGER, I PROMISE YOU THAT!

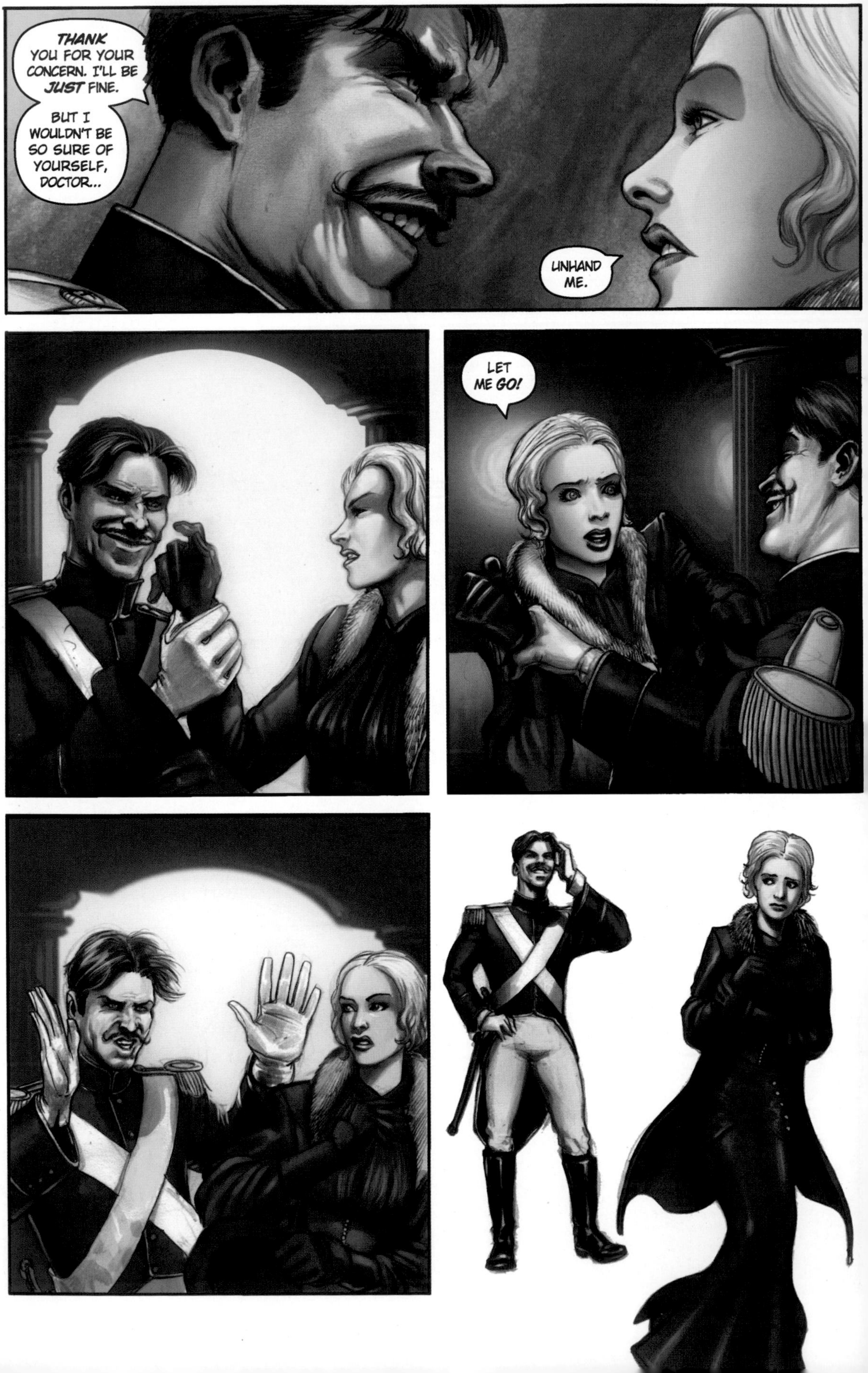
THANK YOU FOR YOUR CONCERN. I'LL BE JUST FINE.
BUT I WOULDN'T BE SO SURE OF YOURSELF, DOCTOR...
UNHAND ME.
LET ME GO!

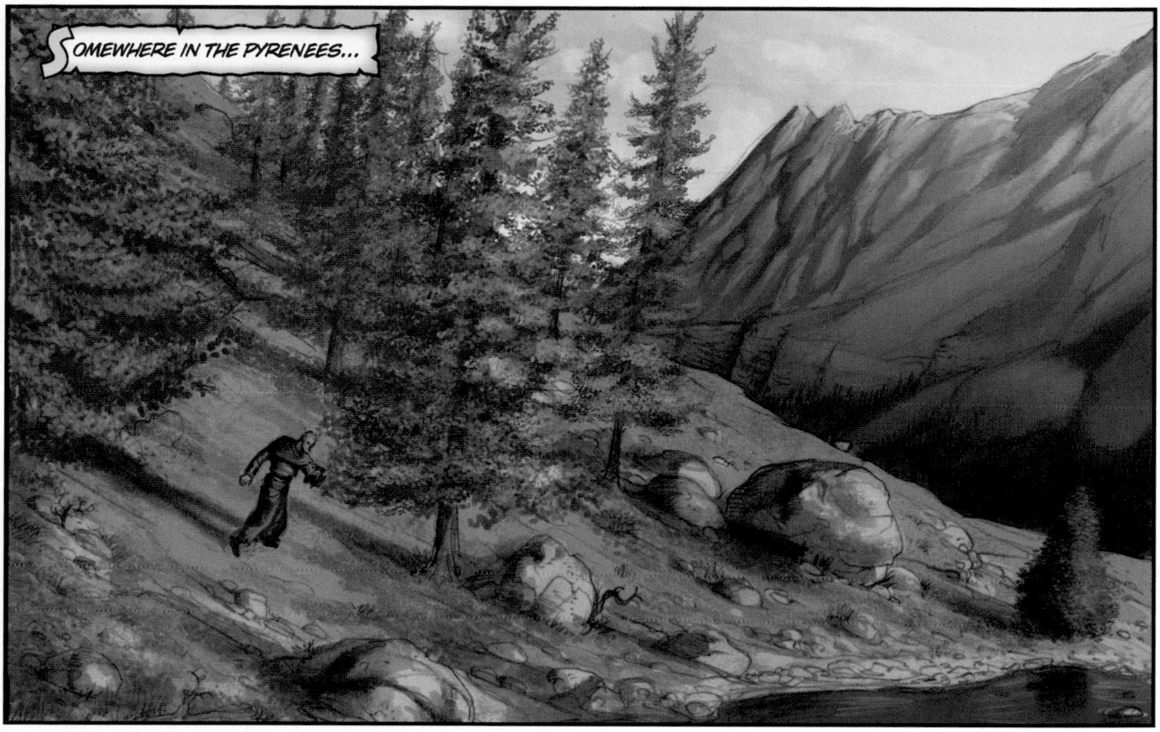
SOMEWHERE IN THE PYRENEES...

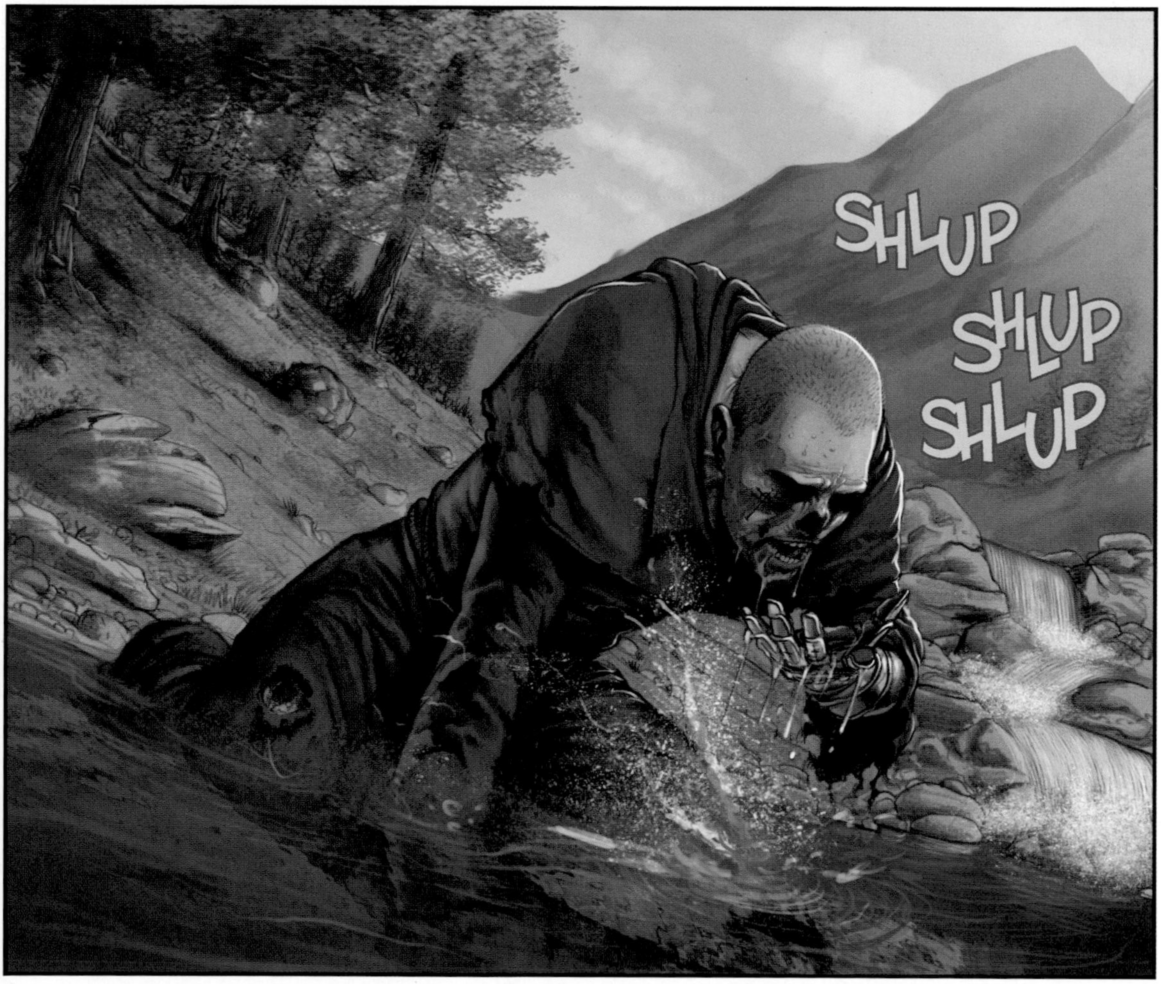
SHLUP
SHLUP
SHLUP

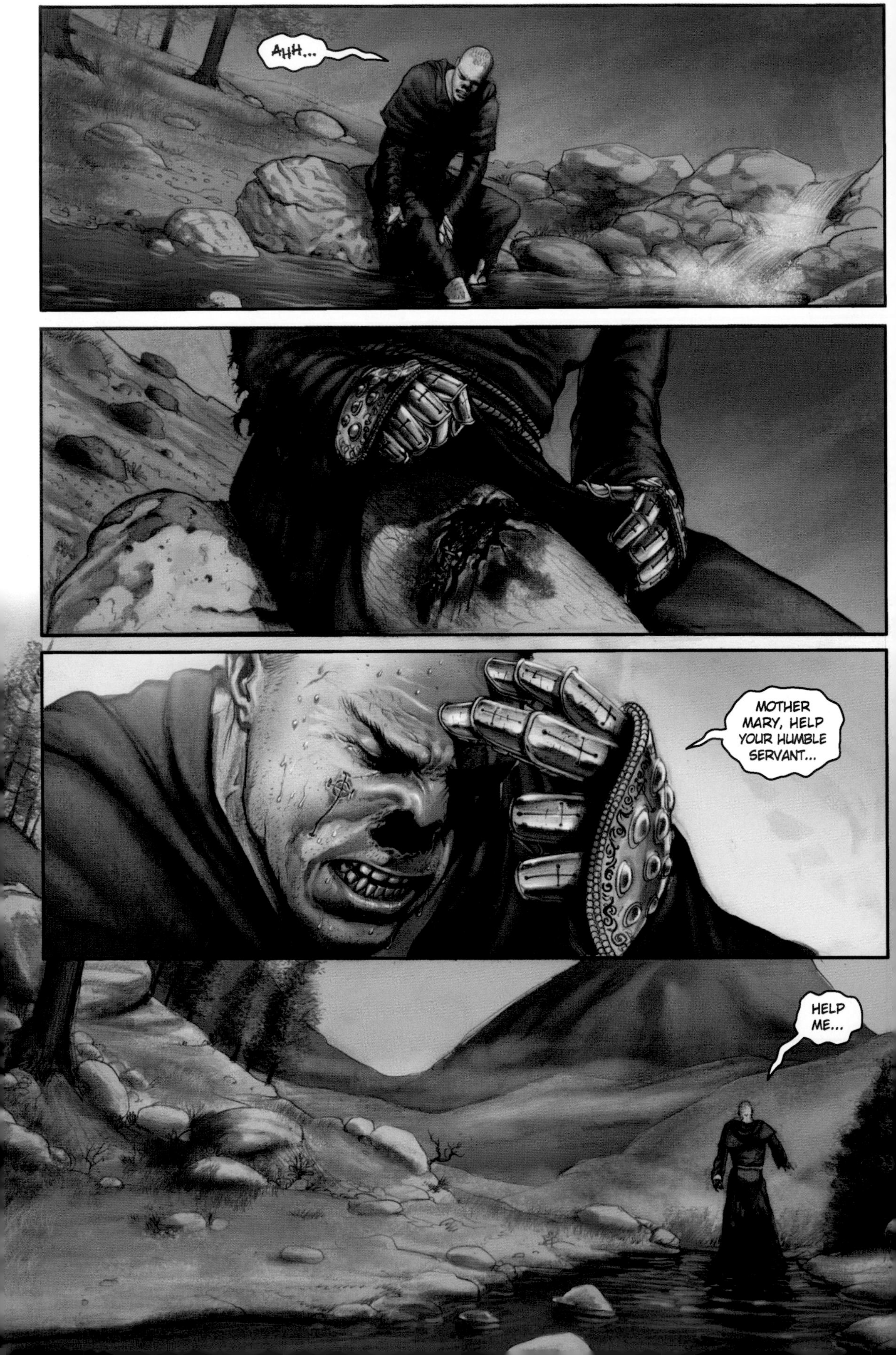
AHH...
MOTHER MARY, HELP YOUR HUMBLE SERVANT...
HELP ME...

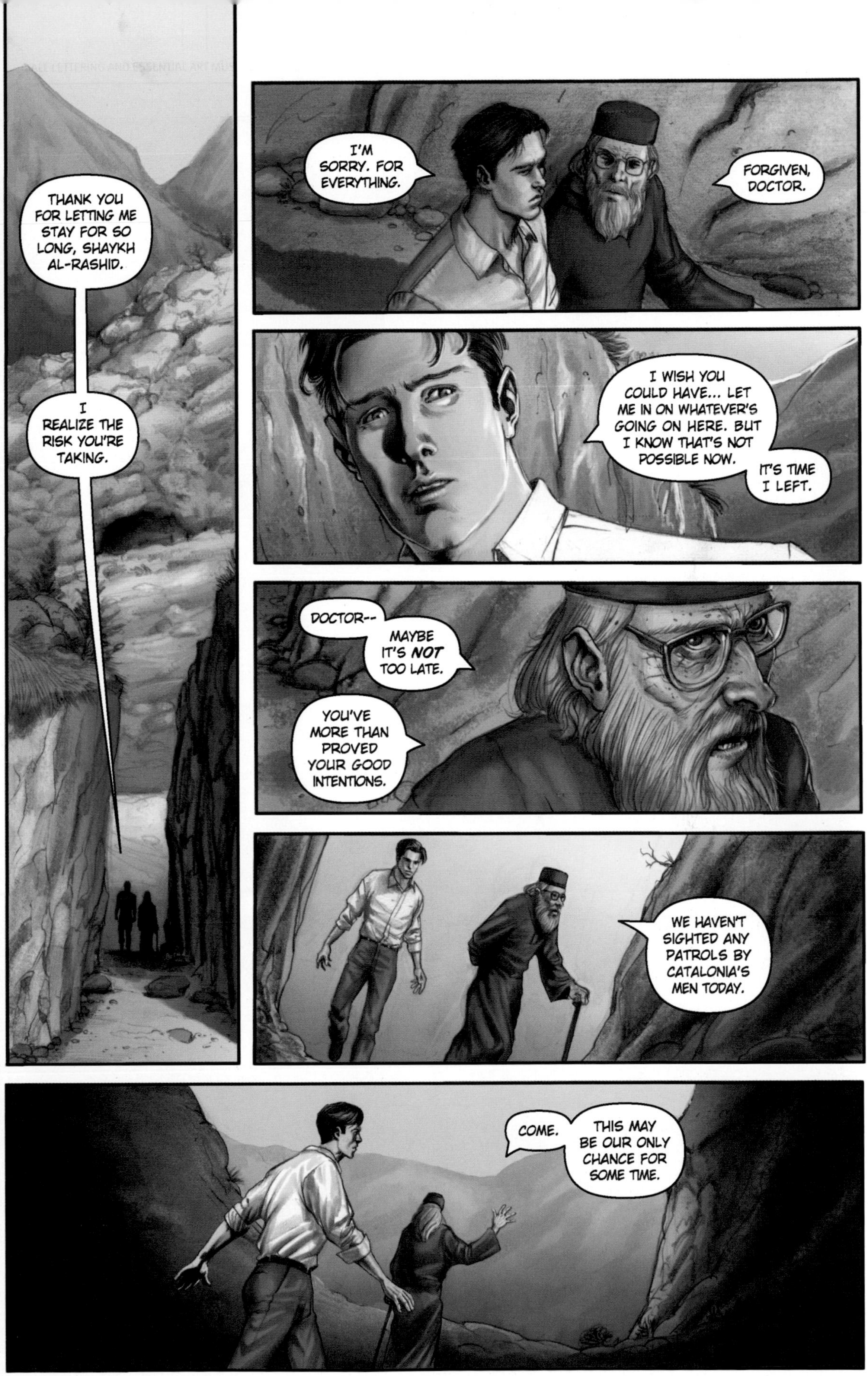
THANK YOU FOR LETTING ME STAY FOR SO LONG, SHAYKH AL-RASHID.
I REALIZE THE RISK YOU'RE TAKING.
I'M SORRY. FOR EVERYTHING.
FORGIVEN, DOCTOR.
I WISH YOU COULD HAVE... LET ME IN ON WHATEVER'S GOING ON HERE. BUT I KNOW THAT'S NOT POSSIBLE NOW.
IT'S TIME I LEFT.
DOCTOR--
MAYBE IT'S NOT TOO LATE.
YOU'VE MORE THAN PROVED YOUR GOOD INTENTIONS.
WE HAVEN'T SIGHTED ANY PATROLS BY CATALONIA'S MEN TODAY.
COME.
THIS MAY BE OUR ONLY CHANCE FOR SOME TIME.

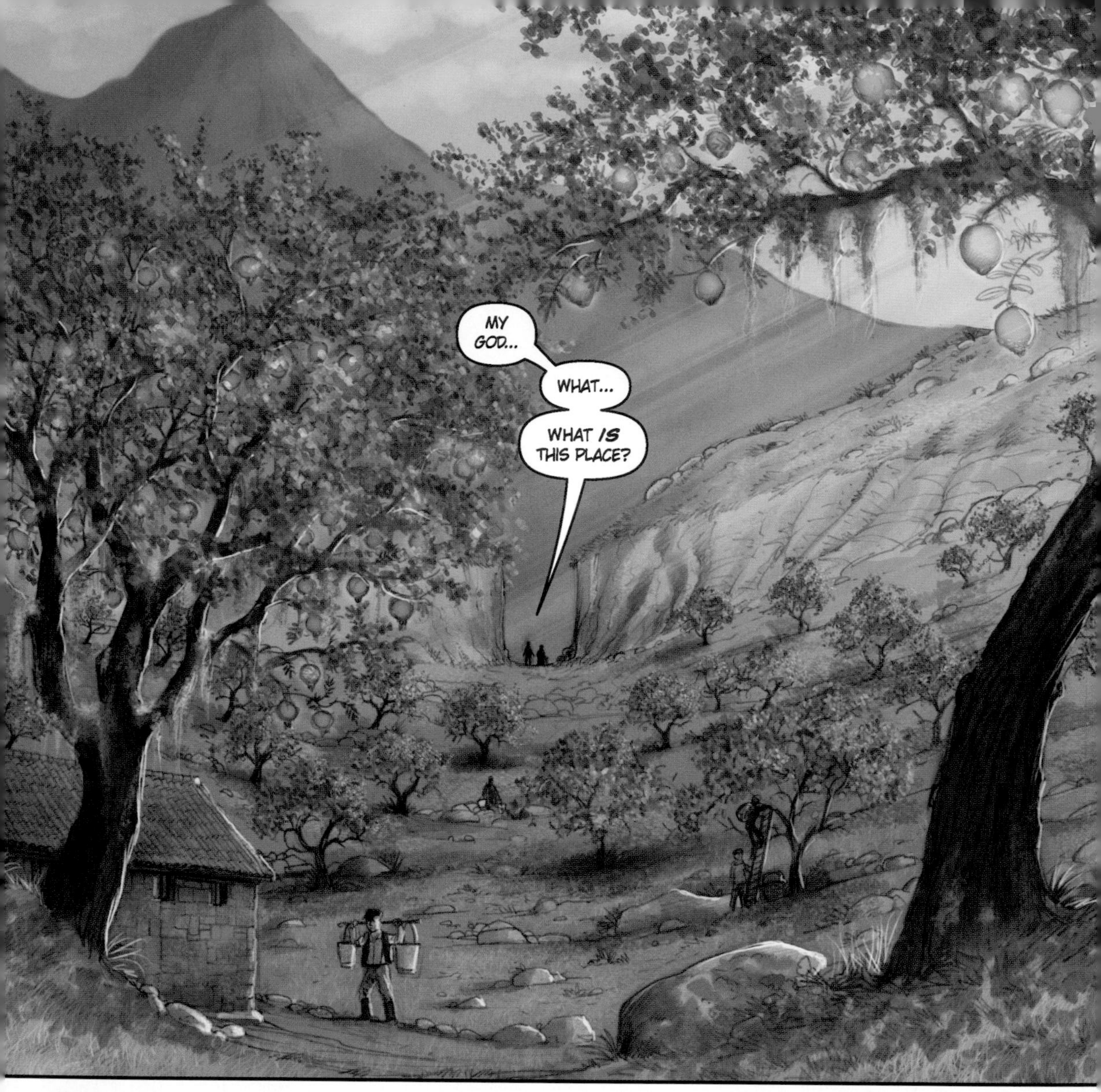
MY GOD...
WHAT...
WHAT *IS* THIS PLACE?

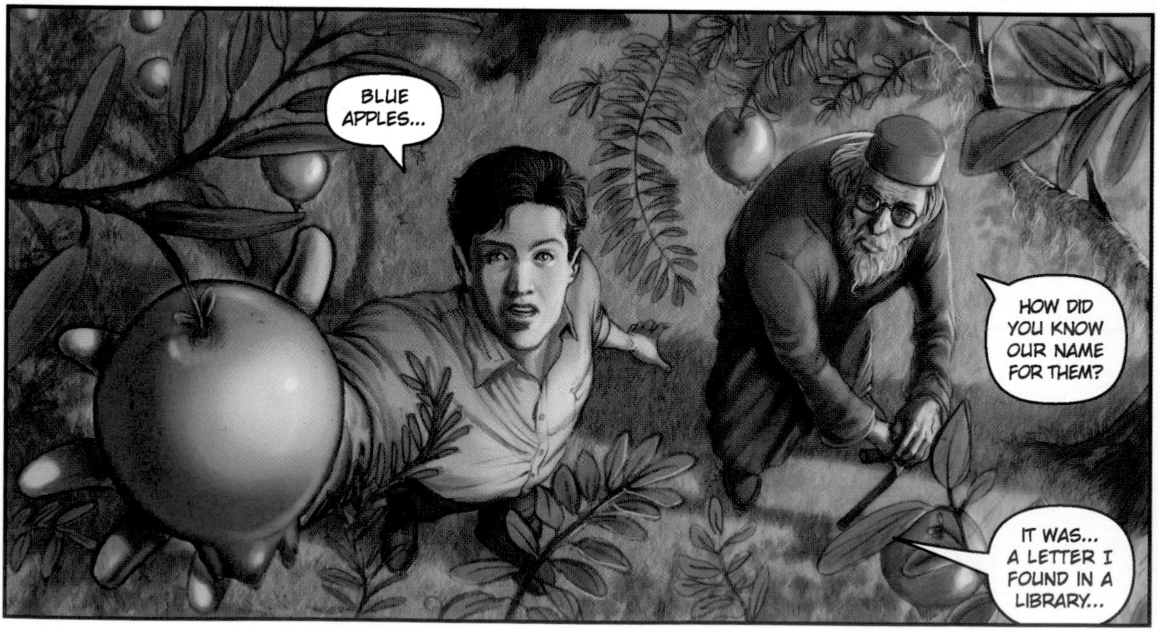
BLUE APPLES...
HOW DID YOU KNOW OUR NAME FOR THEM?
IT WAS... A LETTER I FOUND IN A LIBRARY...

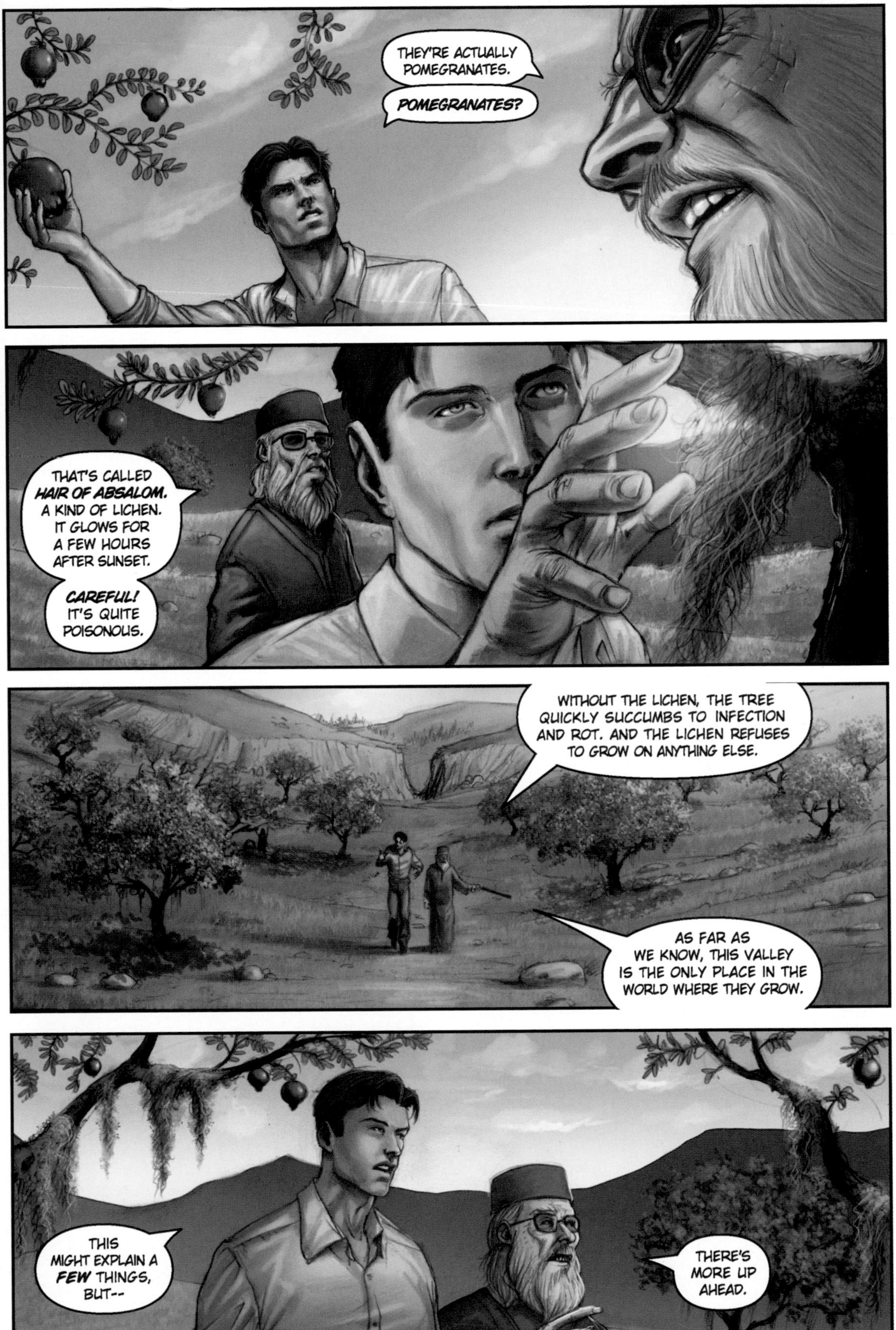
THEY'RE ACTUALLY POMEGRANATES.
POMEGRANATES?
THAT'S CALLED ***HAIR OF ABSALOM.*** A KIND OF LICHEN. IT GLOWS FOR A FEW HOURS AFTER SUNSET.
CAREFUL! IT'S QUITE POISONOUS.
WITHOUT THE LICHEN, THE TREE QUICKLY SUCCUMBS TO INFECTION AND ROT. AND THE LICHEN REFUSES TO GROW ON ANYTHING ELSE.
AS FAR AS WE KNOW, THIS VALLEY IS THE ONLY PLACE IN THE WORLD WHERE THEY GROW.
THIS MIGHT EXPLAIN A ***FEW*** THINGS, BUT--
THERE'S MORE UP AHEAD.

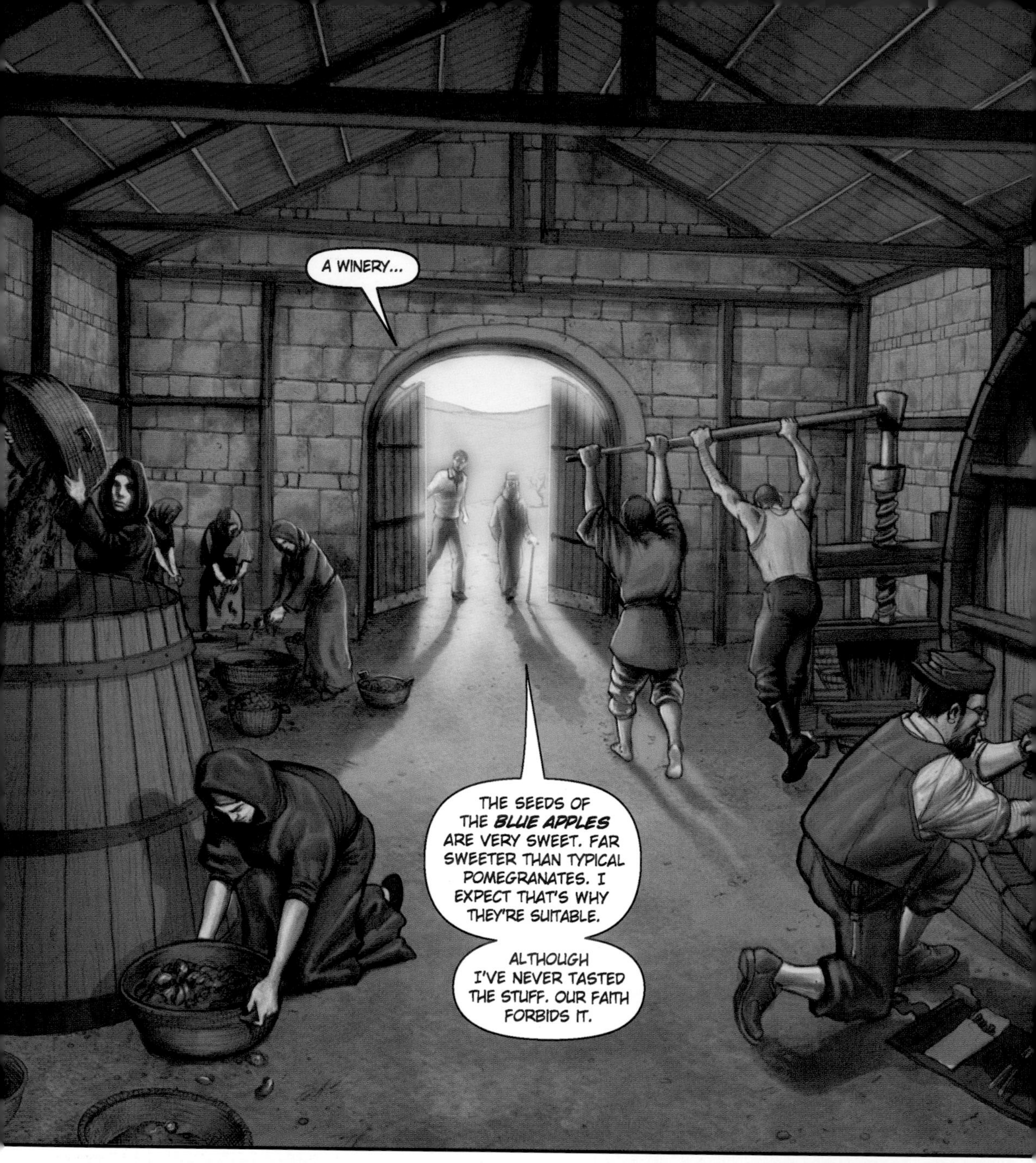
A WINERY...
THE SEEDS OF THE BLUE APPLES ARE VERY SWEET. FAR SWEETER THAN TYPICAL POMEGRANATES. I EXPECT THAT'S WHY THEY'RE SUITABLE.
ALTHOUGH I'VE NEVER TASTED THE STUFF. OUR FAITH FORBIDS IT.

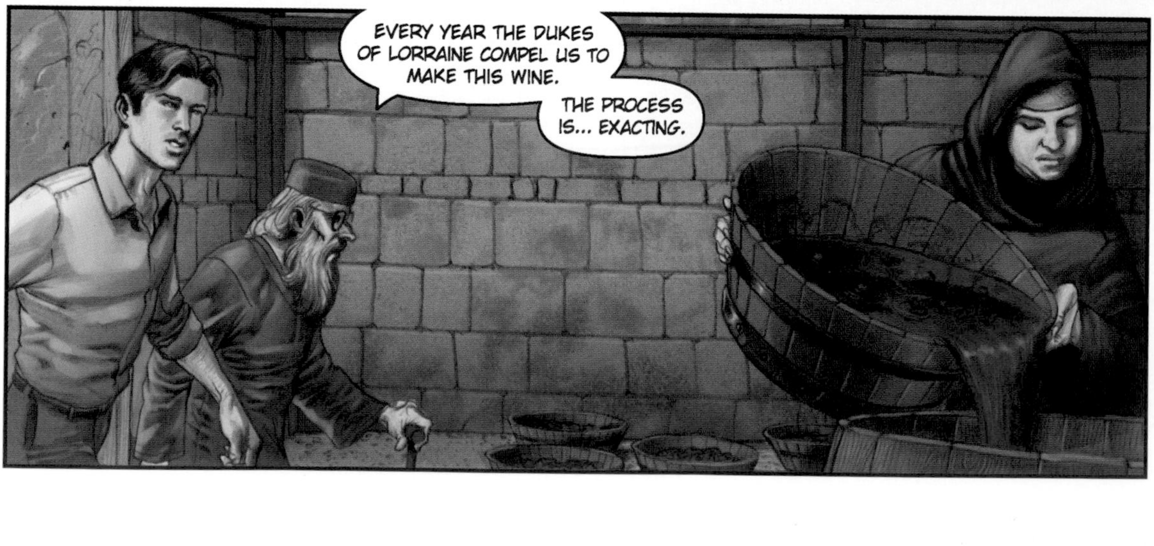
EVERY YEAR THE DUKES OF LORRAINE COMPEL US TO MAKE THIS WINE.
THE PROCESS IS... EXACTING.

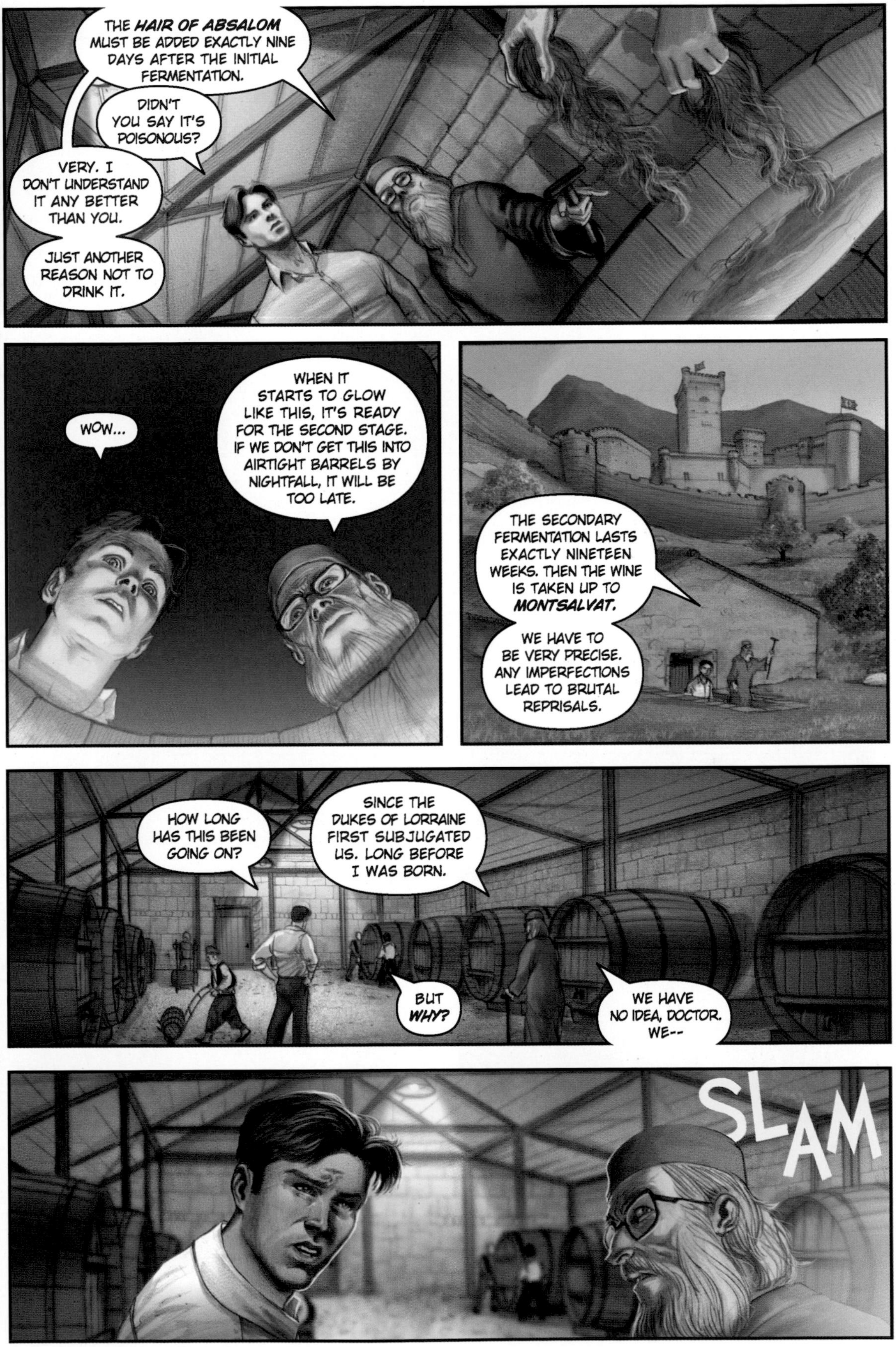
THE *HAIR OF ABSALOM* MUST BE ADDED EXACTLY NINE DAYS AFTER THE INITIAL FERMENTATION.
DIDN'T YOU SAY IT'S POISONOUS?
VERY. I DON'T UNDERSTAND IT ANY BETTER THAN YOU.
JUST ANOTHER REASON NOT TO DRINK IT.
WOW...
WHEN IT STARTS TO GLOW LIKE THIS, IT'S READY FOR THE SECOND STAGE. IF WE DON'T GET THIS INTO AIRTIGHT BARRELS BY NIGHTFALL, IT WILL BE TOO LATE.
THE SECONDARY FERMENTATION LASTS EXACTLY NINETEEN WEEKS. THEN THE WINE IS TAKEN UP TO *MONTSALVAT.*
WE HAVE TO BE VERY PRECISE. ANY IMPERFECTIONS LEAD TO BRUTAL REPRISALS.
HOW LONG HAS THIS BEEN GOING ON?
SINCE THE DUKES OF LORRAINE FIRST SUBJUGATED US. LONG BEFORE I WAS BORN.
BUT *WHY?*
WE HAVE NO IDEA, DOCTOR. WE--
SLAM

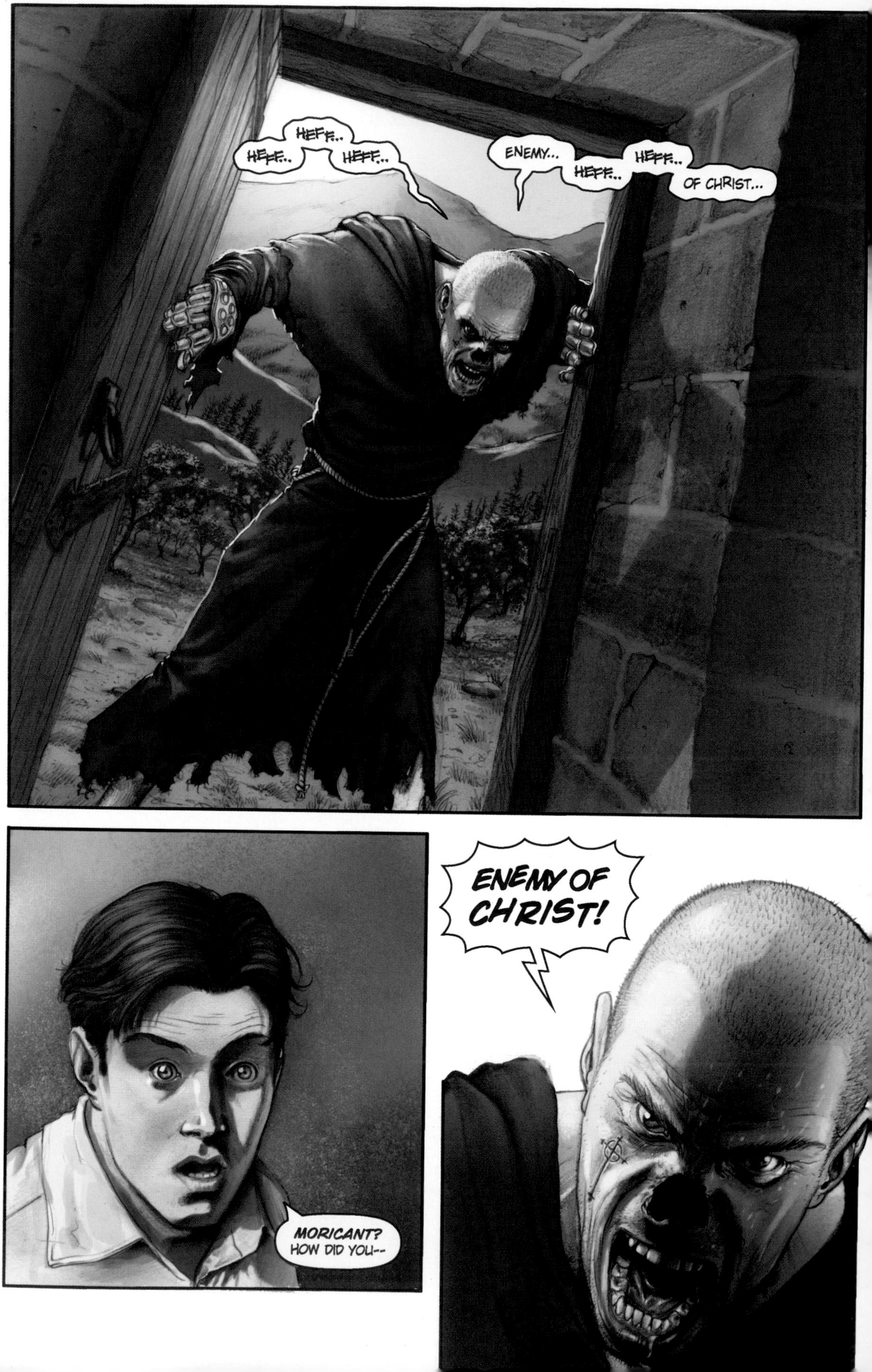
HEFF.. HEFF.. HEFF..
ENEMY... HEFF... HEFF... OF CHRIST...
MORICANT? HOW DID YOU--
ENEMY OF CHRIST!

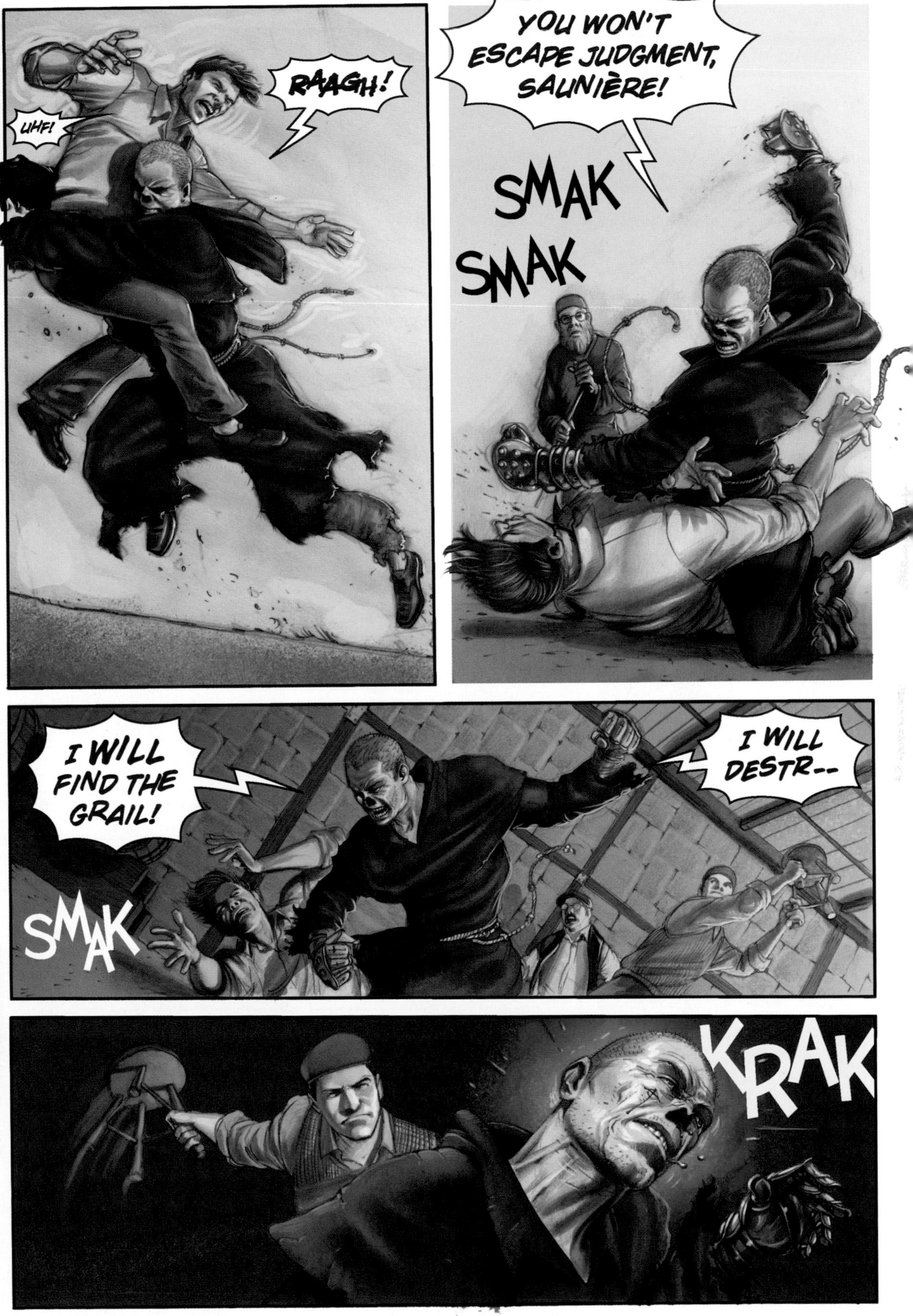
UHF!
RAAGH!
YOU WON'T ESCAPE JUDGMENT, SAUNIÈRE!
SMAK
SMAK
I WILL FIND THE GRAIL!
I WILL DESTR--
SMAK
KRAK

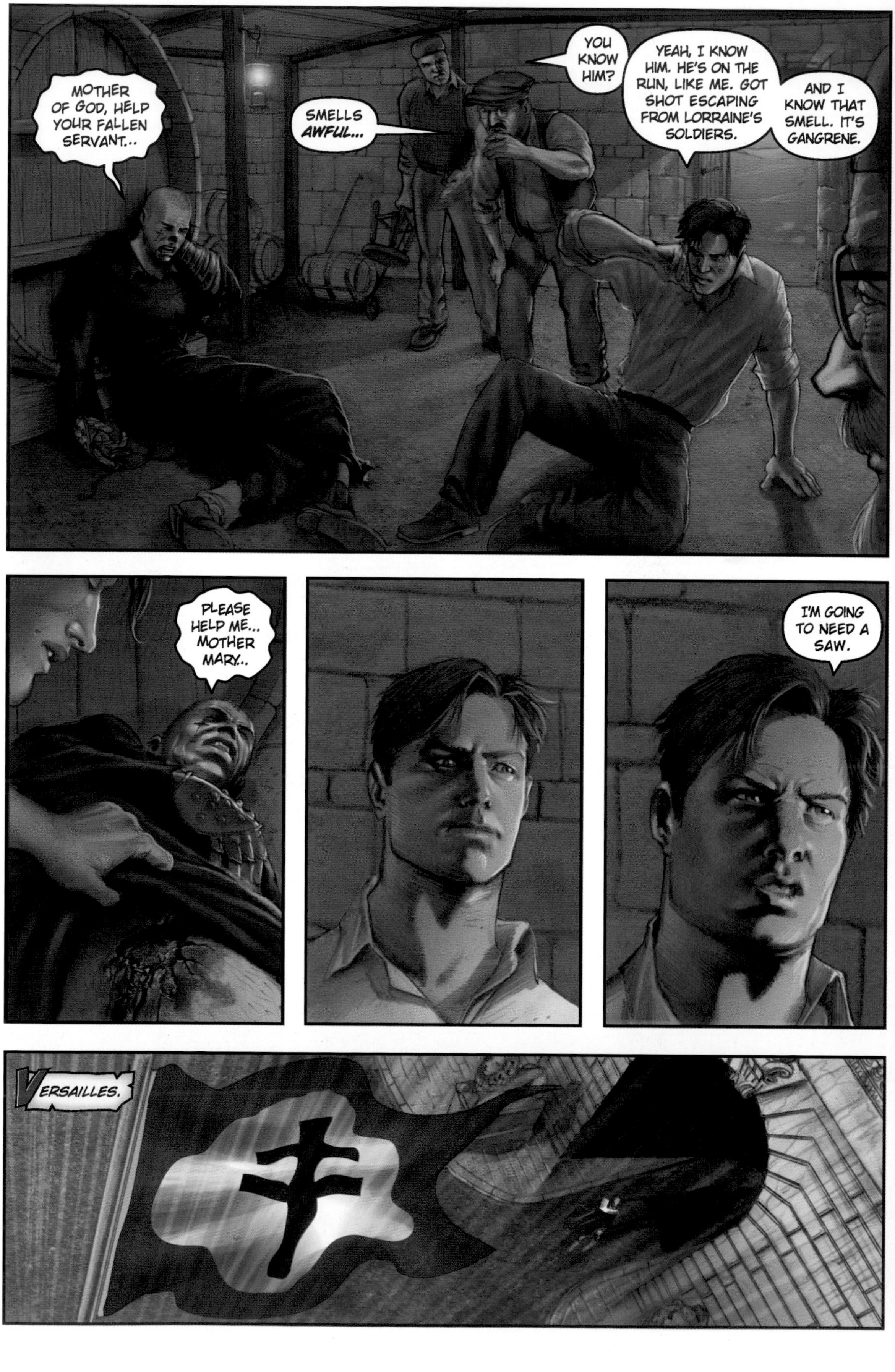
MOTHER OF GOD, HELP YOUR FALLEN SERVANT...
SMELLS AWFUL...
YOU KNOW HIM?
YEAH, I KNOW HIM. HE'S ON THE RUN, LIKE ME. GOT SHOT ESCAPING FROM LORRAINE'S SOLDIERS.
AND I KNOW THAT SMELL. IT'S GANGRENE.
PLEASE HELP ME... MOTHER MARY...
I'M GOING TO NEED A SAW.
VERSAILLES.

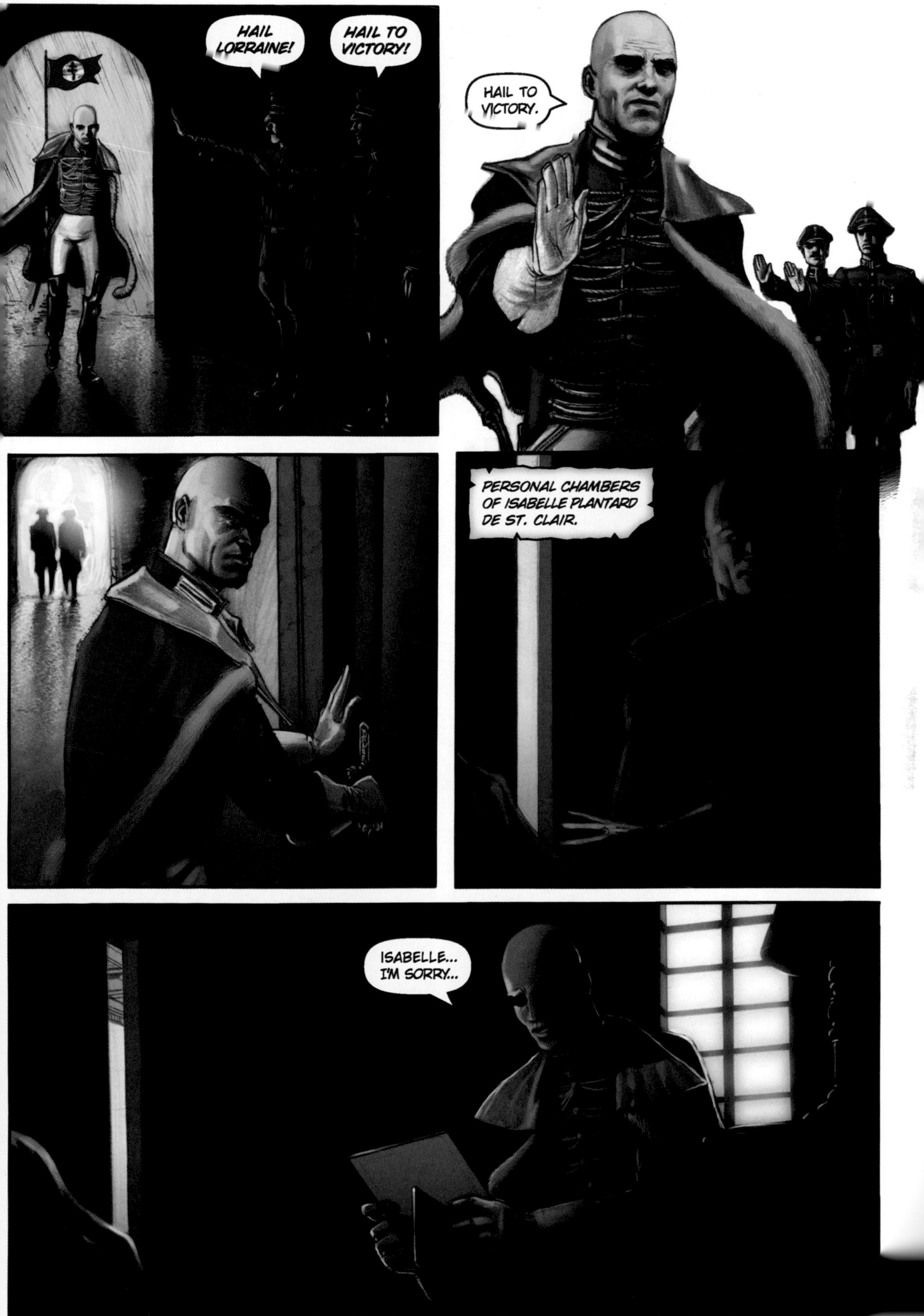
HAIL LORRAINE!
HAIL TO VICTORY!
HAIL TO VICTORY.
PERSONAL CHAMBERS OF ISABELLE PLANTARD DE ST. CLAIR.
ISABELLE... I'M SORRY...

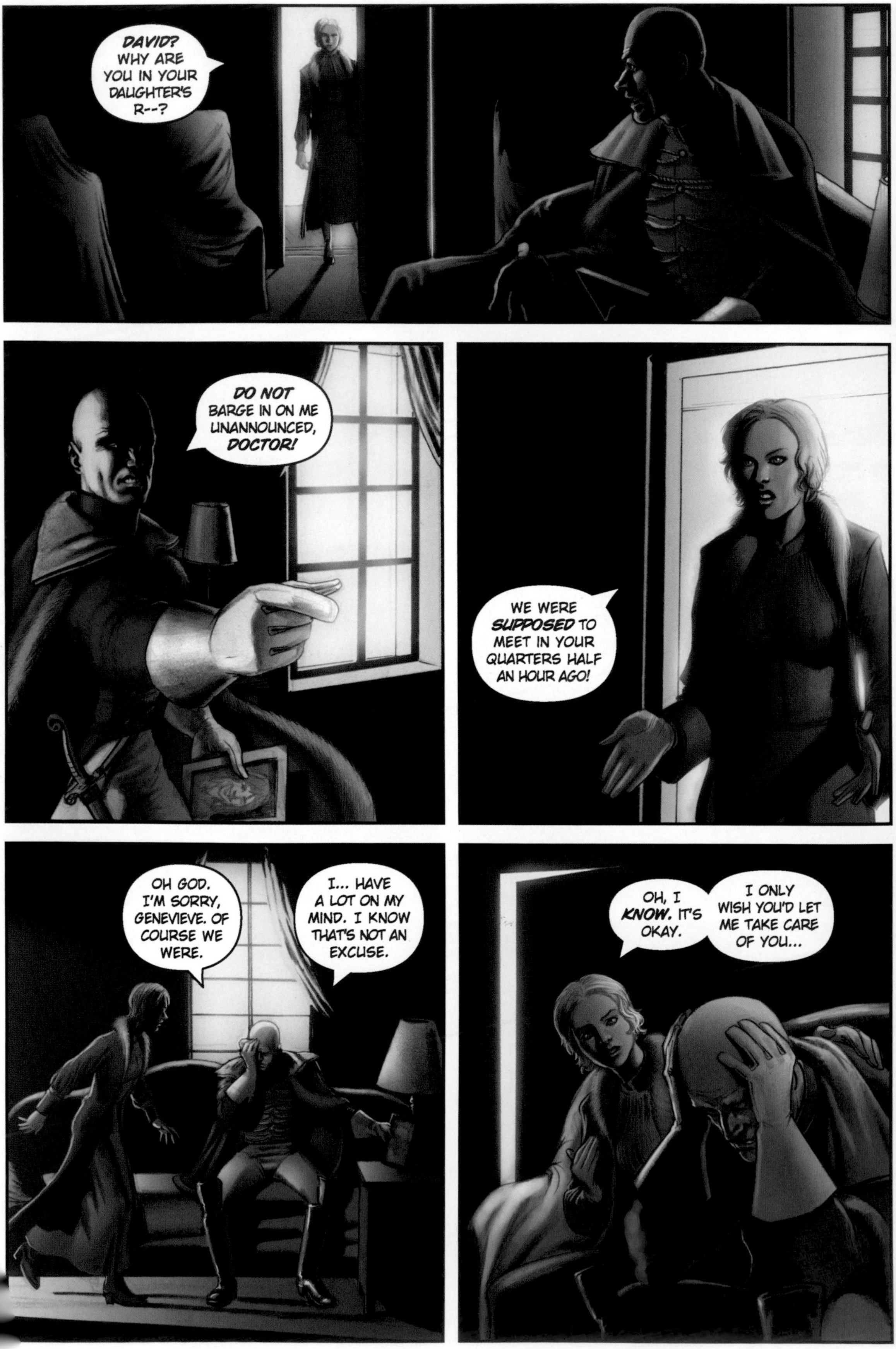
DAVID? WHY ARE YOU IN YOUR DAUGHTER'S R--?
DO NOT BARGE IN ON ME UNANNOUNCED, DOCTOR!
WE WERE SUPPOSED TO MEET IN YOUR QUARTERS HALF AN HOUR AGO!
OH GOD. I'M SORRY, GENEVIEVE. OF COURSE WE WERE.
I... HAVE A LOT ON MY MIND. I KNOW THAT'S NOT AN EXCUSE.
OH, I KNOW. IT'S OKAY.
I ONLY WISH YOU'D LET ME TAKE CARE OF YOU...

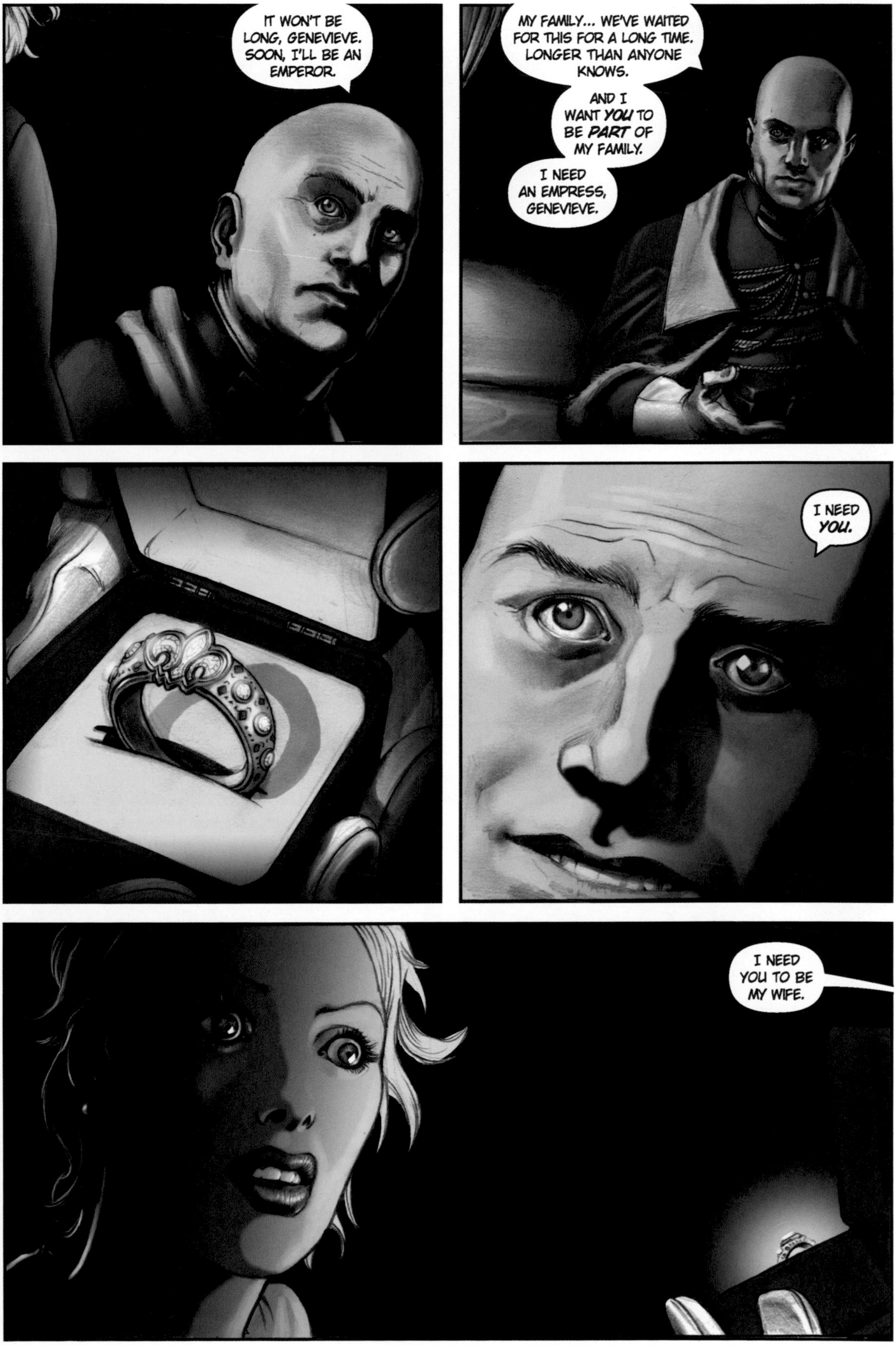
IT WON'T BE LONG, GENEVIEVE. SOON, I'LL BE AN EMPEROR.
MY FAMILY... WE'VE WAITED FOR THIS FOR A LONG TIME. LONGER THAN ANYONE KNOWS.
AND I WANT *YOU* TO BE *PART* OF MY FAMILY.
I NEED AN EMPRESS, GENEVIEVE.
I NEED *YOU.*
I NEED YOU TO BE MY WIFE.

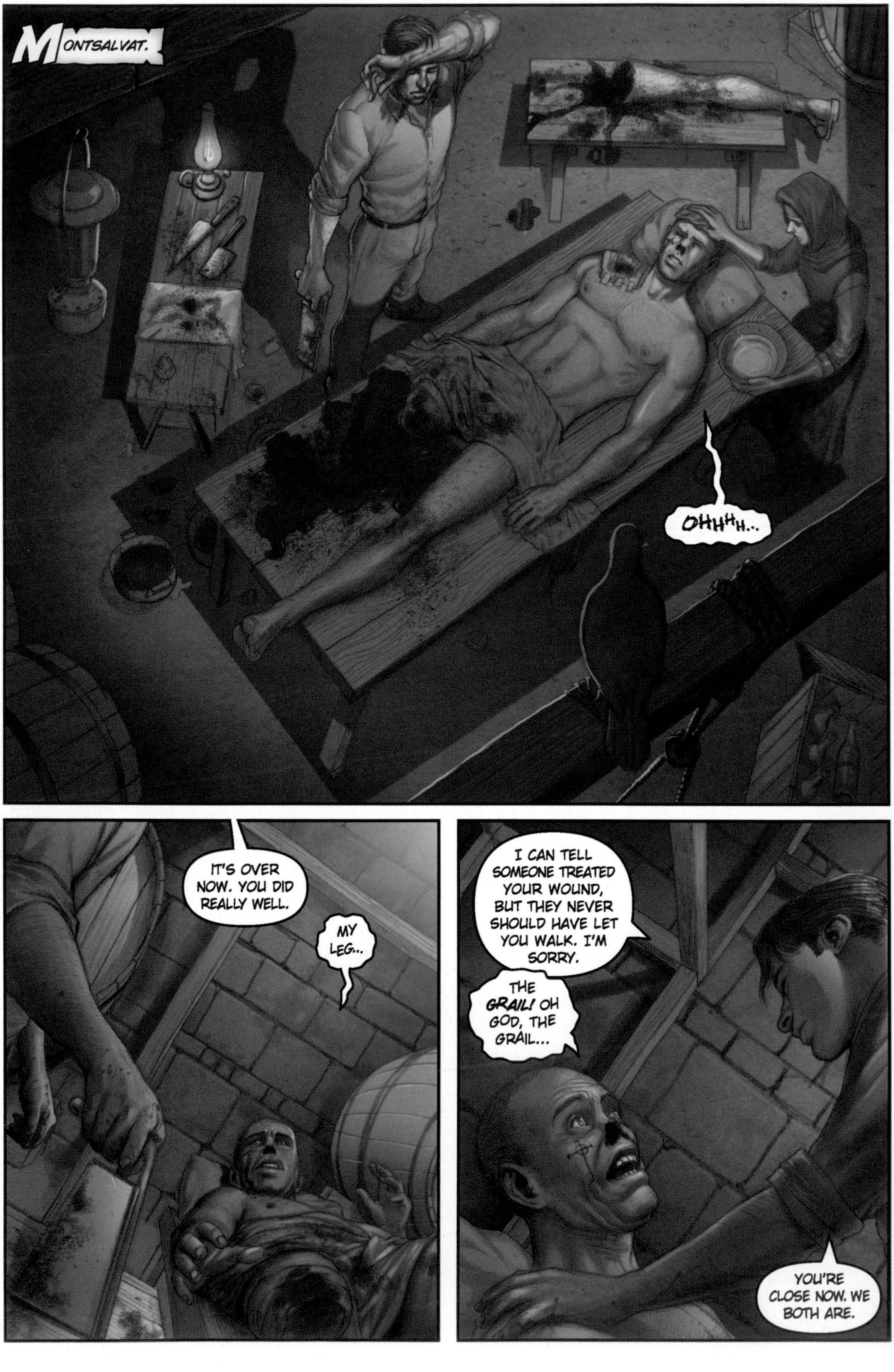
MONTSALVAT.
OHHHH...
IT'S OVER NOW. YOU DID REALLY WELL.
MY LEG...
I CAN TELL SOMEONE TREATED YOUR WOUND, BUT THEY NEVER SHOULD HAVE LET YOU WALK. I'M SORRY.
THE GRAIL! OH GOD, THE GRAIL...
YOU'RE CLOSE NOW. WE BOTH ARE.

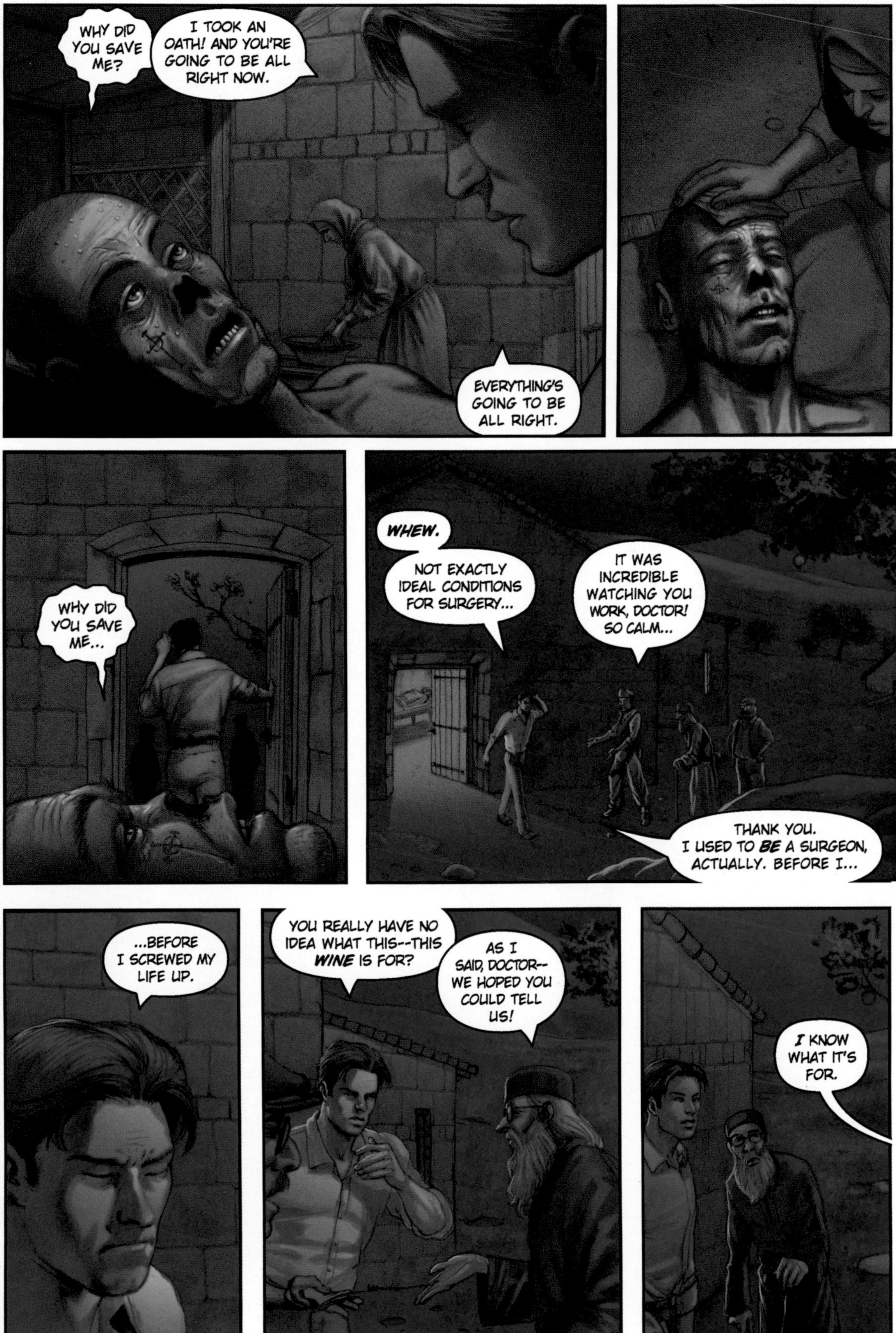
WHY DID YOU SAVE ME?
I TOOK AN OATH! AND YOU'RE GOING TO BE ALL RIGHT NOW.
EVERYTHING'S GOING TO BE ALL RIGHT.
WHY DID YOU SAVE ME...
WHEW.
NOT EXACTLY IDEAL CONDITIONS FOR SURGERY...
IT WAS INCREDIBLE WATCHING YOU WORK, DOCTOR! SO CALM...
THANK YOU. I USED TO BE A SURGEON, ACTUALLY. BEFORE I...
...BEFORE I SCREWED MY LIFE UP.
YOU REALLY HAVE NO IDEA WHAT THIS--THIS WINE IS FOR?
AS I SAID, DOCTOR-- WE HOPED YOU COULD TELL US!
I KNOW WHAT IT'S FOR.

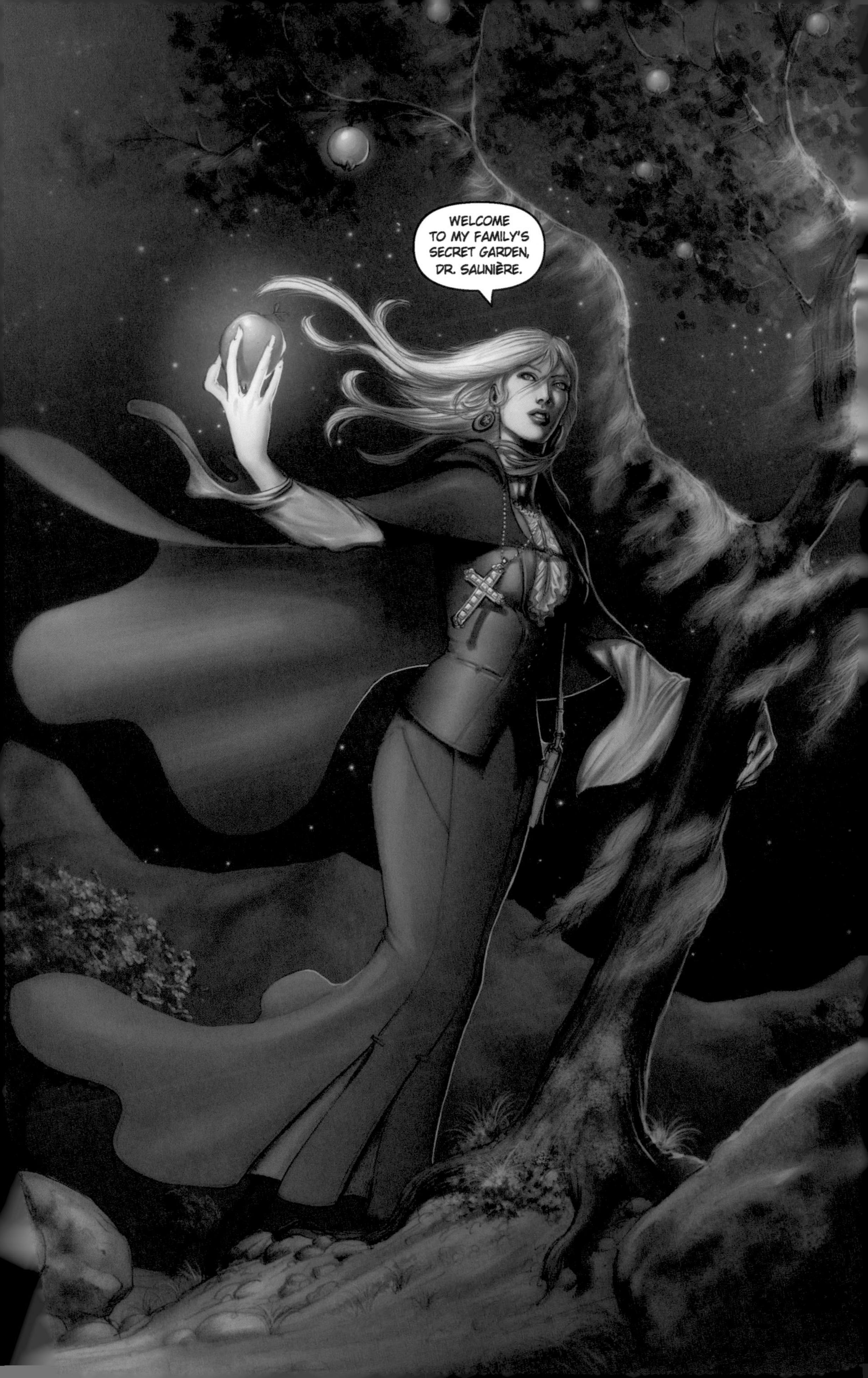
WELCOME TO MY FAMILY'S SECRET GARDEN, DR. SAUNIÈRE.

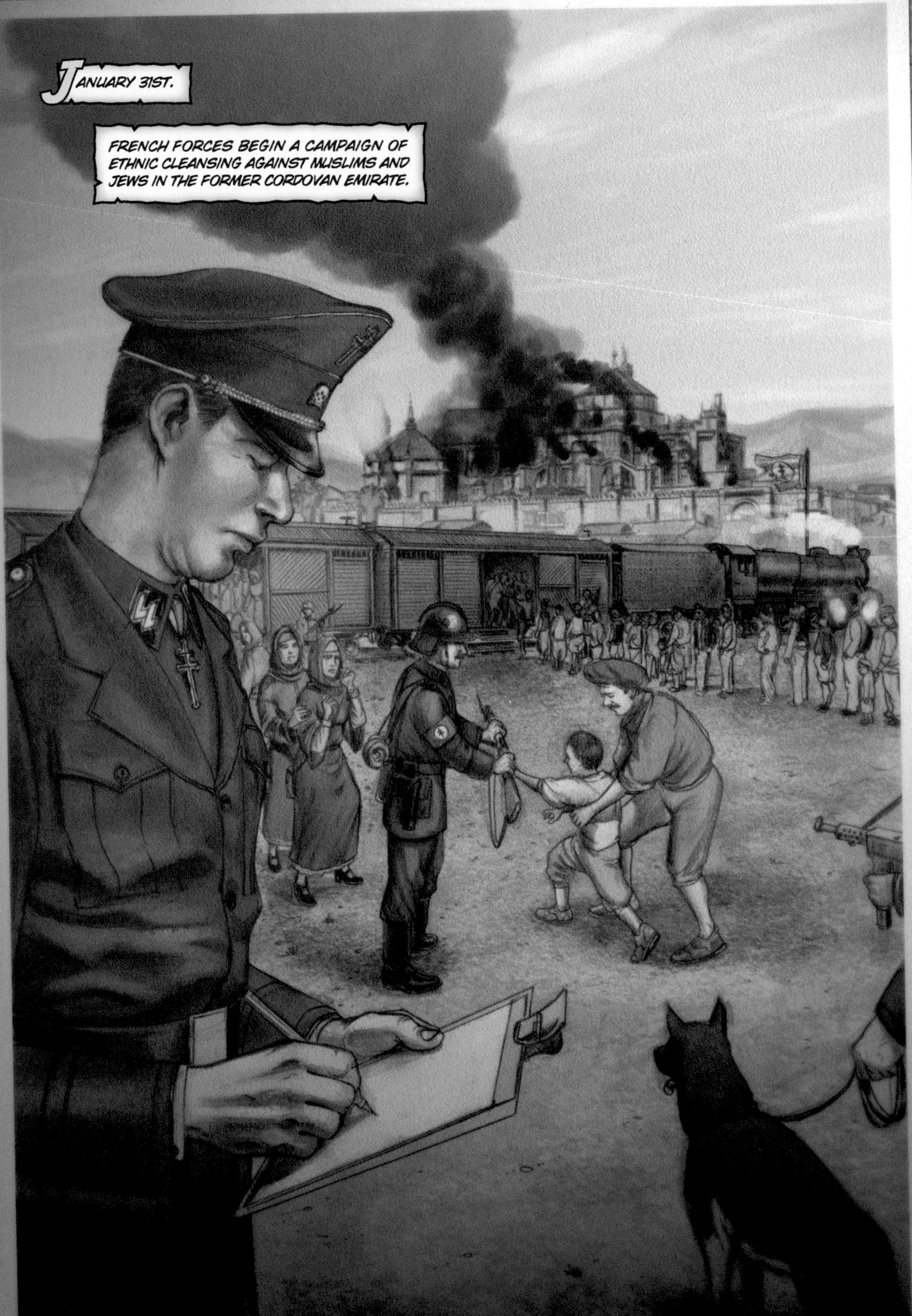
JANUARY 31ST.
FRENCH FORCES BEGIN A CAMPAIGN OF ETHNIC CLEANSING AGAINST MUSLIMS AND JEWS IN THE FORMER CORDOVAN EMIRATE.

Le Journal de la Liberté

Paris's leading anglophone newspaper • vol. 205, no. 171 • Feb. 1, MCMXXXIV

Editors in Chief: M. Michael Richardson, M. Scott Allie, M. Ryan Jorgensen. **Story Editor:** M. Arvid Nelson. **Art Editor:** M. Juan Ferreyra. **Photography Editor:** M. Eugène Atget. **Layout Supervisor:** M. Cary Grazzini. **Editors Emeritus:** M. Clark A. Smith, M. Howard P. Lovecraft, M. Robert E. Howard. *Le Journal de la Liberté* is printed under the benign auspices of his eminence David-Louis Plantard de St. Clair, Duke of Lorraine and First Consul of the Empire of France.

Official seal of

the First Consul

❖ **GOD SAVE LORD LORRAINE** ❖

The Prussian cruiser Wiesbaden *founders under heavy French fire. Sailors rushed over the side to an uncertain fate.*

"FRANKISH UNITY" MOVEMENT GROWING IN PRUSSIA, AUSTRIA

Hamburg, Prussia – As the French army continues its march into the Prussian heartland, more and more of the Kaiser's subjects are redefining their loyalties.

The Duke of Lorraine, First Consul of France, gave a public address in Hamburg's Stadtpark yesterday to a crowd estimated at over 100,000.

Lorraine said it was his goal to unite German and French people into a "new Holy Roman Empire, a true Holy Roman Empire."

"Only together can we reclaim the bloodright of our race," he said in his address.

This idea of "Frankish Unity" resonates deeply with many people, both inside France and in France's newly won territories. Increasingly, Prussians and Austrians are looking on Lorraine not as a conqueror, but a unifier.

"We have a common racial heritage and a common racial destiny," Lorraine said. "We are, all of us, descendants of the holy warriors who conquered Jerusalem for Christ in the First Crusade. We are Franks."

"Lorraine is a leader," Udo Gnaß, a day laborer listening to the address, said. "When I listen to him, I want to be part of something bigger than myself."

"Why should we fight each other? Isn't that exactly what the Mohammedans and the Jews want?" said Josef Odemar, a hotel owner. "Our culture is under siege. It's time to fight back."

Lorraine appeals to deep-seated popular mistrust of the Prussian Kaiser.

"The German people did not want war with France. We understand they only fight at the compulsion of a corrupt tyrant. We ourselves recently swept away a decayed monarchy," he said.

French troops have dealt gently with the Prussian territory under their control, distributing desperately needed food and fuel, and providing public safety and order. This is despite a harrowing opening to the war, in which the Prussian army captured Paris and nearly defeated Lorraine at Carcassonne.

The mercy and generosity of the French is in stark contrast to the massive Russian army invading Prussia from the east.

The Prussian forces trying to halt the advance have buckled under the pressure, and a deluge of refugees has flooded westward, bringing with them stories of horrific atrocities committed by the Russians.

"They treat us worse than animals. Not a single one of our women has escaped their predations," said Ernst von Stein, mayor of the East Prussian town of Heilsburg. The Russians sacked the town.

News of Russian brutality is only adding interest in the idea of Frankish Unity. While France and Russia are allies, that might change very soon.

"Together, I promise we will show the Slavs their place in the world," Lorraine said.

"Russia would bury France in a large-scale armed conflict. Lorraine's comments are therefore arrogant in the extreme," the Russian war minister said.

Lorraine was not concerned. "The blood of a single Frankish peasant is nobler than all tzars of Russia," he said.

Indeed, denizens of Austria-Hungary and the Prussian Empire might soon have no alternative to Lorraine's proposed unification. And for many, that day can't come soon enough. ⚜

Decisive French Victory Over Combined German Fleet Off Coast of Denmark

The North Sea – A combined Prusso-Austrian fleet clashed with the French Navy for several days in a titanic battle on the frigid swells of the North Sea. The two fleets totaled over 200 ships between them.

It was the largest naval battle in history.

The battle began when Vice-Admiral Ludwig von Reuter attempted to force the French fleet commanded by Admiral François Joseph Paul de Grasse, through a gauntlet of submarines and into the massive firepower of the main fleet.

But Admiral de Grasse maneuvered around the trap and engaged the slightly larger German fleet around sunset on Jan. 29.

Casualty estimates range in the thousands on both sides, but in the end the Germans suffered more heavily and were forced to retreat. The French sank 14 ships, including three battlecruisers, while losing only nine of their own, including a single battlecruiser.

"This effectively ends the contest for the high seas," Admiral de Grasse said.

The naval victory is the latest *continued on next page*

continued on next page

East Prussian peasants forced from their homes, now living in a rude shelter. Civilians bear the brunt of the Russian advance through Prussia.

CHAPTER SIX

THE KING OF THE WORLD

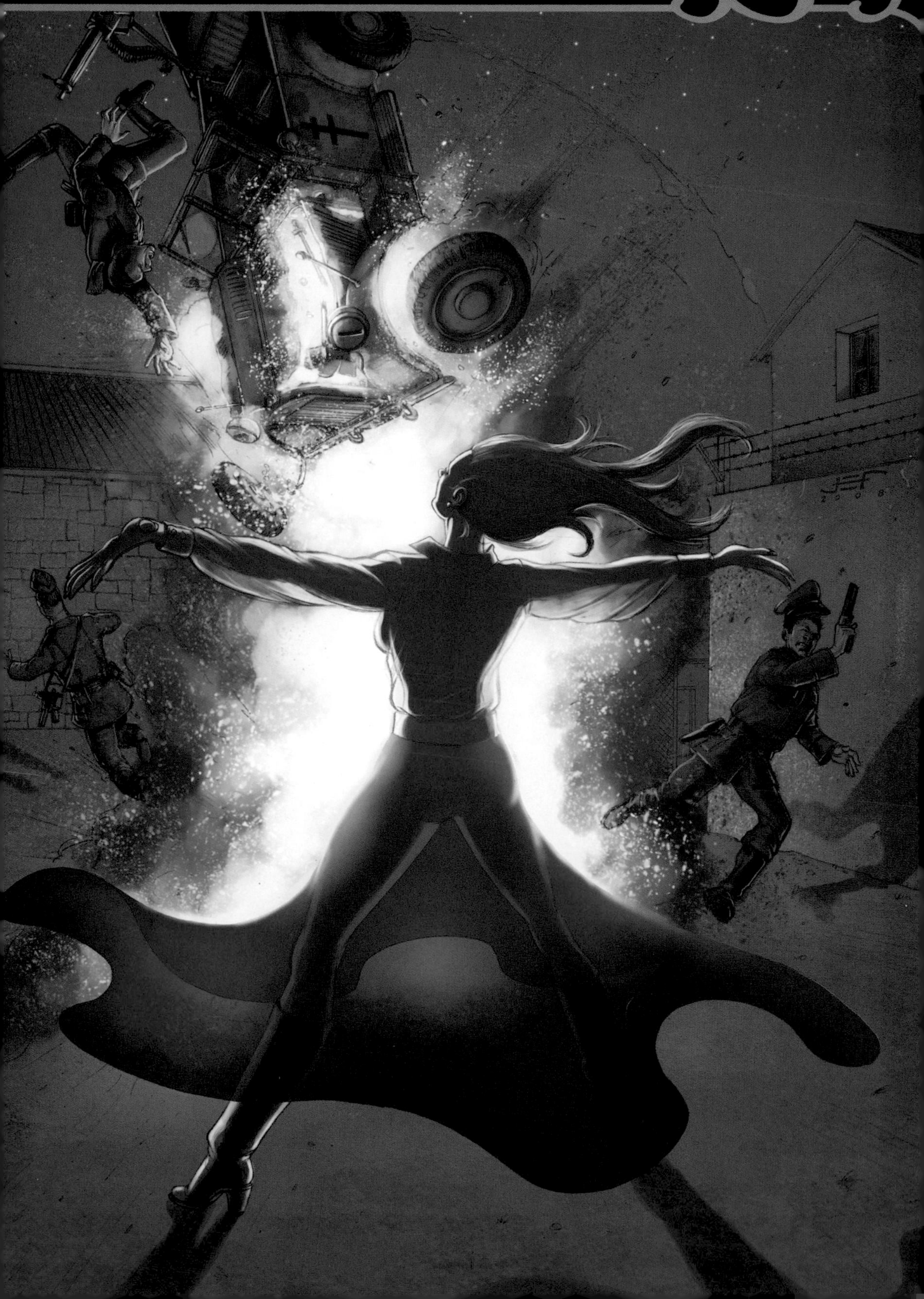

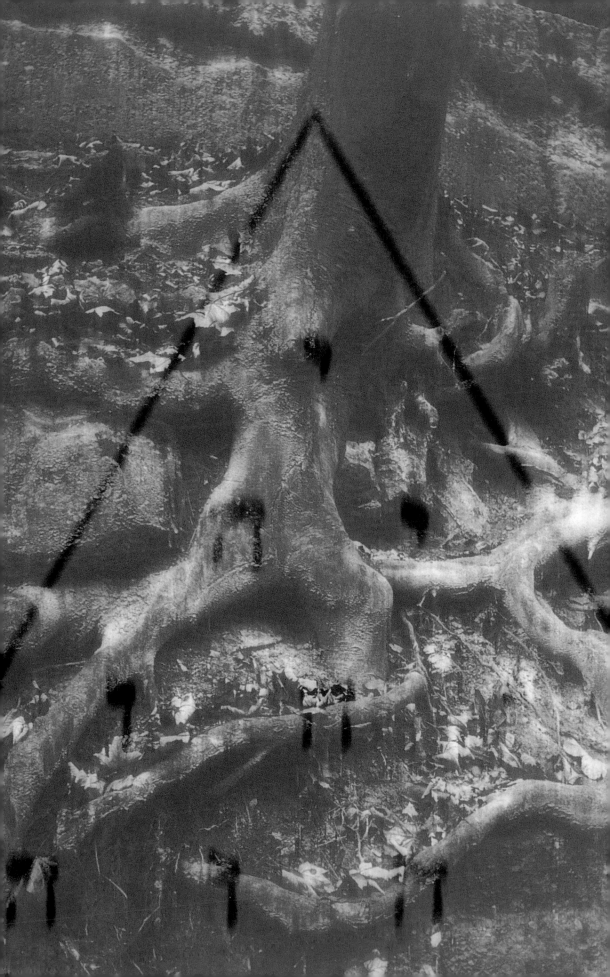

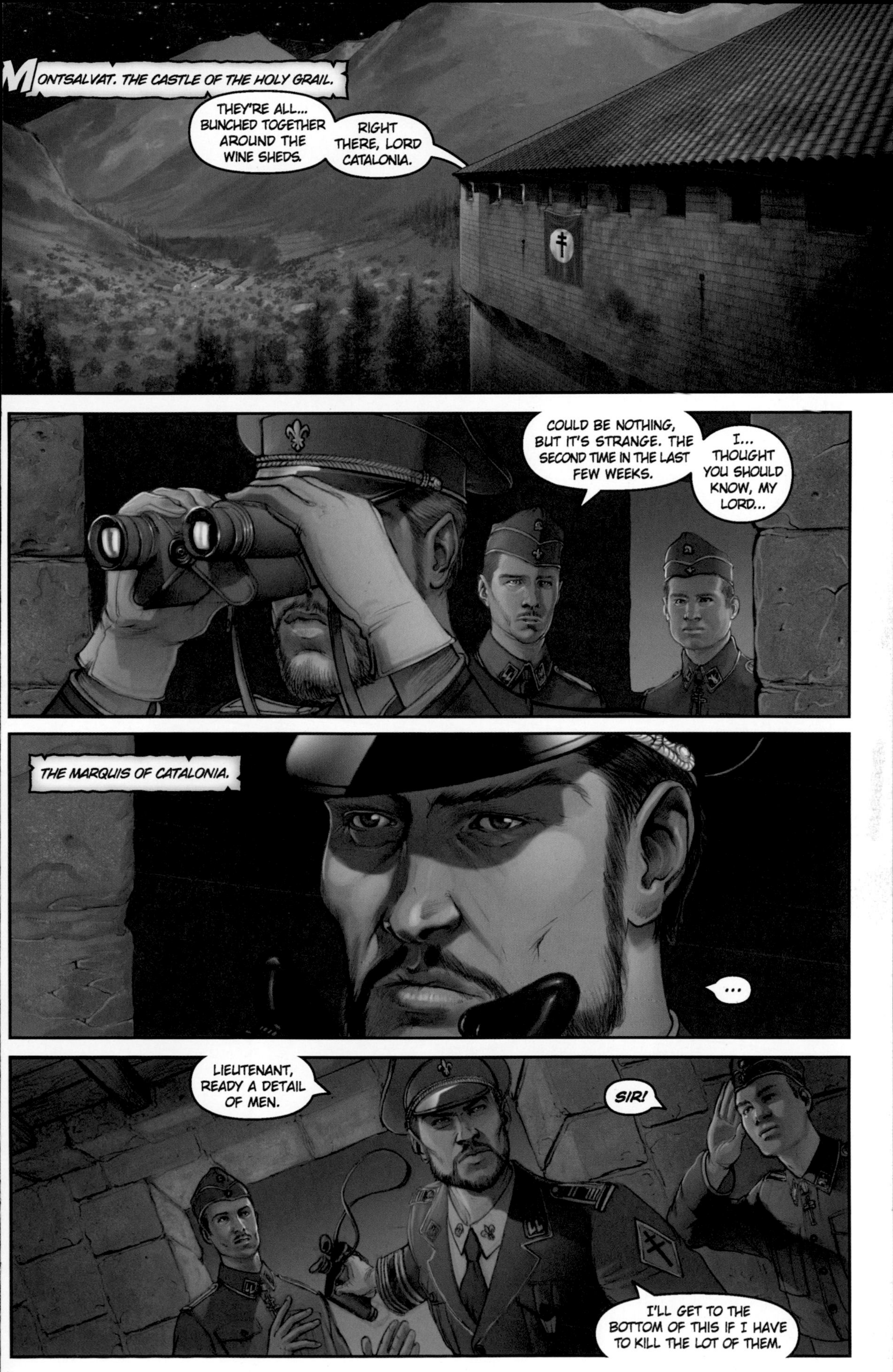
MONTSALVAT. THE CASTLE OF THE HOLY GRAIL.
THEY'RE ALL... BUNCHED TOGETHER AROUND THE WINE SHEDS.
RIGHT THERE, LORD CATALONIA.
COULD BE NOTHING, BUT IT'S STRANGE. THE SECOND TIME IN THE LAST FEW WEEKS.
I... THOUGHT YOU SHOULD KNOW, MY LORD...
THE MARQUIS OF CATALONIA.
...
LIEUTENANT, READY A DETAIL OF MEN.
SIR!
I'LL GET TO THE BOTTOM OF THIS IF I HAVE TO KILL THE LOT OF THEM.

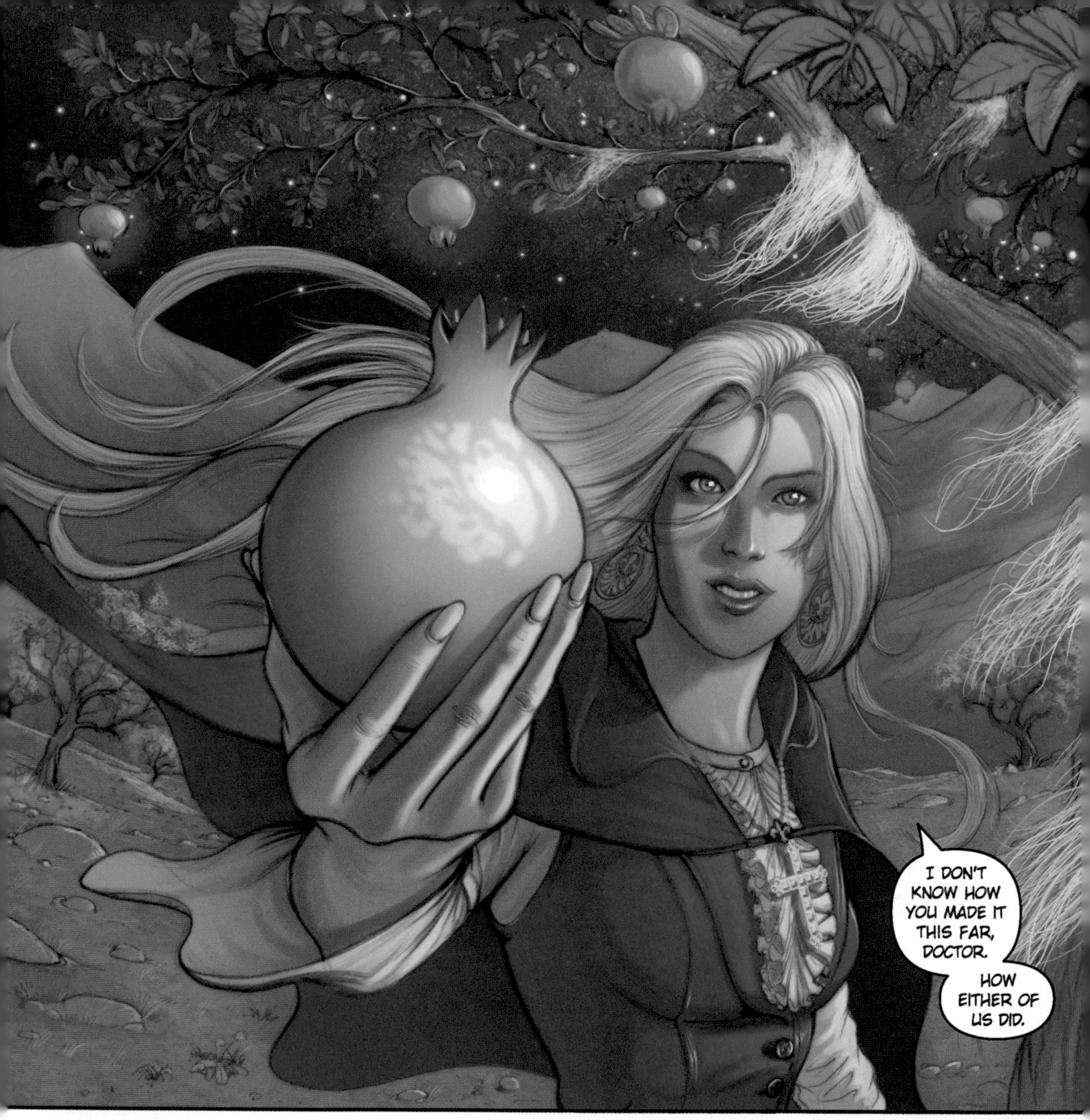
I DON'T KNOW HOW YOU MADE IT THIS FAR, DOCTOR.
HOW EITHER OF US DID.

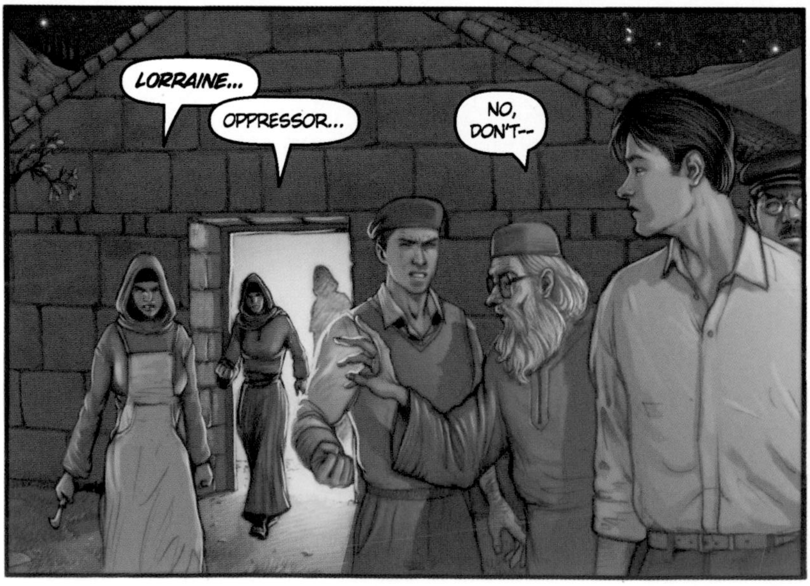
LORRAINE...
OPPRESSOR...
NO, DON'T--

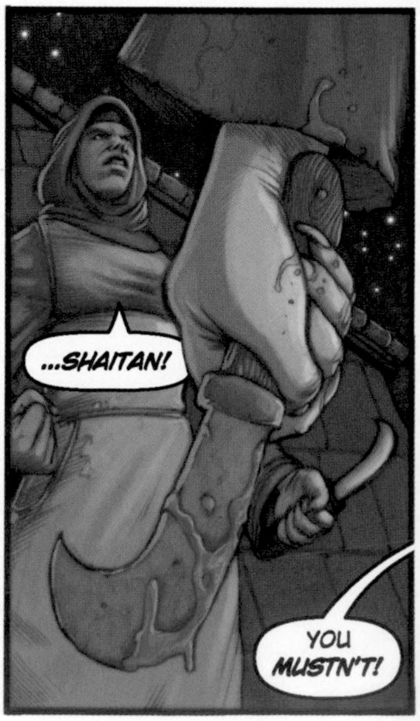
...SHAITAN!
YOU MUSTN'T!

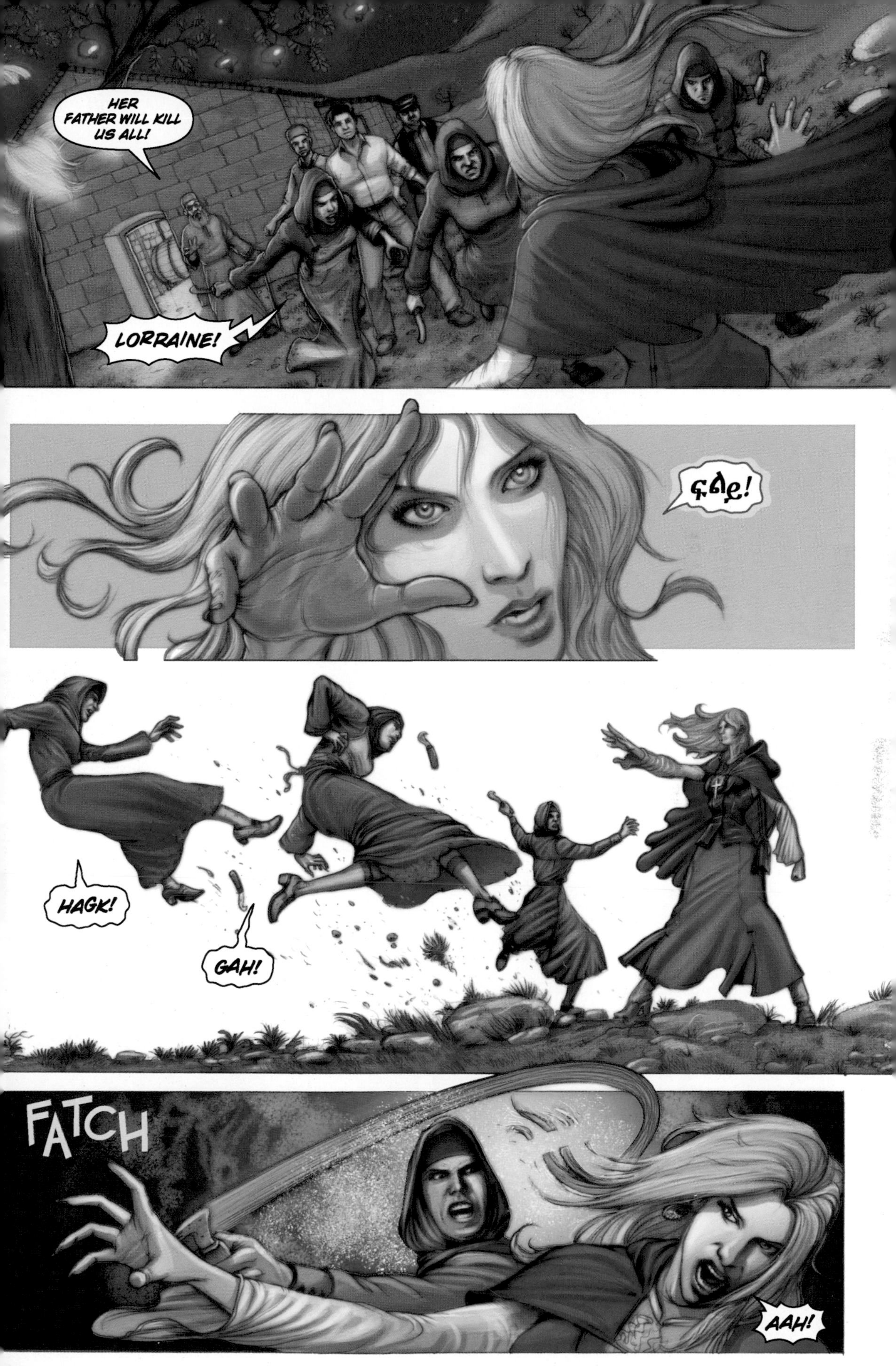
HER FATHER WILL KILL US ALL!
LORRAINE!
ፍሊይ!
HAGK!
GAH!
FATCH
AAH!

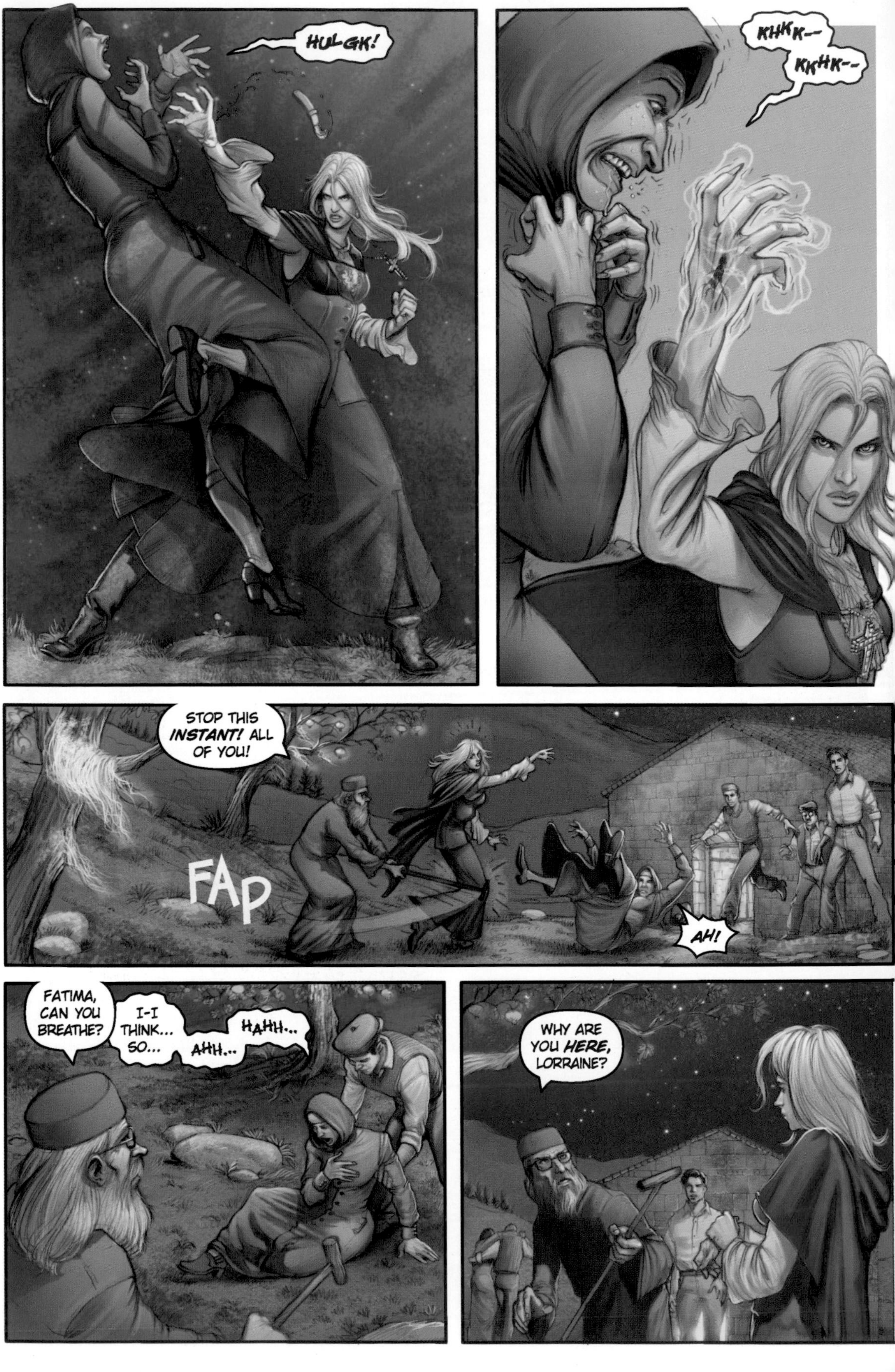
HULGK!
KHKK--
KKHK--
STOP THIS INSTANT! ALL OF YOU!
FAP
AH!
FATIMA, CAN YOU BREATHE?
I-I THINK... SO...
AHH...
HAHH...
WHY ARE YOU HERE, LORRAINE?

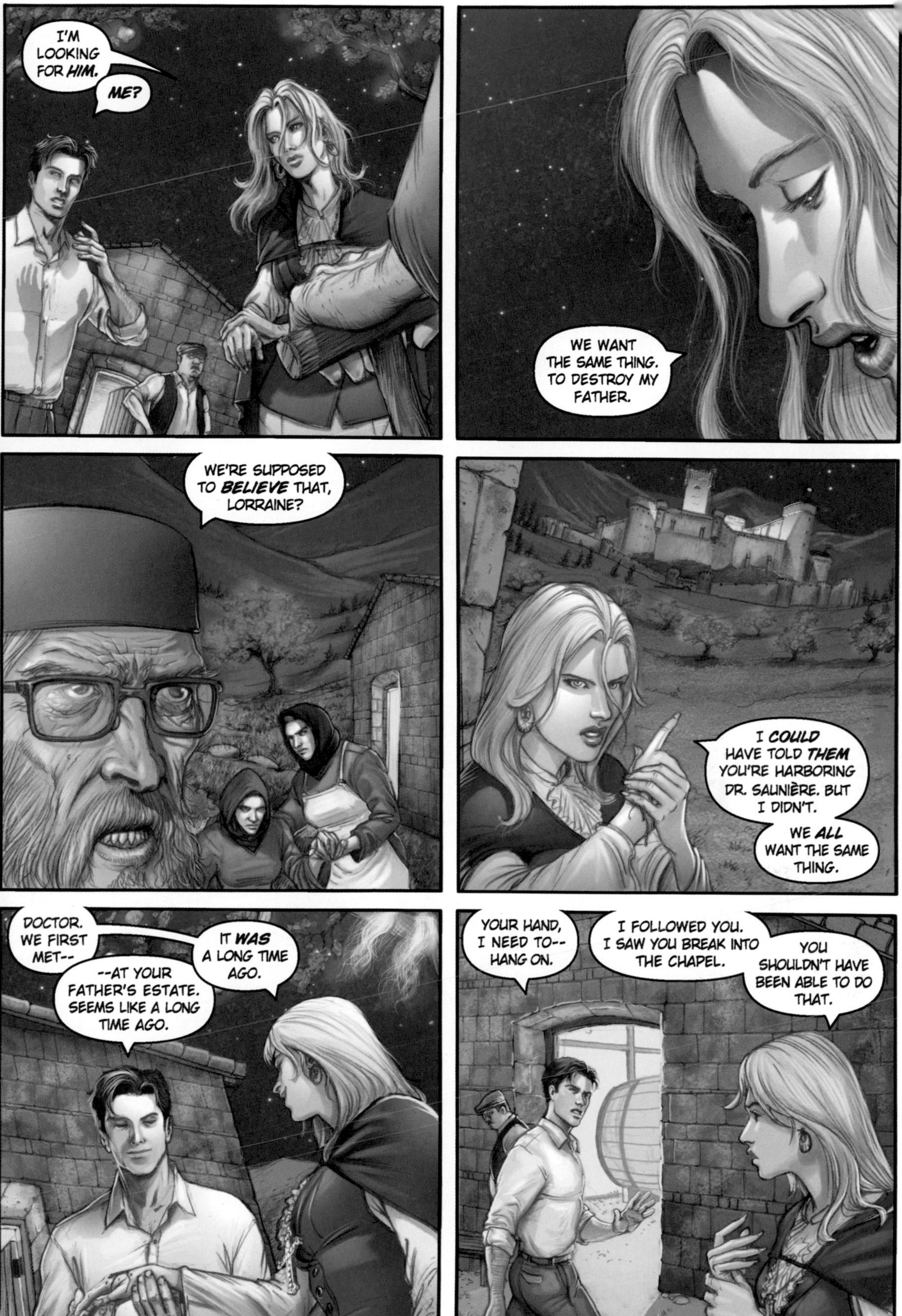

I'M LOOKING FOR HIM.
ME?
WE WANT THE SAME THING. TO DESTROY MY FATHER.
WE'RE SUPPOSED TO BELIEVE THAT, LORRAINE?
I COULD HAVE TOLD THEM YOU'RE HARBORING DR. SAUNIÈRE. BUT I DIDN'T.
WE ALL WANT THE SAME THING.
DOCTOR. WE FIRST MET--
--AT YOUR FATHER'S ESTATE. SEEMS LIKE A LONG TIME AGO.
IT WAS A LONG TIME AGO.
YOUR HAND, I NEED TO-- HANG ON.
I FOLLOWED YOU. I SAW YOU BREAK INTO THE CHAPEL.
YOU SHOULDN'T HAVE BEEN ABLE TO DO THAT.

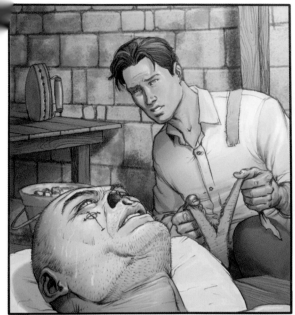

I'M STILL TRYING TO FIGURE THAT ONE OUT.

ME TOO.

AND YOU KNOW WHO MY FATHER IS.

WHO HE *REALLY* IS.

SO WHY ARE YOU *HERE*? WHAT'S YOUR PLAN?

PLAN?

I DON'T... HAVE ONE.

WHAT?

HOLD STILL.

YAAH!

SSS

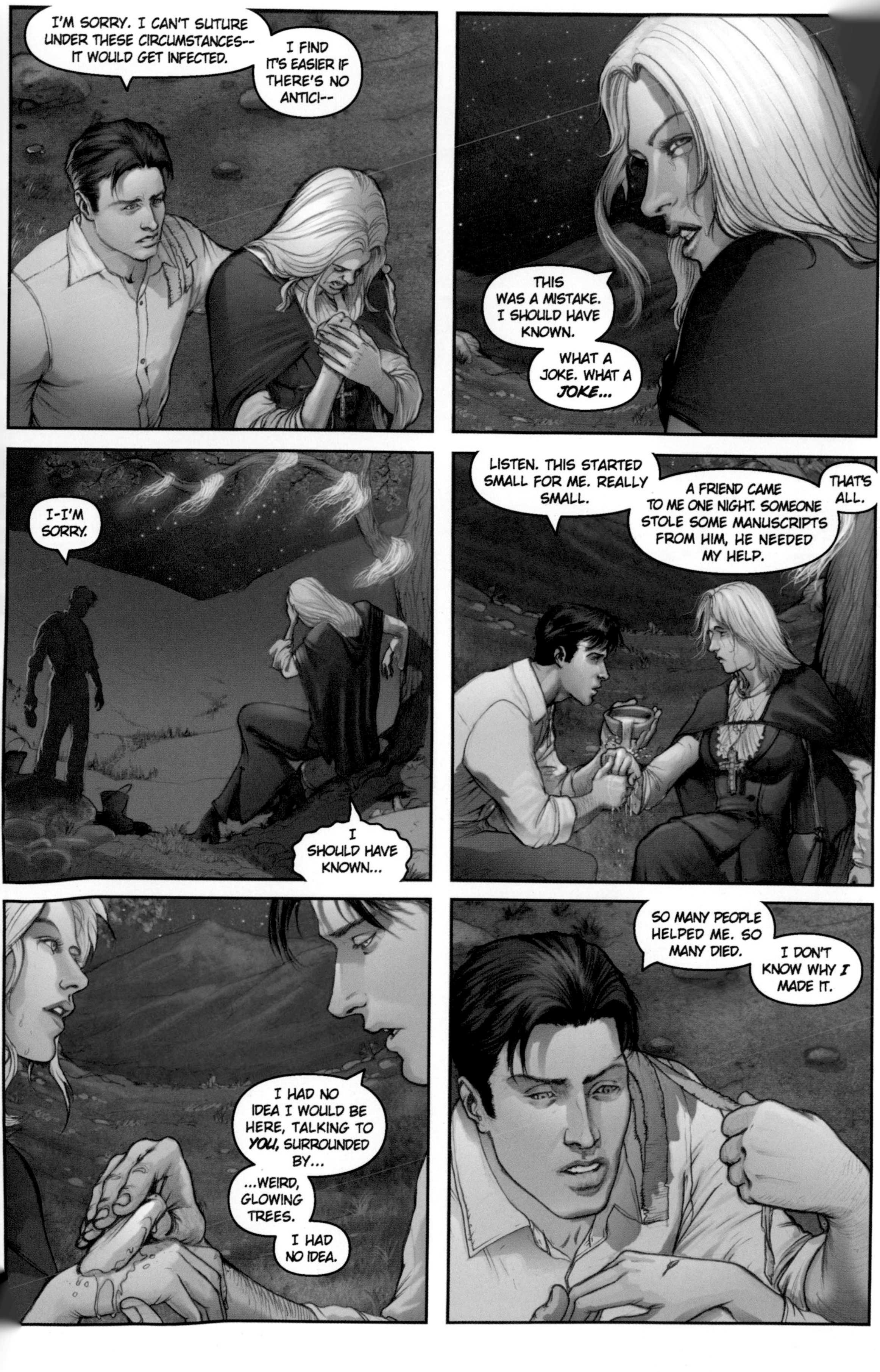
I'M SORRY. I CAN'T SUTURE UNDER THESE CIRCUMSTANCES-- IT WOULD GET INFECTED.
I FIND IT'S EASIER IF THERE'S NO ANTICI--
THIS WAS A MISTAKE. I SHOULD HAVE KNOWN.
WHAT A JOKE. WHAT A *JOKE*...
I-I'M SORRY.
I SHOULD HAVE KNOWN...
LISTEN. THIS STARTED SMALL FOR ME. REALLY SMALL.
A FRIEND CAME TO ME ONE NIGHT. SOMEONE STOLE SOME MANUSCRIPTS FROM HIM, HE NEEDED MY HELP.
THAT'S ALL.
I HAD NO IDEA I WOULD BE HERE, TALKING TO *YOU,* SURROUNDED BY...
...WEIRD, GLOWING TREES.
I HAD NO IDEA.
SO MANY PEOPLE HELPED ME. SO MANY DIED.
I DON'T KNOW WHY *I* MADE IT.

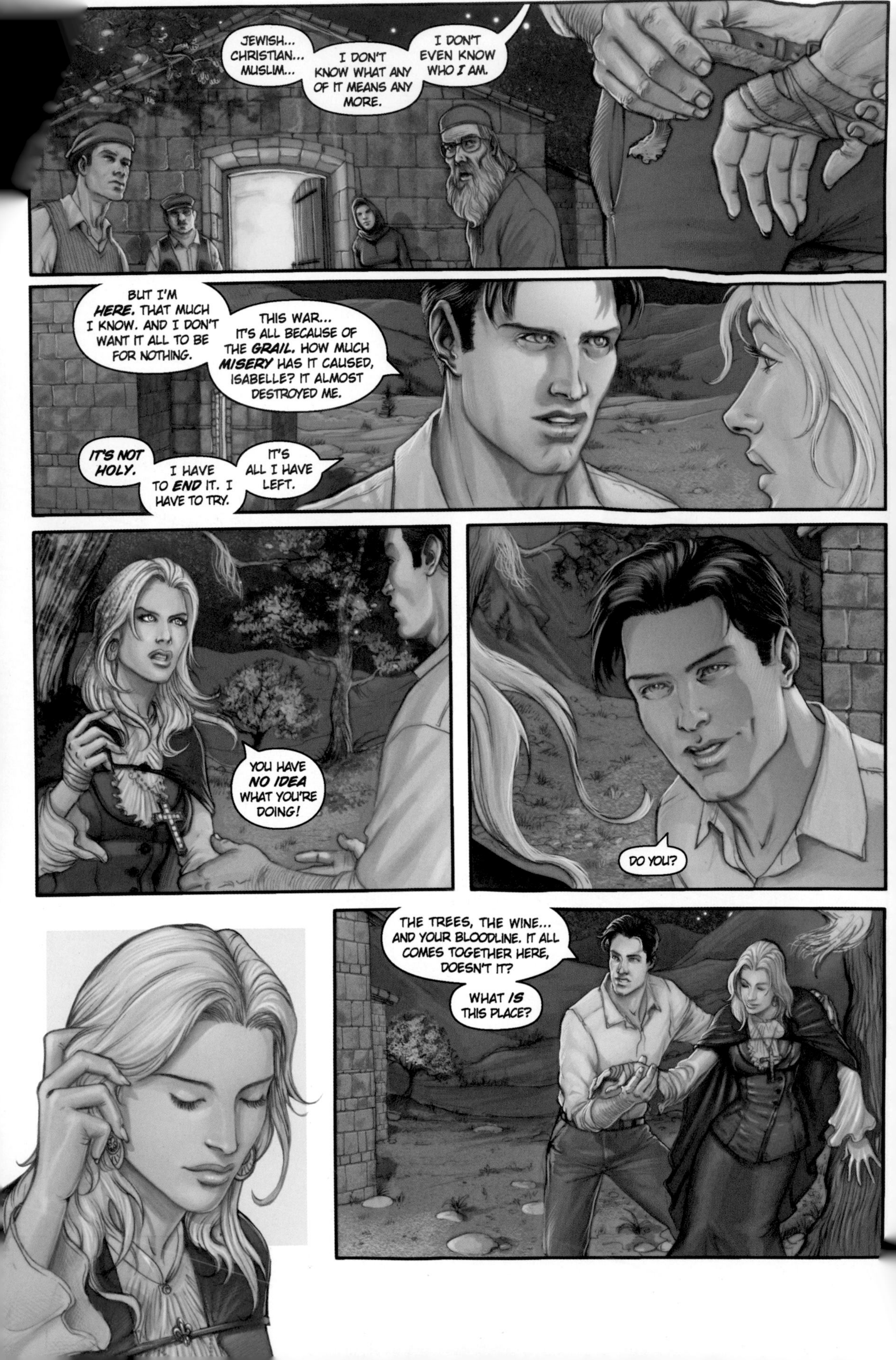
JEWISH... CHRISTIAN... MUSLIM...
I DON'T KNOW WHAT ANY OF IT MEANS ANY MORE.
I DON'T EVEN KNOW WHO *I* AM.
BUT I'M *HERE*. THAT MUCH I KNOW. AND I DON'T WANT IT ALL TO BE FOR NOTHING.
THIS WAR... IT'S ALL BECAUSE OF THE *GRAIL*. HOW MUCH *MISERY* HAS IT CAUSED, ISABELLE? IT ALMOST DESTROYED ME.
IT'S NOT HOLY.
I HAVE TO *END* IT. I HAVE TO TRY.
IT'S ALL I HAVE LEFT.
YOU HAVE *NO IDEA* WHAT YOU'RE DOING!
DO YOU?
THE TREES, THE WINE... AND YOUR BLOODLINE. IT ALL COMES TOGETHER HERE, DOESN'T IT?
WHAT *IS* THIS PLACE?

I DON'T KNOW FOR SURE. I DON'T THINK ANYONE DOES.

THERE ARE ONLY STORIES. STORIES PASSED DOWN IN MY FAMILY FOR A LONG TIME.

ACCORDING TO ONE, THESE FIRST APPEARED TO MOSES WHEN GOD SPOKE TO HIM IN THE WILDERNESS.

IT'S EASY TO SEE WHY SOMEONE MIGHT MISTAKE ONE OF THESE FOR A *BURNING BUSH.*

ANOTHER VERSION HAS IT THE QUEEN OF SHEBA GAVE THE BLUE APPLES TO SOLOMON--ALONG WITH THE SECRET OF THE WINE--IN EXCHANGE FOR THE *ARC OF THE COVENANT.*

HOW OR WHERE *SHE* FOUND THEM, I DON'T KNOW.

BUT *THIS* IS MY FAVORITE STORY.

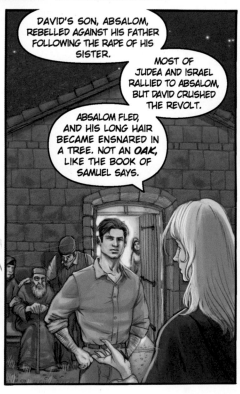

DAVID'S SON, ABSALOM, REBELLED AGAINST HIS FATHER FOLLOWING THE RAPE OF HIS SISTER.

MOST OF JUDEA AND ISRAEL RALLIED TO ABSALOM, BUT DAVID CRUSHED THE REVOLT.

ABSALOM FLED, AND HIS LONG HAIR BECAME ENSNARED IN A TREE. NOT AN *OAK,* LIKE THE BOOK OF SAMUEL SAYS.

A POMEGRANATE TREE.

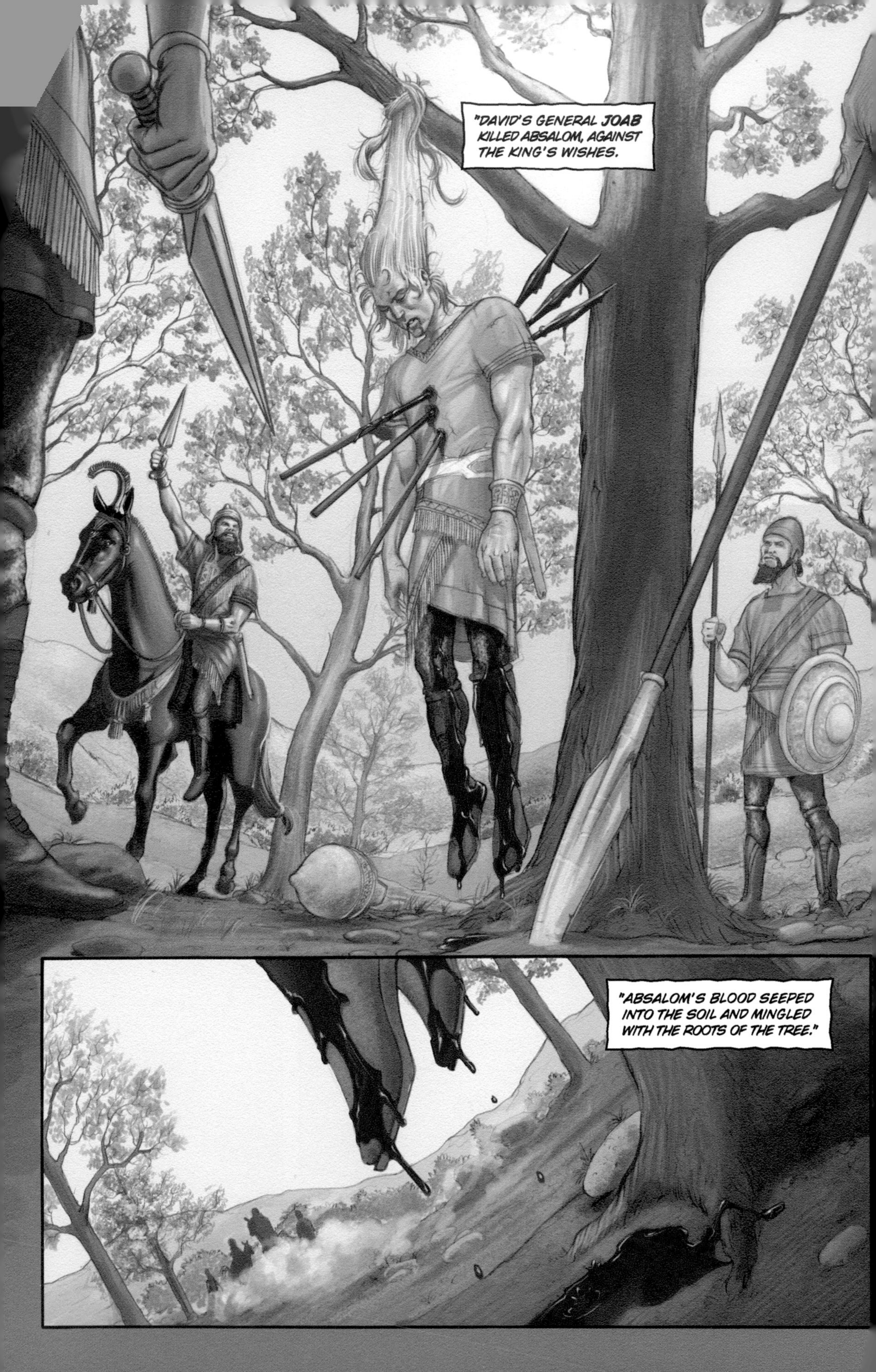
"DAVID'S GENERAL JOAB KILLED ABSALOM, AGAINST THE KING'S WISHES.
"ABSALOM'S BLOOD SEEPED INTO THE SOIL AND MINGLED WITH THE ROOTS OF THE TREE."

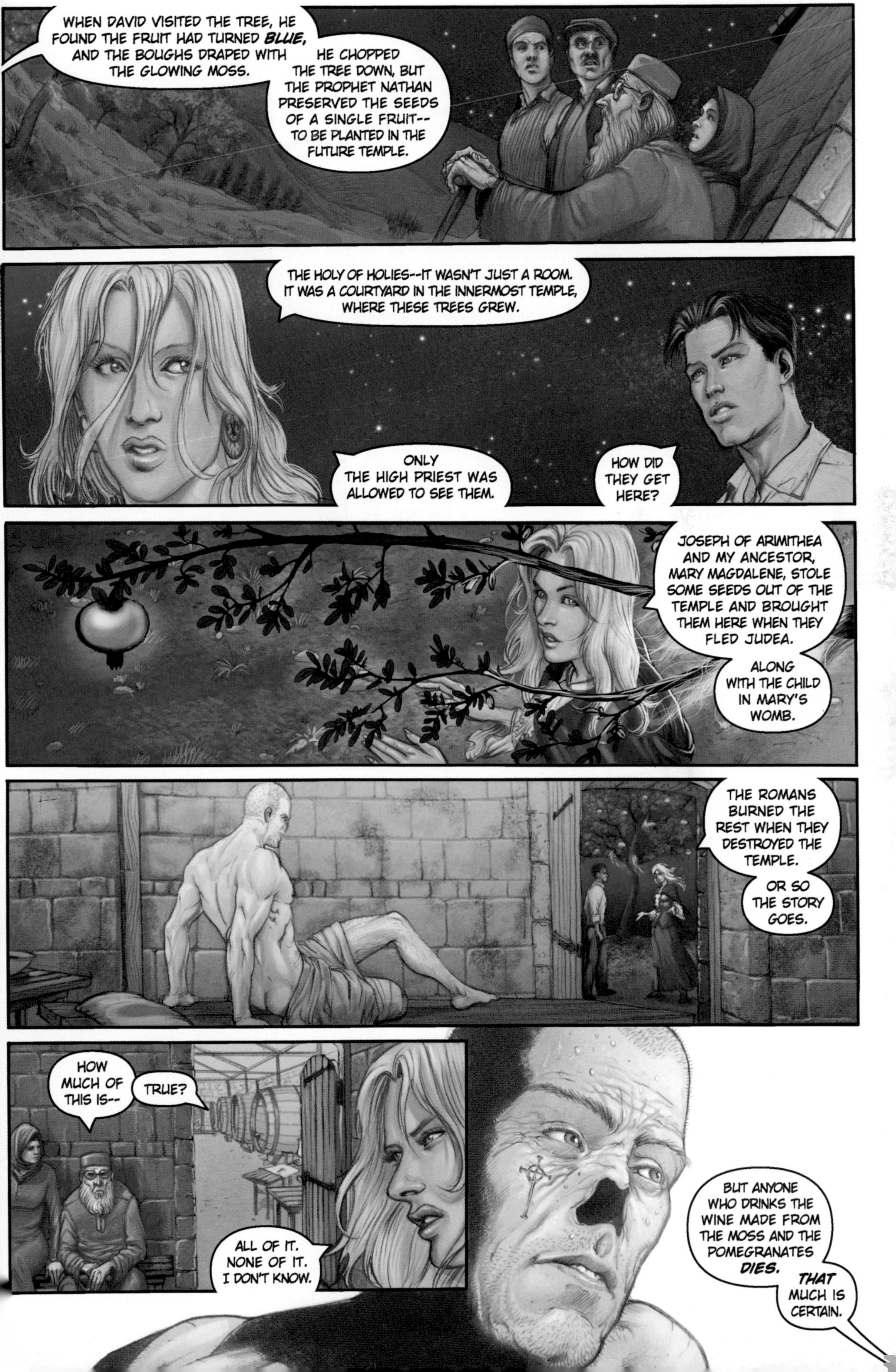

WHEN DAVID VISITED THE TREE, HE FOUND THE FRUIT HAD TURNED ***BLUE,*** AND THE BOUGHS DRAPED WITH THE GLOWING MOSS.
HE CHOPPED THE TREE DOWN, BUT THE PROPHET NATHAN PRESERVED THE SEEDS OF A SINGLE FRUIT-- TO BE PLANTED IN THE FUTURE TEMPLE.
THE HOLY OF HOLIES--IT WASN'T JUST A ROOM. IT WAS A COURTYARD IN THE INNERMOST TEMPLE, WHERE THESE TREES GREW.
ONLY THE HIGH PRIEST WAS ALLOWED TO SEE THEM.
HOW DID THEY GET HERE?
JOSEPH OF ARIMITHEA AND MY ANCESTOR, MARY MAGDALENE, STOLE SOME SEEDS OUT OF THE TEMPLE AND BROUGHT THEM HERE WHEN THEY FLED JUDEA.
ALONG WITH THE CHILD IN MARY'S WOMB.
THE ROMANS BURNED THE REST WHEN THEY DESTROYED THE TEMPLE.
OR SO THE STORY GOES.
HOW MUCH OF THIS IS--
TRUE?
ALL OF IT. NONE OF IT. I DON'T KNOW.
BUT ANYONE WHO DRINKS THE WINE MADE FROM THE MOSS AND THE POMEGRANATES ***DIES.***
THAT MUCH IS CERTAIN.

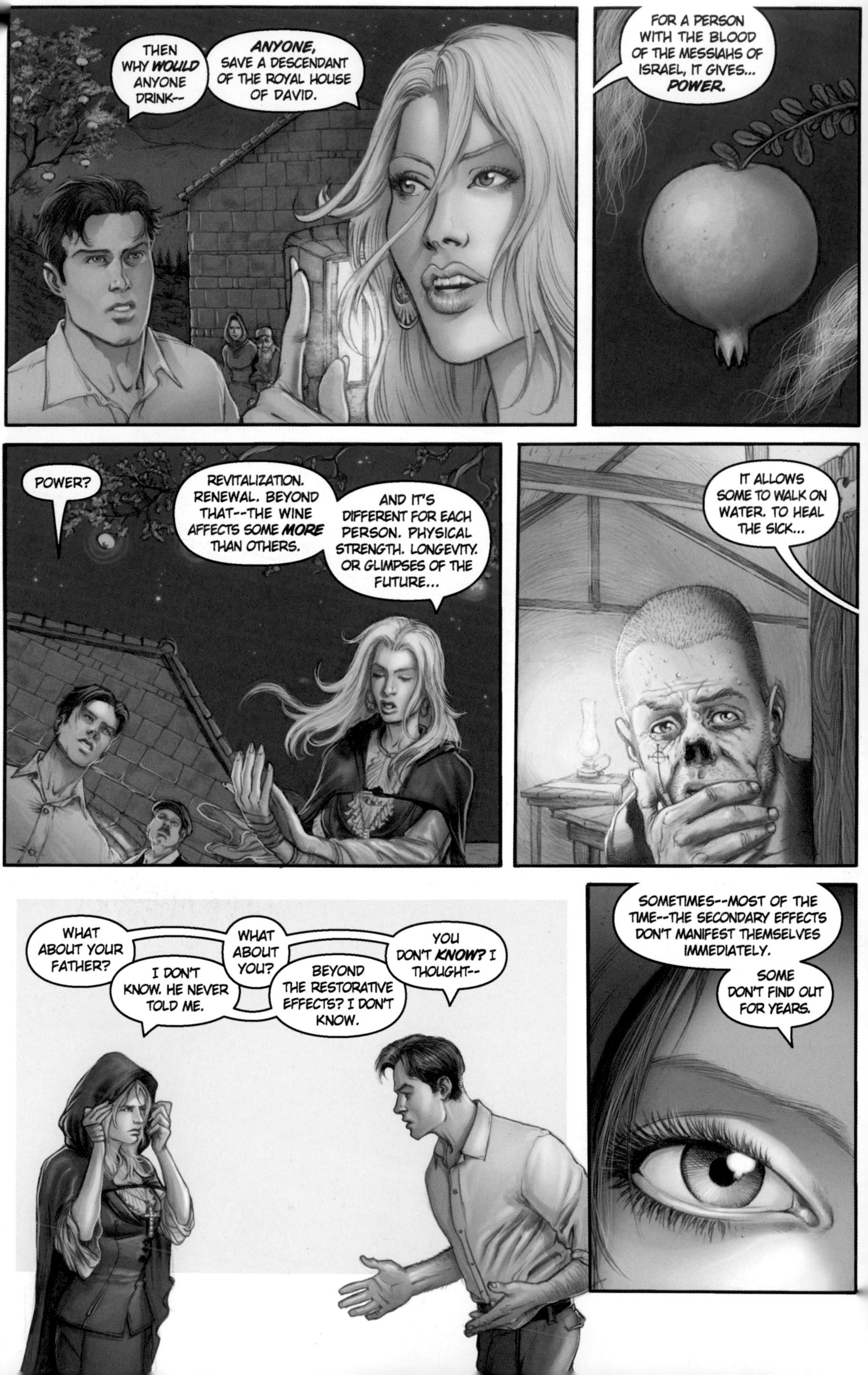
THEN WHY *WOULD* ANYONE DRINK--
ANYONE, SAVE A DESCENDANT OF THE ROYAL HOUSE OF DAVID.
FOR A PERSON WITH THE BLOOD OF THE MESSIAHS OF ISRAEL, IT GIVES... *POWER.*
POWER?
REVITALIZATION. RENEWAL. BEYOND THAT--THE WINE AFFECTS SOME *MORE* THAN OTHERS.
AND IT'S DIFFERENT FOR EACH PERSON. PHYSICAL STRENGTH. LONGEVITY. OR GLIMPSES OF THE FUTURE...
IT ALLOWS SOME TO WALK ON WATER. TO HEAL THE SICK...
WHAT ABOUT YOUR FATHER?
I DON'T KNOW. HE NEVER TOLD ME.
WHAT ABOUT YOU?
BEYOND THE RESTORATIVE EFFECTS? I DON'T KNOW.
YOU DON'T *KNOW?* I THOUGHT--
SOMETIMES--MOST OF THE TIME--THE SECONDARY EFFECTS DON'T MANIFEST THEMSELVES IMMEDIATELY.
SOME DON'T FIND OUT FOR YEARS.

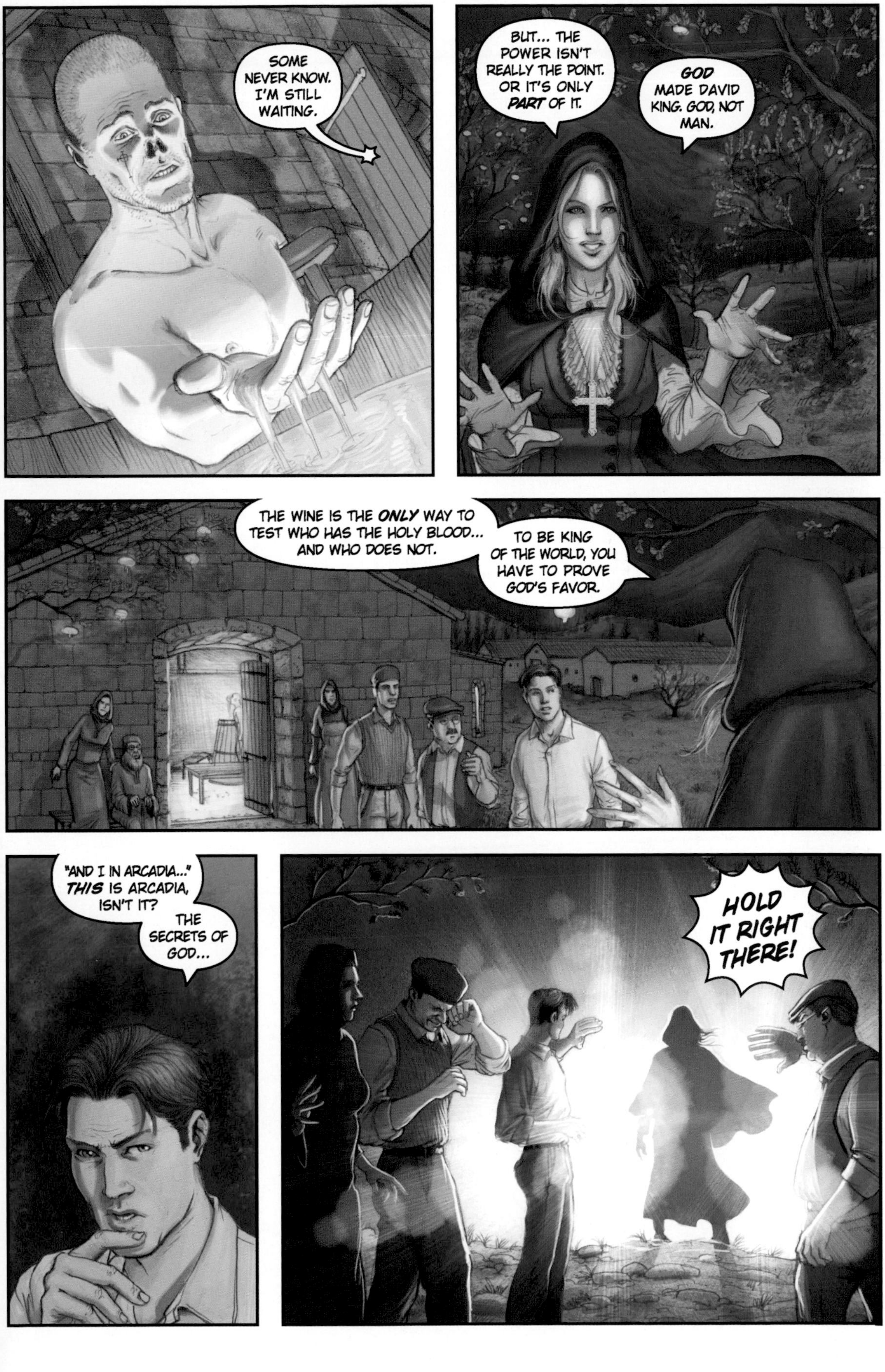
SOME NEVER KNOW. I'M STILL WAITING.
BUT... THE POWER ISN'T REALLY THE POINT. OR IT'S ONLY PART OF IT.
GOD MADE DAVID KING. GOD, NOT MAN.
THE WINE IS THE ONLY WAY TO TEST WHO HAS THE HOLY BLOOD... AND WHO DOES NOT.
TO BE KING OF THE WORLD, YOU HAVE TO PROVE GOD'S FAVOR.
"AND I IN ARCADIA..." THIS IS ARCADIA, ISN'T IT?
THE SECRETS OF GOD...
HOLD IT RIGHT THERE!

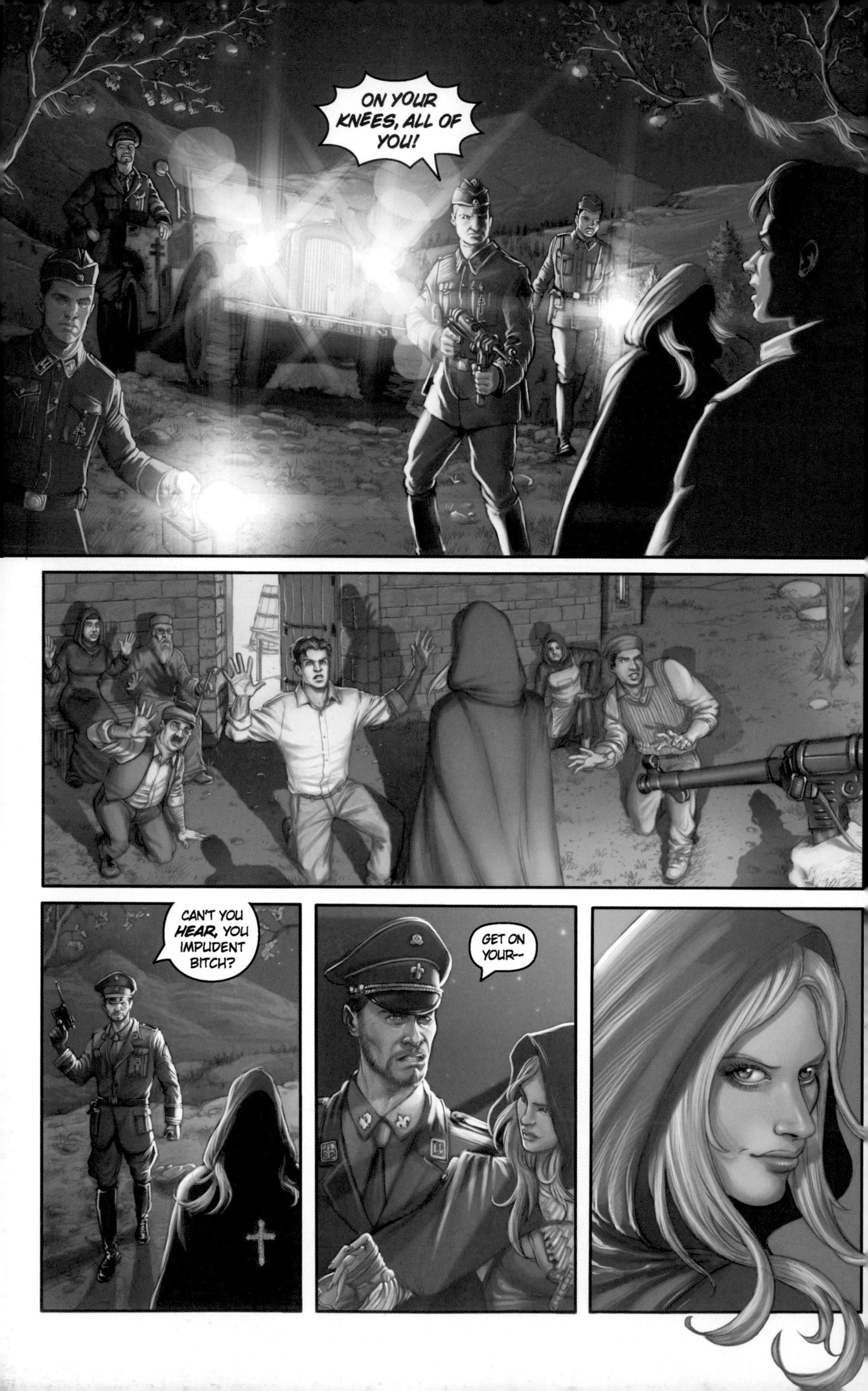
ON YOUR KNEES, ALL OF YOU!
CAN'T YOU HEAR, YOU IMPUDENT BITCH?
GET ON YOUR--

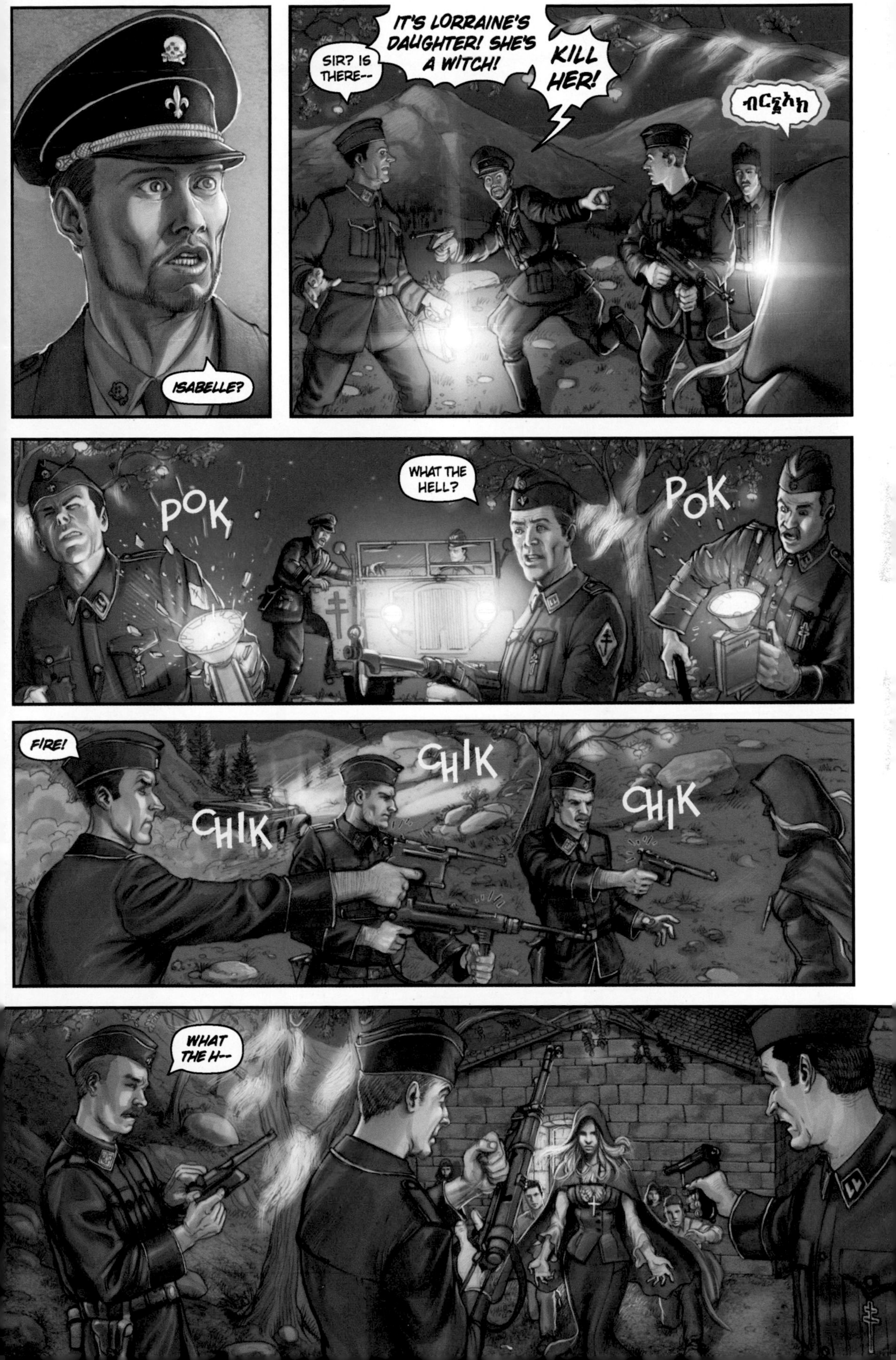
ISABELLE?
SIR? IS THERE--
IT'S LORRAINE'S DAUGHTER! SHE'S A WITCH!
KILL HER!
POK
WHAT THE HELL?
POK
FIRE!
CHIK
CHIK
CHIK
WHAT THE H--

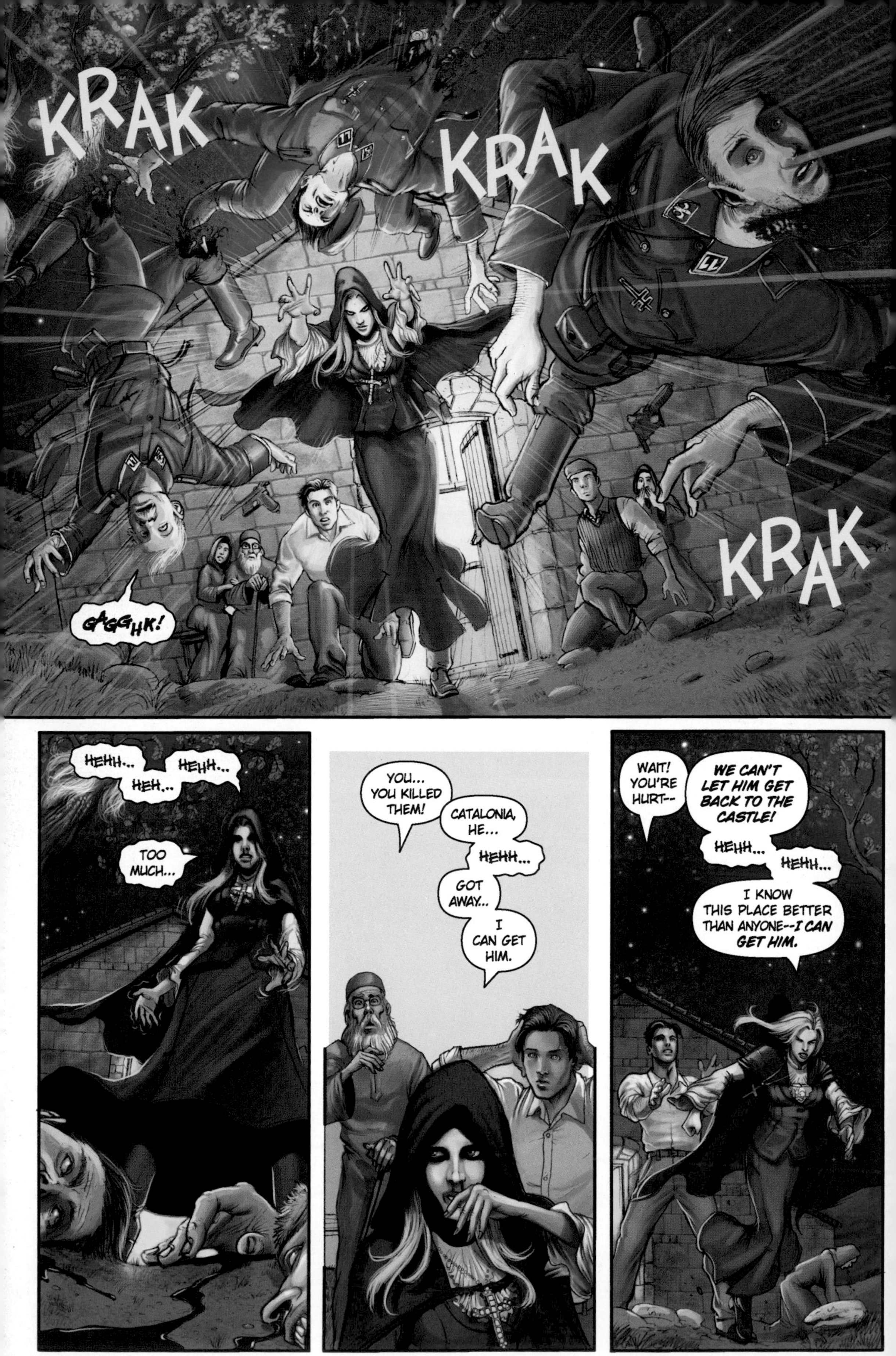
KRAK
KRAK
KRAK
GAGGHK!
HEHH... HEH... HEHH...
TOO MUCH...
YOU... YOU KILLED THEM!
CATALONIA, HE...
HEHH...
GOT AWAY...
I CAN GET HIM.
WAIT! YOU'RE HURT--
WE CAN'T LET HIM GET BACK TO THE CASTLE!
HEHH... HEHH...
I KNOW THIS PLACE BETTER THAN ANYONE--I CAN GET HIM.

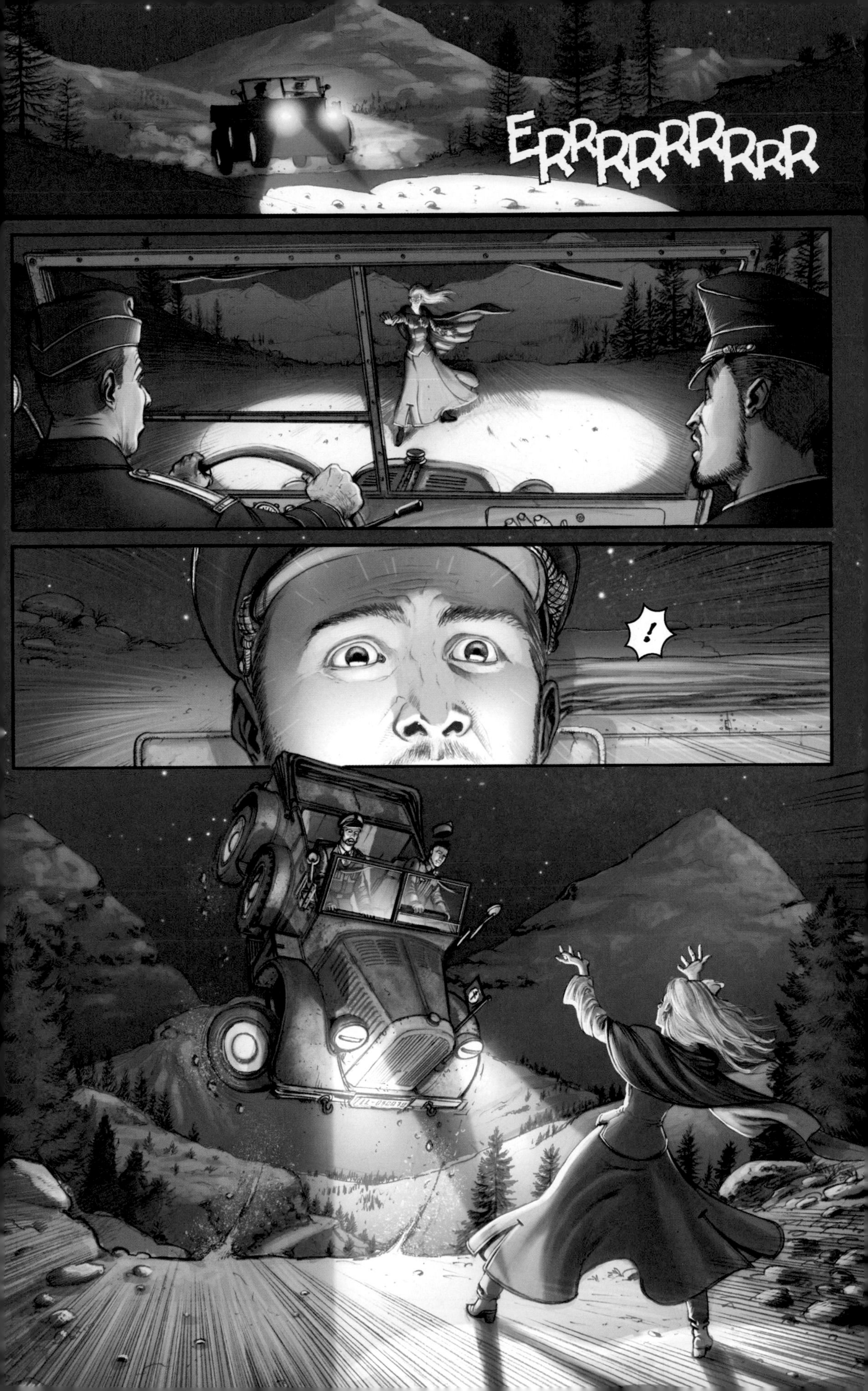

ERRRRRRRRRR
!

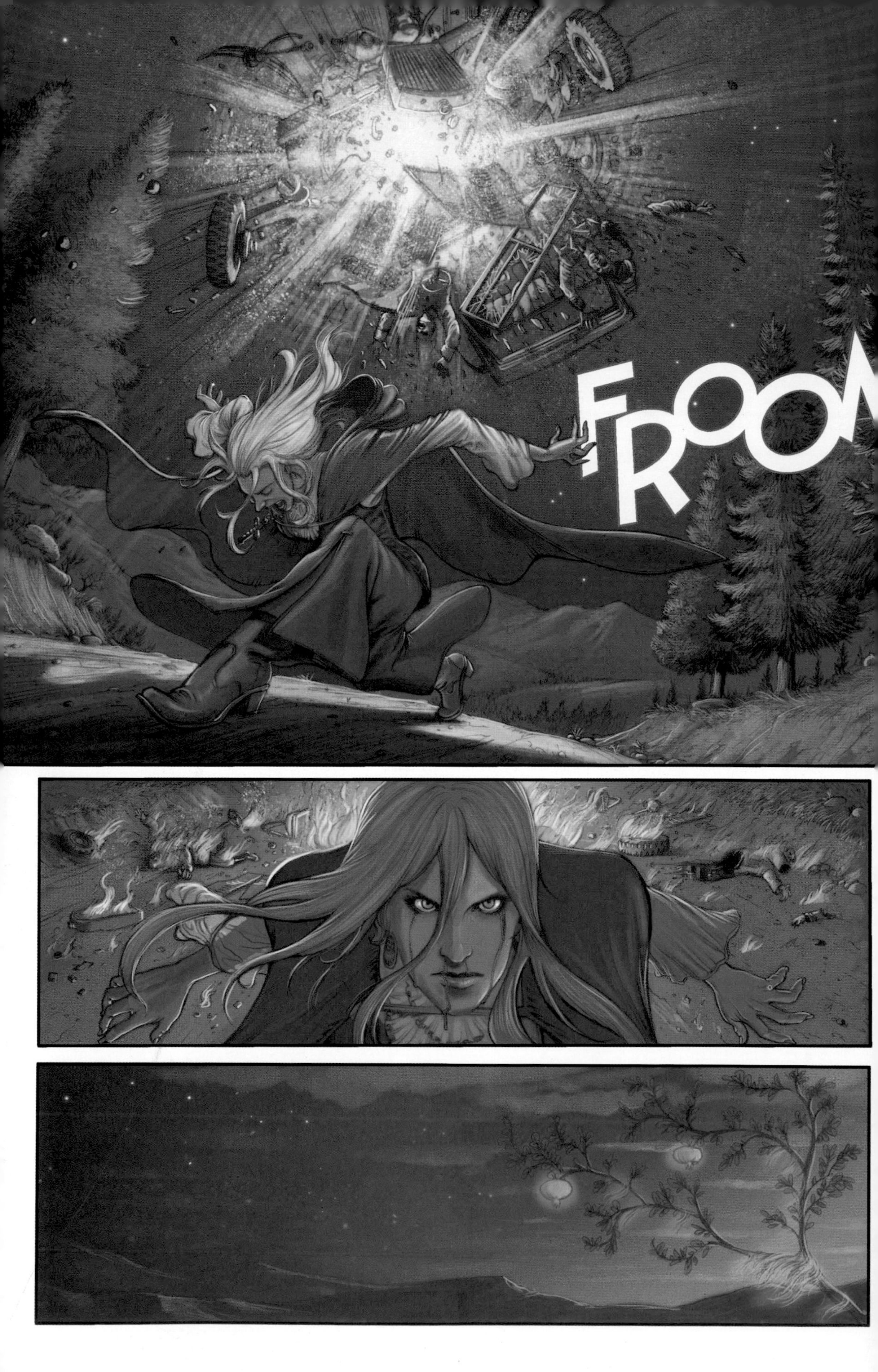
FROOM

ISABELLE!

THAT... SOLVES THE QUESTION OF A PLAN...

MY FATHER, HE'LL BE... COMING...

DOCTOR, WE NEED YOU RIGHT AWAY.

IT'S THE MONK!

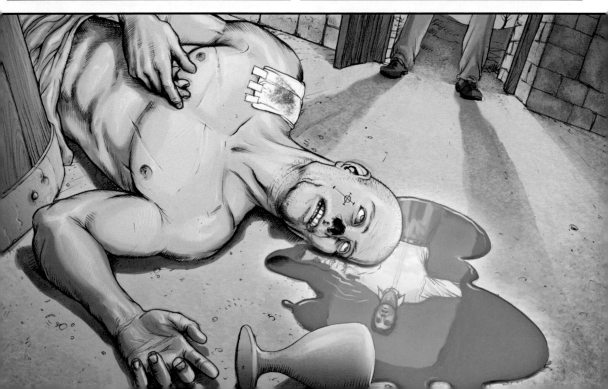

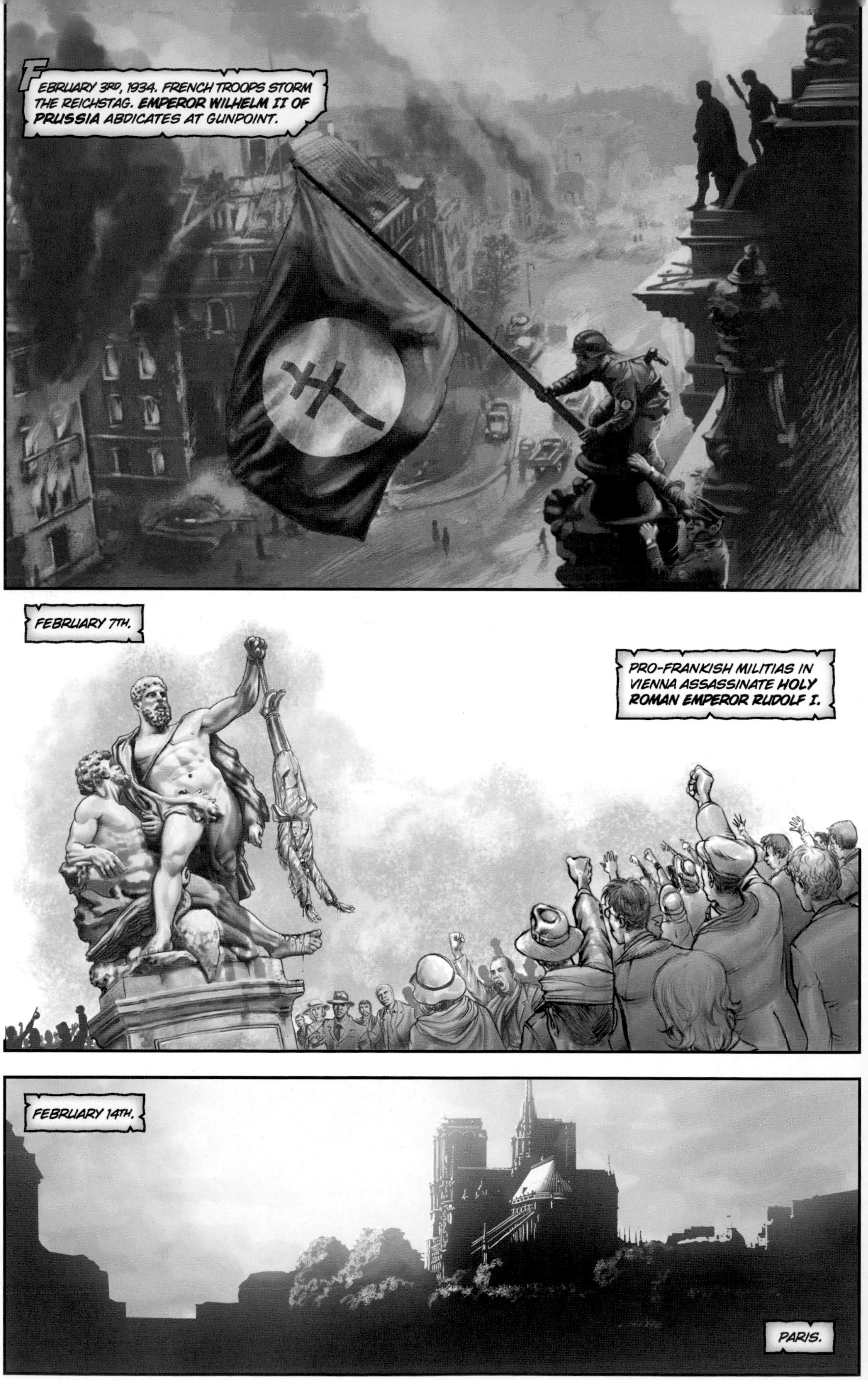
FEBRUARY 3RD, 1934. FRENCH TROOPS STORM THE REICHSTAG. EMPEROR WILHELM II OF PRUSSIA ABDICATES AT GUNPOINT.
FEBRUARY 7TH.
PRO-FRANKISH MILITIAS IN VIENNA ASSASSINATE HOLY ROMAN EMPEROR RUDOLF I.
FEBRUARY 14TH.
PARIS.

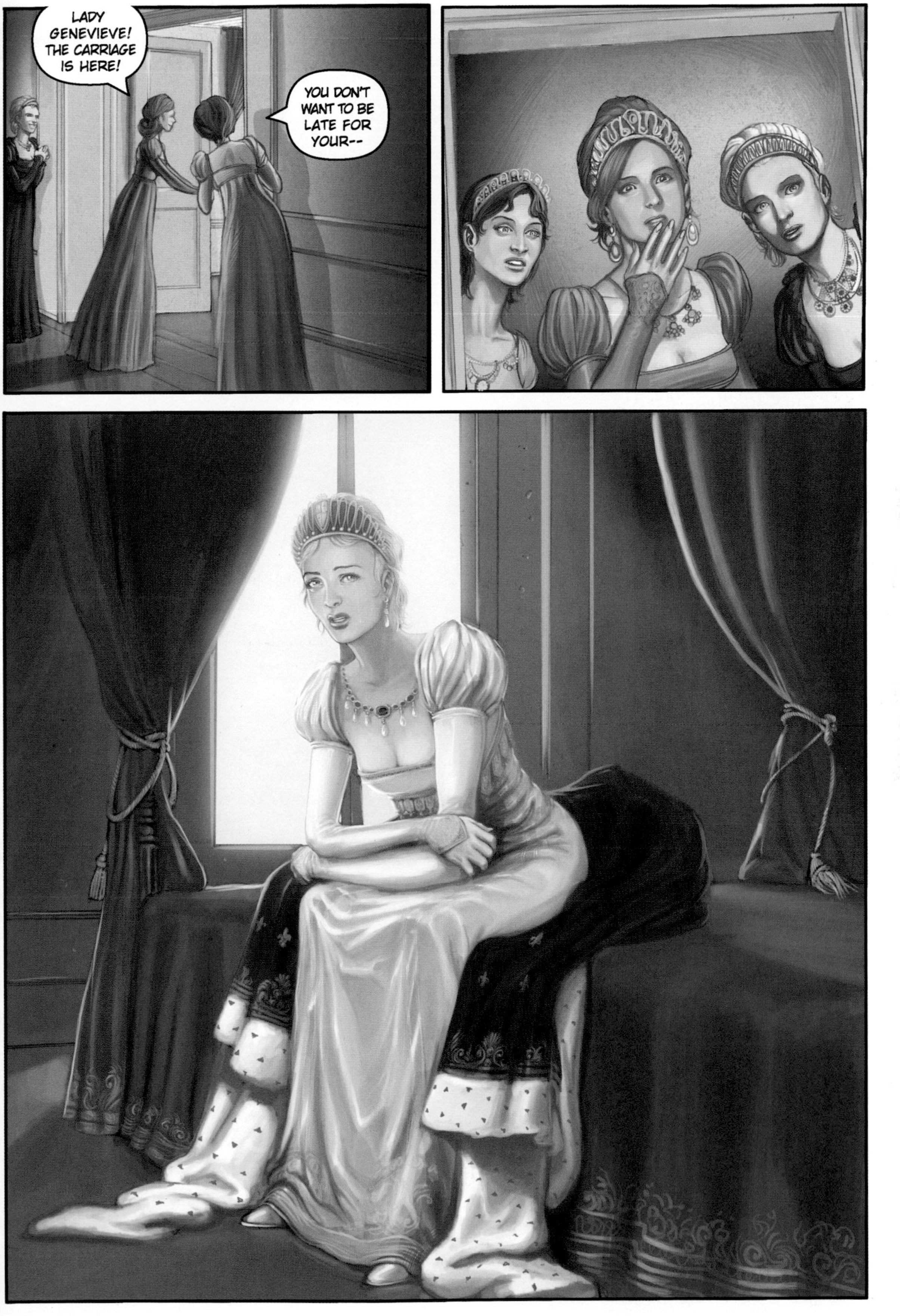
LADY GENEVIEVE! THE CARRIAGE IS HERE!
YOU DON'T WANT TO BE LATE FOR YOUR--

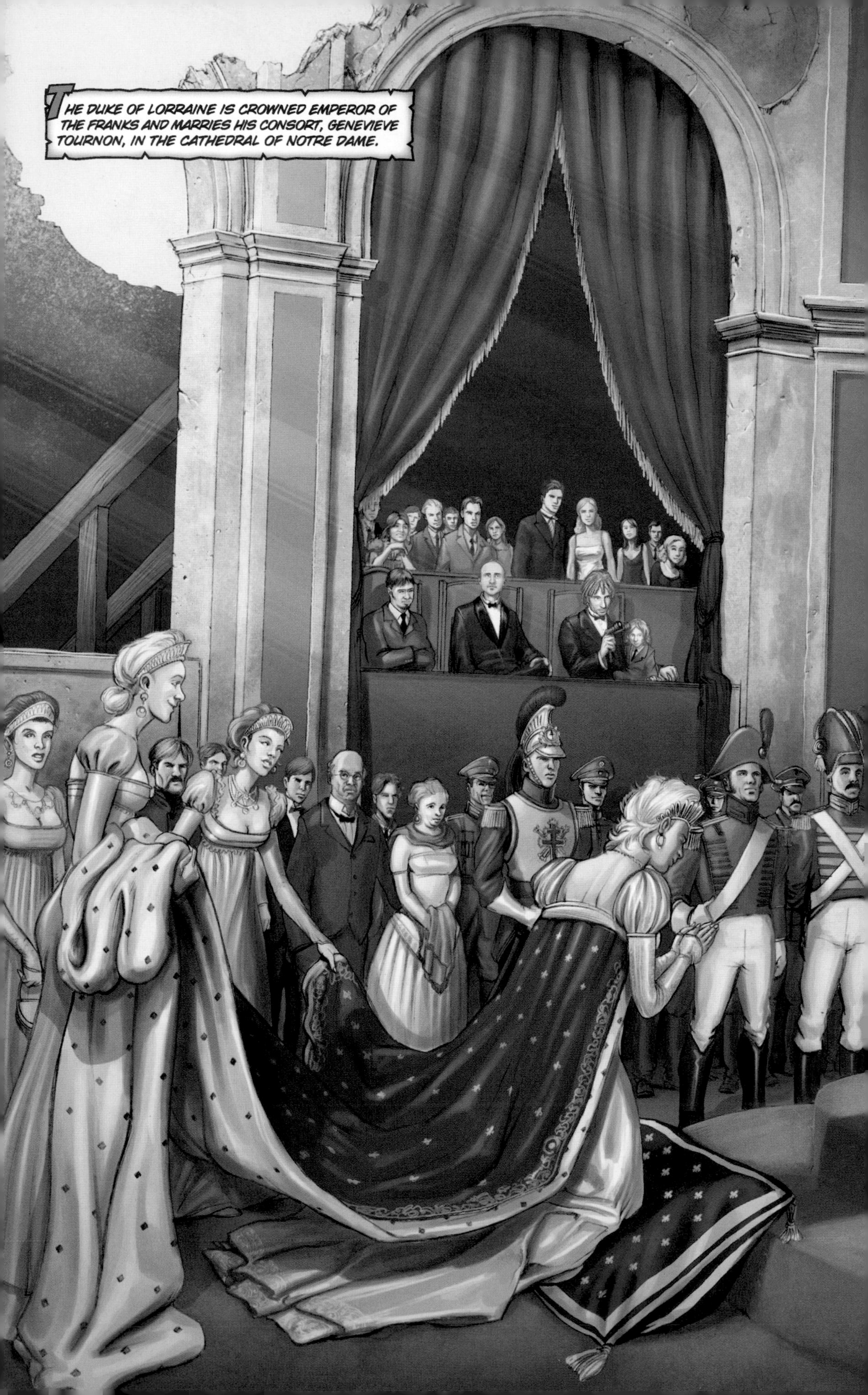
THE DUKE OF LORRAINE IS CROWNED EMPEROR OF THE FRANKS AND MARRIES HIS CONSORT, GENEVIEVE TOURNON, IN THE CATHEDRAL OF NOTRE DAME.

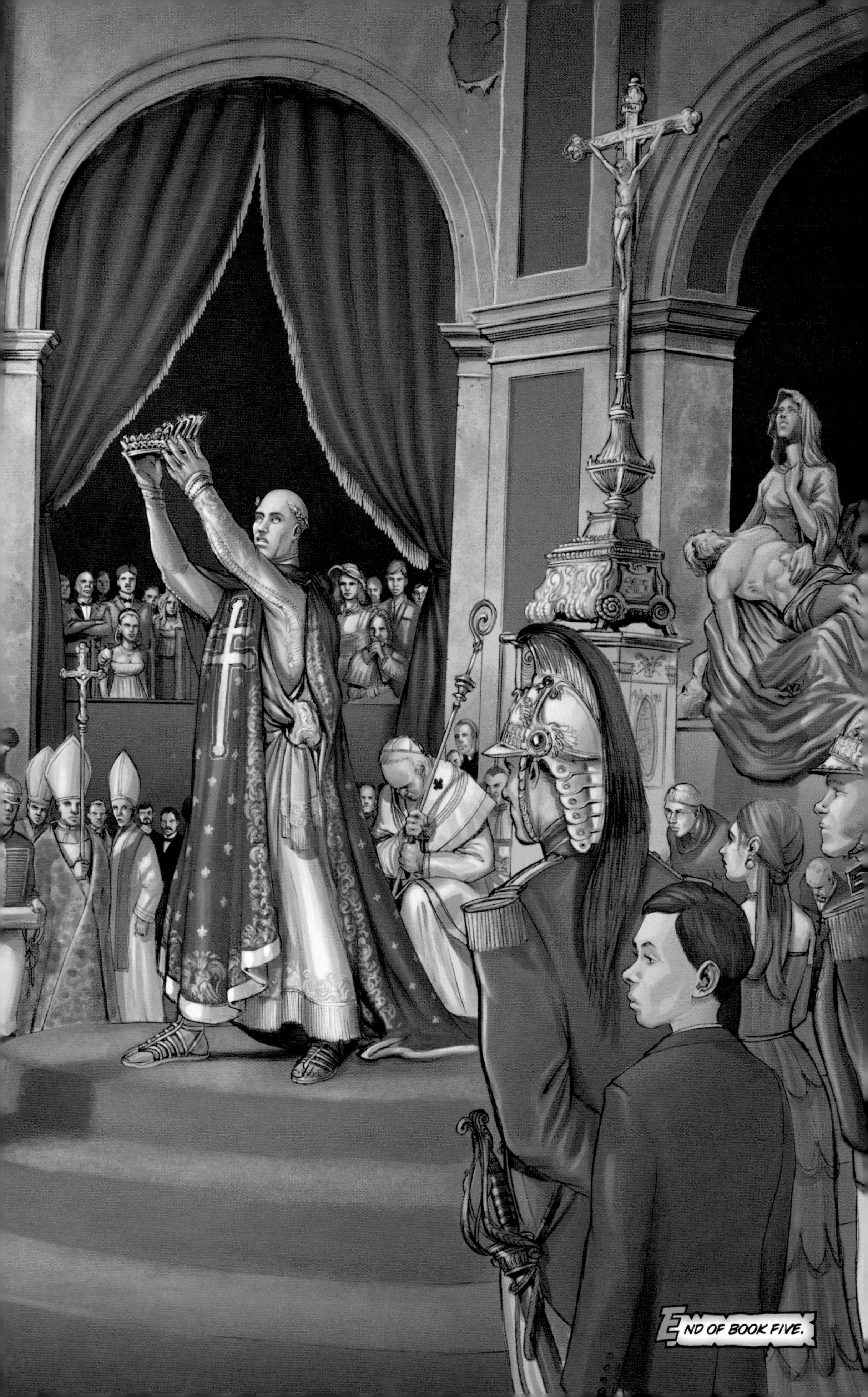
END OF BOOK FIVE.

Le Journal de la Liberté

Paris's leading anglophone newspaper • vol. 205, no. 171 • Feb. 15, MCMXXXIV

Editors in Chief: M. Michael Richardson, M. Scott Allie, M. Ryan Jorgensen. **Story Editor:** M. Arvid Nelson. **Art Editor:** M. Juan Ferreyra. **Photography Editor:** M. Eugène Atget. **Layout Supervisor:** M. Cary Grazzini. **Editors Emeritus:** M. Clark A. Smith, M. Howard P. Lovecraft, M. Robert E. Howard. *Le Journal de la Liberté* is printed under the benign auspices of his eminence David-Louis Plantard de St. Clair, Duke of Lorraine and First Consul of the Empire of France.

Official seal of

the First Consul

✣ GOD SAVE LORD LORRAINE ✣

KING OF THE WORLD

Lorraine Crowned Emperor of the Franks, Wedded to Longtime Companion Lady Genevieve Tournon

Paris – It was a coronation the likes of which the world has not seen since ancient Rome.

David-Louis Plantard de St. Clair crowned himself Emperor of the Franks yesterday in the cathedral of Notre Dame de Paris. Members of the royal houses of Hohenzollern and Hapsburg-Lorraine attended to swear loyalty to their new emperor.

At the same time, Lorraine married his longtime companion Dr. Genevieve Tournon. The union marks, in the words of the Duke of Nevers, "the founding of a thousand-year dynasty to preside over a true and eternal Holy Roman Empire."

The cathedral still bore marks of devastation weathered during the Prussian assault on Paris months earlier. But the jagged gaps in the walls admitted a ray of sunshine, starkly illuminating Lorraine and his new empress.

"It was just one of many incredible details in Lorraine and Lady Genevieve's fairy-tale romance," society writer Baroness Emmuska Orczy said.

The coronation comes after many setbacks for Lorraine. He was pushed into war with Austria and Prussia and then forced to abandon Paris.

"Genevieve has helped me through all of my hardships," Lorraine said. "She will be a fine wife and a worthy empress."

Indeed, Lorraine rallied his broken men and crushed the invading armies. Soon, French troops were marching through Berlin and Vienna.

"We never wanted war with our racial allies, the German people," Lorraine said. "And now our people are at last united under one emperor."

Lorraine's first wife died in 1920 due to consumption. His daughter, Isabelle, could not attend the ceremony, due to "pressing engagements elsewhere." ✣

Russians Refuse to Cede Territories Gained in Recent Offensive

Danzig – Russia and France are uneasy allies in the best of circumstances. Now tensions between the two are mounting, over the territories Russia gained in its advance across East Prussia.

Prussia has united with France under the flag of Lorraine's newly founded Frankish Empire. The Russian-captured territories that once belonged to the kaiser are now Lord Lorraine's.

Lorraine has demanded an immediate halt to the Russian offensive and a withdrawal to prewar boundaries.

The Russian troops have halted while the Tzar "considers his options," according to Yuri Zolutkin, the Tzar's spokesman. But the invasion force has not withdrawn from the front lines.

Lord Lorraine is adding French reinforcements to the German troops on the eastern front, and some in his command staff are even considering an assault on their Russian allies.

"The longer the delay, the longer they have to entrench," the Duke of Orleans said.

continued on next page

FLEETS MASSING IN AEGEAN SEA, ENGLISH CHANNEL

The English Channel – French warships numbering in the "hundreds" are gathering in the waters off England and Asia Minor.

"The fleet movements should not be taken as a precursor to an invasion," Vicomte Jean-Paul de Grasse, secretary of the Imperial French Navy, said.

But tensions between Great Britain and France have been high ever since Queen Elizabeth pulled British troops out of the siege of Carcassonne. Many in the Imperial French War Ministry are openly calling for war with England.

"England is a nation of shopkeepers," Lord Lorraine said in a speech to the Imperial War College the other day.

The naval maneuvers follow a decisive victory against a combined Prussio-Austrian fleet weeks earlier. Prussia and Austria are now part of Lorraine's continent-spanning empire, and their fleets are being absorbed into a combined Frankish naval force.

"The Frankish fleet will be the largest, the most formidable force on the high seas. The era of British naval dominance is over," Vicomte de Grasse said.

The Ottoman Empire might also find itself in the crosshairs of Lorraine's imperial ambitions. He has made colonization of the Holy Land a cornerstone of his foreign policy ambitions since his early days as Speaker of the Hall of the Sword.

Although the Ottoman Turks were allied with the German powers, Lorraine has declared the partnership "null and void."

"Christ shall reign again in Jerusalem," Lorraine said. ✣

French battleships lurking outside the fortified Ottoman port of Smyrna.

❧ Society Pages ❧

Lucky Thirteen

Forget the glamorous, glitzy world of international celebrities. All the excitement *these* days is taking place in American politics! From the sunny bayous of the Confederate States of America to the bustling cities of the Federal Republic in the North, trouble is brewing. Are we talking about a complex political crisis with profound implications for the future? Of *course* not! Just who do you take us for? We're talking about *sex!*

That's right — governors all over the former United States are getting into trouble the oldest way men know how — by letting their little heads do the governing for their big heads. Most prominent of the lot is Eliazer Schutzer of New York, who paid as much as fifteen dollars a night for a call girl barely older than his eldest daughter.

Fifteen dollars? That's more than most Americans earn in an entire *week!*

Apparently Schutzer had visited the young lady in question a total of *thirteen* times by the time investigators figured out why he was secreting large sums of money in and out of his personal accounts.

"We thought it had something to do with bribery or corruption," said an agent working on the case. "Imagine our surprise when we found out it was just hookers!"

The revelations are all the more surprising because Schutzer made a name crusading against corporate monopolies. He was even prosecuting a prostitution ring while carrying out his pay-by-the-session trysts.

All the same, Northerners are expressing frustration about the furor, especially in light of the misconduct on the part of CSA senators Harold Craig and Marcus Foley, both accused of homosexual improprieties — in Foley's case, of harassing fifteen-year-old male pages in the capitol building of Richmond, Virginia.

"Say what you will, but at least in the North our scandals always involve grown women," said a disgruntled Connecticut state legislator.

Cruisin' for a Bruisin'

Things just get weirder and weirder for American talkie star Thompson Cruz. First his… *abrupt* marriage to young, impressionable starlet Kaitlin Combs, then an… *enthusiastic* series of public outbursts, and now the latest: the unauthorized release of a "private" film reel in which the dashing star extols the virtues of his unusual spiritual beliefs.

> "WE THOUGHT IT HAD SOMETHING TO DO WITH BRIBERY OR CORRUPTION. IMAGINE OUR SURPRISE WHEN WE FOUND OUT IT WAS JUST HOOKERS!"

People have reacted to the reel — now all the rage in private projection salons across Europe and America — with a mix of amusement and vague unease.

"I don't understand what he's talking about," one viewer said. "But it seems really important to him."

The reel was intended as a "members-only" advocacy piece for Cruz's religion, Mormontology™. Some believe the clip's wider release raises serious questions about Cruz's nouveau-faith, founded in the 1800s by American dime-novelist-turned-prophet Joseph Ron Smithard.

"I'm not sure anyone knows what Mormontologists™ really believe," said religion expert Clarence Darrow. "Something about Jesus teleporting to the New World to annihilate evil undead alien spirits in volcanoes four trillion years ago."

"All I know is, never join a religion founded in America by a white person."

> "NEVER JOIN A RELIGION FOUNDED IN AMERICA BY A WHITE PERSON."

Some Fairy Tales Do Come True

Will the fantasy *never* end for Genevieve Tournon, girl from the wrong side of the river who made good?

It all began as a steamy romance with the bald, sexy Duke of Lorraine. "I don't know what it is about him," one of Lady Genevieve's ladies-in-waiting said. "Maybe it's his confidence. Maybe it's his muscles, or his snappy uniforms. But women swoon when they see the light reflecting off of his shiny scalp. Lord Lorraine is hot!"

And what started as animal attraction has blossomed into eternal love. Genevieve Tournon became *Lady* Genevieve yesterday when she tied the knot with Lorraine in a spectacular ceremony in Notre Dame.

"Lady Genevieve gets to live out every woman's fantasy — a girl of humble birth falls madly in love with the handsome prince, and he makes her his princess. It's a real-life fairy tale so glamorous it puts Beauty and the Beast to shame!" socialite Madame Marie de Tourvel said.

Does all this come with resentment on the part of common people? Far from it! The new Lady Lorraine is proving to be a big hit with crowds, drawing throngs of admirers after the ceremony yesterday.

"People see themselves in her. It's like she's doing it for all of us!" one well-wisher said.

Lady Genevieve is already being hailed as the "people's empress". And rumor has it the people's princess might be carrying Lorraine's love child!

"It doesn't take away from the beauty of it," Madame Tourvel said. "In fact, it only makes it more sweet. It's part of the fairy tale."

The future looks bright for Lady Genevieve — and her child!

American Idol Ashleigh Timmsdale Declares "No More Plastic Surgery"

Yes, the star of the popular moving-picture serial "Grammar School Musical" has sworn off cosmetic surgery for good. In a related story, thousands of children starve to death every day in Africa! ⚜

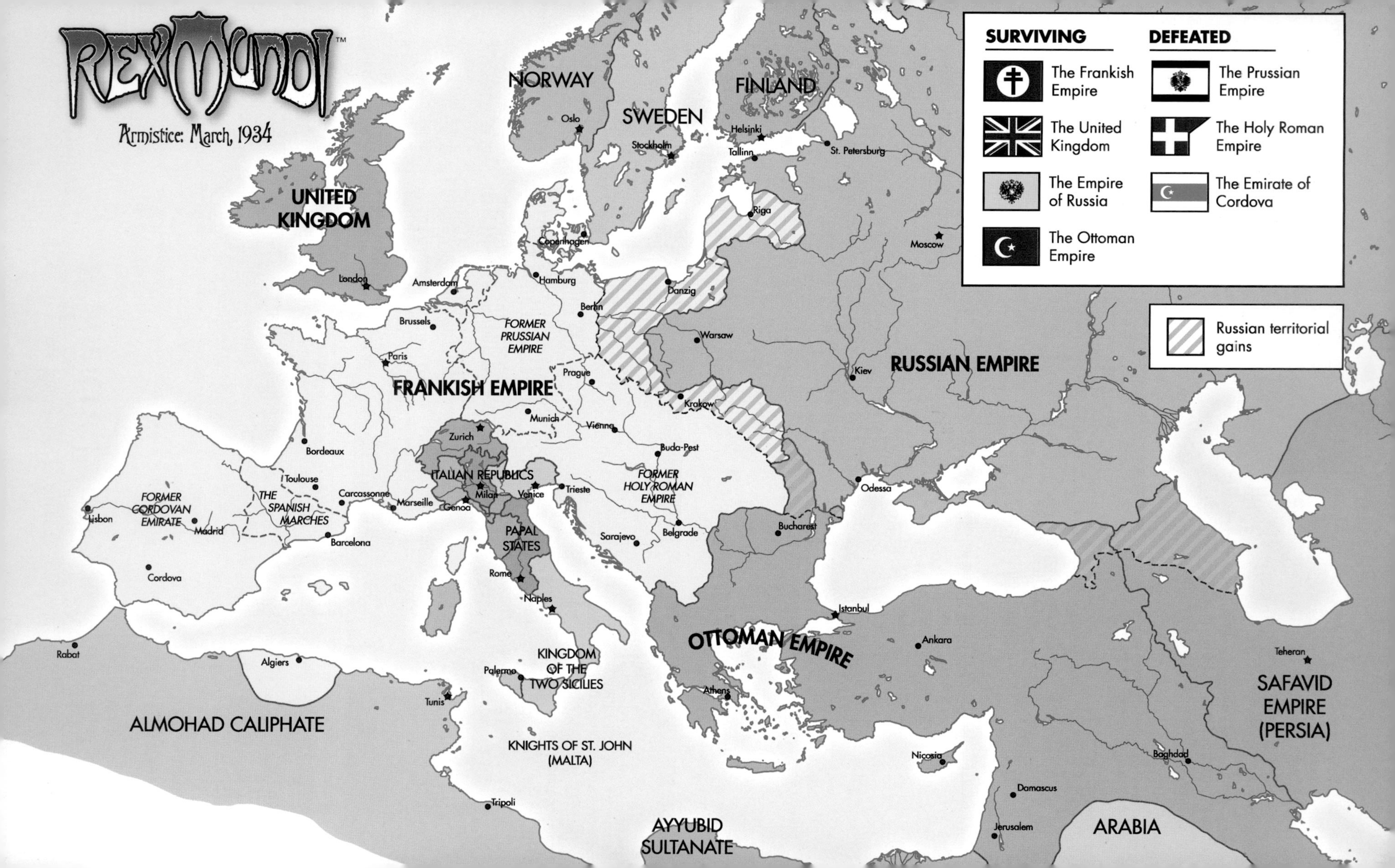
REX MUNDI™
Armistice: March, 1934
SURVIVING
The Frankish Empire
The United Kingdom
The Empire of Russia
The Ottoman Empire
DEFEATED
The Prussian Empire
The Holy Roman Empire
The Emirate of Cordova
Russian territorial gains
UNITED KINGDOM
NORWAY
SWEDEN
FINLAND
RUSSIAN EMPIRE
FRANKISH EMPIRE
FORMER PRUSSIAN EMPIRE
FORMER HOLY ROMAN EMPIRE
ITALIAN REPUBLICS
PAPAL STATES
KINGDOM OF THE TWO SICILIES
FORMER CORDOVAN EMIRATE
THE SPANISH MARCHES
OTTOMAN EMPIRE
ALMOHAD CALIPHATE
KNIGHTS OF ST. JOHN (MALTA)
AYYUBID SULTANATE
ARABIA
SAFAVID EMPIRE (PERSIA)
London
Oslo
Stockholm
Helsinki
Tallinn
St. Petersburg
Riga
Moscow
Copenhagen
Hamburg
Amsterdam
Danzig
Berlin
Brussels
Warsaw
Paris
Prague
Kiev
Krakow
Munich
Vienna
Zurich
Bordeaux
Buda-Pest
Toulouse
Milan
Venice
Trieste
Odessa
Carcassonne
Marseille
Genoa
Lisbon
Madrid
Barcelona
Bucharest
Sarajevo
Belgrade
Cordova
Rome
Naples
Istanbul
Ankara
Rabat
Algiers
Palermo
Tunis
Athens
Teheran
Nicosia
Baghdad
Damascus
Tripoli
Jerusalem

FRAILTY

introduction by Arvid Nelson

Greetings, Dear Reader, to the end of the penultimate volume of *Rex Mundi*. It's been an enduring act of devotion in my life for a long time now.

Speaking of devotion . . .

Scott, my editor, asked me to do a *Rex Mundi* Valentine's Day story for MySpace in 2007. "Frailty" is what came of it: a short poem, a little snippet from Julien and Genevieve's past.

I tried to show some of the things Julien and Gen loved about each other when they were younger . . . and some of the things that tore them apart.

By now you've spent more time reading this introduction than it will take to read "Frailty," Dear Reader, so I'll not waste any more of your time. Thank you for reading Book Five.

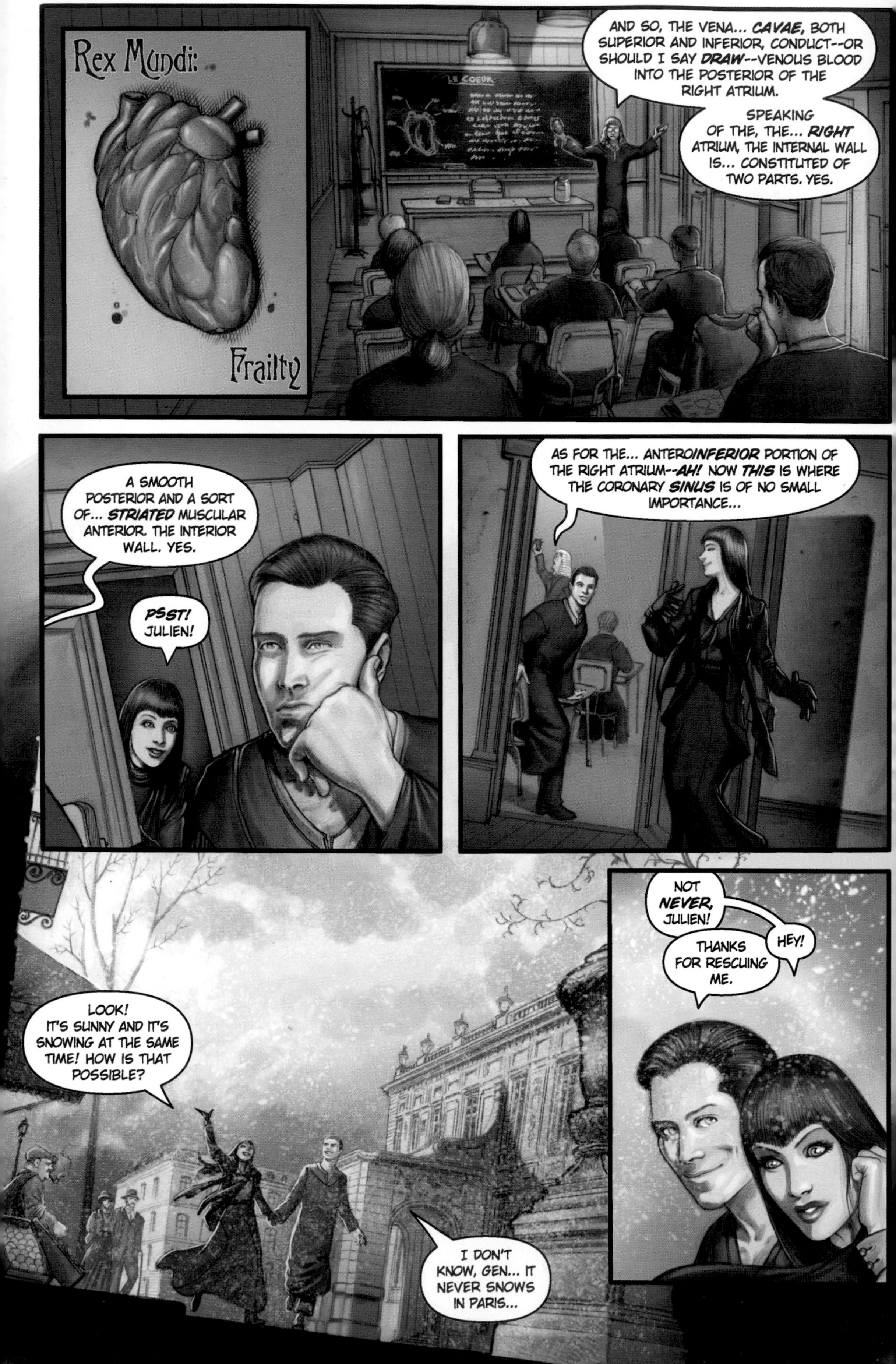
Rex Mundi:
Frailty
AND SO, THE VENA... CAVAE, BOTH SUPERIOR AND INFERIOR, CONDUCT--OR SHOULD I SAY DRAW--VENOUS BLOOD INTO THE POSTERIOR OF THE RIGHT ATRIUM.
SPEAKING OF THE, THE... RIGHT ATRIUM, THE INTERNAL WALL IS... CONSTITUTED OF TWO PARTS. YES.
LE COEUR
A SMOOTH POSTERIOR AND A SORT OF... STRIATED MUSCULAR ANTERIOR. THE INTERIOR WALL. YES.
PSST! JULIEN!
AS FOR THE... ANTEROINFERIOR PORTION OF THE RIGHT ATRIUM--AH! NOW THIS IS WHERE THE CORONARY SINUS IS OF NO SMALL IMPORTANCE...
LOOK! IT'S SUNNY AND IT'S SNOWING AT THE SAME TIME! HOW IS THAT POSSIBLE?
I DON'T KNOW, GEN... IT NEVER SNOWS IN PARIS...
NOT NEVER, JULIEN!
HEY!
THANKS FOR RESCUING ME.

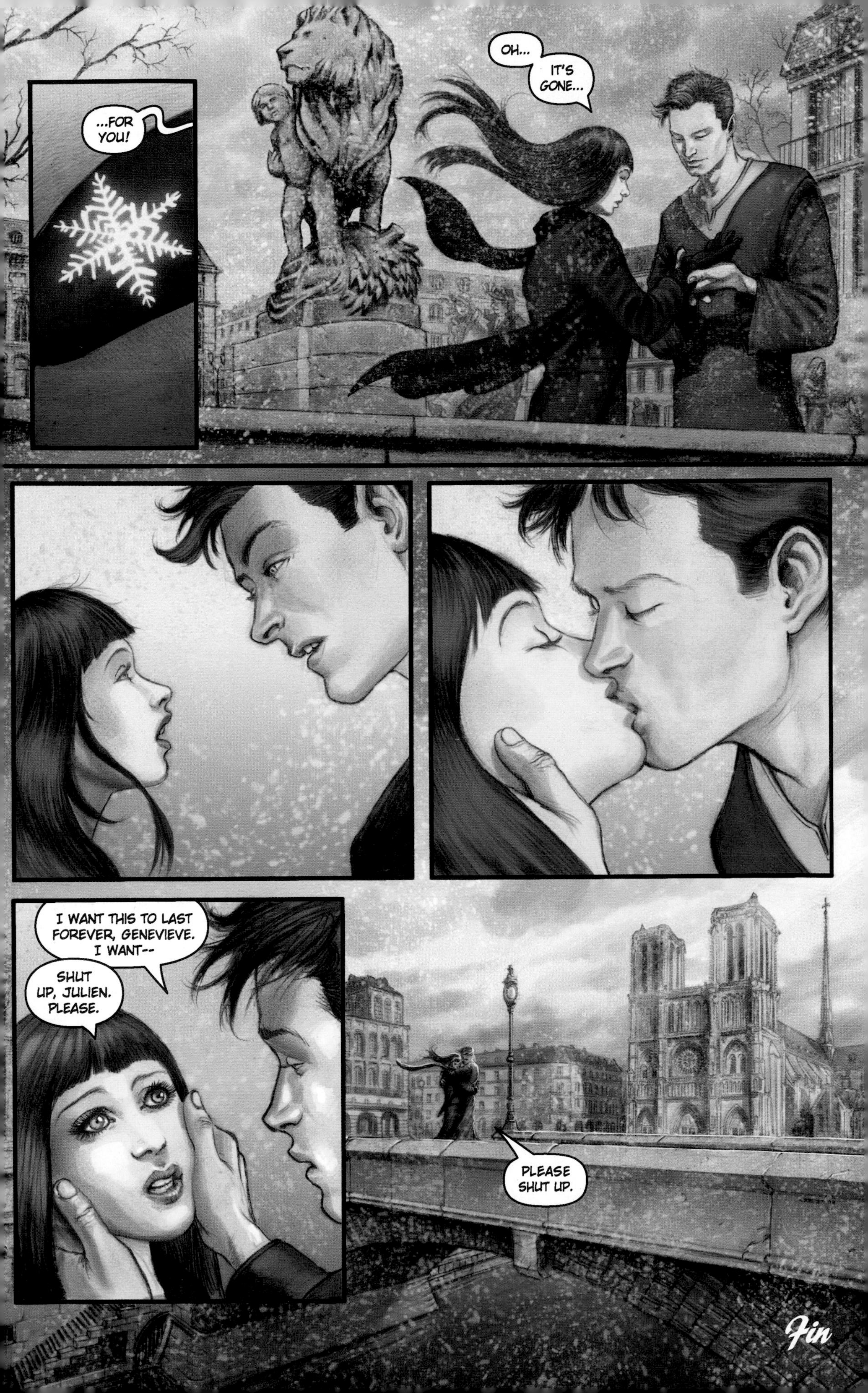
...FOR YOU!
OH...
IT'S GONE...
I WANT THIS TO LAST FOREVER, GENEVIEVE. I WANT--
SHUT UP, JULIEN. PLEASE.
PLEASE SHUT UP.
Fin

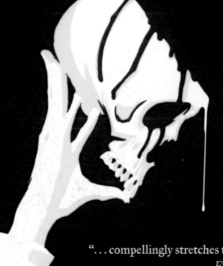